ROUTLEDGE LIBRARY EDITIONS: DEMOGRAPHY

Volume 16

ESSAYS ON AFRICAN POPULATION

ESSAYS ON AFRICAN POPULATION

Edited by
K. M. BARBOUR AND R. M. PROTHERO

Routledge
Taylor & Francis Group

LONDON AND NEW YORK

First published in 1961 by Routledge & Kegan Paul Ltd.

This edition first published in 2024
by Routledge
4 Park Square, Milton Park, Abingdon, Oxon OX14 4RN

and by Routledge
605 Third Avenue, New York, NY 10158

Routledge is an imprint of the Taylor & Francis Group, an informa business

British Library Cataloguing in Publication Data
A catalogue record for this book is available from the British Library

ISBN: 978-1-032-53819-8 (Set)
ISBN: 978-1-032-54818-0 (Volume 16) (hbk)
ISBN: 978-1-032-54820-3 (Volume 16) (pbk)
ISBN: 978-1-003-42764-3 (Volume 16) (ebk)

DOI: 10.4324/9781003427643

Publisher's Note
Some of the material in this book contains terms or views that were acceptable in the period in which they were written, but may no longer be considered appropriate. These terms do not necessarily reflect the views of The Publishers. The original text will remain available for historical context.

Disclaimer
The publisher has made every effort to trace copyright holders and would welcome correspondence from those they have been unable to trace.

ESSAYS ON

AFRICAN POPULATION

edited by

K. M. BARBOUR

B.Litt., M.A., Lecturer in Geography,
University College London

and

R. M. PROTHERO

M.A., Lecturer in Geography,
University of Liverpool

LONDON

ROUTLEDGE & KEGAN PAUL

First published 1961
by Routledge & Kegan Paul Limited
Broadway House, 68–74 Carter Lane
London, E.C.4

Printed in Great Britain by
Butler & Tanner Limited
Frome and London

Contents

Maps

(FIGURES)

Maps

Notes on Contributors

K. M. BARBOUR, B.Litt., M.A. Lecturer in Geography, University College London, and formerly at the University of Khartoum (1948–55). Author of *The Republic of the Sudan—a Regional Geography* (1961) and of maps of the distribution and density of population in Sudan.

A. T. GROVE, M.A. Lecturer in Geography, University of Cambridge. Author of *Land Use and Soil Conservation (South-east Nigeria)* (1951), *Land Use and Soil Conservation (Jos Plateau)* (1952), *Land and Population in Katsina Province* (1957) and *The Benue Valley* (1958).

T. E. HILTON, M.A., Ph.D. Senior Lecturer in Geography, University College, Ghana. Author of *A Population Atlas of Ghana* (1960).

C. J. MARTIN, B.A. Statistical Adviser to the East African Governments, Director of the East African Statistical Department and Economist to the Kenya Government. Member of the Scientific Council for Africa with special responsibilities for statistics. Author of papers and reports on demography and statistics.

N. C. MITCHEL, M.A. Lecturer in Geography, Queen's University, Belfast and formerly at the University College, Ibadan (1951–7).

J. C. MITCHELL, B.A., D.Phil. Professor of African Studies, University College of Rhodesia and Nyasaland and formerly Director of the Rhodes-Livingstone Institute. Author of *The Lamba Village* (1950), *African Urbanization in Ndola and Luanshaya* (1954), *The Yao Village* (1956) and *The Kalela Dance* (1956).

R. M. PROTHERO, M.A. Lecturer in Geography, University of Liverpool and formerly at University College, Ibadan (1950–4) and the West African Institute of Social and Economic Research (1954–5). Member of the Special Commission on a World Population Map of the International Geographical Union (1958–) and consultant on some population problems in Africa to the Division of Malaria Eradication, World Health Organization (1960).

Notes on Contributors

J. R. H. Shaul, M.Sc. (Econ.), B.Com. (London). Research Fellow at the University College of Rhodesia and Nyasaland, and formerly Director of Statistics, Northern Rhodesia, and Director of the Central African Statistical Office. Author of papers and reports on demography and statistics.

A. W. Southall, M.A., Ph.D. Professor of Sociology at Makerere College, University College of East Africa, and Director of the East African Institute of Social Research. Author of *Alur Society* (1956) and (with P. C. W. Gutkind) *Townsmen in the Making: Kampala and its suburbs* (1957) and editor of *Social Change in Modern Africa* (1960).

R. W. Steel, B.Sc., M.A. John Rankin Professor of Geography, University of Liverpool, and formerly Senior Lecturer in Geography and Fellow of Jesus College, University of Oxford. Drapers' Company Research Scholar, Sierra Leone (1937–9) and member of the Ashanti Social Survey (1945–6) and the Colonial Social Science Research Council (1945–). Editor (with A. F. Martin) of *The Oxford Region: a Scientific and Historical Survey* (1954) and (with C. A. Fisher) of *Geographical Essays on British Tropical Lands* (1956).

The maps in this volume were drawn by K. Wass and A. G. Hodgkiss and the staffs of the drawing offices in the Departments of Geography of University College London and the University of Liverpool. Grateful acknowledgement is made to them for their work.

1

Introduction

THESE essays on African population have been written from a variety of points of view and brought together by two geographers who have both worked in University Colleges in British African dependencies since the Second World War. Both editors have worked in the field of human rather than physical geography, yet both are convinced that there is no clear division to be drawn between the two fields of research, since in the study of most problems the two prove to be intimately interwoven. More than this, in the field of population studies they are of the opinion that workers in the social sciences are engaged in the pursuit of common objectives, and need to work together to avoid misdirected efforts and wasted energies.

At the present time, with far-reaching changes taking place in many of the countries of inter-tropical Africa,[1] it is especially important that all political, social or economic policies should pay heed to the number, distribution, characteristics and inclinations of the population. New technical developments may be made possible by advances in scientific knowledge and its application and an adequate supply of capital is clearly indispensable in the development of projects of major importance. Yet the course of ordered evolutionary development will also depend on the availability and use of sufficient knowledge of the people of Africa themselves. There is a need for integrated studies, undertaken by workers from several

[1] So rapid and numerous have been these changes that the Editors have thought it best not to try to attain a transient topicality. Instead, both in the text and in the maps, use has been made of the established names of countries such as are more likely to be found in atlases and other works of reference.

disciplines, since it seldom happens that the information required for the solution to any specific problem lies wholly within the competence of a single investigator.

Workers who engage in population studies include social anthropologists, demographers, economists, geographers and others, whose approaches may differ, but who also share a great deal of common ground. This, it is hoped, will be illustrated by the essays that appear in this volume, which are all primarily concerned with territories now or formerly under British rule. That the collection has been confined to these territories should not be taken to imply that similar studies have been neglected in French, Belgian and Portuguese territories. In fact collections of equal interest and diversity could be made which omitted British Africa altogether. In practice, however, the colonies of the various European powers in Africa have tended to pursue their several objectives in striking isolation from one another, and even on the academic level relatively little heed is paid by scholars to work in languages other than their own. In the future the easy movement of foreign scholars from one African country to another may be diminished. At the same time the small but increasing number of Africans working in the field of population studies will begin to make itself felt and a future volume of this nature would certainly be strengthened by drawing on their work.

Within the broad field of population study the theme selected to draw these studies together is the editors' acceptance of the view, now increasingly prevalent among geographers and other workers in the social sciences, that a quantitative approach can and must be made to human problems which hitherto have been treated on a less precise basis. Just as the years since the war have seen the rapid extension of aerial survey over most of Africa, making accurate large-scale topographic maps available for wide areas previously covered by little more than rough field traverses, so censuses of various kinds are bringing more precision to our knowledge of the numbers, age structure, occupations, ethnic and other characteristics of the many peoples who inhabit the continent. The analysis and interpretation of these figures constitute the major part of this volume, and lead to a final chapter which considers the political implications of this approach in relation to the boundaries that divide the present-day political units.

For many of the essays the principal statistical material has come from the first post-war population censuses. These date mostly from the last decade, and while often leaving much to be desired have yet been a great advance on what has gone before. It is hoped that this volume will be published before the spate of new census data which will become available in the 1960's, for these will in turn provide the data for further studies and comparisons. In some African territories—Ethiopia, Liberia and the former Somaliland Protectorate—the first censuses have still to be attempted and only rough estimates of their populations exist. In almost all African territories population data are limited by the problems involved in organizing their collection. In some the range and scope of censuses are limited and their effectiveness is reduced by the reluctance or inability of governments to provide enough funds for them. In this respect Ghana has set a commendable example by spending in 1960 nearly £300,000 on its census, nearly ten times the figure spent in 1948. This indicates a recognition, by a newly independent country, of the need for sound population data as a basis for planning social and economic development.

Yet to be of the greatest value it is not sufficient for a census to be planned with a generous budget and be able to draw upon a fund of experience. There is a real need for international co-operation in the drawing up of questionnaires, so as to achieve the standardization of data and to make direct comparative studies possible. To this end important roles should be played by the United Nations Economic Commission for Africa and the Scientific Council for Africa, each of which has a statistical section concerned with demography, and by bodies such as the International Geographical Union. By way of example of such co-operation we may cite the study of migrant movements in Ghana, Côte d'Ivoire, the Republic of Mali, Haute Volta and Niger which has been sponsored during the last four years by the Human Sciences Committee of C.C.T.A. In this project studies have been carried out under the direction of Dr. Jean Rouch of the Musée de l'Homme, Paris, both in the home areas of the migrants and in the areas to which they

Introduction

migrate. These studies have been supported by the governments of the countries concerned.[1]

In the essays in this volume three lines of approach may be observed. There are those which discuss methods of population study, those which present a broad survey of work that has been done in particular fields and those which apply the results of population enquiries to the solution of particular problems. In the first category we may place Prothero's account of censuses in West Africa, while for East Africa and the Federation of Rhodesia and Nyasaland Martin and Shaul are also concerned with basic population data, not only describing census-taking but also summarizing the results of the latest censuses and commenting on them. Martin also provides a first study of the changes to be observed between two post-war censuses of East African territories. Shaul draws attention to the value of sampling techniques, which he was the first to use in Africa and has shown how large countries can overcome their natural disadvantages for census-taking.

Prothero's account of population mapping in Africa is a general survey of the work that has been done in this field. Hilton and Barbour, who tell strikingly different tales of how they undertook the production of population maps in Ghana and Sudan on the basis of post-war censuses, both make the point that the accuracy of population maps can be no better than that of the topographic maps on which they are based.

The two rural studies illustrate the use of census material in conjunction with other lines of investigation, but approach the fundamental question of man/land relationships from two rather different points of view. Grove in Northern Nigeria has worked in an area that is physically almost uniform, and is able to demonstrate within it the effects of human and economic factors, particularly the density of population, on the differing patterns of land use. Barbour, on the other hand, has chosen his examples from geologically varied portions of Central Sudan, in an attempt to determine how far the distribution of population by age and sex is related to cultural factors, and how far to the possibility of providing a balanced diet from local resources. Both studies clearly suggest that official poli-

[1] For general reports on the progress of these investigations see *Africa*, xxviii, 1958, 156–9, and xxix, 1959, 417–19.

4

cies of soil conservation or of improving rural water supplies need to pay heed to more than merely agronomic or hydraulic considerations.

The studies of population mobility by Southall and Mitchell take the latest census results, together with a great deal of other historical and economic information, and use them to investigate changes and movements of population in East Africa and the Federation of Rhodesia and Nyasaland. In the former, where economic development has been much less than in the Federation, the census data allow the study of movements of members of individual tribes in response to the pull of wages and the push of overcrowding at home. In the Federation, on the other hand, the census of Africans in employment deals with them on the basis of their nationality, using the term in the sense of Southern Rhodesian, Portuguese East African, etc. In either instance it is clear that the maintenance of a stable and contented labour force to work in mines or factories or on farms will, in a changing political situation, require the type of careful analysis undertaken in these essays.

Moreover, unless catastrophic political upheavals should bring financial confidence and investment to an end, the major mining and industrial centres in Africa will experience a steady increase of urban growth in the second half of the twentieth century. For this reason Steel's description of African town development, and of the broad lines of urban study now being pursued in the continent, is of considerable topical value. At the same time it is good to be reminded that there are one or two areas in Africa where in the past social as much as economic factors have been responsible for town growth, and Mitchel's account of Yoruba towns shows that it is important not to think of all Africans as having been peasants or nomads until they came under European rule.

The last essay takes a new look at the hurried division of the African continent, in the latter part of the nineteenth century, into a number of separate states and dependencies. In this division Africans themselves had very little or no say. Barbour's study of the political geography of inter-tropical Africa discusses the types of boundary line used between countries, and considers how these lines are related to tribal distributions and population densities. To understand the significance of African boundaries, it is suggested, the human geography of the frontier zones requires a detailed study of the kind that is only now becoming possible, as new techniques of mapping and population study are being extended to more and more of the continent.

The conclusion is inescapable. In this era of change from colonies to independent states in Africa, the need for research into problems concerned with the population of the continent will not disappear but will become more acute. On the political plane, it will be for African statesmen to ensure that co-operation between states is not impeded but rather intensified; on the academic plane, scholars interested in the continent will have the duty of continuing their own investigations and of training African scholars to plan and undertake research of their own.

2

Post-war West African Censuses

R. MANSELL PROTHERO

KUCZYNSKI's West African volume[1] in his monumental survey of the demography of the British Empire will remain for all time a classic in the analysis and assessment of census and other demographic data for the territories of Nigeria, Ghana (Gold Coast), Sierra Leone and Gambia. Published in 1948, it surveyed the data available from the earliest records, in some instances (particularly Sierra Leone) going back to the nineteenth century, up to the decade before the outbreak of the Second World War. Much of this data was unsatisfactory, it was often fragmentary and incomplete, based on assessment rather than on enumeration and with inevitable discrepancies and inaccuracies resulting from the methods and circumstances of compilation. To all these features Kuczynski drew attention and his conclusions are generally valid. Nevertheless one may not invariably agree with his assessment and interpretation.[2] He does not always seem to have appreciated the enormous problems involved in the collection of this data; it was most remarkable in some instances that there should be any data at all available for criticism. His work surveyed the first era of the collection of West African demographic data which came to an end with the 1939/45 war. The censuses that have taken place since the war differ in many respects, not only in the methods used but also in the circumstances under which

---

[1] R. R. Kuczynski, *Demographic Survey of the British Colonial Empire*, I, West Africa, London, 1948.

[2] R. Mansell Prothero, "The population census of Northern Nigeria, 1952: problems and results", *Population Studies*, x, 2, 1956, 166.

they were conducted.[1] Though at least one further set of censuses will be required before there are data for a further study on the same scale as that of Kuczynski, the variety of post-war censuses offers scope at this stage for a review of progress in the collection of demographic data in West Africa during the last decade. In this review specific references are made to Nigeria, with comparative references to Ghana and other West African territories.

The decennial pattern of census-taking which had been adopted in British West African territories was interrupted in 1941 by the war. At that time only rough estimates of population were available which were in no way comparable in accuracy and detail with the assessment of population in Britain based on National Registration. Furthermore, the data which had been collected in the 1931 censuses in British West Africa were for the most part suspect and so could not be used as a base-line for any accurate estimates of subsequent population growth. The 1931 census in the Gold Coast had attempted to enumerate the population but the report on this census, while suggesting that there had been a 5 per cent understatement in 1921 and some further understatement in 1931, made no attempt at a numerical assessment of the error in the results. Nigeria's 1931 census was even more unsatisfactory from the point of view of its probable accuracy. Its scope was severely curtailed due to administrative difficulties and lack of money and the data were collected for the most part by assessment and not by enumeration. While there were inaccuracies in the data for total population it must be remembered that data relating to sex, age, tribal affiliation, religion, etc., were even more inaccurate. Even if the 1931 data had provided an acceptable base-line for calculations of population growth these were impossible owing to the absence of vital statistics and assessments of emigration and immigration for calculating rates of increase. All that was known was that since 1931 there had probably been progressive increases in popula-

[1] It will be obvious to the reader that the censuses taken in West Africa and in similar underdeveloped territories are in few respects comparable with those taken in developed areas of the world (e.g. U.K., U.S.A.). "No African censuses can be classified as being in all cases universal, nominative and simultaneous." Council for Technical Co-operation in Africa (C.C.T.A.) *Second Conference of African Statisticians*, 1957, Part III, 2.

tion but only general ideas existed as to their magnitude. In the post-war period there was a pressing need for more up-to-date population data for a variety of reasons. New political developments resulting in extensions of the franchise required greater knowledge of the size and condition of populations, as did programmes for economic expansion and improvements in education, medical and social services and public works.

The Gold Coast, with the advantage of its small size and population and with relatively favourable resources, was able to take its first post-war census in January and February 1948. Nigeria, with a much greater area and a population which turned out to be a little less than eight times larger than that of the Gold Coast, required a longer time to plan its census. The Acting Government Statistician in Nigeria in 1948 judged that it might be politically impossible to take even a simple census throughout the whole of the country. This view was fortunately not held by his successor and after favourable experience in the census of Lagos in 1950[1] plans were made for a census of the whole of Nigeria. The census was taken in the Northern Region in May, June and July 1952, in the Western Region in December 1952 and January 1953 and in the Eastern Region in May, June and August 1953. This staggering of the census was necessary so that the Department of Statistics, which was responsible for the central census organization, would be able to handle the great amount of data coming in for tabulation.

In both the Nigerian and the Gold Coast censuses there were significant advances in organization, methods and results on any previous census held in these countries. In Nigeria for the first time an attempt was made to enumerate the whole population and not to rely on estimates based on data from other sources (e.g. lists of taxpayers). Data, however, were recorded for households and not for individuals as in the censuses of more advanced countries. In the Gold Coast census individual enumeration was possible in some of the larger settlements in the Colony and Ashanti. Population data for other West African territories were obtained in the first post-war decade by various methods which are summarized in the following table.

In almost every instance where a census was taken there was a considerable advance in collection of demographic data on

[1] *Census of Lagos, 1950.* Department of Statistics, Lagos, 1952.

R. Mansell Prothero

Table 1: Methods of collecting Demographic Data[1]

By census	By administrative enumeration	By sample census	By estimate or by population count
Gold Coast (1948)	French territories (every 4 years)	French Guinea (1954/55)	Sierra Leone— Protectorate (1948)
Portuguese Guinea (1950)	Gambia—Protectorate (annual)	Ivory Coast (1955)	
Sao Tomé and Principe (1950)			
French territories— Europeans (1951)			
Gambia—Colony (1951)			
Nigeria (1952/53)			

Note: In Gambia the census was limited to the Colony and applied to only 30,000 of the population; the majority, over 250,000, in the Protectorate were counted by a less reliable method. In French West Africa administrative enumeration was a continuous process, four years being required to complete the task.

what had gone before. The collection of data was controlled by a central census organization working through the civil administration to the supervisors and enumerators responsible for the initial collecting of data in the field. In all censuses the small number of literate persons available made it difficult to find sufficient competent enumerators at the lowest but, nonetheless, the most important level of the census organization.[2] Shortages of enumerators, which required many of them to be responsible for counting over large areas even though the numbers to be counted might not be great, necessitated the censuses being extended over longer periods of time than are normally considered to be desirable. In spite of these and other problems

[1] Census results and demographic data are given in the following publications:
Gold Coast. *Census of Population 1948.* Accra, 1951.
Portuguese Guinea. *Censos da Populaçao de 1950* (Vol. II, Populaçao nao civilizada). *Annuario Estatistico 1951–2.*
Sao Tomé and Principe. *Annuario Estatistico 1954.*
French West Africa. *Recensement de la population non-autochtone de l'A.O.F. Annuaire Statistique de l'A.O.F. Population du Sénégal 1956. Recensement démographique de Dakar 1955. Enquête démographique de Guinée et de Bougouanou (Côte d'Ivoire).*
Gambia. *Report of the Census Commissioner for the Colony 1951* (1952).
Nigeria. *Census of Population 1952/53.* Department of Statistics, Lagos, 1953/57.
[2] Prothero, *loc. cit.*, 169.

the census results were without doubt much superior to anything previously obtained. The superiority of this new data over that obtained from administrative enumerations, estimates and counts is demonstrated by the following figures which show the percentage difference between the pre-census estimates and the census returns in respect of total population.

Table 2

Portuguese census 1950		Nigerian census 1952/53	
	%		%
Cape Verde	+ 8·9	Northern Region	+ 20·0
Guinea	+ 12·7	Eastern Region	+ 34·0
Sao Tomé and Principe	+ 1·2	Western Region	+ 33·0

There is much to be said in favour of a sample census which, because of its application to limited numbers of people, can be conducted with greater accuracy and in greater detail with adequate supervision by trained personnel. In the sample census of French Guinea (now Republic of Guinea) 16 statisticians, medical and administrative officers controlled the work of 108 enumerators, while in the sample census in the Ivory Coast there was an even higher proportion of 6 senior supervisors to 30 enumerators. Sampling units were chosen by random selection and were stratified according to the ethnic and economic characteristics of the selected population in French Guinea and according to the distribution of population by villages in the Ivory Coast. The sampling fraction ranged from one-eighth to one-tenth, but was one-fifth in the towns and one-thirteenth in the Fouta Jallon area of French Guinea. The scope of the schedule used in French Guinea (to include data on race, sex, age, marital status, polygamy, number of sons born, nature of residence, occupation, industrial status and branch of activity) was more extensive than that used in the Ivory Coast which omitted race, nature of residence, industrial status and branch of activity. Both schedules were more extensive than those used in the 1950 Rhodesian census (data collected on age, sex and fertility) and the 1948 East African census (data collected on age, sex, fertility, place of birth, marital status, occupation and level of education). In French Guinea and the Ivory Coast vital statistics for the previous 12 months were also recorded. Adequate checks on error and the calculation of its extent are both possible under controlled sampling. The margin of error for all data collected in the Ivory Coast was calculated as 3 per cent.

In Nigeria, apart from the very brief comments on the census data contained in the final census reports, there has been little further analysis of it, either published or unpublished. Though considerable use of the census data must have been made both directly and indirectly by government departments on many occasions (e.g. in the allocation of revenue on a per capita basis; in the preparation of voters' lists) the absence of specific official demographic analyses is regrettable. Two un-official commentaries on the census results of the Northern and Eastern Regions of Nigeria have been published.[1] The latter is based on a geographical analysis. Much more analysis was made of the data of the 1931 census in Nigeria in the census reports, and this was done at a time when the official statistical organization was in no way comparable with what it is at the present day.

The situation has been similar in Ghana with no official demographic studies based on the 1948 census data. They have been used by the Department of Statistics as a basis for house-hold budget surveys undertaken in Accra (1953), Akuse (1954), Takoradi-Sekondi (1955), Kumasi (1955) and among cocoa-producing families in the Oda-Swedru-Asamankese area (1955/ 56). In 1956 a survey of population and rural economy was undertaken in Ashanti but this has not yet been published.[2] Dr. T. E. Hilton of University College, Ghana, has undertaken a considerable cartographic analysis of the 1948 census which is to be published as an atlas of the population of Ghana; and he writes of some of this work in an essay in this volume.[3]

The report of the second conference of statisticians from

[1] Prothero, *loc. cit.*, and " The population of Eastern Nigeria", *Scot. Geog. Mag.*, LXXI, 3, 1955, 165–70.

[2] Information from the Government Statistician, Accra, May 1960.

[3] See also T. E. Hilton, "The population of the Gold Coast", *Natural resources, food and population in Inter-Tropical Africa, International Geographical Union,* London, 1956, 43–9. Hilton's *Atlas of the Population of Ghana* is now published (January 1961).

territories in Africa south of the Sahara states that the results of the first post-war censuses in these territories are considered to be generally satisfactory. The estimates of margin of error for those taken in West Africa ranged from 1 per cent for the census of the total population of the Colony of Gambia to 10 per cent for the enumeration of the native population of French territories. If these estimates are correct, though the methods by which they were calculated are not always clear, they underline further the important advances that have been made in the collection of demographic data. Errors still remain considerable—for example, the estimated margin of error of 5 per cent for the total population of Nigeria represents over 1,500,000 people. It is hoped that past reliance on administrative enumerations and estimates for demographic data will cease and that censuses in the future will ". . . take the form of exhaustive censuses of the classical type or of sampling censuses". Detailed sampling would seem to be an obvious need in Nigeria where there is such a dearth of reliable data on population increase. The virtual absence of vital and migration statistics suggests the need for the sampling of fertility and the determination of a national growth ratio similar to that used in the Federation of Rhodesia and Nyasaland as an alternative means of calculating inter-censal estimates.

Where a large measure of simplicity in the census schedules is required, so that they will not exceed the capacity of the enumerator to complete them, there are obviously severe limitations placed upon the range and variety of data that can be collected. Table 3 shows the categories of data collected in the various post-war West African censuses. As much uniformity as is possible between the different territories in the types of data collected would seem to be desirable to allow for comparative studies. At the same time within each territory there may well be the need for the collection of particular categories of data.

Co-ordination in the timing of censuses is also necessary. The first post-war censuses for the West African territories were taken over a period of years from 1948 to 1955 thus making impossible comparisons between them for any particular set of demographic data in one particular year. It was recommended in 1957 that to eliminate this problem in the future

Table 3: Summary of Major Post-war Censuses in West Africa
(Data collected for indigenous populations)

Country	Unit of enumeration	Duration of enumeration	Data collected										
			Place of enumeration	Birth place	Duration of stay	Nationality	Tribe	Sex	Age	Marital status	Religion	Occupation	Educational level
A.O.F.	individual	4 years	*	*	*	*	*	*	*	*	*	*	*
Portuguese Guinea	household	30 days	*		*	*	*	*					
Gambia	individual	31 days	*	*	*	*	*	*	*	*		*	*
Gold Coast (Ghana)	individual and household	Northern Territories 3 weeks Ashanti 4 days Colony 1 day	*				*	*	*	*			
Nigeria	household	4/14 days	*				*	*	*		*	*	*
Sierra Leone	individual		*				*	*	*				*

Post-war West African Censuses

preference should be given for taking censuses in the year ending in "o". Present plans are for the next census to be taken in Ghana in 1960 and in Nigeria in 1962.[1] Contemporary political events and resulting changes in status for many of the territories in West Africa will inevitably influence the advanced planning of censuses which is essential.[2] When these changes have taken place it is to be hoped that a regular pattern of census-taking will become established.

[1] Advice on the organization, conduct and analysis of the 1960 census was given by a United Nations expert on loan to the Ghana Government. For some time to come the West African countries will require expert advice and assistance in the taking of censuses and in developing demographic studies. Under the U.N.O. regional centres for demographic research and training are being established in Asia and Latin America (in response to initial requests for assistance from India and Chile). They will train demographers to plan and carry out such population studies as may be requested by governments to assist in the planning of development programmes. The 9th Session of the Population Commission of the U.N.O. (1957, E/2957 E/CN 9/144) requested the Secretary-General to explore the desirability and feasibility of establishing similar centres in Africa. It also noted the need for organizing population seminars in the Middle East and Africa and for establishing pilot demographic studies. A colloquium on African demography was held in Paris in 1959 under the auspices of the Union Internationale pour l'Étude Scientifique de la Population and a report was published in *Problems in African Demography*, Paris, 1960.

[2] In this respect it is interesting to note that the plebiscite to decide whether Ghana should become a republic was postponed for three weeks in order that the census should be completed.

3

Population Census Estimates and Methods in British East Africa

C. J. MARTIN

UNTIL the late nineteenth century the three mainland territories of British East Africa, now designated Kenya Colony and Protectorate, the Trusteeship Territory of Tanganyika and the Protectorate of Uganda, were hardly known to the western world and no records existed of population trends or other economic or social behaviour. Zanzibar was known throughout history and was a base used by explorers such as Livingstone for the preparation of their journeys into the hinterland, but no reliable records existed to allow one to estimate population totals prior to the early twentieth century. Before 1911 no censuses or serious estimates of total populations are available. Such guesses as were made have hardly any validity and even since 1911 many of the estimates were based on most unreliable data.

Estimates of the population of the mainland territories have been made ever since explorers and then the administrators of the British East African Company travelled through the country. Stanley in 1878 estimated the population of Uganda proper at some 780,000 persons and in 1879 the estimate had risen to over 5 million. Later in the century Sir Arthur Harding estimated the population of Kenya Protectorate at 2½ million persons, while Portal thought the population could not be larger than 450,000.[1]

---

[1] For other examples see R. R. Kuczynski, *Demographic Survey of the British Colonial Empire*, East Africa, 1949, 144 and 237.

Other estimates, varying in size, but possibly equally inaccurate, continued to be made until comprehensive censuses were carried out throughout British East Africa for the first time in 1948. Some population counts of differing standards of accuracy and with different degrees of coverage were made in the East African territories from 1911 onwards. Generally these counts applied to the non-African population, although in Uganda and Tanganyika some attempts were made to count the total African population during the 1930's. The following sections describe the methods of estimation used prior to 1948, followed by details of the methodology used in the censuses of 1948 and subsequent censuses, together with descriptions of and comments on the methods of sample surveys being undertaken as supplementary to the census studies. A brief description is also given of other useful studies which have been made.

Estimates

It was the custom until recent years to estimate the population in the East African territories on the basis of a hut tax or of the male poll-tax paying population. The former was often related more to the number of wives rather than to the number of adult males. In recent years the calculation of the total population has been made in a number of different ways. In Kenya it was based on factors for women and children, it being accepted that the female population represented 49 per cent of the total adult population and that 37 per cent of the total population were children. In Tanganyika the estimates were based on the average number of dependants per adult male and the calculations were made on the assumption that there were $3\frac{1}{2}$ dependants per adult male included in the tax registers. In Uganda estimates were based on the periodic counts adjusted by the statistics obtained from the birth and death registers which are maintained in that territory.

The Secretary of State for the Colonies requested that a population census should be held throughout the Colonial Dependencies during 1931, but little money was available to make such a study. In the case of Kenya Colony no official count was made and the statistics, based on the methods described above, were included in the report on the non-native

Population Census Estimates in British E. Africa

census of 1931. A population count was attempted in Tanganyika and the system used was explained in the Report of the Census of the Native Population, 1931. According to this report, the district commissioners were informed that a full count of the population was needed and they were given a number of months in which to estimate their population. Test checks were made by actual enumeration in selected and typical villages, with a single date being fixed for the termination of these investigations and the compilation of returns. No explanation was given as to whether the count should be by individual enumeration or of groups residing in huts, and the only firm instruction was that the closing date was July 1st. The comparison between the totals from the poll tax register and the number of adult males from the census differed by only 0·3 per cent, and it was stated that the accuracy of each was substantiated.[1] It became obvious from personal studies and from talking with headmen that the poll tax registers were used as the basis of the census totals.

A census of the population carried out on one day was attempted in Uganda Protectorate on the 28th May 1931. Quite detailed instructions were issued on the method of completing the form and the schedule asked for information by the smallest administrative unit, the *butongole*. It is considered from the census results that this small administrative unit included up to 500 persons. Such an area was under an unpaid headman, and each headman was considered to know the area of his *butongole* and the number of persons residing there. This area could not be described accurately on any map, nor was its physical size in square miles known. The schedule asked for the numbers of men and women, with an analysis by age, for males: (a) below one year, (b) 1–7 years, (c) 7–18 years, and (d) of age to pay tax, and (e) aged; there were slight variations in age groups for the female population. Further questions were included on marital condition and religion, occupations of males and on infirmities. The problem was to collect this information by groups, since the population had to be marshalled

---

[1] For comments on this see Kuczynski, *op. cit.*, 330, and for a detailed description of methods of estimating the population in Tanganyika prior to 1948 see "The Population of Tanganyika", *Reports on the Populations of Trust Territories*, No. 2, United Nations, 1949.

C. J. Martin

differently for each characteristic and recounted each time. The males were divided from the females and then each group was re-divided by ages and the numbers counted; then there had to be a reshuffle on marital condition. It is considered that a fairly accurate census was achieved by a rather complex method, forced on the Protectorate because of the small number of qualified and educated enumerators available at that time. It is not believed that the census was in fact taken in one day, and it is likely that areas were omitted, that there was double-counting in certain places, and that some young children and elderly persons were omitted.

The estimates of population, based on the varying systems in operation in East Africa, are compared in Table 1 with the 1948 census results. As will be seen from these comparisons, a large number of persons was discovered, mainly adult females and children. The large increase in population resulted from the inadequacy of the factors used in the past in Kenya and Tanganyika and the under-registration of births and deaths recorded in Uganda Protectorate.

Table 1: Comparison of Estimated Population of 1947 and Census Totals 1948

Territory	Estimated population, 1947, total	Census, 1948, total	Absolute difference
Kenya Colony	4,055,000	5,373,000	1,318,000
Tanganyika Territory	5,917,000	7,332,000	1,415,000
Uganda Protectorate	3,967,000*	4,917,000	950,000
Total	13,939,000	17,622,000	3,683,000

* End 1946.

Census Methods, 1948

The methods used in the 1948 population census of British East Africa have been described in the reports on the population censuses and elsewhere.[1] In these full details of the methods

[1] C. J. Martin, "The East African population census; planning and enumeration", *Population Studies*, III, 3, 1949, 303–20.

used and descriptions of the forms and system of training were given. The main problems facing the organizers of a population census were (*a*) the time factor in counting, (*b*) the difficulty of obtaining literate staff capable of completing the census schedule, (*c*) the great expense of undertaking such a study over such a vast area with a widely scattered population, (*d*) the natural suspicion of the population, and (*e*) the number of questions which had to be asked. The season of the year when the census could be taken was fixed almost automatically because the "rainy seasons" prevented a census being taken at those times. It was finally decided to hold the census at the time of the harvest in August.

In the East African territories the population does not live in small villages; the population is scattered in agricultural holdings all over the countryside and although the Africans belong to known administrative units, their huts are hidden throughout the mountainside, or in the case of Buganda are covered almost completely by banana trees, as they nestle in gardens of coffee and cotton. One of the main problems was finding the huts and working out systems of travel which reduced to a minimum the number of miles to be covered by enumerators.

The main aim of the census was to count the total population in the shortest possible period of time. To do this required a large number of enumerators, which reduced the acceptable standard, while the need for speed and the semi-literacy of certain enumerators necessitated a very simple form. It was decided, after pilot studies had been made, that a general population census should be held, the main aims of which were to count the total population over the shortest period of time and to obtain the simplest characteristics. This census should be followed by a sample census of some 10 per cent of the population, the aim of which would be to collect detailed demographic characteristics using the best enumerators with the highest qualifications. Time was not of importance in this second study.

The data called for by all government departments and outside bodies were enormous. They were pruned to certain basic questions on tribe, sex, age group and marital condition. A preliminary schedule was sent to all district commissioners, asking for the main details about their district including the number of literate staff in government departments and schools, together with estimates of population totals, geographical size of the district and estimates of the length of time each officer thought the census should take. When all this information had been analysed, it was obvious that only a most simple census could be achieved, to be followed by the sample census where detailed characteristics would be obtained.

Supervisors chosen by the Administration were trained for a period of three weeks on how to take a census at central schools in two of the territories and at provincial schools in the other. The reasons for the census were explained to them and they became thoroughly indoctrinated in census methods. They had to carry out small test studies themselves in addition to enumerating each other. When their training was completed, they were sent to their districts to undertake the training of the enumerators who were brought together in groups by the district commissioners, either at the district headquarters or at certain schools and other centres. The Census Officer, who was a senior administrative officer of the territory, from time to time checked on the supervisors' ability as teachers. The sample census form was not described to the sample census enumerators until after the general census had been completed.

A total of some 25,000 enumerators was used throughout the territories. Some were not very literate and mistakes were made. In the very densely populated areas the population was counted in a period of one day, but in more sparsely populated areas the census took up to a week and among the wandering nomadic tribes it took even longer.

The sample census was an individual enumeration by hut. The name of each person residing in the hut was recorded, together with details of his or her estimated age if known, marital condition, occupation, religion, tribe, place of birth, the number of children each woman had borne and certain details on education and infirmities. The enumerators for the sample census were chosen from the best supervisors and enumerators in the general census and they were allowed sufficient time to carry out the study. Different results were obtained in the general and sample censuses, particularly for ages, but some indication of the comparability of the general and sample censuses

Population Census Estimates in British E. Africa

was given in the *Reports on the Populations of Trust Territories*, No. 2, Supplement "Additional information on the population of Tanganyika" (pages 23-5). The comparability between the two censuses was quite satisfactory, particularly in view of the absence of a frame on which to plan the sample census in 1948.

The analysis of the census was carried out centrally, using all the advantages of a factory system with progress chasers and supervisors controlling the work of a large number of clerical staff whose task was simple and routine.

Census Methods, 1957

The system adopted in the census of Tanganyika in 1957 was similar to that used for the East African territories in 1948. It was found that a general enumeration, with a sample census, would meet best the requirements of government departments especially since the same details were required for small administrative areas. For the sample census the Statistical Department had an advantage because it had certain information available to it from the 1948 census, which allowed a frame to be prepared and a random sample study to be made. The general enumeration covered the same subjects as in 1948, with the exception of marital condition. It was decided that this item should be omitted as very little useful information had been obtained. In order that a population density map of Tanganyika could be prepared, the Department divided the area of Tanganyika into some 563 territorial census areas, and it was decided that analyses should be made by these areas. The size of each territorial census area was known by the Survey Department and so it was possible to include densities for a much larger number of areas than had been possible in 1948. The densities in 1948 could only be worked out for areas such as chiefdoms and districts. On each form the name of the territorial census area was stamped prior to its despatch to enumerators and by this means it was possible to analyse the results quickly. In all other respects, including the training of supervisors and enumerators, the general census followed the lines described earlier in this chapter and in other publications in regard to the 1948 censuses.

The sample census was on a smaller scale than in 1948 and

it was decided that the information to be collected should be significant for provinces and not for districts. While it was hoped that certain information could be made available at the district level, the Statistical Adviser to the East African Governments decided that to provide information on a sample basis which would be accurate at district level would necessitate a much larger sample and would increase the cost greatly. A two-stage sampling scheme was planned. Territorial census areas which had already been defined were used as the basis of the first stage of sampling with a sampling fraction of one-fifth. From all the territorial census areas which were included in the sample, a list of headmens' areas was prepared with the aid of the local administration and a random sample of headmens' areas was produced. These areas then formed the sample for the study of roughly 5 per cent of the population of the territory. As might be expected many areas which were drawn in the sample were many miles from roads and some of course were relatively uninhabited with the result that various officers were not in favour of these areas being included. However it was explained to them as necessary and that no substitution was possible if the random sample nature was to be maintained. A detailed report on this census will be published by the East African Statistical Department.

The Tanganyika general census involved the use of some 10,000 enumerators, the majority of whom were schoolteachers and schoolchildren. The use of schoolchildren on a large scale was experimented with first in Zanzibar in 1948, and with the expansion of schools and school facilities it was decided to use the Education Department for the collection of information in the 1957 census. The children were taught mainly in school by their schoolmasters and this proved successful.

The analysis of the general population census was completed within a period of ten and a half months, the total population as reported amounted to 8·6 million people, an increase of 1·2 million over the 1948 census, or an annual geometrical increase of 1·75 per cent per annum. The analysis of the sample census is continuing at the time of writing this chapter. The analysis of any population census of East Africa is made more complicated by the desire for administrative purposes to have distributions by up to seven races and an analysis of the African population by as many as 140 tribes. The tribal analysis is complicated, and is made more so by the fact that often persons enumerated give clan names rather than tribal names. In some territories different tribes have the same name and this causes further complications, made worse by the fact that no one at the present time can agree on the spelling of most tribal names. All population analyses in Africa are prolonged due to this complicated tribal division which is required by administrators, sociologists and anthropologists, but which from a demographic viewpoint, while interesting, is not vital. It would be of the greatest value if a tribal classification for Africa could be developed and accepted as standard for census and other sociological studies in the same way as the international trade classification or the international classification of occupations are accepted.

The 1957 census of Tanganyika and the 1958 census of Zanzibar and the proposed 1959 census in Uganda, together with the prospective 1961 census in Kenya, will meet the requirements as given in "Studies in Methods. Series F. No. 5: Handbook of population census methods", Statistical Office, United Nations, New York, 1954, for coverage and will also cover the minimum range of subjects recommended at the W.H.O./C.C.T.A. conference on vital and health statistics held in Brazzaville in November 1956. In the report of this conference it was stated that the minimum coverage for every census should be (*a*) either the *de facto* or *de jure* population by geographical sub-divisions, (*b*) the relationship to the head of household, (*c*) sex, (*d*) age or age group, and (*e*) tribe or race. It was decided that the relationship to the head of the household was not important in East Africa and time should be devoted to trying to get the other basic characteristics. In accordance with the recommendations of the same conference, sample surveys were to be carried out which, as stated in the report, "may provide a greater wealth of detail and more accurate information, also facilitating the fieldwork and simplifying computation analysis".

In addition to these censuses, which are costly in time and manpower, an attempt has been made in the East African territories to commence sample surveys on a limited scale. These are in accordance with the suggestions put forward for the collection of vital statistics together with population totals in underdeveloped territories and these in turn would allow rates to be calculated on comparable bases.[1] The danger with the calculation of most rates at the present time in East Africa is that the basic information is collected relatively accurately, but the secondary data on the population to which the information refers are only known, except at census intervals, with a wide margin of error. To date no actual studies except of a pilot nature have been made, but it is thought that in one or two of the East African territories this method will be put into operation when finance permits since it is generally accepted that this scheme will give better results than the taking of periodic censuses.

Certain sample studies have already been carried out, one of the most notable being a sample study of the population of the city of Nairobi. This study was an attempt to obtain an estimate of the total population of Nairobi city for planning purposes and to discover the growth in the size of the city since 1948. It had been discovered that in Tanganyika in many of the towns the population had grown at a rate of about 7 per cent per annum and it was necessary to have some idea of the growth of the largest urban centre in East Africa. The method used was to prepare a sample, based on geographical areas of the city, and on varying sample fractions. The work was carried out by schoolchildren over a period of time and fairly accurate results were obtained. For the total population of Nairobi it is estimated that for all sampling areas the probable limits of error were plus or minus less than 5 per cent, the greatest limits of error being found in the European population dwelling in flats. At the time of this survey the East African Statistical Department was not fully cognizant of the great changeover to flat dwelling and it was this which biassed the results most. It is believed that the experience gained in this first attempt will make any further studies much easier, and it is hoped to carry out these urban sample censuses at annual intervals in other areas of East Africa.[2] The growth of urban populations is a

---

[1] C. J. Martin, "The collection of basic demographic data in underdeveloped countries", *Bulletin of the International Statistical Institute*, XXXIV, 3, 1953.

[2] East African Statistical Department, *Sample Population Census of Nairobi, 1957/58. An experiment in sampling methods*, June 1958.

most important factor in general development and since the majority of this growth comes from migration from surrounding rural areas, it cannot be estimated except by direct recording.

In addition to these demographic studies, census material has been collected as part of sample studies carried out by the East African Medical Survey and also by the East African Institute of Malaria and Vector-borne Diseases in the Taveta-Pare area. Studies have also been undertaken by sociologists and anthropologists, but here a much more direct questioning of the population by the controller of the scheme has been possible because of the small numbers involved. The development of vital statistics registration has been slow, although committees have sat on the subject, notably a committee in Uganda as the result of the Fraser report on health services in Uganda.

The Protectorate of Zanzibar

In the Protectorate of Zanzibar population censuses of differing standards have been held since 1911. In 1924 a group enumeration of the African population was attempted, but in total only fifty clerks were available to undertake the task and although it was possibly the most accurate census or enumeration available to that date, it is not thought that the total population was covered.[1] The first individual enumeration was made in 1948, when individual ages were requested from every inhabitant in the islands, together with details of birthplace, nationality, occupation and also size of family for women. A sample census was unnecessary because the detailed characteristics were obtained from each person in the course of the general census. The age distribution of the population was found on analysis to be most inaccurate, but this was mainly due to the inability of the population to define ages, and in a relatively non-numerically minded society it was found that some people could not differentiate between 17 years of age and 70 years of age. In the 1958 census an age-grouping method was adopted and in total eight age-groups were used. Historical events and other aids were brought in to achieve a better age distribution. Even then it has been found very difficult to

[1] *Report on the Native Census, Zanzibar, 1924*, 4.

reconcile some of the ages given with normal age distribution for an underdeveloped country.

The census was controlled by a Census Officer and some 1,000 enumerators were used. The majority of these were schoolchildren who were trained in school by their schoolmasters before spending four days prior to the census date enumerating each person individually and then going round the houses on the night of the census or the morning after and revising the census schedules. Because of the small distances to be covered by the enumerators and the large number of persons available to undertake this work, it was possible to carry out an individual enumeration successfully.

Conclusions

Development of census methods in the East African territories has followed the growth of the standard of education and the expansion of services throughout the territories. In areas such as the Protectorate of Zanzibar, where there are large numbers of people in relationship to land areas and where it is possible for enumerators to move quickly, a system of individual enumeration was put into force in 1948 and was adopted again in 1958. In such areas it was discovered that attempts to obtain individual ages met with little success in a general enumeration and therefore in 1958 an age-group method was adopted and enumerators were trained by the use of historical events, etc., to question the population and to put down ages based on categories.

In the mainland territories methodology has depended on the availability of educated enumerators, together with the standard of literacy of the population. The advance in the number of children at school since 1948 has made it possible to have a larger number of enumerators at work under the control of schoolteachers. The census has become almost a combined operation of the Statistical Department, the local Administration and the Education Department. It was decided that the best use which could be made of the increased standard of enumerator, together with the increased numbers of enumerators, was to try to carry out a sample enumeration more accurately and more quickly and so no development has been made

on the expansion of the general census schedule in the East African territories. The basic questions suggested at the Brazzaville conference, which were sex, age, race or tribe or division, are the ones used in the old and new censuses of the East African territories. The development of a statistical frame for sampling, based on the 1948 population censuses, has allowed a smaller census fraction to be used in the sample censuses. Where previously a 10 per cent sample was used, it is thought now that not more than 5 per cent is necessary, since the analyses are presented for provincial areas only and not for districts. In addition to the development of sampling methods at census intervals, schemes have been prepared for continuous sample censuses throughout areas of the territories in which census totals would be obtained together with details of vital events which would allow a number of important rates, particularly death rates, to be collected for a number of years in the hope that with the development of these sample censuses it would be possible to organize better systems of birth and death registrations throughout the territories. The development of census methods and registration systems to the standard of an individual enumeration, with a complementary territory-wide system of birth and death registration, will depend on the expansion of educational facilities and the development of the national income of the territories to a state where such studies can be afforded.

LIST OF CENSUSES TAKEN IN THE TERRITORIES OF KENYA, TANGANYIKA, UGANDA AND ZANZIBAR, TOGETHER WITH TITLES OF REPORTS

Kenya Colony and Protectorate

(1) E. A. Protectorate Census Return, 1911.
(2) Report on the Census of Non-Natives held on 24th April 1921.
(3) Report on the Non-Native Census Enumeration made in the Colony and Protectorate of Kenya on the night of 21st February 1926.
(4) Report on the Non-Native Enumeration made in the Colony and Protectorate of Kenya on the night of 6th March 1931.
(5) Report on the Non-Native Population from analyses of information obtained from the issue of Series V Ration Books during January 1947.
(6) Report on the Census of Non-Native Population of Kenya Colony and Protectorate taken on the night of 25th February 1948.

C. J. Martin

(7) Geographical and Tribal Studies: analyses prepared from the census results of the African Population of Kenya Colony and Protectorate taken in August 1948.

Tanganyika

(1) Report on the Native Census, 1921.
(2) Census of the Native Population, 1931.
(3) Report on the Non-Native Census taken in the Territory on the night of 26th April 1931.
(4) Report on the Census of Non-Native Population of Tanganyika taken on the night of 25th February 1948.
(5) Geographical and Tribal Studies: analyses prepared from the census results of the African Population of Tanganyika taken in August 1948.
(6) Report on the Census on the Non-African Population taken on the night of 13th February 1952.
(7) Report on the Census of Non-African Population taken on the night of 20th/21st February 1957.
(8) Reports on the General African Census taken in August 1957:
    (a) Analysis by sex and age.
    (b) Analysis by tribe and district.
    (c) Analysis by tribe and territorial census area.

Uganda

(1) Census Returns, 1911.
(2) Census Returns, 1921.
(3) Census Returns, 1931.
(4) Report on the Census of Non-Native Population of Uganda Protectorate taken on the night of 25th February 1948.
(5) Geographical and Tribal Studies: analyses prepared from the census results of the African Population, 1948.

Zanzibar Protectorate

(1) Report on the Non-Native Census, 1921.
(2) Report on the Native Census, 1924.
(3) Report on the census enumeration of the whole population on the night of 28th/29th March 1931.
(4) Notes on the Census of the Zanzibar Protectorate taken on the night of 25th February 1948.

4

Demographic Features of Central Africa

J. R. H. SHAUL

THE Federation of Rhodesia and Nyasaland has an area of 475,000 square miles, which is only 50,000 square miles less than that of Spain, France, Belgium and the Netherlands combined, and is slightly more than that of the four provinces of the Union of South Africa. With an estimated total population of 8 millions, the Federation is little more than half as densely populated as the Union, and has barely one twelfth as many persons to the square mile as the states referred to in Western Europe.

The Federation was formed in 1953, bringing together the Protectorate of Nyasaland, the Colony and Protectorate of Northern Rhodesia and the self-governing colony of Southern Rhodesia. These three territories lie within the tropics, and embrace the greater part of the drainage system of the Zambezi Basin, together with the headwaters of the River Congo and a portion of the north bank of the River Limpopo. A large part of the area consists of the Central African Plateau, and is suitable for permanent European settlement above 3,000 feet. Though the whole of the Federation lies within the tropics, the effect of altitude is to produce a wide range of climates, which range from the tropical in the larger valleys to the temperate in the highest parts of the plateau.

The first census of the Federation took place on 8th May 1956, and showed that there were 248,000 Europeans, 19,081 Asians and 10,855 persons of mixed race living in the federal state, and that some 1,037,343 Africans were employed by the persons enumerated in the census. It did not cover Africans not so employed, who were estimated at the census date to number about 6,173,000 persons. Comparison with earlier territorial enumerations showed that the African population of the Federation was growing at a rate of about 2½ per cent per annum. The figure for Europeans, wherein the effects of both immigration and natural increase played their part, was about 6 per cent per annum between 1953 and 1958; the present rate is 3 per cent and it is generally considered that the rate of growth in the present decade will not exceed 5 per cent. No comparable figure can be given for Asians and persons of mixed race because of changes in the method of classification.

Before the creation of the Federation the three territories conducted their censuses separately, and followed no consistent or co-ordinated policy, whether in the selection of census dates or in the drawing up of questionnaires. In consequence it is difficult to make valid comparisons between the three. In the following pages an account will be given first of the several censuses that have been conducted in the three territories, and then an analysis will be made of their findings and of the differences and similarities revealed between the constituent parts of the Federation.

Census Taking

The first census conducted in what is now the Federation was in Southern Rhodesia in 1901, and was followed by two further censuses there, in 1904 and 1907, before censuses came to be taken in each of the three territories in 1911. This may seem surprising in view of the fact that the first European settlement occurred in Nyasaland in 1884, four years before the start of the European occupation of Southern Rhodesia. In Nyasaland, however, the establishment of a British Protectorate in 1891 led to a check in the granting of land concessions to foreigners, and since little mineral wealth has been found in the country the number of Europeans in the country has risen quite slowly to its present figure of about 9,000 only. With little taxable wealth the country lacked at first both the means and the motive for census taking. In Southern Rhodesia, on the other hand, extensive land grants and the development of mining have proceeded rapidly, so that in all about half the

country has been alienated to Europeans or reserved for occupation by the European population, which now numbers about 225,000 persons. In Northern Rhodesia, where European settlement began a few years later than further south, censuses were at first taken at intervals of ten years or longer. It has been in the last fifteen years only that the resources of the territory have come to be in any way comparable with those of Southern Rhodesia, and censuses are now being taken at five-year intervals. All current censuses refer to residence at the time of the census rather than to place of domicile, since they relate to midnight of the census date.

In Southern Rhodesia, then, the first census was held in 1901, followed by censuses at irregular intervals—1904, 1907, 1911 and 1921—after which a census has been held every five years up to 1956. Except in 1907, when only Europeans and Asians were enumerated, the census has included all races, but counts of the whole African population were made in 1904, 1911 and 1921 only. From 1926 onwards only Africans in employment have been enumerated. The first reliable figures of the African population and its vital statistics were obtained by the sample demographic surveys of the Africans held in 1948 and 1953–6.

The population characteristics of Northern Rhodesia are less well known. The first census was held in 1911, and altogether five censuses have been held since then, in 1921, 1931, 1946, 1951 and 1956. Since 1946 the Central African Statistical Office has been taking a quinquennial census concurrently with that in Southern Rhodesia. In 1911 only European and Asian persons were counted, but from 1921 onwards the census has covered these groups and persons of mixed race. No census has been taken of the African population, but a sample demographic survey of Africans was taken in 1950.

In Nyasaland, too, the first census was taken in 1911, followed by further censuses in 1921, 1926, 1931, 1945 and 1956. Up to 1945 the census distinguished between Europeans, Asians and Africans. In 1945 the group "Other Non-Europeans" was introduced to include persons of mixed race who paid the Protectorate poll tax as distinct from the African poll tax.

In the Federal census of 1956 a group entitled "persons of mixed race" was distinguished, being defined similarly in all three territories as "persons whose parents are of different race and who live after the same style as a European". While the demographic characteristics of the African population of the two Rhodesias has been determined by sample surveys, little is known about the demographic characteristics of the African population of Nyasaland for there has been no sample survey. Counts of the African population of Nyasaland and of their principal characteristics were taken at the census dates 1921, 1926, 1931 and 1945. Dr. Kuczynski considered that either the two earlier counts understated, or that the 1931 count over-stated, the totals, since the persons employed in taking the census had no qualifications for the work, and after a necessarily quite perfunctory check by an administrative officer a clerk in the Census Office did nothing more than add up the numbers in the enumeration tables. Kuczynski thought the counting of the *de facto* African population in 1945 was a great improvement on those earlier counts, and in particular that it threw a much clearer light on the age composition of the native population than any earlier count.[1]

The Population of the Federation

The total population of the Federation on 30th June 1959 was estimated to be 8,134,000 persons, made up as follows:

Table 1

Race		Total	Percentage
Europeans		297,000	4
Asians	}	37,000	—
Mixed race			
Africans		7,800,000	96
Total		8,134,000	100

These were by no means evenly divided throughout the three territories. In 1959, 72 per cent of all the Europeans lived

[1] R. R. Kuczynski, *Demographic Survey of the British Colonial Empire*, II, East Africa, 1949.

in Southern Rhodesia, where they constituted 7·1 per cent of the total population; 25 per cent lived in Northern Rhodesia, where they represented 3·1 per cent of the Northern Rhodesian population, and the remaining 3 per cent were in Nyasaland, where they made up only 0·32 per cent of the Nyasaland population. Asians were even less significant numerically, their highest percentage of a territorial population being in Northern Rhodesia and Nyasaland, and there they amounted to only 0·3 per cent of the territorial total. The numerical preponderance of the Africans is thus a feature of all the territories, being relatively least in Southern Rhodesia, where in 1959 they made up 92·0 per cent of the whole, and most in Nyasaland,

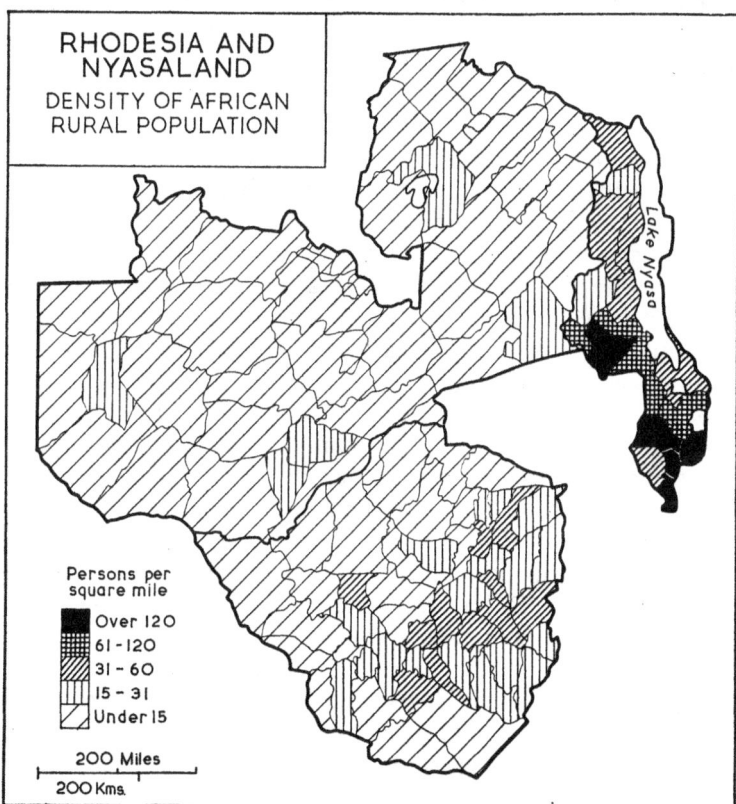

Fig. I. The density of African rural population in the Federation of Rhodesia and Nyasaland, 1959.

where they constituted 99·4 per cent of the Protectorate's inhabitants[1] (Fig. I, p. 35).

The Population of Southern Rhodesia[2]

(a) *European Population.* The European population of Southern Rhodesia in 1901 was 11,070, in 1921 it was 33,780, in 1941 69,330, and in 1956 it had risen to 178,000. During the period covered by the censuses the European population has displayed waves of growth, dominated largely by the volume of immigration. Up to 1904 the population was growing at a rate of just under 5 per cent, between 1904 and 1907 at 3 per cent, between 1907 and 1911 at the high annual rate of over 15 per cent and between 1911 and 1921 at 3·6 per cent per annum. Between 1921 and 1926 the rate increased to 5 per cent but declined to 2·1 per cent in the depression years 1931 to 1936. Up to the close of the last war the European population was growing at the rate of 4 to 5 per cent a year, but after 1946 there was a great surge forward and between 1946 and 1956 the European population more than doubled from 83,500 to 178,000. Taking a forward view of 10 years it seems reasonable to adopt an annual increase of 5 per cent a year for population projection estimates, but in view of the fluctuations revealed it is inadvisable to project at this rate for a longer period of years.

Besides immigration natural increase plays an important part in the growth of the population. Compulsory registration of births and deaths of persons other than "aboriginal natives of Africa" was made effective from 1st April 1904. In urban areas the registration of deaths of all races is compulsory. Since no body can be buried without a burial certificate very few deaths escape registration. The frequent censuses already described provide an important means of checking the completeness of the birth registration and show that registration of European births is very accurate. Registration of Asians and persons of mixed race are unsatisfactory in earlier years but for a short period ending in 1953 state maternity grants were made

[1] Central African Statistical Office, *Monthly Digest of Statistics*. Articles on the Federal Census of Population, 1956, 1956–8.
[2] *Report of the Census of Population of Southern Rhodesia*, 1951.

dependent on the production of birth certificates and during that period the registration coverage was good.

Records of European births and deaths have been published since 1906. The birth rate has always been high and is one of the highest among countries inhabited by persons of European stock.

In 1906, when the death rate was naturally much higher than at the present day, the natural increase of the European population was 10·6 per 1,000. Twenty years later, although the birth rate had fallen from 25·4 to 23·8, natural increase had risen to 15 per 1,000 due to the death rate falling from 14·9 to 8·8 per 1,000. By 1946 the birth rate had risen to 25·7 again and the natural increase to 17·2 per 1,000. In recent years the birth rate has risen further, reaching 27 per 1,000 in 1959; in that year the death rate was 6 per 1,000 and the natural increase 21 per 1,000. Over the period there has been a remarkable improvement in European infant mortality. In 1906 the rate was 150 per 1,000, in 1926 49 per 1,000, in 1946 30 per 1,000 and in 1959 17 per 1,000. Taken as a whole these figures show a substantial fall in the death rate at all ages and indicate a healthy climate for Europeans. The Southern Rhodesian Life Tables for 1936 give an expectation of life at birth of 58·52 years for males compared with 58·74 in England and Wales, the corresponding figures for women being 62·57 and 62·88. The most recent figures suggest an improvement at about the same rate as in England and Wales.

The net production rate, which measures the rate at which women of child-bearing age are being replaced, is 1·55 and is higher than in most centres. If continued at this level this index would reflect a 55 per cent increase in population due to natural causes in a generation. Since 1936 each census year has shown a relatively marked increase in the rate, and under the conditions of rising births and declining deaths already described this increase should continue.

The favourable vital statistics so far described are not attributable purely to a healthy climate. The European population is dominated by the immigration of a young and vigorous population with the result that the proportion of Europeans in the child-bearing ages is high and the proportion of old people is low. Thus in 1956, 31 per cent of the population were under

15 years of age, only 7 per cent over 59 years, the remaining 62 per cent being between 15 and 60 years.

Reference has been made to the effect of immigration on the vital statistics and age structure of the population. Since 1915, when immigration figures were first kept, there has been a number of waves of high immigration, namely the years 1919 to 1921, 1925 to 1930, 1935 to 1939, 1946 to 1952 and 1955 to 1957. In 1957 and subsequent years immigration has been regulated by quota, and in 1957 amounted to 16,431 persons of whom 16,380 were Europeans. The ever-increasing size of the natural increase will ultimately reduce the dominating effect of these waves of immigration on the relative growth of the total population, but it will be many years before this position is reached.

(*b*) *Asians and Persons of Mixed Race.* In 1911 there were 880 Asians in Southern Rhodesia. By 1926 the number had risen to 1,460, by 1946 to 2,940 and by 1956 to 5,127. Immigration is not an important determinant of the rate of growth of the Asian population. Birth registrations have always been unreliable, but in any case the total population is too small for the purpose of determining reliable vital statistics, net reproduction rates and life tables. During the period 1951 to 1956 the population has been growing at the rate of 3·6 per cent per annum. The age pyramid of the Asian population is regular with a relatively wide base of persons under 15, the proportion under 15 in 1956 being 41 per cent and only 5 per cent being 60 years and over, the remainder being between 15 and 60 years of age.

The census of population defines a person of mixed race as one whose parents are of different race and who lives after the same style as a European. Other persons of mixed race are classified as Africans. It follows that the numbers shown by the census are recruited from three sources, (1) immigration from African areas to the European area; (2) the natural increase of the population and the rate of miscegenation; (3) migration from other territories. In May 1911 there were only 2,042 persons of mixed race in Southern Rhodesia, in 1926 2,158, in 1946 4,559 and in 1956 8,079 persons. As in the case of the Asian population, birth registrations are too incomplete to warrant the publication of birth rates or the estimation of net reproduction rates. The census of population classifies the population by race of parents, and shows that the principal source of increase is from families in which both parents are of mixed race. Thus in 1956 out of 8,079 persons, 4,869 had parents who were both of mixed race. The age pyramid of the population is regular with a wide base for the ages 15 and under who represented 52 per cent, and the numbers over 59 years 2·2 per cent of the population in 1956.

There are high concentrations of Asian and Coloured persons in Salisbury and Bulawayo, there being 3,340 Asians and 4,640 persons of mixed race in these two towns in 1956. Asians tend to congregate in towns even more than persons of mixed race, and the total number of Asians in the Municipalities between 1921 and 1956 varied from 73 to 85 per cent of the Asian population, as compared with 47 to 63 per cent for persons of mixed race.

(*c*) *African Population.* Until the organization of the sample demographic surveys of the African populations of Southern Rhodesia in 1948 and 1953-5 and of Northern Rhodesia in 1950 little was known of the population characteristics of the Africans. The adoption of the new statistical method of study was the pioneer model for a series of similar investigations in many African territories which have resulted in a considerable widening of knowledge of the demography of the African.[1] Earlier estimates of the African population were originally based on the number of registered huts subject to hut tax, but in later years the basis was changed to the number of registered taxpayers. To these figures a coefficient was applied to form an estimate of the total men, women and children concerned. The estimates were made by administrative districts and then added up for the whole country. As may readily be imagined the quality of the estimates by districts varied not merely with the degree of conscientiousness displayed by the district officer but also with the accuracy of the coefficients employed from time to time to accord with current conditions. The first sample demographic survey showed that in 1948 estimates for the whole country were remarkably good and fell within sampling limits established for the survey.

[1] J. R. H. Shaul, "Designing African demographic sample surveys in Central Africa", *Central African Journal of Medicine*, 1, 3, 1955, 120-4.

J. R. H. Shaul

The accuracy of a sample survey of this nature is dependent upon the accuracy of the frame used as a basis for sampling. The survey adopts for a frame not the registers of African taxpayers but a list of villages drawn up from the register. It is considered that while the list of taxpayers is incomplete owing to evasion, it is very unlikely that any African village escapes representation on the register and for that reason the results are considered reasonably accurate. The 1948 sample comprised 2,561 out of 23,370 sample units or a little more than 11 per cent. In designing the sample a sample error of 5 per cent for each African district was sought but in general the error exceeded 5 per cent, while that for the whole country was 1·4 per cent.[1]

The densest African population in Southern Rhodesia is found in a belt running north and south parallel to and a little to the west of the eastern border. Density declines progressively in the direction of the eastern border and in the direction of the Zambezi. There is another region of dense population round the Lundi River and in the neighbourhood of Shabani and Fort Victoria. Population declines progressively from these districts in the direction of the Limpopo River, the south-western boundary and the Zambezi. Fig. I (p. 35).

The sample survey provided the first estimates of the natural increase of the population. The birth rate in 1948 was 46·2 per 1,000 (sample error, 0·75), the infant mortality 131 (sample error, 0·8) per 1,000 births and the death rate 18·1 (sample error, 0·3) per 1,000, the natural increase being 28·1 per 1,000. The latter figure represents a doubling of the population every 25 years. Past estimates of population have shown it doubling every 30 years. These characteristics resemble those of the Mexican population, which has a birth rate of 46 per 1,000 and a death rate of 16 per 1,000 in 1950. The death rate of Africans aged 1 year and over was 12·1 per 1,000 compared with 11·0 in the United Kingdom and 11·4 in Mexico.[2]

The 1953–5 sample survey aimed at securing small sample errors of birth, death and infant mortality rates in order to

---

[1] J. R. H. Shaul, "Statistical research and African vital statistics", *C.A.J.M.*, 1, 2, 1955, 83–5; "Vital statistics of Africans living in Southern Rhodesia, 1948", *C.A.J.M.*, 1, 4, 1955, 145–50.
[2] *United Nations Demographic Year-book*, 1959.

compare changes in these rates with those obtained in 1948.[1] Preliminary results relating to 14 administrative districts gave a birth rate of 41·8 compared with 44·8 per 1,000 in the same area in 1948. The change in the birth rate was not statistically significant. The death rates were 12·6 compared with 19·0 per 1,000 and showed a significant decline. The infant mortality rates showed no significant change, being 120 as compared with 123 per 1,000 live births. The natural increase was 2·9 per cent. Dr. C. A. L. Myburgh, who has made a special study of the vital statistics of African population, estimates that the net reproduction rate of Southern Rhodesia is 2·0 compared with 1·5 in Ghana and 1·6 in Swaziland. He estimates the African mean expectation of life at birth as 48 for Southern Rhodesia, 38 for Ghana and 48 for Swaziland.[2]

Little is known regarding the age structure of the African population. The 1948 sample survey gave 52 per cent of the males as below and 48 per cent above puberty. Of the women 50 per cent were below and 50 per cent above puberty. The 1953–5 survey endeavoured to obtain a more detailed breakdown of ages. The age of puberty for men was found to be 16·6 and for women 15·3 years. The survey also suggested that the 1948 survey failed to obtain a full coverage of the adult population.

As a result of the 1953–5 sample surveys tentative models of the age structure of the African population of the 14 districts already mentioned were made from the age of 0 to 45 as follows:

Table 2: Age Group as a percentage of the Total Population

	0–4	5–9	10–14	15–19	20–24	25–29	30–34	35–39	40–44	45 and over
Males	17	15	13	12	10	8	6	4	2	13
Females	17	15	13	11	10	8	6	4	3	13

[1] J. R. H. Shaul, "Preliminary results of the second demographic survey of the African population in Southern Rhodesia", *C.A.J.M.*, I, 5, 1955, 246–9.
The 1953–55 Demographic Sample Survey of the Indigenous Population of Southern Rhodesia.
[2] C. A. L. Myburgh, "A brief comparison of the fertility and mortality rates of Africans in various countries", *C.A.J.M.*, II, 4, 1956, 155–9.

J. R. H. Shaul

Attention has been drawn to the resemblance between the vital statistics of Mexico and of the African population of Southern Rhodesia. The resemblance also extends to the age structure of the populations, that of Mexico for males and females being as follows:

Table 3: Age Group as a percentage of Total Mexican Population, 1950

	0–4	5–9	10–14	15–19	20–24	25–29	30–34	35–39	40–44	45 and over
Males	16	15	13	10	8	8	6	6	5	13
Females	15	14	12	11	9	8	5	6	5	15

The estimates show that the proportion of African women of child-bearing age (15–44) is 42 per cent of the total number of women. The corresponding figure for Mexico is 44 per cent, for Venezuela 45 per cent and for the Maori population of New Zealand 42 per cent. Similar figures for England and Wales are 41 per cent, Northern Ireland 42 per cent, Scotland 42 per cent. The high birth rates of the African population in Southern Rhodesia are therefore due to high fertility rather than to a high proportion of potential mothers.

The Population of Northern Rhodesia[1]

(a) *European Population.* This numbered 1,497 in 1911 and in 1921 it was only 3,634. From 1931 onwards the effects of mining development became apparent, for the European figure for 1931 was 13,846, for 1946 21,907, for 1951 37,079 and for 1956 64,810. The discovery of rich copper deposits occurred in 1925 in the north-west of the territory. There was a great wave of immigration from then onwards, and the European population rose to a peak of 13,846, after which it declined to a figure which Kuczynski places in the neighbourhood of 12,000 in 1935. In the twelve years between 1935 and 1946 there was a heavy gain attributable to immigration, and since 1946 the European population has continued to grow rapidly from the same source. Between 1946 and 1951 the population increase consisted of

[1] *Report of the Census of Population of Northern Rhodesia, 1951.*

3,300 excess of births over deaths, the remainder being due to the net migration of Europeans. Between 1946 and 1956 European population has been growing at the rate of 11 per cent per annum compound interest, but it is clear that this rate cannot be maintained indefinitely. For a long-period forecast of ten years a rate of 6 per cent would appear reasonable, but in view of the rapid developments within the country, both political and economic, it would be unwise to attempt any projection of the European population more than a decade ahead.

Compulsory registration of births and deaths of Europeans was introduced into Northern Rhodesia in 1905 and in North-Western Rhodesia in 1909. Since 1914 when the two territories were amalgamated, registration has been governed by the Births and Deaths Registration Ordinance. Registration is obligatory for persons of European, American or Asiatic descent. Kuczynski doubted whether the statistics were reliable up to 1943, and pointed out that the rates were worked out on inappropriate population estimates; he re-worked corrected figures for 1924–43. Since 1948 the statistics have been prepared by the Central African Statistical Office, which has drawn a proper distinction between European, Asian and Coloured populations and has worked the rates on the correct population estimates. Up to 1939 the figures concerned were too small to enable any sound conclusion to be drawn, since a small evasion of registration could produce a disproportionate error in the rates. This is not the case after 1946, and for 1946 and 1951 the Central African Statistical Office estimated the net reproduction rate of Europeans at 1·41 and 1·58 respectively. The latter figure is similar to that of Southern Rhodesia.

As with Southern Rhodesia the high fertility of the European population in Northern Rhodesia is due to the high proportion of women of child-bearing age. The age-population pyramid is very similar to that of Southern Rhodesia, the proportion of females to males being rather lower. In 1956 the proportion of persons under 15 years of age was 33 per cent and of those aged 60 or over 4 per cent, some 63 per cent being between 15 and 60. Emigration figures have never been kept, but the figures of inter-censal increases since 1946 show the dominant part of immigration not only as a source of population growth but also accounting for the very small proportion of the population of 60 years or over.

(b) *Asians and Persons of Mixed Race.* In 1911 there were only 39 Asians in Northern Rhodesia, and it was not until the census of 1946 that the number (1,117) exceeded 1,000. In 1951 the numbers had increased to 2,524 and in 1956 to 5,400. Immigration of Asians into the territory was not controlled until the establishment of the Federation, and the increase of the population has been dominated by net immigration. The numbers are too small to justify the estimation of reliable vital statistics. As regards the age structure, 40 per cent of the Asians were under 15 and 2 per cent were 60 and over in 1956, the remainder being between 15 and 60 years.

In the census of 1911 persons of mixed race were classed as Africans. The total number in this group in 1921 was 145, in 1931 it was 425, in 1946 804, in 1951 1,112 and in 1956 it had reached 1,577. The analysis of the population by race of parents shows that of these 1,577 persons 785 were the descendants of parents of mixed race, 375 were due to miscegenation of European and African persons, 135 of Europeans and persons of mixed race and the remainder of various mixed races. Over half (51 per cent) of these persons were under 15 years and about 1·0 per cent were over 59 years of age.

In general Asians tend to live in urban areas, and persons of mixed race in the rural areas and townships.

(c) *African Population.* No census has yet been taken of the African population. Kuczynski has pointed out how unsatisfactory the estimates of the population were at the time of his studies. The first firm basis for studying the demographic characteristics was provided by the Demographic Sample Survey of the Africans relating to the year 1950.[1] The sample survey confirmed Kuczynski's criticisms, in that it gave a total African population of 1,837,000, as compared with the official estimates of 1,674,000 for 1950. The method employed was similar to that of Southern Rhodesia, namely a sample of the villages recorded in the tax registers; the sample error for the whole country was 1·24 per cent. The areas of densest African population in Northern Rhodesia are the Luapula valley and

[1] J. R. H. Shaul, "Results of the demographic sample survey of the African population of Northern Rhodesia", *C.A.J.M.*, I, 6, 1955, 307–11.

Demographic Features of Central Africa

parts of Fort Jameson, Petauke, Mongu and Kalobo districts. Fig. I (p. 35).

The birth rate of the Africans in Northern Rhodesia was higher than in Southern Rhodesia, being 56·8 per 1,000 persons. Infant mortality was very high, being 259 per 1,000 live births. These figures are in accordance with the evidence surveyed by Kuczynski. The African death rate was also much higher than in Southern Rhodesia, being 32 per 1,000, and the natural increase was 24·6 per 1,000 or a little lower than in Southern Rhodesia. The rate of natural increase showed that the population was doubling every 28 years compared with every 25 years for Southern Rhodesia. Myburgh estimates the mean expectation of life at birth of the African in Northern Rhodesia as 37 years and the net reproduction rate as 1·7, both being lower than in Southern Rhodesia.[1] The sample survey obtained only 3 age divisions, namely under 1, 1 year to puberty and over puberty. The relative number of Africans under puberty is less than in Southern Rhodesia where the proportions in 1953 were 49 per cent for males and 47 per cent for females, compared with 45 and 41 per cent respectively for Northern Rhodesia. On the basis of surveys conducted in Northern Rhodesia Professor Clyde Mitchell has published estimates of the age structure of the African population.[2] For comparison with Southern Rhodesia and Mexico the distribution is given below.

Table 4: Age Group as a percentage of the Total Population

	0–4	5–9	10–14	15–19	20–24	25–29	30–34	35–39	40–44	45 and over
Male	17	13	11	8	8	7	7	6	5	18
Female	15	13	11	10	10	8	7	5	4	17

[1] C. A. L. Myburgh, "Estimating the fertility and mortality of African populations from the total number of children ever born and the number of these still living", *Population Studies*, x, 1956, 193–206.

[2] J. C. Mitchell, "An estimate of fertility in some Yao hamlets in the Liwonde District of Southern Nyasaland", *Africa*, xix, 1949, 293–308.

J. R. H. Shaul

The Population of Nyasaland[1]

(a) *European Population.* In 1901 there were 314 Europeans in Nyasaland, in 1911 there were 766, in 1921 1,486, in 1926 1,656 and in 1931 the figure had reached 1,975. Since the last war immigration has been large and the total population has grown rapidly, being 1,948 in 1945 and 6,730 in 1956. The numbers of births and deaths are naturally small and the reliability of the corresponding rates would be materially affected by any registration omissions. In 1959 275 births and 41 deaths of Europeans were registered. As regards age distribution, 27 per cent are below 15 and 5 per cent are 60 years and over, the remaining 68 per cent being between 15 and 60.

(b) *Asians and Other Non-Europeans.* Up to 1945 the censuses of Nyasaland distinguished only Europeans, Asians and Africans. Other Non-Europeans were enumerated as such in the territorial census of 1945, and in the 1956 federal census the group "persons of mixed race" was introduced. There were 115 Asians in 1901, 481 in 1911, 563 in 1921, 850 in 1926, 1,591 in 1931, 2,804 in 1945 and 8,504 in 1956. The Asian population has been growing more rapidly than the Europeans, mainly through immigration, but since the establishment of the Federation Asian immigration has throughout the Federation been limited to persons related to Asians already living in one of the territories. Some 48 per cent of the Asians are 15 years of age or under, and 2 per cent are aged 60 and over. In 1945 there were 455 Other Non-Europeans and in 1956 persons of mixed race numbered 1,190. Of the persons of mixed race 52 per cent are under 15 years of age and 2 per cent are over 59. Some 480 were born of parents of mixed race, 145 of a European and an African parent, 145 of an Asian and a person of mixed race, 216 of an Asian and African parent and the remainder of various mixed marriages.

(c) *African Population.* The number of Africans enumerated in Nyasaland in 1945 was 2,178,013, and the latest estimate of the African population published by the Central African Statistical Office for 30th June 1959 is 2,750,000. The most densely populated area of Nyasaland is the region south of the Lake, the density of population in 1945 in the Lower Shire District having

[1] *Report of the Census of Nyasaland,* 1945.

been 90, in Chiradzulu District 310 and in Zomba District 201 per square mile. For the whole of the Southern Province the density is 83, and for the Northern Province 27 per square mile. Fig. I (p. 35).

Kuczynski considers that the report on the 1945 count throws a much clearer light on the composition of the native population than any earlier count. Four age groups were distinguished, 0–1, 1–5, 5–18, and 18 and over. The numbers in the first age group were probably double the true figure, and the numbers aged 1–5 were also apparently over-stated, but it seemed probable that the numbers aged 5–18 were not seriously wrong.

The 1945 count gave the number of Africans under 18 in Nyasaland as 50 per cent. In an interesting enquiry in the Liwonde District of Nyasaland Dr. Clyde Mitchell found the proportion of Africans under 15 to be 45 per cent, those aged 15–49 44 per cent and the remainder 11 per cent.[1] The enquiry gave a net reproduction rate of 2·0 and concluded that the population was doubling every 25 years. These conclusions are not at variance with the results of the sample surveys in the two Rhodesias. It is therefore reasonable to conclude that in the absence of more reliable data the average results of the Southern and Northern Rhodesia enquiries relating to the African population may be regarded as representative of the fertility conditions and age structure of the Nyasaland African population.

Addendum

THE 1953–5 DEMOGRAPHIC SAMPLE SURVEY OF THE AFRICAN
POPULATION OF SOUTHERN RHODESIA

The final results of this survey have now been published. The total indigenous population in September 1954 was estimated to be 2,047,000 of which 1,023,000 were males and 1,024,000 females. Some 49 per cent of the males were below the age of puberty (16·4 years) compared with 46 per cent of the females (15·1 years).

---

[1] J. C. Mitchell, "A note on the age and sex distribution of the African population of Northern Rhodesia" in D. Mathews and R. Apthorpe (ed.), *Social Relations in Central African Industry*. Proceedings of the Twelfth Conference of the Rhodes-Livingstone Institute, Lusaka, 1958.

The age distribution of the whole country was as follows:

	0–4	5–9	10–14	15–19	20–24	25–29	30–34	35–39	44–45	45 and over
Males	17	15	13	12	10	8	6	4	2	13
Females	17	15	13	11	9	8	6	3	2	16

The birth rate for the whole country was 44·8 per 1,000, the death rate 14·4 per 1,000 and the infant mortality rate 122 per 1,000 live births. Corresponding rates in 1948 were birth rate 46·2, death rate 18·1 and infant mortality 131 per 1,000 live births. The opinion is expressed that the 1953–5 survey is more reliable than that of 1948, and that the fall in the death rate is probably over-stated. The rate of natural increase has risen from 2·81 to 3·04 per cent per annum. The net reproduction rate is given as 2·1 and the expectation of life is estimated at 48·76 years.

5

Estimates of Population Growth in East Africa, with Special Reference to Tanganyika and Zanzibar

C. J. MARTIN

ANALYSES of population growth require periodic and systematic information on population totals and the regular collection of birth and death records, together with data on migratory movements.

Unfortunately, for the East African territories of Kenya, Tanganyika, Uganda and Zanzibar, information of this nature is not available in the form of a long series. The population counts made in the past are not of identical standards of accuracy and therefore can be used only with caution to estimate changes in population growth. Birth and death records, at present collected in Uganda and Zanzibar, have not been controlled systematically in the past, with the result that the data are not susceptible to statistical analysis and cannot be used for drawing conclusions on changes in natural increase. Information on the migratory movements of the non-African population is available, but very little can be gleaned on the African, particularly on movements to and from other parts of Africa, which are important in certain territories.

The value of population estimates and counts for early years in East Africa has been assessed in an earlier essay in this book. Examination of the records, which show fluctuating figures of population growth, is of no real value in studying the changes of population and it is therefore impossible for a student of East

African demography to hope to do more than reconstruct very tentatively a growth line for the African population.

The factors affecting the population growth in East Africa in the early years of the twentieth century were mainly three in number. It is believed by some demographers, including myself, that the population of East Africa changed very little in size until the end of the First World War. There were increases and declines depending on good seasons, good rainfall, on pestilences, plagues and drought, and on migratory movements. Overall, however, it is thought that there had been very little change over a century.

The early years of the twentieth century brought little expansion in the total African population of Kenya, Tanganyika and Uganda. With the exploration and development of the territories and the expansion of railway facilities opportunities for the prevention of famine existed. But insufficient food was produced on a commercial basis throughout the greater part of the area of 680,000 square miles to allow large-scale transport movements in time of famine while transport facilities were in their infancy. The African population was then living in similar conditions to those which had been experienced for many hundreds of years. The exploration of German East Africa resulted in a number of rebellions and the savage subjugation of the Maji Maji rebellion in Tanganyika in 1905–6 is believed by some to have resulted in half a million deaths, mainly from starvation as a result of a "burnt earth" policy which the Germans adopted. In the British parts of East Africa although there were minor rebellions, nothing of this nature took place. However, the African population still was susceptible to the diseases which came with the immigrant communities, while remaining susceptible also to those which were endemic. The development of medical services was, of course, an extremely slow process throughout such a large area.

The war years from 1914 to 1918 found East Africa a battlefield and a large number of the African male population was used by Germany and by the Allies as porters as well as askaris. Estimates of the numbers who died from dysentery, malaria, etc., vary widely and in all probability estimates are wildly exaggerated, but certainly the death rate increased, while the very activity of enemy troops throughout the area resulted in a reduction in food production with the concomitant dangers of famine and disease.

As an example of writings on the subject of population growth in the East African territories, the following quotations are from Kuczynski's *Demographic Survey of the British Colonial Empire*, Vol. II, East Africa. In this volume is assembled much of the information appertaining to population growth up to the end of the Second World War. He quotes from the missionary Wilson who said in 1879, "The diseases to which the Waganda are subject make a formidable list. Smallpox is one of the most fatal, coming at intervals in epidemics and carrying off thousands of victims. Syphilis is extremely common and is a very frequent complication in other diseases."[1] For the first period of British administration Commissioner Johnson said in 1900 that for the Protectorate as a whole "Civil wars, invasions, and in some districts, famines, have of late years caused an evident decrease in the population".[2] Some people have estimated that in the years around 1900 some 100,000 people died as a result of these causes, but in fact there is little direct evidence. It is considered that between 1900 and 1906 sleeping sickness killed approximately one-tenth of the population of the Uganda Protectorate.

Similar remarks were made about Tanganyika. In 1930 the Director of Medical Services stated that in the period preceding the establishment of the German Protectorate in 1885 the population had been decreasing and that the situation did not change essentially in the following 35 years. As late as 1913 the German Government was doubtful whether even in times of peace the population was increasing and it was believed to be certainly not greater in 1920 than in 1913. The consequences of the war were continuing in the period 1921 to 1925 and any increase which might have come was most likely from 1921 to 1931. Most of the official documents of the period expressed the opinion that the population was fairly stagnant at that time.

In Kenya it was often believed that the population was increasing faster than in the other territories. In the early part of the century all the commissioners were of the opinion that the population was low but could be expected to increase. Famines

---

[1] Kuczynski, *op. cit.*, 314.
[2] *Preliminary Report on the Protectorate of Uganda*, April 1900, 51.

and smallpox, however, killed off a large number, and after the First World War there was a general opinion that the population was stationary or, if anything, was declining. Such available population estimates did little to satisfy statisticians that any real knowledge was available on population growth.

In the inter-war years from 1920 to 1939 medical facilities improved. By means of roads and further rail development it was possible, when famine developed, to send food from other areas. This was particularly true with the expansion of commercial farming by the British community in the Kenya Highlands. The development of African farming for markets meant that as time went on more food became available for sale and although famines did occur, their severity was lessened. Even with this improvement the death rate on account of famines and droughts was still high. The attempt to eradicate such diseases as sleeping sickness, bubonic plague and smallpox came mainly during this inter-war period. Large areas of East Africa are subject to tsetse fly and the main method of eradicating sleeping sickness is by removing the inhabitants from the tsetse-infected area. This action was taken in Tanganyika and Uganda and the reports of the Tsetse Reclamation Departments showed that numbers of people were moved and strict control was instituted over sleeping sickness settlements. With vaccination and the development of dispensaries and health services, the mortality from other causes fell. However it is not thought that mortality declined greatly as the result of general activities of health services. It was famine control and the eradication wherever possible of the major epidemics and diseases which reduced mortality in the earlier years of the twentieth century. The number of doctors and the size of the budgets for health services in East Africa did not permit of enormous expansion of facilities and in all probability the main activity was to get sick people better more quickly rather than to save a great number of patients who were liable to die.

The war years of 1939 to 1945 brought with them the use of East Africa as a base and the education of the African soldier in the use of medical facilities and drugs. Intensified research on malarial problems, particularly in regard to the Burma campaign, meant that drugs were developed to reduce the effect of this disease and reduce the death rate from it. At the end of the war years there was an upsurge and expansion in the general economy, the majority of the African population possessed higher incomes, a higher standard of living and a better knowledge of hygiene and other things. All of these helped to reduce mortality.

It can be estimated that between 1920 and 1948 the increase in East Africa of the African population was from not more than ½ per cent rising to 1½ per cent per annum. In some areas, such as the Central Province of Tanganyika and other places where rainfall is sporadic and the dangers of famine still exist, the increase in the population was possibly very slight indeed. In other areas where people lived at high altitudes, where plentiful rainfall and satisfactory health conditions allowed them good living, the mortality rate was most likely smaller, with the result that there was a regular increasing rate of growth. I think this is particularly true of high-altitude districts such as Tukuyu, the Kilimanjaro slopes, Kigezi, part of the Kikuyu areas in Kenya, and the Mount Elgon area of Uganda. Here there are fairly heavy densities of population, but it is my belief that these heavy densities of population have come from a slow but positive rate of natural increase over many many years and not from any terrific upsurge in recent times. The population data which allow these estimates to be made are scanty, but sufficient is known for one or two areas to make rough estimates.

The 1948 population census was really the benchmark from which estimates of population can be made for the whole of East Africa. Many individual studies were made in the 1920's and in the 1930's, but the population examined differed in coverage on each occasion, with the result that no real comprehensive statement could be made. Unfortunately since 1948 it has not been possible to undertake the demographic research which was contemplated when the censuses were planned. To have been successfully accomplished, demographic research projects should have included a series of repetitive population censuses, the organization of birth and death records in many areas of East Africa and studies of migration. At the present time, however, only two new censuses have been made, in Tanganyika and Zanzibar. These can be considered as a second series, conducted on a comparable basis to the censuses of 1948. They allow some estimates to be made of population growth, giving changes in population characteristics. However, the most important population characteristic, age, is still very badly recorded in population censuses. For Tanganyika in 1948 and in 1957 the age classification, while comparable, is not completely satisfactory. In Zanzibar in 1948 an attempt was made to obtain individual ages. This project was not found to be successful, so in 1958 age groupings were used. Although the groupings were more numerous than in the general population census of the mainland territories, comparisons were not possible because of the differing methods which had to be used.

In August 1957 the second census of Tanganyika was taken. The population, which in 1948 was recorded as 7,410,000, increased to 8,665,000, which was an increase of 16·9 per cent, or a gross rate of increase of 1·75 per cent per annum. Part of the increase was from the immigration of peoples from Kenya, Uganda and Belgian Congo. Allowing for this migratory increase, natural increase was of the order of 1·65 per cent per annum. Details of immigration are not available, but the increase of numbers in the immigrant tribes between 1948 and 1957 was more than would have been expected from the natural rate of increase. The provincial rates of growth are shown in the following table.

Table 1: Total Census: African Population by Provinces, 1948 and 1957

Province	Population in thousands		Percentage increase
	1948	1957	1948–57
Total	7,410*	8,665*	+ 16·9
Lake	1,845	2,228	+ 20·8
Western	946	1,053	+ 11·3
Central	816	879	+ 7·8
Eastern	909	1,040	+ 14·4
Southern Highlands	845	1,024	+ 21·1
Southern	914	1,008	+ 10·3
Tanga	547	671	+ 22·7
Northern	585	759	+ 29·7

* Including persons in transit.

Estimates of Population Growth in East Africa

All provincial areas were comparable between 1948 and 1957, the main alterations being in district boundaries which therefore cannot be used for comparison. The largest increases recorded between the censuses were found in the Lake, Tanga, Southern Highlands and Northern Provinces. In two of these, at any rate, there was a large influx of population, mainly migratory labourers. In Dar es Salaam also, in the Eastern Province, there was an increase, though this increase was not out of line with those of other areas. Of the four provinces which showed increases higher than the average for the territory (16·9 per cent), the Northern Province showed 29·7 per cent, the Tanga Province 22·7 per cent, the Southern Highlands Province 21·1 per cent, and the Lake Province 20·8 per cent. There were four provinces which recorded figures lower than that for the territory. The Eastern Province showed 14·4 per cent, the Western Province 11·3 per cent, the Southern Province 10·3 per cent, and the Central Province 7·8 per cent. Areas where population increases were greatest were those with immigration. This was particularly true of the Northern Province. An indication of the increase in numbers of the tribes of non-Tanganyika origin in the territory is given in the following table. Provincial figures are not readily available.

Table 2: Tanganyika: Growth of Certain Immigrant Tribes, 1948–57

Tribe	Population 1948	Population 1957	Net increase	Percentage increase
Zigua	112,113	134,406	22,293	+ 20
Rundi	90,312	122,233	31,921	+ 35
Luo	58,844	82,876	24,032	+ 41
Nyasa	36,346	65,514	29,293	+ 80
Ruanda	20,263	35,175	14,912	+ 74
Manyema	18,670	26,878	8,208	+ 44
Wemba	9,644	11,438	1,794	+ 19
Kamba	2,348	10,865	8,517	+ 363

This table shows that although different tribal classifications were used in the two censuses, there being 201 tribes distinguished in 1948 compared with 127 in 1957, an attempt being made in 1957 to classify the population in Tanganyika more

C. J. Martin

satisfactorily, the increases in the non-Tanganyika tribes were considerable. It is because of this that I expressed the view that the natural increase for the territory has been generally of the order of 1·50 per cent, the remaining 0·25 per cent being due to immigration into the territory. Migration between the provinces was considerable also and may have accounted for the very low figure of increase in certain provinces. Internal migration is a subject which requires considerable study, but it is extremely complex and difficult to undertake.

Tanganyika has been fortunate in having carried out three censuses of urban areas in 1948, 1952 and 1957. The changes in the urban population are shown in the following table.

Table 3: Tanganyika: Urban Population, 1948–52–57

	1948	1952	1957
Number of gazetted townships	27	31	33
Africans	152,435*	204,894	279,606
Non-Africans	44,831	64,947	84,466
Total	197,266	269,841	364,072
Net increase		72,575	94,231
Percentage increase		37	35

* Includes an estimated 3,000 for the African populations of Musoma and Songea townships, not shown separately from surrounding chiefdoms in 1948 Geographical and Tribal Studies.

The increase in the urban population between 1948 and 1952 was of the order of 37 per cent and between 1952 and 1957 of 35 per cent. The annual rate of growth over the nine-year period was 8·5 per cent per annum. The total number of townships recorded over this period increased from 27 to 33 and by 1957 the urban population represented some 4 per cent of the total. It is interesting to note that the growth figure of 8·5 per cent is very similar to that obtained from other studies of urban growth in East Africa. The estimate for the population of

56

Table 4: *Total Censuses: African Population, by Two Main Age Groups; Provincial Analysis, 1948 and 1957*

Province	1948					1957				
	Figures in thousands			Percentage		Figures in thousands			Percentage	
	Total	Children	Adults	Children	Adults	Total	Children	Adults	Children	Adults
Total	7,408	3,326	4,082	45	55	8,665	3,841	4,824	44	56
Lake	1,845	806	1,039	44	56	2,229	982	1,247	44	56
Western	946	398	548	42	58	1,053	444	609	42	58
Central	816	386	430	47	53	879	400	479	46	54
Eastern	909	373	536	41	59	1,040	421	619	40	60
Southern Highlands	846	450	396	53	47	1,024	521	503	51	49
Southern	914	408	506	45	55	1,008	432	576	43	57
Tanga	547	236	311	43	57	671	292	379	44	56
Northern	585	269	316	46	54	759	349	410	46	54

Note: Both sexes are combined.

Nairobi based on a census in 1948 and a sample census in 1958 showed a growth figure of the same order of magnitude.

The comparison of the age distribution of the population of Tanganyika as recorded in the two censuses is complex. A table is given below showing for the total population the distribution of adults and children. This table possibly shows too high a percentage of children because it is thought that, particularly among the male population, too many persons were included as children in the general census. However, since the two censuses were taken on similar lines general comparisons are of interest. It is hoped that when the sample census of Tanganyika has been analysed it will be possible to do more studies and describe in greater detail the comparison of the age distribution in 1948 and 1957.

The table below gives for 1957 alone the estimated age distribution from the general population census, together with sex ratios. The sex ratios are considered to be fairly reliable.

In Zanzibar the census of 1948 was repeated in 1958, but in the 1958 census the racial analysis was made more difficult due to the fact that some of the population did not describe themselves as requested on the form. The total growth in the population of Zanzibar Protectorate between the two censuses was 1·25 per cent per annum. In the main this population was African. In 1948 over 70 per cent of the population was African and it is believed that the population distribution has not changed greatly since then. The growth of the population of Pemba and Zanzibar has been slightly different, with an increase of about 16·8 per cent in Pemba as against 10·5 per cent in Zanzibar. The annual rate of growth was 1·57 per cent and 1·0 per cent respectively. These results are similar to the figures obtained in 1948 from fertility studies, although part of the increase in Pemba may be due to migration since a large number of Africans come to Pemba each year for clove picking and many do not return to the Tanganyika mainland. An age distribution of the population on a comparative basis cannot be given since in 1948 individual ages were requested while in 1958 age groups were required. However, some figures are given.

Table 5: Tanganyika General African Census, 1957: Provincial Populations by Sex and Estimated Age Group in thousands

Province	Age group	Under 1	1–5	6–15	16–45	Over 45	Total*
Central	Males No.	27	77	96	167	43	409,131
	Females No.	30	82	90	216	52	470,290
	Total No.	57	159	184	383	96	879,421
	Sex Ratio	89·9	94·8	105·1	77·0	83·1	87·0
Eastern	Males No.	25	82	104	246	60	518,376
	Females No.	28	86	97	254	57	521,415
	Total No.	53	168	201	501	117	1,039,791
	Sex Ratio	88·3	95·8	107·9	96·8	107·0	99·4
Lake	Males No.	66	194	230	440	135	1,066,608
	Females No.	73	202	216	516	154	1,161,877
	Total No.	139	396	447	956	289	2,228,485
	Sex Ratio	91·2	96·1	106·4	85·2	87·7	91·8
Northern	Males No.	21	67	89	173	36	384,921
	Females No.	22	70	80	161	41	374,039
	Total No.	42	137	169	333	76	758,960
	Sex Ratio	94·9	95·2	111·8	106·8	86·9	102·9
Southern	Males No.	24	83	106	208	58	479,845
	Females No.	28	86	105	250	59	528,201
	Total No.	52	169	211	458	118	1,008,046
	Sex Ratio	88·6	96·0	101·8	83·0	97·9	90·8
Southern Highlands	Males No.	39	100	119	167	43	468,025
	Females No.	45	108	111	237	56	555,780
	Total No.	85	208	229	403	98	1,023,805
	Sex Ratio	87·5	92·8	107·2	70·4	77·1	84·2
Tanga	Males No.	17	58	75	162	40	352,834
	Females No.	19	59	64	144	33	318,547
	Total No.	35	117	139	306	73	671,381
	Sex Ratio	91·7	97·7	117·0	112·8	123·3	110·8
Western	Males No.	30	88	103	206	57	485,361
	Females No.	33	92	97	275	70	567,434
	Total No.	64	180	200	481	127	1,052,795
	Sex Ratio	90·4	96·0	105·8	75·1	81·9	85·5
Tanganyika Territory†	Males No.	250	749	921	1770	473	4,166,746
	Females No.	277	784	859	2055	521	4,498,590
	Total No.	526	1534	1781	3824	994	8,665,336
	Sex Ratio	90·1	95·5	107·2	86·1	90·8	92·6

* Including those with ages not stated (5,990).
† Including those in transit (2,652).

Table 6: *Zanzibar Protectorate: Total Population by Sex and Age Group,
as at Census Date, 19th March 1958*

Age group in years	Total males		Total females		Grand total	
	Number	Percentage	Number	Percentage	Number	Percentage
Not stated	158	0·1	126	0·1	284	0·1
0–1	5,266	3·3	5,011	3·5	10,277	3·4
1–4	15,625	9·9	15,818	11·2	31,443	10·5
5–9	21,925	13·9	21,332	15·1	43,257	14·5
10–14	12,282	7·8	9,478	6·7	21,760	7·3
15–19	11,744	7·5	16,730	11·8	28,474	9·5
20–45	65,152	41·4	57,285	40·4	122,437	40·9
46 and over	25,350	16·1	15,829	11·2	41,179	13·8
Total	157,502	100·0	141,609	100·0	299,111	100·0

The census totals by major administrative areas for the two censuses are given in Table 7. More information on population growth will be available when the census has been completely analysed.

Conclusions

It can be stated that population increases before 1939 were fairly small, although in certain areas there may have been annual natural increases of over 1 per cent per annum. In the era since 1946, with the development of the territories, the expansion of health services and improvement of the standards of living of the people, it is likely that in certain areas the population has been increasing at a rate of more than 2 per cent per annum. From the two population censuses carried out in Tanganyika with a nine-year interval, the gross rate of increase of 1·75 per cent was calculated, while in Zanzibar in the total population there was an increase of 1·25 per cent, with Pemba island showing an increase of 1·57 per cent and Zanzibar island 1 per cent. The rates of increase recorded in the provinces of Tanganyika ranged from over 2 per cent in the Lake Province to less than 1 per cent in the Central Province. These figures show that the beginning of the population expansion has

Estimates of Population Growth in East Africa

Table 7: Zanzibar Island: Population Growth by Mudiria, 1948–58

Mudiria	Population 1948	Population 1958	Net increase	Percentage increase
Northern	47,910	50,795	2,885	6·0
Magharib	19,020	19,402	382	2·0
Central	22,235	21,230	− 1,005	− 4·5
Southern	15,126	15,903	777	5·1
Zanzibar Town	45,284	57,923	12,639	27·9
Total Zanzibar Island	149,575	165,253	15,678	10·5
Zanzibar Island excl. township	104,291	107,330	3,039	2·9

Pemba Island: Population Growth by Mudiria, 1948–58

Mudiria	Population 1948	Population 1958	Net increase	Percentage increase
Kondwe	18,840	20,615	1,775	9·4
Wete	29,182	37,435	8,253	28·3
Chake	39,016	45,691	6,675	17·1
Mkoani	27,549	30,117	2,568	9·3
Total Pemba Island	114,587	133,858	19,271	16·8

started in Tanganyika. In Zanzibar the rate of increase was low and might be lower than would have been expected. It is of interest that the sea coast of Tanganyika showed equally low rates. When the Uganda and Kenya censuses have been completed it will be possible to discuss more fully the question of population growth in East Africa, but at the present time it would seem that the population is increasing at a substantial rate, but not at the rates recorded for the Asian population of East Africa, which is over 2·5 per cent per annum, or at the rates at present recorded in many other parts of the world. The beginning of the demographic boom has only recently started in East Africa.

6

Population Maps and Mapping in Africa South of the Sahara

R. MANSELL PROTHERO

A REALIZATION of the practical need to count the population, for the purpose of tax assessment if for no other reason, accompanied the establishment of European rule in Africa. At the same time the existence of important relationships were recognized between people and the land which they occupy. Throughout most of the continent the economy is still dependent on these relationships. However, in spite of the collection of population data and the recognition of the importance of population/land relationships there have been few attempts until recently to map in detail the distribution of population, or to consider quantitatively its relationship with unit area in terms of density per square mile or per square kilometre. Before 1939 there were few population maps of African territories other than those which covered very large areas on very small scales.[1] These were of value for their general representation of population patterns but, through inevitable generalization, maps on these scales have tended to produce errors and misconceptions that are repeated and which are only gradually eliminated. For example, as a result of inadequate mapping, densities in the Eastern Region of Nigeria have been

[1] S. J. K. Baker, "The distribution of native population over East Africa", *Africa*, x, 1937, 43.

Stanley D. Dodge, "The distribution of population in Northern Nigeria", *Papers of the Michigan Academy of Science, Arts and Letters*, xiv, 1936, 297.

C. R. Niven, "Some Nigerian population problems", *Geog. Journ.*, LXXXV, 1935, 54.

frequently understated, the highest figure quoted being "over 300 persons per square mile". In fact between a third and a half of the total area of the Region has average densities of over 300 persons per square mile and 10 per cent has densities of over 500 persons per square mile.[1] Recent mapping of the population of Eastern Nigeria on a larger scale than previously has shown that there are areas with densities of over 1,000 persons per square mile.[2] These may well be among the highest rural population densities anywhere in Africa south of the Sahara. Their size and extent can be revealed only through the process of detailed mapping and their significance in terms of population/land relationships can only be fully appreciated in this way.[3]

It is not difficult to specify some of the reasons for the neglect of large-scale population mapping. In the first four decades of this century there was an absence of practising geographers in Africa and of people trained to think and work geographically. Population data has been incomplete and inaccurate and base-maps, on which to plot patterns of distribution and density, have either not existed or have been inadequate. These short-comings may be advanced with the argument that with in-adequate material for compilation population maps would have been far from perfect. This is true, but to use it as an excuse for no work is only to evade the issue. Many years will pass before population mapping in Africa will be possible with adequate and accurate data and base-maps; but population maps of limited accuracy, constructed from data which is only partly accurate on inadequate base-maps, are better than no maps at all. Once maps have been drawn they can be progressively improved as the means to do so become available. What is important is that their limitations shall always be made apparent and if possible specified in order to give some indica-tion of reliability. This is not always done and even to imply

[1] R. Mansell Prothero, "The population of Eastern Nigeria", *Scot. Geog. Mag.*, LXXI, 1955, 165.

[2] J. H. Jennings, "A population distribution map of the Eastern Region of Nigeria", *Geog. Journ.*, CXXIII, 1957, 416.

[3] A map published in 1960 by the Uganda Lands and Surveys Department, *Uganda 1/1,250,000, Population Densities by Gombololas* (1959 census), shows clearly for the first time that in considerable areas of Kigezi, Buganda, Busoga, Bukedi and Bugisu the population density ranges between 400 and 1,000 persons per square mile.

that population maps of Africa are comparable in accuracy with those of developed countries is gravely misleading. The methods of construction are not always clear from the maps themselves and it is not always possible to obtain information on how they were constructed. In 1949 the Survey Department of Nigeria published a dasymetric map of population density on the scale of 1 : 3,000,000 based on the 1931 census. Apart from its small scale and lack of detail it was of limited value in that it failed to show in their true magnitude the densities of population in areas of intense concentration. Enquiries made at the Survey Department in 1954 and 1955 failed to produce any information relating to the construction of this map as there was no record. It should be incumbent on all who construct population maps to accompany them with a statement of how they were compiled, unless the method is clearly implicit in the map itself.

Population mapping in Africa south of the Sahara has been summarized in Fig. II (pp. 66–7). With one exception these are maps which have been compiled since 1945 and the majority of them are on scales of 1 : 1,000,000 or larger. 1 : 1,000,000 is not a large scale in the strict sense, but in terms of the great area of Africa and the problems of suitable base-maps it is considered as the largest scale on which complete coverage is possible and practicable. Proposals for such a coverage will be discussed later.

The one pre-war map which demands consideration is Clement Gillman's 1 : 3,000,000 map of population distribution in Tanganyika, published in 1936.[1] It was an important pioneer effort and there is still nothing comparable to it for many parts of Africa at the present day. It should be studied, together with the published notes on its compilation, by anyone contemplating the construction of population maps in underdeveloped territories. Gillman's many years of experience of Tanganyika as a railway and water engineer, coupled with an ability and willingness to think geographically, made the high quality of his work possible. The need for wide experience and acute observation cannot be over-emphasized in areas with limited census data and poor base-maps. Any map compiled

[1] C. Gillman, "A population map of Tanganyika Territory", *Geog. Rev.*, xxvi, 1936, Plate 2.

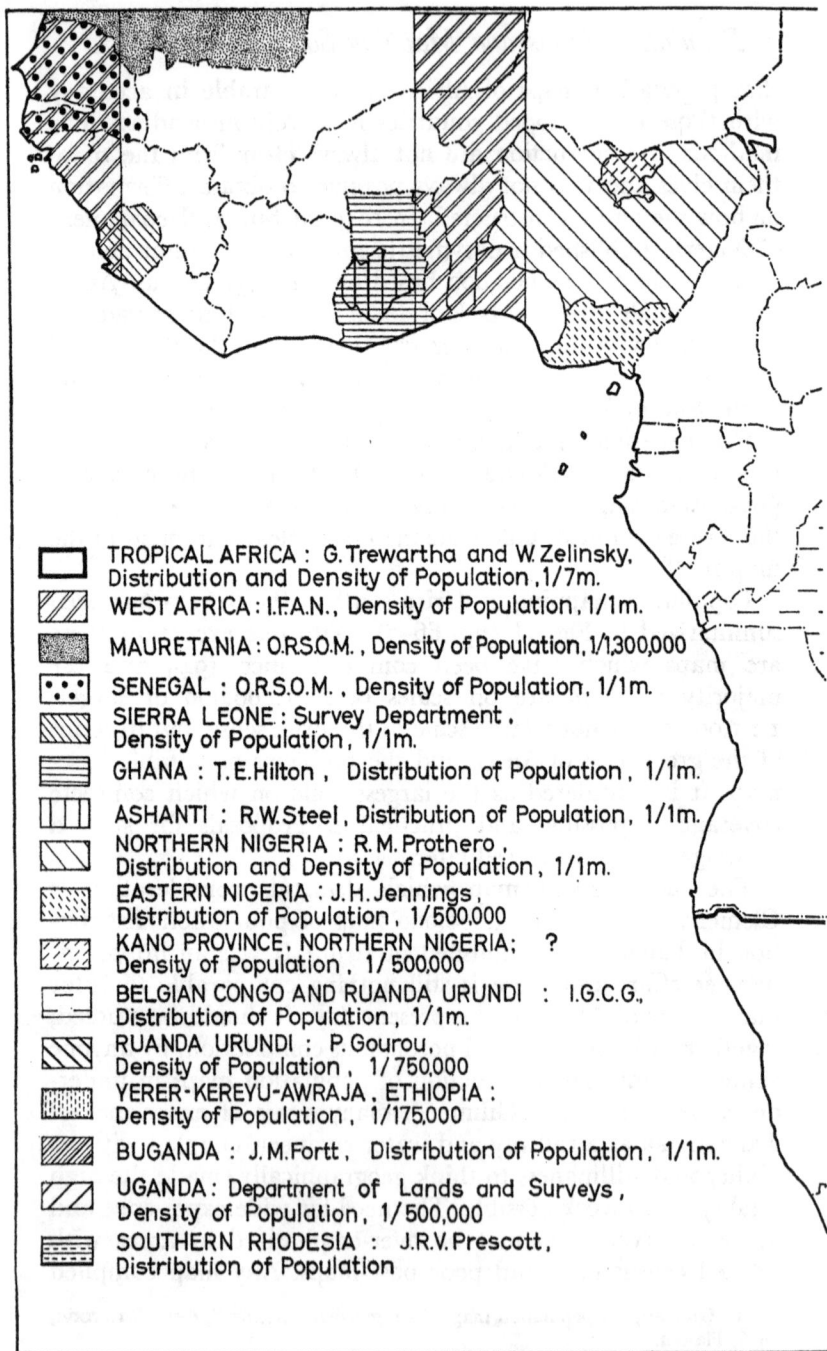

TROPICAL AFRICA : G.Trewartha and W.Zelinsky,
Distribution and Density of Population ,1/7m.

WEST AFRICA : I.F.A.N., Density of Population, 1/1m.

MAURETANIA : O.R.S.O.M. , Density of Population, 1/1,300,000

SENEGAL : O.R.S.O.M. , Density of Population, 1/1m.

SIERRA LEONE : Survey Department ,
Density of Population, 1/1m.

GHANA : T.E.Hilton , Distribution of Population, 1/1m.

ASHANTI : R.W.Steel, Distribution of Population, 1/1m.

NORTHERN NIGERIA : R.M.Prothero ,
Distribution and Density of Population, 1/1m.

EASTERN NIGERIA : J.H.Jennings ,
Distribution of Population, 1/500,000

KANO PROVINCE, NORTHERN NIGERIA;   ?
Density of Population , 1/500,000

BELGIAN CONGO AND RUANDA URUNDI : I.G.C.G.,
Distribution of Population, 1/1m.

RUANDA URUNDI : P.Gourou,
Density of Population , 1/750,000

YERER-KEREYU-AWRAJA, ETHIOPIA :
Density of Population , 1/175,000

BUGANDA : J.M.Fortt , Distribution of Population, 1/1m.

UGANDA : Department of Lands and Surveys ,
Density of Population , 1/500,000

SOUTHERN RHODESIA : J.R.V.Prescott,
Distribution of Population

FIG. II. Post-war population mapping

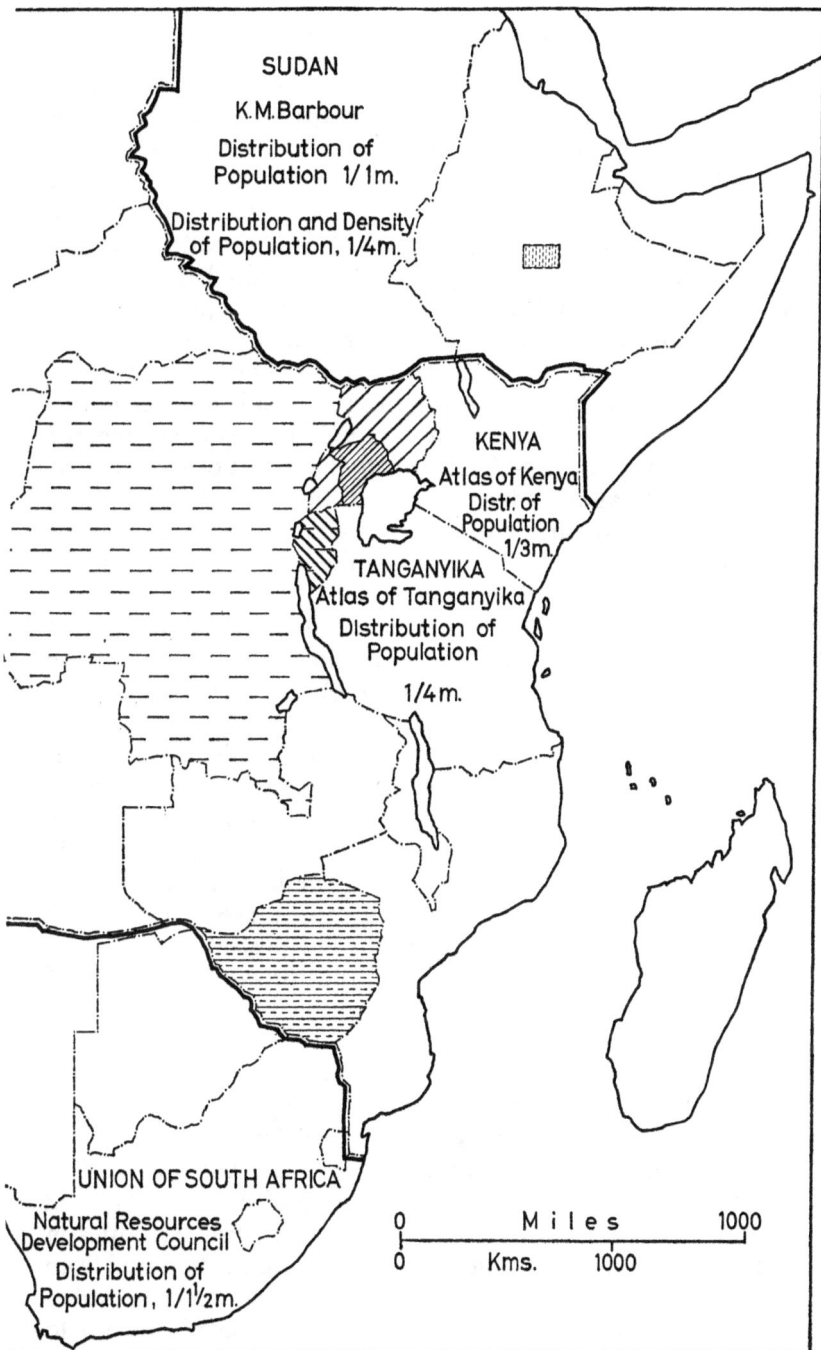

SUDAN

K.M.Barbour

Distribution of
Population 1/1m.

Distribution and Density
of Population, 1/4m.

KENYA

Atlas of Kenya
Distr. of
Population
1/3m.

TANGANYIKA

Atlas of Tanganyika

Distribution of
Population

1/4m.

UNION OF SOUTH AFRICA

Natural Resources
Development Council
Distribution of
Population, 1/1½m.

Miles

0   1000

0   Kms.   1000

in Africa south of the Sahara.

without them must to some extent be suspect. If results are to be satisfactory, detailed population maps of Africa should be compiled *in Africa* by people with extensive field knowledge.

Gillman regarded the use of the dot method (he used dots of standard size, each dot representing 200 persons) as basic for all population maps, an opinion which is held widely, though not unanimously, by geographers. He recognized the problem of massing dots together in areas of dense population with resulting illegibility, and to prevent this he adopted a form of shading on his map for areas with densities of over 400 persons per square mile. Too frequently this problem is not recognized and dots are massed together and superimposed on one another to become meaningless. This defeats the object of the method, which should allow individual dots to be counted so as to give a numerical assessment of the population in any area. After consideration and experiment with the population data to be mapped and the base-map available, it should be possible to devise a dot value and size which will allow accurate and legible representation, with possibly some modification for the higher-density areas such as that used by Gillman.

Post-war contributions to population mapping in Africa have been made by geographers in the African university colleges and other institutions of higher education and research which have been established recently. They have been stimulated by the first post-war censuses taken in the late 1940's and early 1950's and by the production during the last decade of many new maps on varying scales which can be used for mapping population distribution and density. The post-war census data is of notably greater accuracy than that pre-war and many of the new maps are on topographic scales. These topographic maps are not suitable as base-maps on which to plot the population patterns of whole territories but they may be used to assist in the more accurate location of population on smaller scale base-maps. They may also be used for the correction of general topographic information on these base-maps. The 1 : 50,000 and 1 : 100,000 series of maps of the Directorate of Overseas (formerly Colonial) Surveys for British territories in Africa are notable examples of this recent work. Produced from the interpretation of air photographs on a framework provided by ground control, these maps are more detailed and up to

Population Maps and Mapping South of the Sahara

date than would ever be possible from ground surveys of areas which are frequently inaccessible and where movement is difficult. They record accurately the location and to some extent the pattern of settlement and therefore are invaluable as a guide for plotting the distribution of population. For many African territories the coverage of air photographs on large scales is much more extensive than the map coverage (e.g. in Nigeria and Republic of Sudan). Apart from the more complete coverage, the examination of air photographs can provide more information relating to population distribution than can a map. They are less easily manageable because of the large number of photographs involved and greater experience is required for photo-interpretation than for map analysis.

Before considering the post-war population maps of individual territories some reference must be made to recent population maps which show the overall distribution of population in Africa. Professor Friedrich Burgdörfer's map of the whole continent on a scale of 1 : 20,000,000 is included in his distinguished *Atlas of World Population* which was published in 1954.[1] This map was compiled for the most part from population data collected in 1950 and in adjacent years. The rural population is represented by a standard size dot (one to 10,000 persons) and urban population by spheres of proportional volume. The general patterns of distribution which are shown on the map accurately reflect conditions as they are known to exist in different parts of the continent. Even in the areas of densest population the dots can be individually counted. However, if the dots are counted (and the use of this method presupposes that this is a reasonable thing to do, even if a laborious task) it is evident that in some territories there is a considerable discrepancy between the number of dots on the map and the population recorded by the census which Professor Burgdörfer has used. While some margin of error is reasonable, it is disturbing to find it as great as in the case of Gambia. There are only eight dots, representing a population of 80,000, shown in the territory which is known to have a population of at least 250,000. It is obvious that in a territory like Gambia, which occupies only a small area on the map of Africa on a scale of

---

[1] F. Burgdörfer, *Welt-Bevölkerungs-Atlas. Verteilung der Bevölkerung der Erde um das jahr 1950*, Hamburg, 1954.

1 : 20,000,000, it would be difficult to place the number of dots required to represent its population within the frontiers of the territory. This is one of the problems and limitations of the dot method when used for an area the size of Africa. Only a small scale base-map can be used on which must be represented a great variety of population distribution patterns. They range from uninhabited and virtually uninhabited areas to dense concentrations of up to 1,500 persons per square mile. One solution of this problem would be to use a dot of greater value so that fewer dots would be required to represent the population in any area. It is then necessary to guard against the danger of having too few dots with which to be able to represent reasonably the distribution of population. An example of this type of population map, with too few dots, is to be found in the revised edition of Lord Hailey's *African Survey*.[1] The dot value (one to 500,000 persons) is absurdly large and there are far too few dots to accurately represent the distribution of population. On this particular map it would have been possible to use a dot of smaller value and of smaller size and thus have been able to show the distribution of population in much greater detail. The map as it stands, however, is an improvement on that published in the original edition of the *Survey*.

The great post-war American interest in research in Africa is evident in the field of population mapping in the work of Glenn Trewartha and Wilbur Zelinsky of the University of Wisconsin. Their work for the whole of Tropical Africa, followed by more detailed territorial studies, of which that on the Belgian Congo is the most important,[2] is the outcome of Trewartha's plea for further studies in the field of population geography and for a programme of world population mapping.[3] The initiative and resourcefulness shown in this work are commendable. All of the mapping of Trewartha and his associates was undertaken in the U.S.A., and anyone with knowledge of the problems of assembling statistical data and

---

[1] Lord Hailey, *An African Survey, Revised 1956*, London, 1957, 118.

[2] G. T. Trewartha and W. Zelinsky, "Population patterns in Tropical Africa", *Ann. Ass. Amer. Geog.*, XLIV, 1954, 135; "The population geography of Belgian Africa", *ibid.*, XLIV, 1954, 163.
  G. T. Trewartha, "New population maps of Uganda, Kenya, Nyasaland, and Gold Coast", *ibid.*, XLVII, 1957, 41.

[3] G. T. Trewartha, "A case for population geography", *ibid.*, XLIII, 1953, 71.

maps for African population studies will acknowledge their achievement of such useful results. Their maps are all reproduced on small scales and at these scales they portray patterns of distribution effectively and satisfactorily. On larger scales defects in Trewartha's maps would become apparent for there is no doubt that large-scale mapping of population demands some first-hand field knowledge of the area being mapped and of the distribution of population.

The most effective of Trewartha's maps employ the dot method, with a dot value of one to 2,500 persons for the map of the whole of Tropical Africa and values of from one to 400 to one to 500 persons for maps of individual territories. The problem of the dot value and the size of the dot in relation to the scale at which the map is produced is well illustrated in the map of the distribution of population in Tropical Africa. One to 2,500 persons is a low dot value to select when dealing with an area of this size on a single map. It is satisfactory in areas with sparse population, where with a dot of higher value it would be impossible to show anything of the detail of the pattern of distribution. In areas of dense population, however, there are too many dots for these to be shown individually and they merge together on the map and become meaningless. This also happens in some of Trewartha's maps of individual territories, though in these the fault lies not so much in the value of the dot as in the small scale of the map.

Trewartha's choropleth maps of population density are not particularly satisfactory because of the large size of many of the administrative units on which they are based. These maps, for example, give little indication of the high densities of rural population which occur in some parts of Tropical Africa (in Ruanda-Urundi or in Eastern Nigeria). The one dasymetric map, of population density in Ghana, is also highly generalized and is of little interest from the point of view of mapping technique.

Recent population maps of territories in Africa south of the Sahara on scales of 1 : 1,000,000 or larger display a wide variety of methods of presentation with varying degrees of success. A choropleth map of population density of Kano Province, Northern Nigeria,[1] deserves mention only as a

---

[1] *Population map of Kano Province, 1/500,000.* Printed by the Survey Department, Lagos. No date.

cartographic monstrosity and as an example of how a population map should not be presented. Various enquiries have failed to determine how it was constructed. J. H. Jenning's map of the distribution of population in the Eastern Region of Nigeria on a scale of 1 : 500,000 is of a very different calibre.[1] It is a more detailed representation of the population patterns in this most interesting area than anything previously attempted. The high concentrations in Owerri and Calabar Provinces are shown clearly and there is an accurate indication of the high densities found there. The dot value (one to 1,000 persons) is high for the scale of the map and it would be possible in an area this size to map in greater detail by using a dot of lower value (e.g. one to 200 persons). In this way greater accuracy could be achieved for it would be possible to show that, though the population is dense over considerable parts of the Region, in some of the areas of concentration it has a dispersed pattern of distribution; the people live in individual compounds or in small groups of these rather than in large villages or towns.[2]

Following proposals for an international atlas of West Africa made at the Conférence Internationale des Africanistes de l'Ouest at Dakar in 1945, the Institut Français d'Afrique Noire (I.F.A.N.) launched a scheme for the preparation of a series of *Cartes ethno-démographiques* on a scale of 1 : 1,000,000.[3] Plans for this scheme were drawn up by Jacques Richard-Molard, chief of the geographical section of the Institut, and he completed the first sheet in the series before his death in 1951. Ethnographic and demographic data are presented on separate maps and up to the present time sheets have been published which cover Senegal, Gambia, Portuguese Guinea and parts of the Republic of Guinea and of Sierra Leone (Sheet 1) and Dahomey, Togoland and parts of Ghana, Nigeria, Haute Volta, Niger and Mali (Sheet 5). Sheet 6 which covers Niger and parts of Northern Nigeria is in preparation. The ethnographic maps are non-quantitative in character and show the ethnic

[1] J. H. Jennings, *Nigeria, Eastern Region Population (1953 Census), 1/500,000.* Federal Survey Department, Lagos.

[2] W. B. Morgan, "The 'grassland towns' of the Eastern Region of Nigeria", *Transactions and Papers of the Institute of British Geographers,* XXIII, 1957, 213–24.

[3] J. Richard-Molard *et al., Cartes ethno-démographiques de l'Afrique Occidentale.* Institut Français d'Afrique Noire, Dakar. Sheets 1 and 5 have been published and Sheet 6 is in preparation.

differences in the population in a somewhat bewildering variety of symbols and colours. The demographic maps show the density of population per square kilometre by the dasymetric method. They were compiled from choropleth maps, based on the smallest administrative units whose boundaries could be mapped and their areas calculated and for which there were population data available. These administrative units are man-made and frequently bear little relation to basic physical and human factors. In most underdeveloped territories the boundaries of the smallest administrative units can only be shown tentatively on maps as they have not been surveyed. The derivation of a dasymetric map from a choropleth map based on such units is inevitably a subjective procedure, depending for accuracy on the local knowledge of the person constructing the map. In the case of the sheets so far published by the I.F.A.N. this was very considerable, for the individual authors were able to supplement their own extensive experience with that of their colleagues in the Institut. However, in most instances in underdeveloped territories it would certainly be better to derive population density maps from dot distribution maps, provided that all possible precautions are taken to ensure the accuracy of the latter. In this way they may be almost entirely objective. This has been attempted with the writer's 1 : 1,000,000 population maps of the Northern Region of Nigeria, based on the 1952 census.[1] In this census, data were recorded and published for administrative units (*provinces, divisions, districts* and *village areas*) which were areas and not settlements. It was therefore impossible to devise a map of population distribution using symbols relating to variations in the size of settlements. Instead the distribution of population was shown by standard size dots, each dot representing 200 persons. As an aid to the preparation of the distribution map, a base-map was drawn showing the *district* boundaries. With this as a base, a choropleth map of population density

[1] The map of the distribution of population has been published by the Directorate of Overseas Surveys, Surbiton, *Northern Region, Nigeria, 1/1,000,000, Distribution of Population* (1952 census), D.O.S. (Misc) 237, 1960. The map of the density of population will be published in the near future. The compilation of these maps is discussed in a paper by the writer, "Problems of population mapping in an underdeveloped territory (Northern Nigeria)", *Nigerian Geographical Journal*, III, 1960, 1–7.

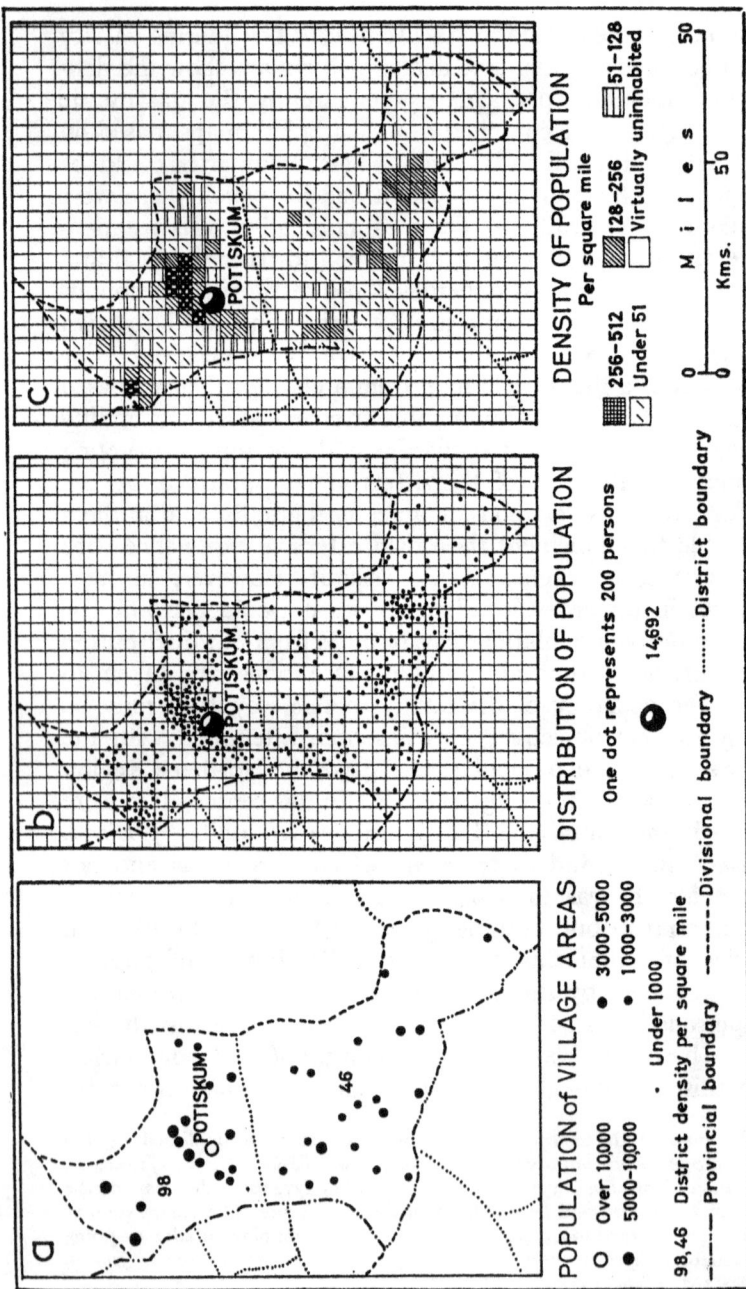

Fig. III. Stages in the construction of population maps of Potiskum Division, Northern Nigeria. The distribution of population (b) is derived from (a), and the density of population (c) is in turn derived from (b). (Reproduced by kind permission of the Editor of the *Nigerian Geographical Journal*.)

POPULATION of VILLAGE AREAS

○ Over 10,000   ● 3000–5000
● 5000–10,000   ● 1000–3000
                       · Under 1000

98,46 District density per square mile
———— Provincial boundary ————— Divisional boundary ········ District boundary

DISTRIBUTION OF POPULATION

One dot represents 200 persons

◕ 14,692

DENSITY OF POPULATION
Per square mile

▨ 256–512   ▤ 51–128
▩ 128–256   ☐ Virtually uninhabited
▨ Under 51

Miles
0   50
Kms.
0   50

was prepared which turned out to be a great improvement, in the amount of detail shown, on any previous map of population density of Northern Nigeria.[1] It was not an entirely satisfactory map for several reasons. It was not possible to locate the *district* boundaries and to calculate the areas enclosed within them with precision, though every effort was made to achieve the best results with the material available. The areas of some of the *districts* are so large (e.g. over 2,000 square miles) that within them there are great variations in the density of the population and a figure of average density for a whole *district* may therefore be of little significance. In order to improve on this choropleth map a detailed map of population density was prepared directly from the dot distribution map by super-imposing on it a grid, each square of which equalled 4 square miles (*c.* 10 square kilometres), and calculating the densities within each square of the grid. Fig. III (p. 74). This method very largely eliminates the subjective element in the preparation of a density map. Sharp and sudden changes in density can be adequately shown and areas in different categories of density, for all or for any part of the map, can be calculated without difficulty. Fig. IV (p. 76) compares three methods of mapping population density and demonstrates the degree of detail which it is possible to achieve with the method discussed above.

Apart from the maps discussed, and those of K. M. Barbour and T. E. Hilton which are discussed in separate essays in this volume, there are two other examples of population mapping to which brief reference must be made. Pierre Gourou's maps of the Belgian Congo and Ruanda-Urundi are of outstanding importance and are well documented.[2] Some of them are unsatisfactory from the point of view of their cartographic presentation; for instance, the selection of colours for different categories of density in a map in the *Atlas du Congo Belge* is particularly unpleasing and meaningless. The 1 : 1,500,000 map of population distribution in the Union of South Africa

[1] *Northern Nigeria, 1/2,000,000, Density of Population* (1952 census). Federal Survey Department, Lagos, 1958.
[2] Pierre Gourou, *Carte de la densité de la population, 1/5,000,000. Atlas du Congo Belge,* Institut Royal Colonial Belge, Bruxelles, 1951. *Répartition de la population indigène, 1/1,000,000.* Institut Géographique du Congo Belge, Léopoldville, 1949.

based on the 1951 census[1] is interesting for the way in which it reflects official policy by attempting to distinguish clearly between the different racial groups which make up the Union's population. Dots of different colours, for African, European, Coloured and Asian peoples, are used for the rural population

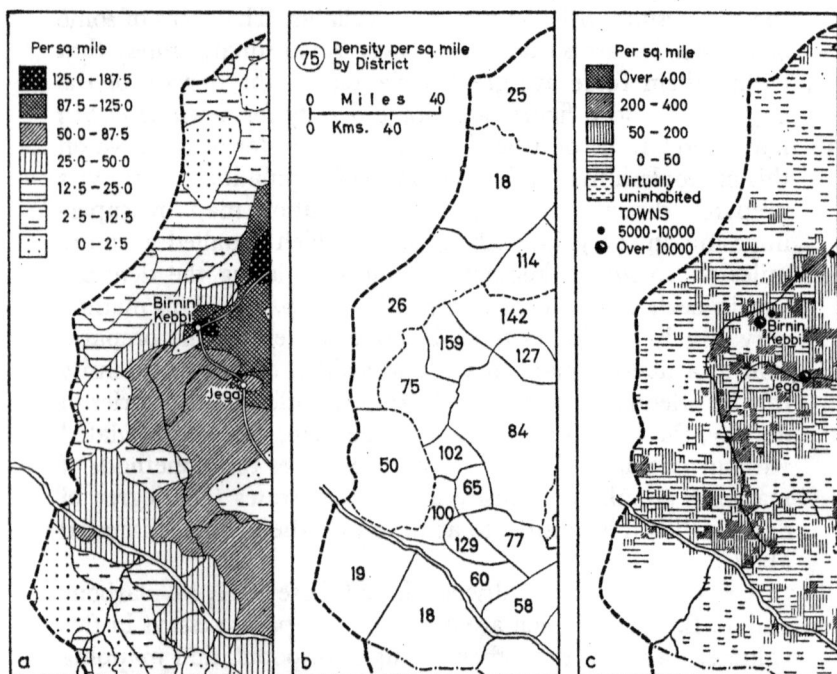

FIG. IV. Three methods of mapping the density of population in part of Sokoto Province, Northern Nigeria. Map (a) is based on Cartes Ethno-démographique, Sheet 5, Institut Français d'Afrique Noire, Dakar. (b) and (c) are based on maps compiled by the writer.

and proportional circles representing the urban population are coloured in accordance with the numerical importance of the four racial elements in a town's population. The use of four different coloured dots does not always give a very clear picture

[1] *Population distribution map of the Union of South Africa, 1/1,500,000*, Natural Resources Development Council.

and it is particularly difficult to distinguish minority elements in areas of dense population.

In the post-war mapping of population in Africa south of the Sahara there have been important advances on what was previously available, but nonetheless the present situation is not satisfactory. Large parts of West Africa and French Equatorial Africa and most of British East Africa and the Federation of Rhodesia and Nyasaland lack population maps on scales of 1 : 1,000,000 or larger. Where there is now coverage in Africa, it has resulted from the isolated efforts of institutions and individuals and it inevitably lacks co-ordination in methods of compilation and in the styles of the completed maps. Thus even if maps on a common scale exist, comparisons of patterns of distribution and density between one territory and another are difficult and sometimes impossible. Comparisons are desirable and the need for a common and a single style was discussed and recommended by the Inter-African Committee on the Social Sciences of the Council for Technical Co-operation in Africa South of the Sahara which met at Bukavu in 1955. To follow this up, geographers representing Belgium, France, Portugal, the Union of South Africa and the United Kingdom met at Brussels in July 1956 to make preliminary recommendations for the compilation and presentation of uniform maps of population distribution and density.[1] They confirmed that these should be on a scale of 1 : 1,000,000 and suggested that the International 1 : 1,000,000 Map should be used as a base. They recommended that the base-map should be in half-tone with the population distribution in black; using dots for the rural population and proportional circles for the urban population. Wherever possible the original compilation should be carried out on maps on scales larger than 1 : 1,000,000 (e.g. 1 : 200,000 or 1 : 250,000) and should show localities listed in the census returns together with their populations. In addition the meeting recommended that a coloured 1 : 2,000,000 map of the density of population should be made "to synthesize the data of the 1 : 1,000,000 map". The technical details of the compilation of this map were not considered. Delegates of the

[1] C.C.T.A./C.S.A., London (56), 150, 17/9/56. Preliminary meeting of geographers for the drawing of maps showing the density and distribution of population, 5th and 6th July 1956.

R. Mansell Prothero

various member governments to the Inter-African Committee on the Social Sciences were suggested as the organizers of the mapping programme within their own territories. Co-ordination of the work was to be carried out through a committee under the chairmanship of Pierre Gourou who would also edit the maps. Three years have passed since these recommendations were made and there has been no further information forthcoming of this very desirable proposal. The need to proceed with it is urgent in view of the forthcoming censuses of the early 1960's but to translate it into fact and to bring it to a successful conclusion is a considerable undertaking.

If the C.C.T.A. proposal should come to nothing it is reasonable to query the prospect of success for a much larger scheme for uniform mapping which would include Africa. This scheme for population mapping throughout the world on a scale of 1 : 1,000,000 was proposed and discussed by the International Geographical Union in the 1930's but any progress in implementing it was prevented by the war. At the Congress of the I.G.U. at Rio de Janeiro in 1956 it was decided to re-establish a Special Commission on a World Population Map[1] which should make recommendations to the 1960 Congress at Stockholm for carrying on the work. The Commission met three times, at Zurich in 1958 when it was assisted by a number of expert corresponding members, and at Stockholm in 1959 and 1960. At the Stockholm School of Economics a series of experiments have been carried out and are being continued to determine suitable map scales, the types of symbols to be used and the representation of nomadic population.

The report of the Commission was presented and discussed by the I.G.U. Congress at Stockholm in August 1960. It recommends the use of the 1 : 1,000,000 scale as a standard for population maps, with other scales being used when they are either necessary or desirable. A series of tests was carried out in conjunction with the Department of Psychology in the University of Stockholm to investigate on a theoretical basis the efficiency of area and volumetric symbols for representing population.[2] The results suggest that area symbols are pre-

---

[1] The members of the Commission are Professors W. William-Olsson, Stockholm (Chairman), F. Burgdörfer, Munich, S. Kiuchi, Tokyo, and R. M. Prothero.
[2] G. Ekman and K. Junge, "Psychological relations in the perception of visual

ferable to volume symbols but the findings are of a tentative nature and further experiments are to be made, particularly with different types of volume symbols (spheres and cubes). Unfortunately for practical population mapping the use of area symbols presents great difficulties in many parts of the world because of the wide range in the size of the symbols required.

The smallest value represented by a symbol at the map scale of 1 : 1,000,000 should be either 100 or 200 persons.[1] The committee of the C.C.T.A. has recommended 100 persons for the smallest value but for much of Africa it is probable that that of 200 persons is more realistic. In an underdeveloped territory with inaccuracies and inadequacies in the population data and a dearth of large-scale maps for detailed plotting, it would be difficult to place the dots of lower value with reasonable accuracy. If dots of a value of one to 100 persons had been used on the writer's 1 : 1,000,000 map of population distribution in Northern Nigeria this would have only doubled the number of dots on the map. With the statistical and map resources that were available it would have been impossible to show the distribution of population with any greater accuracy.

The Commission has made recommendations for the mapping of nomadic population. It suggests that a special symbol should be used for mapping nomads and that areas over which they migrate should be shown by a distinctive shading. These symbols should be placed in the areas where the nomads concentrate at certain times of the year and if this is not their practice, or if these areas are not known, the symbols should be distributed evenly over the whole of the areas in which the nomads migrate. There are no comparable recommendations for nomadic population made by the C.C.T.A. committee and this is an unfortunate omission for Africa south of the Sahara where there are still important nomadic elements in the populations of many territories. There are special problems involved in the mapping of nomadic population. Census data relating to

length, area and volume, with special regard to the interpretation of certain map symbols", Ms. Psychological Institute, Universities of Stockholm and Oslo, 1960. See also J. I. Clarke, "Statistical map-reading", *Geography*, XLIV, 2, 1959, 96–104.

[1] At the 1/1,000,000 map scale with the use of volume symbols, if 100 persons are shown by a symbol with a diameter of 0·5 mm. it is possible to range with the same scale of symbols to represent the largest cities in the world.

nomads is frequently less accurate than that for sedentary population. By the nature of their life these people are more difficult to count and being generally conservative in outlook they are reluctant to be enumerated. The 1952 census of Northern Nigeria separately enumerated nomadic "cattle Fulani" in the *districts* where they were found. An examination of the numbers recorded in relation to other information suggests that this group was under-counted and that they were in fact not separately enumerated in some *districts*. In the writer's map of Northern Nigeria they are not differentiated from the rest of the population.

No specific recommendations are being made by the I.G.U. Commission at this stage for the compilation of population density maps. The Commission feels that it will be a major achievement to produce anything approaching world coverage with population distribution maps on a scale of 1 : 1,000,000 and that all energies should be concentrated in an attempt to achieve this. However, it has stated the opinion that density maps should be derived from distribution maps and that they should not be compiled separately as choropleth maps.

Co-operation between the two schemes proposed for population mapping in Africa south of the Sahara is obviously desirable. Neither of them is unrealistic with the material that is available at the present time. In many of the African countries there are already people competent to undertake the work on a voluntary basis since neither the C.C.T.A. or the I.G.U. are able to contemplate the employment of full-time workers. Even if the work is to be undertaken on this basis it must have, if it is to succeed, official recognition and some material aid from governments in the territories concerned. This aid should come during the preparation of the maps and after. In the first stage, contributions towards the cost of field work are essential and the need for field work, both intensive and extensive, has been stressed. Reasonable access to official documents which may be relevant to the work and assistance from government officers with knowledge of particular areas are desirable. Adequate publication of the final results will require official financial assistance.

In approaching governments for aid it will be necessary to be able to indicate the positive and material advantages to be gained from supporting the work of population mapping. Both Barbour and Hilton refer to the assistance that they have received and the co-operation achieved with the governments of Sudan and Ghana. Reference has already been made in this essay to the need for knowing the accurate location of population when planning political, social and economic developments. The writer has recently been advising the Division of Malaria Eradication of the World Health Organization on certain problems relating to population in schemes for the eradication of malaria in Africa. At present these schemes are limited to relatively small areas and populations. It is hoped to expand them in the near future to cover whole territories. Whether eradication is carried out by attacking the malaria vector with residual insecticides or by the administration of anti-malarial drugs to people, or by a combination of these methods, an accurate knowledge of the location of population is a *sine qua non*. The exclusion of even a relatively small part of the population from treatment may result in a reservoir of infection being maintained. For this work large-scale population maps, on scales of 1 : 50,000 and 1 : 100,000, would seem most desirable. This type of mapping will require experiment for as far as can be determined there are no population maps on these scales in Africa at the present time. Nomadic and other population movements in Africa present particular problems in malaria eradication and the existence of maps showing the distribution of nomadic and migrant population (possibly in a series for different times of the year) would be of inestimable value.

There is no doubt of the practical value of population maps on scales of 1 : 1,000,000 and larger; their full value however can become apparent only after they have been constructed and are available for use. The first half of the twentieth century has seen the development and improvement of census data in Africa and the production of suitable base-maps for the plotting of population distribution and density. These are the bases for effective population mapping in which uniformity is most desirable and in which therefore planning and control by organizations such as the C.C.T.A. and the I.G.U. are very necessary.

Note: I.G.C.G. (Fig. II, p. 66) *should read* I.G.C.B.

7

Population Mapping in Ghana

T. E. HILTON

Introduction

THE first census of the population of the Gold Coast was taken in 1891. Further censuses were taken in each tenth year until war conditions interrupted the sequence in 1941. The census of 1948 was the sixth.

From mid-1950, when the Government Statistician was kind enough to make available the proofs of the 1948 census report, until 1955 the writer was engaged in a study of population in the Gold Coast. The main portion of the project consisted of the preparation of maps of the distribution of population in the country in 1931 and 1948, and provisional maps of population density for 1948. In addition maps were prepared showing densities and inter-censal changes by administrative sub-divisions in the periods 1921–31 and 1931–48. It was also possible to investigate some of the changes and movements of population that had taken place after 1950, using the limited amount of statistical information available.

The results of these investigations are now published in an *Atlas of Population of Ghana*. The present essay describes how the problems involved were approached in the light of the sources available, the field investigations which were necessary, and the methods of mapping which were employed.

Primary Source Material

The 1931 census was the first in which the population was individually counted. In the report on this census it was

83

suggested that there had been 5 per cent understatement of the population in 1921, and that there was also some understatement, to an uncertain extent, in 1931. In 1948 careful preparations were made to ensure accuracy, and it was hoped that the house-to-house count, coupled with the decreasing likelihood of there being unknown and undiscovered villages, would have resulted in there being no significant error in the count due to accidental omission of population. For some areas this hope was probably optimistic.

Minor difficulties were experienced in using the 1931 tables. The populations of the Navrongo and Zuarungu Districts, for example, were returned only under their larger unit headings; thus in the former, with a population of 120,870, 36 units only were listed in 1931 as against 196 in 1948. As the approximate boundaries of the larger sub-divisions were available, and many of the smaller units listed in 1948 are farming communities in scattered compounds which are grouped for convenience under names but rarely have well-defined boundaries, it was possible after field work to map the distribution of the population with reasonable accuracy.

Considerable reliance had also to be placed on topographical maps. Though the quality and reliability of the published maps of Ghana vary, the country is better off than most West African territories, including Nigeria. Nevertheless the 1 : 250,000 maps are the only ones covering most of the country on a scale larger than those of the 1 : 400,000 wall map or the 1 : 500,000 road map. Part of the former Trusteeship Territory of Togoland between 7° 30′ N. and 9° 30′ N. is not mapped on any scale larger than 1 : 400,000; this includes part of the eastern trunk route through a developing food-producing area and a portion of the area of expanding cocoa production north and east of Jasikan. Town plans and a 1 : 5,000 air survey map of the Volta gorge and delta are available, and these were used in addition to the topographic maps.

The location of places listed in the census returns proved difficult for some areas. In Kusasi only 28 places out of 277 listed in the 1948 census, involving 7 per cent of the population, could not be located on the maps, but this was exceptional. In Lawra, covered by a war-time 1 : 250,000 sheet, 129 place names appear on the map, as against 254 places listed in the census. A similar state of affairs exists for Ashanti and the south; in Akwapim-New Juaben, for example, less than a third of the settlements enumerated were identifiable, and similarly only about a half of those in Volta River District nearby could be found on the map. It was usually possible to remedy this deficiency for 1948 by consulting index cards kept at the Government Statistician's Office on which most settlements were located with reference to 1-minute co-ordinates. These cards were also invaluable in distinguishing between settlements of similar name in the same district or Native Authority area (Wasaw Confederacy has 11 places named Nyamibechere and 10 Domiabras). Field checks showed a fair standard of accuracy in the locations given. For some restricted areas, including a group of Ga villages north-west of Accra, co-ordinates were not given and positions were ascertained by interrogation. Cards were not available for the 1931 census, and the positions of some smaller settlements which had disappeared or changed their names between then and 1948 could not be ascertained.

Preliminary Work with Census and other Material

It was decided to carry out preliminary mapping on the largest scale map available for each area. Traces were prepared with a 5-minute graticule, as used on the topographical maps. For the Togoland area, which is not covered by the normal series, an enlargement of the relevant portion of the 1 : 400,000 map was prepared. The populations of all settlements identifiable on the maps were entered in their correct places and ticked off in the census volumes. To facilitate comparisons and to assist the formulation of possible lines of enquiry, all populations showing an inter-censal increase greater than the national average were ringed in black on the 1948 traces, while those showing an increase less than this were ringed in green, and all decreases were ringed in red. Similarly coloured dots were placed opposite the settlement names in the census tables. From the census cards the populations of most places enumerated in 1948 and missing from the topographical maps (and those of some places enumerated in 1931) were entered on the traces according to the co-ordinates given. These gave a set of working maps.

The following analyses were then made from the census tables:

(a) absolute and percentage numbers of settlements of specified sizes in the various administrative units.

(b) numbers and percentage of the population by administrative units counted in settlements of the specified sizes.

These analyses were found invaluable in the final study of the population, and they would have been even more useful had the census methods of classifying and enumerating the smaller units been uniform.

The vigorous growth of new hamlets and villages, mostly small, and their subsequent decline are characteristic of areas being developed for the cultivation of cocoa. In the decade or two before 1931, Akwapim as a "pioneer" cocoa-growing state was an area of growing population and expanding settlement. The 1931 census recorded 814 settlements on Akwapim land, of which 499 contained 25 persons or less. Today many cocoa farms in this area are in decay, and in parts even food-farming suffers on the exhausted soil. The small hamlets which sprang up in such numbers are disappearing; Akwapim in 1948 comprised 429 settlements only, 27 per cent of them being of 25 persons or less. In contrast western Ashanti has large areas of recently developed cocoa land, and new farms are continually being cleared and planted. Though exact comparisons are more difficult here due to minor boundary changes, significant increases in numbers of settlements are seen in areas of recent development where smaller units were separately recorded in the censuses, e.g. in the sub-divisions of Sunyani sub-district. Here, for instance, the 1931 census lists 30 settlements in Odumasi-Sunyani sub division, 7 of them with 25 persons or fewer; in 1948, 61 out of the 91 listed were of 25 people or less. In nearby Nkwanta N.A., in 1948, 80 per cent of its 192 settlements were of the smaller size.

In some areas individual settlements were not recorded so carefully, and smaller hamlets were combined. This happened in Ashanti's boom cocoa area of Ahafo, Bechem and Ahafo Ano, where the population of the main villages was given (e.g. Acherensua 932), and the nearby hamlets were grouped as "Acherensua Cottages" 489. This was not a serious drawback in the final mapping, but it leaves a serious gap in the analysis of settlement sizes. More troublesome was the procedure adopted in a few areas such as the Berekum N.A. (Ashanti) or parts of Ho district, where village populations recorded in 1948 included those of surrounding hamlets. Reasonable estimates of numbers living in outlying settlements could, however, often be obtained from local sources, while "cocoa maps" of the Department of Agriculture, supplemented by this local knowledge, were a guide to their location.

For obvious reasons the often vaguely defined units in the areas of dispersed settlement in the north were omitted from these computations.

Analysis of Tribal Elements by Districts

The 1948 census report gives for each district a return of the African population under 61 tribal divisions, plus ten appellations termed "Others and ill-defined". From this a simplified table was compiled for each district, grouping the African population as belonging to tribes normally indigenous to:

   (i) the local district
  (ii) either the Colony, Ashanti or the Northern Territories
 (iii) French West Africa
 (iv) other countries
  (v) both Ghana and French West Africa.

The last formed a very important group, the large number recorded as belonging to tribes indigenous to both French and British territory underlining the fact that the boundary with French territory so often cuts across tribal divisions, especially in Togoland. In 1948 39·4 per cent of North Togoland's population fell into this category (mainly Bimoba, Chokosi and Konkomba peoples) and 79·5 per cent of the people of South Togoland (nearly all Ewe according to the census classification). In the study of migration these tables proved a valuable supplement to those included in the census in which district populations were classified according to birthplace and, in the case of some larger settlements, duration of residence.

T. E. Hilton

Field Work

All parts of the country were visited. Excluding visits to some places close enough to the University College at Achimota for the return journey to be made in a day, 190–200 days were spent in journeys and visits as described below. Interrogations were carried out and sources consulted at 294 centres (Fig. V, p. 89). Most places were accessible by motor road, others were reached by bicycle, launch or canoe, or on foot. The survey was carried out whilst the change from the old Native Authority system to the present Local and District Council system was taking place. This change did not present many difficulties, as the new administrative sub-divisions generally coincided closely with the sub-divisions or groups of these as shown in the census. More progress had been made in establishing the new system in Ashanti and the south than in the Northern Territories.

For each Local or District Council or Native Authority area a questionnaire was prepared after examination of the 1948 figures, comparison with the 1931 returns, and reference to the traces already prepared. These questionnaires formed the basis of the enquiries which were made at each of the centres visited. The questions were primarily designed to find out whether there were any special circumstances since 1931 which might have caused abnormal changes of population in any town, village or area, for example, new roads, extension of cocoa or food farming, opening up of new industries or closing down of old ones. Other factors such as water supply, the opening or closing of markets, and local politics (the losers in a faction fight had left one large settlement in the inter-censal period) were included. Enquiries were concerned not only with inhabited areas and settlements but also with uninhabited areas and the reasons for their being so, and the reasons behind the disappearance of settlements shown on older maps, e.g. the 1907 Sprigade (German) map of Togoland shows vanished settlements near Kete-Krachi inhabited by former slaves from the north following the depredations of the raider Babatu. Special emphasis was laid upon immigration or emigration as factors in population change. Efforts were made to discover the places of origin or destination of any significant population movement that had taken place.

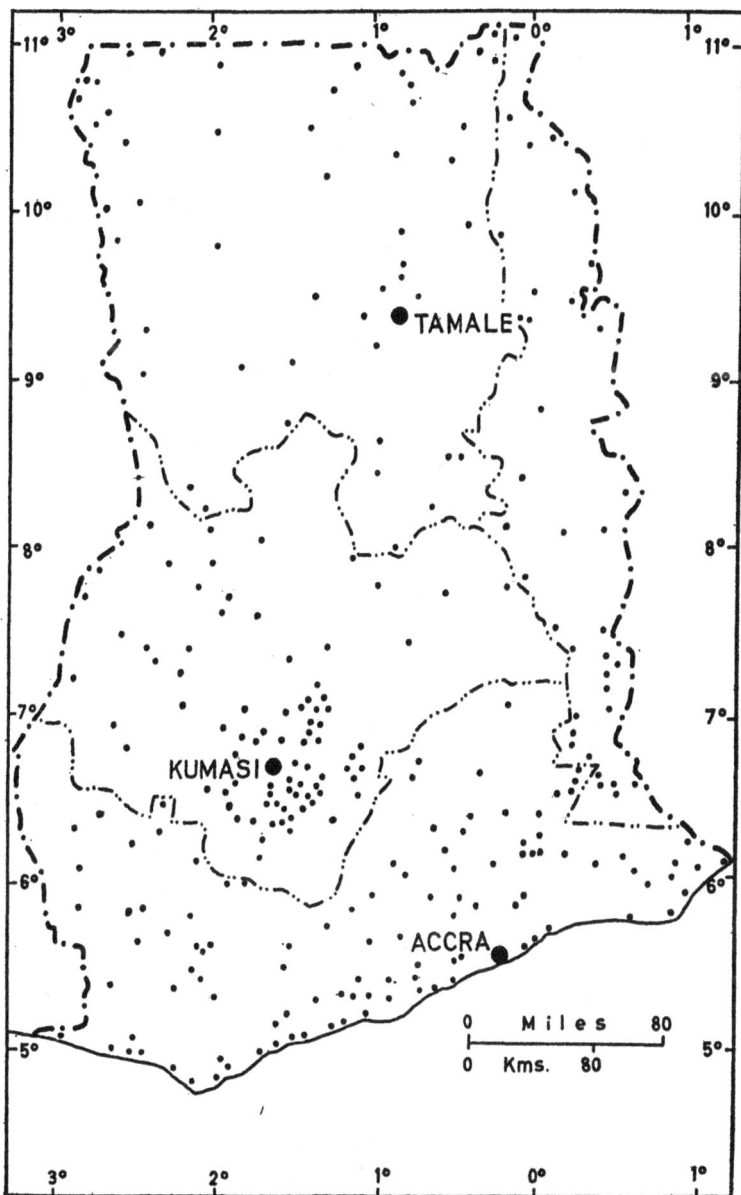

Fig. V. Ghana: places visited for the collection of information on population.

T. E. Hilton

Examination of Nominal Rolls kept at Local Council Offices gave a guide to recent trends in population movement and to the extent of immigration, especially immigration, permanent or temporary, of people from the Northern Territories or French West Africa (Haute Volta, Niger, etc.), since these generally use their tribal designation, e.g. Tongo, Moshi, as their surname. The names of those temporarily absent in the south generally appear in the Nominal Rolls of their Local Councils at home in the North with a distinguishing letter.

For each district or sub-district lists were prepared of any settlements of 200 people and over recorded in the 1948 census which could not be identified on the maps. Their positions when found were compared with those given by the census cards. Enquiries were made as to the locations of settlements enumerated in 1931 which could not be identified. Useful local information was obtained from staffs of schools and Training Colleges, commercial organizations such as the West African Timber Company at Samreboi (Wasaw-Aowin) and the Swiss Lumber Company, from members of Mass Education teams and from Mines Welfare Officers. Wherever possible help was also sought from supervisors and others who had actually taken part in the census.

A stay of some days was made at most District Stations and much valuable material was examined and information gained which was not available elsewhere. It was often possible to examine the old Record Books dating back to the establishment of the station, together with the Informal Diaries kept by District Commissioners or Government Agents as a record of their activities. These included much information on individual settlements. Equally useful were old District files and reports. In some cases these contained rough population maps, memoranda on local history or land tenure, etc. At Agriculture Stations files, annual and other reports, and "cocoa maps", showing both distribution and age of the cocoa farms, prepared by Agriculture Officers and their staffs, were consulted.

The value of studying local lorry movements for determining zones of influence or the attraction of larger settlements is well established. Such checks were carried out at various centres, mainly in the Northern Territories, during the course of the field work, and the results of other checks made by members of the Economics Department of the University College were also used.

In parts of the country economic factors were initially of secondary importance in determining the sites of villages, and it was only later that they became predominant in the evolution of settlements and indigenous political units. Much historical material is available to supplement that given in the standard accounts. Some of it, valuable in the study of the evolution of settlement, exists only in forgotten typescript in scattered stations, or else in the memories of chiefs and their elders. The necessity of locating and recording as much of this as possible was kept in mind.

A less formal but equally valuable part of the field work consisted of an examination of the landscape, together with closer enquiry into selected features of population distribution, such as:

(i) a reconnaissance of depopulated riverine areas in otherwise densely populated areas in north Mamprusi.

(ii) visits to a number of "huza" settlements in the hill country of Krobo west of the Volta and overlooking the eastern Accra plains.[1]

(iii) an examination of land use and agricultural systems in a formerly almost deserted stretch of country in northeastern Mampong district opened up by construction of the Atebubu–Kete-Krachi road in 1927, and investigations into the origins of the immigrant elements of the population.

(iv) village surveys in Tumu district on the northern frontier; at Basiasan, a village near the Navrongo boundary in an area where river blindness is common and population is decreasing through emigration; and at Walembelle, in the south of the district on the Sissili-Kulpawn watershed, a prosperous farming village whose population is increasing.

During all investigations types of settlement were noted and a photographic record of compound and other building types was kept.

---

[1] For a description of these settlements see M. J. Field, "The agricultural systems of Manya Krobo", *Africa*, XIV, 1943–4. Some variations of the pattern described by Field were found.

T. E. Hilton

Mapping

Maps were drawn of the distribution and density of population. By the end of the field work, basic traces on scales ranging from 1 : 62,500 to 1 : 250,000 (with one small area plotted on an enlargement of the 1 : 400,000 map) had been completed,

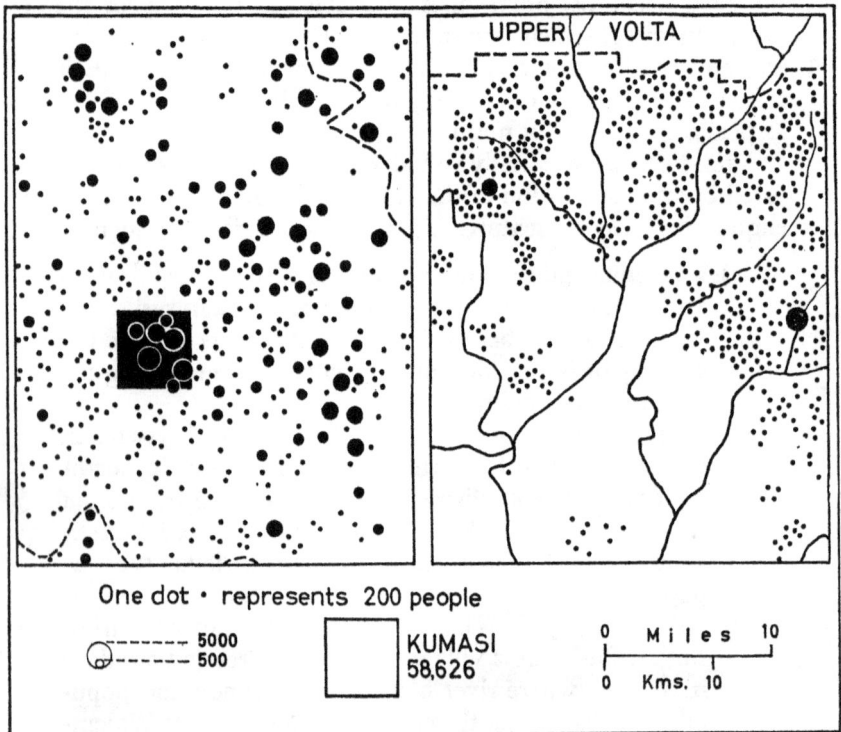

One dot · represents 200 people

⊖------ 5000
⊖------ 500

KUMASI
58,626

UPPER / VOLTA

0   Miles   10
0   Kms.   10

FIG. VI. Contrasting patterns of population distribution in
(a) Ashanti and (b) north-eastern Ghana.

and most of the mapping problems that remained were purely technical.

To show the distribution of population the dot and circle method, with one modification described below, was employed. The first problem to be solved was that of dot value and dot size, bearing in mind that the map was ultimately to be published on the 1 : 1,500,000 scale. Experiments were made with different dot and circle sizes for areas of high population density and different types of settlement.

e.g. (i) Akwapim-New Juaben—387 square miles, average density 287 per square mile, with 67 per cent of the population in settlements ranging in size from 535 to 21,550. Along 17 miles of its main road there were 13 large settlements ranging from 684 to 4,150 people.

(ii) Zuarungu—781 square miles, 340 of which were uninhabited, average density on the remainder 370. Settlement is of the fully dispersed rural type, with one "town", Bolgatanga, of 3,645 people.

After examining maps of selected areas on reduced scales, a minimum dot value of 200 was chosen, as the lowest value practicable for dots large enough and sufficiently well spaced to reduce without blurring in some densely populated rural areas (Fig. VI).

It was considered that settlements of more than 500 persons were large enough to be shown by proportionate circles, since comparatively few units which have not developed some commercial, administrative or similar importance seemed to have reached this size. The numbers of larger sized settlements in the three Administrative Areas in 1931 and 1948 were as follows:

Area	1931 No. of Settlements		1931 Percentage of total Settlements		1948 No. of Settlements		1948 Percentage of total Settlements	
	500–999	1000+	500–999	1000+	500–999	1000+	500–999	1000+
Northern Territories	66	33	2·8	1·4	73	34	4·1	1·9
Ashanti	149	85	6·1	3·5	217	125	6·2	3·6
Colony and Ho	474	261	6·4	3·5	535	358	6·8	3·8

For the smallest dots a diameter of 0·05 of an inch was adopted for the 1 : 400,000 scale. Settlements between 500 and 24,000 were plotted by proportionate circles, and dots and circles of the same sizes were used when the map was redrawn on the 1 : 500,000 scale, so as to make reduction to 1 : 1,500,000 easier.

Three settlements were very much larger than all others: Accra (133,192), Kumasi (58,626) and Takoradi-Sekondi (43,743). To save space and to stress the dominant positions of these three towns, squares of proportionate area were used to map their populations. Kumasi is ringed by suburbs, each of 1,000–3,000 inhabitants, which were enumerated separately in the census though some of them lie only a mile or so from the city centre (Fig. VI, p. 92). At the other end of the scale, there was some loss of accuracy in the distribution pattern in areas with large numbers of small settlements, due to the necessity for adopting a minimum dot value of 200.

Two types of density map were prepared, the first a choropleth map of overall densities of statistical units, the second a more subjective map of densities, based on a dasymetric technique.

In 1931 the Gold Coast was divided into 37 districts; it was in fact possible to compile a table of 44 divisions, ranging in area from 52 to 6,754 square miles, 31 of them being under 2,500 square miles. By 1948 the number of districts had been reduced to 19, including 8 of over 5,000 square miles; as an example of how this process worked, Mamprusi, of 6,376 square miles, incorporated four old districts whose 1948 densities were 117, 209, 92 and 25 per square mile.

One choropleth map was prepared showing densities in the 1948 districts, and five others which traced, from 1921 to 1948, densities and percentage annual rates of increase or decrease in the 44 sub-divisions identifiable for 1931. Changes of boundary had been frequent and much research was needed to establish some of them.

Such maps are valuable in giving preliminary impressions and in suggesting possible lines of enquiry, but their "checkerboard" pattern conceals many density variations and may obscure the essential homogeneity of areas of uniform population density which lie across the administrative boundaries used. A dasymetric density map was therefore constructed on a scale of 1 : 1,000,000 which ignored administrative boundaries and treated density variations, based on the 1948 census figures, on a national basis. Zones of varying density were selected by

Population Mapping in Ghana

examination of topographical maps and working traces, and their areas and densities were calculated. A simple graded shading pattern was used for a scale of densities ranging from "uninhabited" to "over 400 persons per square mile" (Fig. VII, pp. 96–7).

Throughout most of Ghana urban growth is recent. No real or country-wide distinction was made in either 1931 or 1948 between "urban" and "rural" settlements. In 1948 certain towns were enumerated with the aid of a form (Form B) which required detailed occupational returns. Even in southern Ghana (the Colony and Ho) no uniform principle was applied and many important centres were enumerated on Form A, for which less detail was required. Form B was not used at all in Wenchi-Sunyani District (Ashanti) nor in the Northern Territories. It was therefore premature to attempt the classification of an "urban hierarchy" according to function and occupational structure. On the density maps towns of 5,000–10,000 and over 10,000 inhabitants were separately indicated by symbols of different sizes, and their populations were omitted from the density calculations for the areas in which they were located.

Addendum—The 1960 Census of Ghana

Since February 1959 preparations have been in progress for the census of Ghana to be taken in March 1960, directed by Dr. B. Gil, United Nations Population Expert, and for the past eight months (I write in January 1960) members of the staff of the Geography Department of the University College have been working as Geographical Planning Officers for the census, and this is a short account of the part played in the census by geographers. The writer's own concern is with the Northern, Brong-Ahafo and Ashanti Regions.

The first task was to prepare a programme of work and actually to train the field teams which have toured all parts of Ghana, from mid-June to the beginning of the present month, to check the locations and estimated populations of all settlements, large numbers of which do not appear on the published maps. The writer accompanied the teams during their first three weeks in Gonja and north-western Ashanti, and visited them at intervals afterwards.

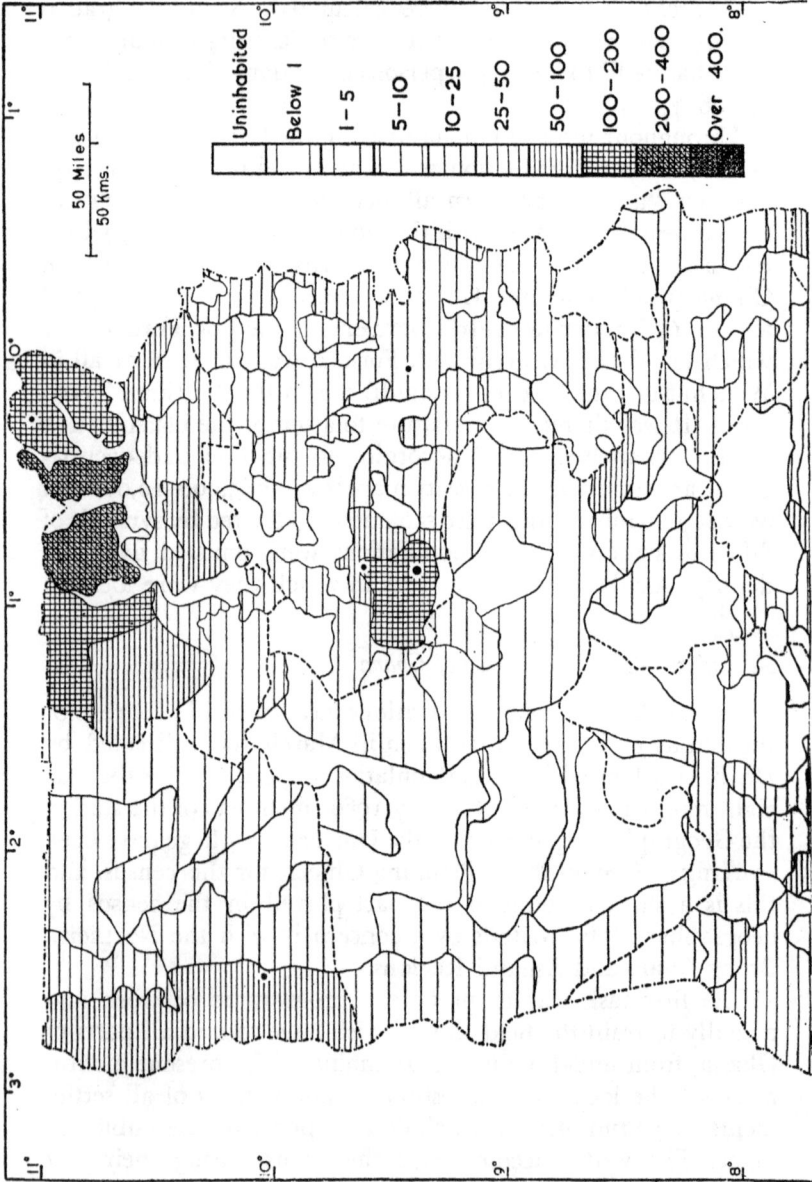

Uninhabited

Below 1

1 – 5

5 – 10

10 – 25

25 – 50

50 – 100

100 – 200

200 – 400

Over 400.

50 Miles

50 Kms.

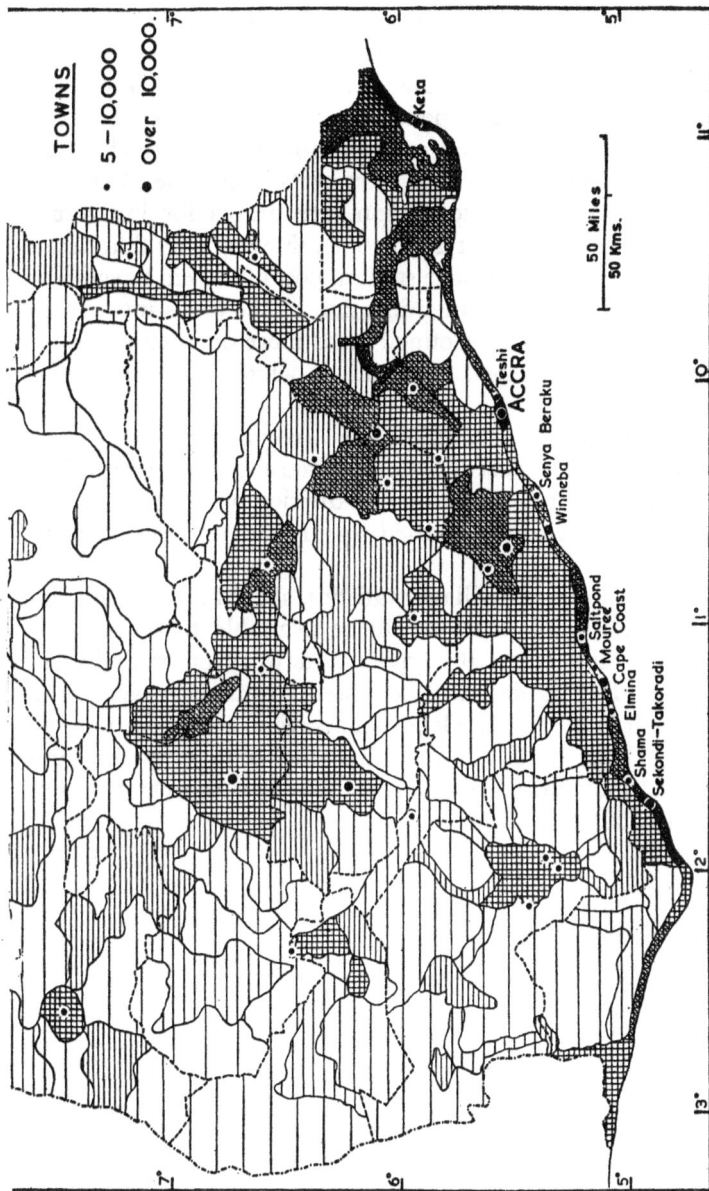

Fig. VII. Ghana: density of population and towns of 5,000 or more inhabitants (1948 census).

T. E. Hilton

In Accra the geographers have lectured to census officers and are preparing maps, one for each Local Council, dividing that Council into "Enumerators' Areas" each containing an estimated 700–1,000 people. Villages and the routes to them are the principal features mapped. The geographer also prepares, on a special form, for each enumeration area, a list of settlements in the area and a description of its boundaries. Skeleton maps, based on field information, are drawn for individual settlements of over about 1,200 people, showing only that detail (main roads and paths, police station, post office, etc.) necessary for the delimitation and identification of the areas into which it is divided. For Urban Council areas more detailed plans are prepared from published town plans, which have first to be brought up to date.

When the maps are completed the geographers will be concerned with such aspects of the preliminary work as instructions to Area Supervisors and a tentative division of the country into socio-economic areas, to be used mainly for purposes of statistical analysis.

The first volume, of village statistics, should appear in mid-1961, but much information will be available to census geographers as and when it arrives, and work on mapping of population distributions will be able to commence very soon after the actual census. Geographers will also take part in preparing both volumes analysing the data obtained and specialized monographs dealing with various aspects of population distribution and movement.

8

Population Mapping in Sudan

K. M. BARBOUR

T HE First Population Census of Sudan was conducted in the winter of 1955/56, and many of its results have since been published in the form of a number of Interim Reports, two popular publications and a Town Planners' Supplement.[1] These results have differed from almost all the census reports brought out in other African territories in that they have been accompanied by a large number of maps drawn to illustrate their findings. The maps constitute a considerable advance in knowledge of the geography of Sudan, for they include several maps that could not be compiled directly from the published figures on maps of administrative or other boundaries. They represent rather the results of an investigation, carried out at the same time as the census, into the distribution of the population within the known administrative areas, and into the most suitable manner of representing the patterns thus revealed on a series of maps.

The story of the production of these maps illustrates a way in which academic geographers have co-operated with government departments in an undeveloped part of the world. To the geographers involved the work was of interest and value for the insight that it brought into the method of conducting a census. It also underlined the need to study all the existing map series

---

[1] Republic of the Sudan, *First Population Census of Sudan 1955/56*, 1st–9th Interim Reports, Khartoum, 1957–8. Philosophical Society of Sudan, *The Population of Sudan*, Report on 6th Annual Conference, Khartoum, 1958. K. J. Krotki, *21 Facts about the Sudanese*, Khartoum, 1958. Republic of the Sudan, *First Population Census 1955/56, Town Planners' Supplement*, Vol. II, 1960.

of a country, and to understand how and why they came to be produced, before attempting to draw new maps of any kind.

The cartographic history of Sudan differs significantly from that of British colonies in the continent, partly because of the country's great size and partly because of the historical links binding the country to Egypt. Though nominally under the joint rule of Britain and Egypt, the Anglo-Egyptian Sudan was really governed by Great Britain alone from 1898 until it became independent at the end of 1955. The mother tongue of some 50 per cent of the Sudanese was Arabic, and that language served as a lingua franca more or less throughout the whole country. Nevertheless English was employed during the Condominium as the official language of government, and all maps and other official publications have until recently been published in English only. In the early days of the Condominium, a complete but largely provisional series of topographical maps of the country was produced at a scale of 1 : 250,000, with a coverage of Darfur added after the Sultanate was subdued during the First World War. Lack of staff and lack of money, however, prevented the survey authorities from doing much to improve this series, or even to keep it up to date, and by the end of the Second World War there were sheets for the poorer and less accessible parts of the country where neither the representation of the relief nor the indication of village and tribal names could be regarded as trustworthy.

To remedy this unsatisfactory state of affairs for the country at large would have involved an enormous effort and expenditure, from which there could have been little immediate return. As part of the first post-war development programme, therefore, it was decided to do little to improve the existing map series, which was anyway on too small a scale to be of much use in the field, and to concentrate on the production of a new series at a scale of 1 : 100,000. This would cover the parts of the country with the best prospects of development, where many new projects were being contemplated such as irrigation schemes, mechanized farms, new water supplies, roads, forest reserves and grazing control measures. For the compilation of these maps a new tool was at hand, the American "Trimetrogon" aerial photographic survey of much of the country that had been carried out during the war. From these photographs it would be possible to plot the drainage and relief features of the country with much greater accuracy than ever before.

The same poverty which prevented Sudan from improving her series of topographical maps was at least in part the reason why no census was carried out during the first 50 years of British rule, since this would have involved the recruitment and training of additional staff when persons with the necessary qualifications were hard to find. It was not until towards the end of this period, moreover, that the adequacy and suitability of a sample as opposed to a complete census was generally recognized.[1] A full census would have been far more expensive, and as the census authorities themselves have pointed out, "in the circumstances of Sudan, there can be no doubt that sampling methods give more reliable results than any attempted full enumeration could do. To have attempted a full enumeration of nomads or of people living in widely scattered *tukls* (huts) could only have led to grossly inaccurate results." [2] The uses of a census are many,[3] but they are more apparent during a period of economic expansion and planned development than when laissez-faire theories and a spirit of strict economy rule in government circles. The British administration, moreover, with its military origins and its senior officials predominantly re-cruited from among students of the liberal arts at the older English universities, was unlikely to feel the need of a precise statistical approach to the problems of government.

The census had been in preparation for some time when in 1955 discussions took place between representatives of the census organization and members of the geography department of the University College (now the University) of Khartoum. It was decided to try to map some of the census results, and to publish the maps as part of the final census report, which was expected to appear at some time in 1958. The list of maps that could be produced depended on two factors, namely, the items included in the questionnaire, which had already been settled, and the size and number of areas for which information was

---

[1] Sudan Government, *The 1953 pilot population census for the first population census in Sudan*, Khartoum, 1955, 12–15.

[2] Republic of the Sudan, *First Population Census of Sudan 1955/56, Supplement to Interim Reports*, Khartoum, 1956, 5 and 6.

[3] C. H. Harvie, "What is the use of the first population census of Sudan?", in *The Population of Sudan*, 1958, 11–19.

to be produced. The areas for which figures were to be produced were of several kinds: in the towns, which were to be enumerated fully, the unit for all information was to be the ward, and naturally no map on which the whole country could be shown on a single sheet would be on a scale large enough for it to be possible to distinguish between wards. In the rural areas, where over 90 per cent of the population lives, the sampling technique employed necessarily produced certain limitations: no figures could be produced for individual villages; for *omodias* or groups of villages overall population figures could be produced of reasonable accuracy, but there could be no breakdown of such figures into special categories, and so for information concerning tribes or occupations or age groups it was necessary to employ the much larger census areas, since otherwise the samples would be too small to be trustworthy.[1]

The boundaries of the 94 census areas were known, for they were in almost every case the same as those of the 92 parliamentary constituencies, which had been determined shortly before in connection with the elections held in late 1953. Many of these followed the boundaries between districts that had been agreed on and surveyed over a number of years, and elsewhere they generally followed the divisions between tribes or sections of tribes. They were shown on a Parliamentary Constituencies map that was produced by the Survey Department in 1953.

The boundaries between *omodias*, on the other hand, were neither recorded nor listed. The *omodia* is originally a section of an Arab tribe, consisting of a number of households and related groups, headed by *sheikhs*, who generally keep fairly close to one another during their migrations and are under the general control of an *omda*; each tribe consists of a number of *omodias*. When an Arab tribe settles on the land, and ceases to lead a migratory existence, or when an Arabic tribal structure is imposed by conquest and assimilation on a previously settled non-Arab population, the Arabs' administrative structure is retained. Each village has a *sheikh* as its headman, and numbers of villages are grouped together under an *omda*, a group of *omdas* being in turn subordinate to a *nazir*. In these circumstances the area cultivated from each village, together with in most instances an area of uncultivated bush, comes under the

[1] *First Population Census of Sudan, Supplement to Interim Reports,* 1956, 13–21.

control of the *sheikh*, who is responsible for granting or with-holding the right to cultivate within it. Similarly all the villages subordinate to an *omda* become his *omodia*, which thus ceases to mean merely a number of persons, and comes to include all the land belonging to the villages also.

Outside the area of Arab cultural dominance the native tribal organizations vary. In Darfur there are petty chiefs known as *shartais*, who in many ways resemble *omdas*, and the same is true of the *meks* or kings in the Nuba Mountains. In the southern provinces, on the other hand, political ties between groups of villages where a common tongue was spoken were usually weaker, a state of affairs only slightly modified by the British when they were in power.

The *omodia*, then, as used in the census and as discussed in this chapter, can have many shades of meaning but consists essentially of a number of nomadic groups of people or of a number of villages which are usually to be found occupying a continuous piece of territory. The diversity of conditions embraced by the term may be indicated by the fact that the largest *omodia*, in Zande District, had a population of 57,896; the smallest, in Dar Masalit, 211 only. The limits of this piece of territory are usually fairly constant, though movements of individuals or even of whole villages often take place. Even in settled areas, it has not been the practice of the Survey Department to record *omodia* boundaries, nor was any record usually made of these boundaries in administrative district head-quarters. This was because the responsibility for determining disputes on such matters between one *omda* and another was usually left to the *nazir*. In a largely illiterate society memory was regarded as a perfectly adequate repository of tradition in such matters, and it was not felt necessary to record on paper what everyone concerned knew perfectly well.

In mapping the census, therefore, there was no possibility of representing by *omodias* even such information as was to be pub-lished on that basis, since without precise limits and areas the distribution or density of population in the *omodias* could not be plotted or calculated. It was apparent, in consequence, that if choropleth density maps of Sudan were to be drawn, they would have to be based on the census areas. Since there were rather less than 100 census areas, and since the area of Sudan as a whole is nearly 1,000,000 square miles, the average size of a census area was about 10,000 square miles, which is not far from the size of Belgium or Basutoland. For general maps of the whole of Sudan such units would be reasonably appropriate to represent information concerning tribal membership, occupations or internal migrations. For maps to show the actual distribution of population, on the other hand, using either dots or isopleths, the census areas would be far too large to reflect the influence of environmental and other factors on the distribution. Moreover they would conceal the fact that in a country with an arid or semi-arid climate very sharp breaks of density often occur, especially along rivers or elsewhere where there are marked contrasts in soil and water conditions.

It was apparent, therefore, that if the best use was to be made of the census figures to map the distribution of population, it would be necessary to determine the distribution of the *omodias*. Even if there were neither the time nor the staff available to determine their precise location on the ground, it would be very helpful to have a general idea of their relative positions within the census areas. The means to do this had apparently been provided by the census authorities. In the course of their preparations they had compiled lists of the names of all the villages in the settled parts of the country, and had grouped them by *omodias*. These had been very carefully checked, since it was a vital element of the sampling technique that the name of every village and the listed number of taxpayers in it should be known, so that the ratio between this listed number and the number of persons eligible for listing could be accurately determined. It seemed, therefore, that all that would be needed to determine the distribution of the *omodias* would be to take the 1 : 250,000 topographical maps, and to mark out on them the boundaries of the census areas; within these areas the new lists of villages could be employed in conjunction with the village names shown on the map, since it should be possible to underline the villages belonging to *omodia* No. 1, No. 2, etc., and so to determine the relative positions of the *omodias*. It was recognized that village names might have changed somewhat since the topographical maps had been compiled, but a preliminary trial in the Gedaref area suggested that the degree of correspondence between the maps and lists would be quite satisfactory; along the settled belts of country the division between one *omodia* and the next proved fairly clear, and though no guide was given to the location of the boundary in waterless and uninhabited stretches of country, this caused little inconvenience, since there was no population to be plotted there. When this technique was applied to the rest of the country, however, its defects and those of the topographic maps became apparent. While there were parts of the country where *omodia* boundaries could be plotted in this way with complete confidence, there were other parts where most but not all of the *omodias* could be located, and others where virtually no correlation between maps and lists was to be found at all.

The best areas for demarcation were in the Northern Province and the irrigated Gezira. In the former there has been very little change in the place names, which are mostly in one of the Nubian languages and not in Arabic. In some instances *omodias* are confined to one bank of the river, in others they occur on both sides, but either way their limits up and down stream are readily determined; how far they, or at least the occupied area, may be regarded as stretching into the desert is a matter that admits of several opinions, but in practice this made little difference to plotting the population in due course. In the area covered by the Gezira scheme an *omodia* map was constructed from the village names, but it subsequently transpired that the areas actually used for the census were those used by the Gezira Board in organizing Blocks and Groups to run the scheme. In effect, therefore, an *omodia* map already existed, namely that published by the Sudan Surveys under the title of Sudan Gezira Board Blocks.[1] No major discrepancies were discovered between this and the map constructed on the basis of the place names, but enough differences appeared to serve as a reminder that even when the village name evidence was very good it was only a poor substitute for a survey of boundaries carried out on the ground.

In the settled belt that stretches across Sudan from east to west, i.e. in Gedaref District, most of the Blue Nile Province, much of central Kordofan and in Darfur, the technique was tolerably successful. With a very few exceptions the only

---

[1] Sudan Surveys 1/250,000, Northern and Southern Gezira. Topo. Nos. S 856-51 and S 848-51 (with "Sudan Gezira Board Blocks" overprint).

omodias that could not be located in this area were those comprising nomads. In southern Blue Nile Province, towards the Ethiopian border, two or three names only were available for the location of each *omodia*, and the boundaries drawn were correspondingly less reliable.

In the Nuba Mountains in southern Kordofan the lists of villages were not available when the *omodia* map was being drawn up, and the boundaries shown on the published map are those reported by the several District Commissioners; there was thus no means of finding out whether the place names had remained reasonably constant. In the districts of western and northern Darfur, i.e. to the west of Jebel Marra and beyond the limits of Arab migration, the task of locating the *omodias* was arduous but unrewarding, for the lists of villages were extremely long, the names shown on the topographical maps were very numerous, and yet there was little similarity between the two. Some of the names were obviously Arabic words, others were apparently transliterations of the many local tongues, and the question inevitably arose whether some of the current Arabic names might not be translations of the original Fur or Zaghawa or other terms. There was, however, no means of putting this to the test. A further difficulty arose from the fact that many of the place names consist of the names of very common features, e.g. Hashaba—the gum tree (*Acacia senegal*) —or Um Suneita—the place of the little *Acacia arabica*—or Abu Mareiga—the place of grain. Such names occur so frequently that it sometimes happens that two or even three names which were listed for a particular *omodia* would be found close together in one part of a given census area, and yet further enquiry would show that the *omodia* in fact lay elsewhere. In this part of the country some three-quarters of the *omodias* could be located on the maps.

In the southern provinces the technique proved virtually useless. In Equatoria it was possible to locate about a quarter of the *omodias* in certain of the census areas, or at least to find one or two villages in those *omodias* without obtaining any clear idea of their limits. The same was true in parts of Bahr el Ghazal round Wau. In the territory occupied by the Nilotes, on the other hand, the maps proved to be completely out of date. It became evident that the names which the Dinka and Nuer give to their summer villages were extremely short-lived, for even where the location of a particular *omodia* was unmistakably known (as happened in the *omodia* near Bor, which is also the headquarters of an administrative district) not one name shown in the current list of villages could be found on the topographical map that had been produced in 1933.

Clearly an *omodia* map of the whole country could not be produced by a collation of maps and village lists alone, even allowing that the nomadic areas would necessarily be omitted. Nevertheless the first tentative *omodia* map that was produced was clearly going to make locating the *omodias* appreciably more accurate than it would have been otherwise. The validity of the technique was well attested by several instances where an *omodia* was found from the map to lie in a different census area from that in which it had originally been listed. When investigated these *omodias* were invariably found to have been wrongly listed by the census authorities.

By the time these investigations had taken place it had come to the notice of various government departments that a map was being produced to show the distribution of *omodias*, and requests for copies began to reach the census authorities. It was therefore decided to call on the provincial and district officials throughout the country to assist the project, and copies of the first draft of the map were sent round with requests for the correction of obvious mistakes and the insertion, where possible, of extra information. The request was interpreted in different ways by various District Commissioners, but in general the initial aim was achieved of recording the relative location of *omodias*, even if the boundaries were not shown consistently or with uniform accuracy. While in parts of Bahr el Ghazal no boundaries were recorded between *omodias* at all, there were parts of Upper Nile and Equatoria where boundaries were indicated around the *omodias* but large areas were left attached to no *omodia* at all. This was no disadvantage for the purpose for which the *omodia* map was being produced, but would prove inconvenient if it were desired to use it for administrative purposes such as the allocation of the right to cultivate or the imposition of the duty to clear and maintain roads.

The completed map location of *omodias*, which was originally drawn on 15 sheets at a scale of 1 : 1,000,000, has been reproduced at that scale, overprinted on topographic sheets using the sheet lines of the International Million Map, as part of the final census report. It has also been reduced to 1 : 2,000,000, and is being produced on 3 sheets as part of the general map series issued at that scale by the Survey Department. While of value as an indication of the relative location of *omodias*, the map can never be used as an authority on their areas, and no densities can be calculated from it.[1]

The original intention was not to publish the *omodia* map at all, but to use it to help locate the distribution of the population within the census areas rather more accurately than would otherwise have been possible. The main purpose was to construct a dot distribution map of the population for the whole country, for which the obvious scale was 1 : 1,000,000, since the International Million Map covers all Sudan in the fairly manageable number of 15 sheets or part sheets. The value of the *omodia* map was to be that instead of being confronted with a whole census area, whose extent might well be more than 10,000 square miles, and with the problem of inserting up to 500 dots within it, the geographer could make a preliminary allocation of dots to the several *omodias*, and so reduce the possibility of error in plotting them. Before plotting began it was learnt that the International Geographical Union's Special Commission on a World Population Map was to make proposals for producing a series of dot maps for the whole world at the scale of 1 : 1,000,000 also, and so it was decided to conform to its system (as anticipated in a personal communication from its chairman) and to use a dot value of 200 persons instead of 250 persons as originally planned.

The problem still remained how to space the dots within the *omodias* so as to represent as accurately as possible the distribution of inhabitants on the ground. For this the principal source of information had to be the 1 : 250,000 series of topographical maps, which for all their unreliability on names could still be regarded as a tolerable authority on the location of inhabited settlements. An effort was therefore made within each *omodia* to reproduce as nearly as possible the pattern of settlements as shown on the topographic series, paying heed at the

[1] K. M. Barbour, "Maps of Africa before Surveys: The 'Location of Omodias Map' of Sudan", *Geographical Review*, LI, 1961, 71–86.

same time to the author's general knowledge of the factors determining the distribution of population in various parts of the country.

Had the plotting work been carried out in Khartoum, as originally seemed likely, use might also have been made of the Trimetrogon air photographs, which are available for much of the country in the Survey Department. At least for the strips across the country that are covered by vertical exposures, these photographs give a striking picture of most of central Sudan in 1943, and they are thus considerably more up to date than most of the topographical maps. This was out of the question in London, however, and indeed it would have been an extremely laborious task for one man to wade through the thousands of prints in the series; use was therefore made instead of the new 1 : 100,000 Rainlands Series of topographical maps that had been compiled for much of central Sudan from the air photographs. For the area they cover these maps are probably at least as good as the photographs: unfortunately the series is being produced primarily to assist development in the clay lands of east-central Sudan, where the 1 : 250,000 maps seem less out of date than elsewhere, and does not cover the parts of Darfur or the southern provinces where additional information was most needed.

For the south, fortunately, a new population map has recently been published as part of the Report of the Southern Development Investigation Team.[1] This map was based on the knowledge of local officials, supplemented by the results of enquiries carried out by members of the team, and it was generally followed. Now that it has been reinforced by the use of the new census statistics, there is reason to believe that a fairly reliable population map of the area has been produced.

In addition to these cartographic sources, use was also made of a more subjective geographical interpretation of the data, based on travelling and observation within the country. In the course of various journeys and studies in central Sudan, the writer had obtained a number of vivid impressions of the significance of soil conditions and water supply on the distribution

---

[1] Sudan Government, *Natural resources and development potential in the southern provinces of the Sudan*, A preliminary report by the Southern Development Investigation Team, Khartoum, 1954.

of the population, and these were used to help complete the map.

Some difficulty was experienced in the representation of the nomadic population. Though listed as inhabitants of particular census areas, many of the nomadic tribes in fact move much more widely, and may even pass beyond the boundaries of the provinces in which they enumerated. It would conceivably be possible, therefore, to draw at least two population maps to distinguish between the distribution of the nomads in the middle of the dry season and that at the height of the rains. For a single general purpose map, however, it seemed more useful to show the nomads of central and northern Sudan more or less evenly dispersed throughout their tribal areas, thus roughly representing the situation that exists during the early part of the rainy season. This policy was consistent with that followed for the population map of southern Sudan, wherein the Nilotic and other semi-nomadic tribes are shown in their summer settlements on the high ground that escapes flooding.

For the urban areas it was resolved to use a system of solid circles, with their areas proportional to the populations of the towns. For convenience of drawing, in view of their extremely small size, circles for towns with less than 10,000 inhabitants were reduced to 3 categories, 500–2,000, 2,001–5,000, and 5,001–10,000 persons. A point to note concerning the urban populations of Sudan is that they are in general rather small, for there is only one city having more than 100,000 inhabitants, while those settlements with less than 3,000 inhabitants would scarcely warrant the title of towns in many other parts of the African continent. In fact the census revealed that there are several settlements in the country, chiefly in the Blue Nile Province, that have larger populations than some of the towns enumerated as such. There is one settlement in particular, called Maiurno, on the west bank of the Blue Nile between Sennar and Singa, where there are more than 14,000 western immigrants, living together in an overgrown village more reminiscent of one in West Africa than of anything in the Sudan.

The actual drawing of the dot map was fairly easy, because in general population densities in Sudan are low; it is only in the narrow strip of alluvial lands along the Nile below

Khartoum that appreciable areas are to be found with more than 100 persons to the square kilometre (250 to the square mile). Throughout most of the country, therefore, no problems arose from the size of dot used, which had a mean diameter of 0·75 mm., and covered an area of 0·5 square kilometre.[1] Along parts of the Northern Province, as at Dongola or near Merowe, the dots had to be spread further from the river than the width of the settled land. A more serious difficulty arose on Aba Island, just north of Kosti, where a total of some 30,000 rural inhabitants were found to be occupying an area of about 60 square kilometres (*c.* 24 square miles). There was no room to insert sufficient dots on the map to represent so many persons without spreading into the White Nile, and so a special triangular symbol representing 10,000 rural inhabitants had to be employed to avoid the overlapping of the dots.

The dot value of 200 persons was quite well adapted to the distribution of the population in the settled parts of the country, for few villages are much smaller than this. In the nomadic areas, on the other hand, the practice of the inhabitants, especially in the rains, is often to move in groups of a few families only, with many groups of less than 200 persons. It should be recognized, therefore, that the map considerably under-estimates the actual number of groups to be found in these areas. Likewise in the Zande area it is the custom of individuals to build their homes at a considerable distance from their neighbours, and so the distribution of population differs from that found in other areas rather more than the map might suggest.

The use of solid circles for the towns raised the problem whether it was better to allow certain nearby dots to be overlapped and disappear, or whether it was better to shift the dots slightly so that they all appeared; in practice it was decided to do the latter. It was unfortunate that several of the country's largest towns are situated so close together at the junction of the Blue and White Niles that their circles had to overlap.

When the initial dot map had been plotted it was used in the construction of a density map, since it was thought that for

---

[1] The relationship between dot size, dot value, linear scale and the greatest density that can be represented without causing dots to merge is discussed by J. Mackay in "Dotting the dot map", *Surveying and Mapping*, IX, 1949, 3–10.

many purposes it might be more useful to have a map of the density of the population, whereon the names of towns and other features could be inserted, than a dot map, which loses its effect when additional extraneous information is inserted. Knowledge of actual densities, moreover, is of great value when studies of the carrying capacity of the land, risk of over-population or need for further governmental services are being undertaken. If densities are known, useful comparisons may also be made both within the country and with other parts of the world.

The density map was first drawn at a scale of 1 : 2,000,000, using a photographic reduction of the original 1 : 1,000,000 dot map; a few fairly broad categories were chosen (0–2, 2–10, 10–50, 50–100 and 100 and over per square kilometre), since it was felt that the accuracy of the original dot map was not of a very high order, and areas were delimited in the following way. A sheet of tracing paper was put over the dot map, and on a separate sheet a number of squares were drawn corresponding to an area of 200 square kilometres; on these evenly spaced dots were inserted to represent critical densities. Thus one square held two dots, representing 400 persons, and indicated the distance between dots that corresponded to a density of 2 persons to the square kilometre; another square with 10 dots represented 10 persons to the square kilometre, and so on. The use of these dummies made it possible over most of the map to see at a glance to which of the five categories adopted any given area should be assigned. In case of difficulty, a plain transparent square could be set over an area, and the number of dots beneath it was then counted.

Lines enclosing areas of the various density classes were then drawn on the large sheet of tracing paper. These lines were not true isopleths, since they did not join points of equal density or numerical value; in population distribution the sharp breaks that often occur between one area and another correspond more nearly to cliffs than to the even slopes that are suggested by contour or other isopleth maps, and the density map of the Sudan may be regarded as an example of a dasymetric map (Fig. VIII).[1]

The distribution and density maps are being produced at a

[1] F. J. Monkhouse and H. R. Wilkinson, *Maps and Diagrams*, 1952, 28 and 237.

scale of 1 : 2,000,000 on three sheets. They have also been drawn as single sheets at 1 : 4,000,000 (involving the conversion of the dot value on the former from 200 to 1,000 persons), and

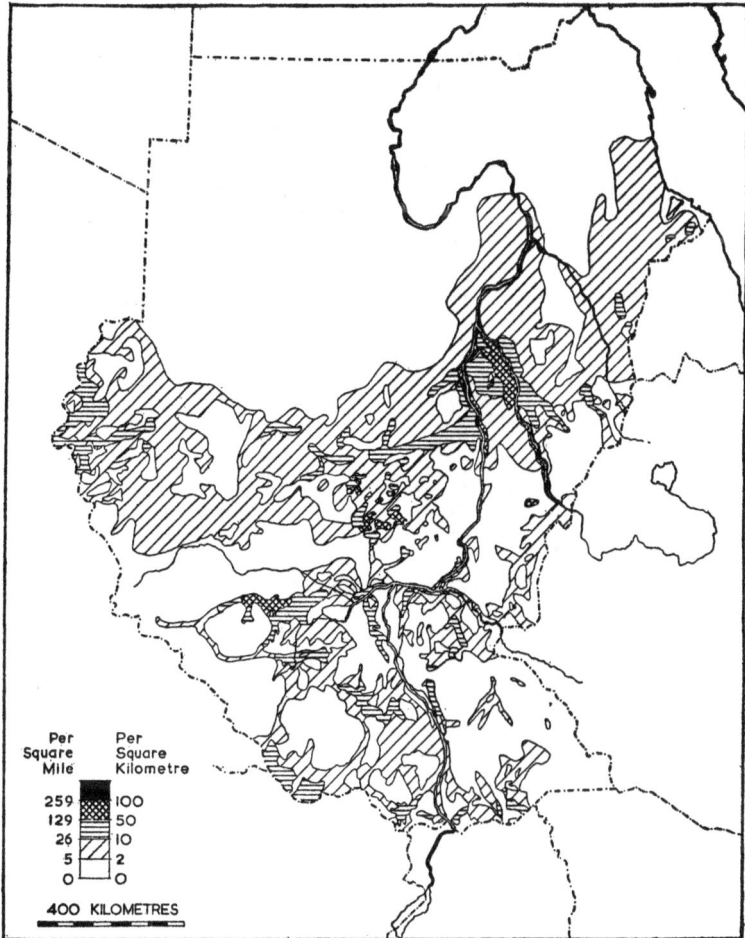

Fig. VIII. Sudan: density of rural population.

are being printed in both English and Arabic. The 1 : 2,000,000 maps are being issued with the final report of the census, while the 1 : 4,000,000 sheets were published earlier with the popular summary of the census results entitled *21 Facts about the*

Sudanese.[1] The other maps that accompany the census reports, including the interesting series of progress maps that were included with the interim reports, were produced directly from the published tables and the map of census areas. They call for no special comment on cartographic policy or technique, except perhaps a note of gratification that the value of mapping the results of the census should have been noted at an early date and have produced such fruitful results.[2]

[1] K. J. Krotki, *op. cit.*, Appendix, 1958.
[2] The complete list of maps published by the end of 1960 was as follows:

Author	Code Number	Title	Scale
H. R. J. and G. M. Davies	Map PC 8	Population density in Sudan	1 : 8,000,000
	Map PC 13	Tribes in Sudan	,,
	Map PC 11	Languages in Sudan	,,
Dept. of Statistics	Map PC 38	Population centres	,,
H. R. J. and G. M. Davies	Map PC 14	West Africans in Sudan	,,
	Map PC 12	Arabic in Sudan	,,
Dept. of Statistics	Map PC 23	Crude birth rates per 1000	,,
	Map PC 24	Crude death rates per 1000	,,
	Map PC 25	Census areas and Interim reports	,,
K. M. Barbour	Map PC 7	Population: Dot distribution	1 : 4,000,000
	Map PC 10	Population density: Isopleth	,,
K. M. Barbour Dept. of Statistics	Map PC 36	Location of Omodias map	1 : 1,000,000
Zein M. Omar	Maps PC 42/ 1122–44/942	68 Town plans	Various scales

9

Population Densities and Agriculture in Northern Nigeria

A. T. GROVE

Most people in tropical Africa are cultivators, depending for their food and much of their cash income on their own cropland and animals. Nearly everywhere there is a broad correlation between population density and intensity of agriculture. Certain systems of shifting agriculture such as those followed by the Bemba of Northern Rhodesia rely on lengthy resting periods between a few years' cropping and are incapable of supporting more than a few people, say 5 or 10 to the square mile. In the semi-arid lands, where pastoralists shift their grazing grounds according to the seasons, population densities are of a similar order. At the other extreme, there are large areas in West Africa and smaller ones in the East where numbers exceed 300 to the square mile and these densities are generally associated with much more efficient use of the land, giving higher production per unit area. The greater numbers of people both require and allow farming to be more intensive.

Agricultural systems vary in character according to the range of crops the climate allows. In West Africa a number of crop belts can be distinguished running east and west and arranged in accordance with the increasing aridity inland from the Gulf of Guinea towards the Sahara. Agricultural systems within each of these belts have several features in common, but they vary one from another because of the differing traditions and heritages of different tribal groups. The selection for study of an area with a single dominant culture and with well-marked climatic characteristics, in this case the Muslim Hausa region of Kano in the Sudan zone of Northern Nigeria, eliminates some of the variables affecting agricultural systems, and the relations between agriculture and population density can thereby be more clearly distinguished.[1]

The physical and cultural characteristics of the Sudan zone, stretching from the Atlantic to the Ethiopian Highlands, are unusually uniform for such an extensive tract of country. The great plains on the southern borders of the Sahara extend over the gentle slopes of the Senegal, Niger and Chad basins, and they owe their homogeneity not only to the low relief and a climate characterized by a short, intense, rainy season but also to a common history of climatic fluctuations over the last several thousands of years. At times during the Quaternary Period the rainfall was greater than at present, as the old high-level shore-lines of Lake Chad clearly testify, and processes of soil formation typical of humid tropical lands were in operation. At other times, dunefields spread far south into lands that are now well-watered, with rainfall totals of more than 30 inches a year, and the soils there are derived from wind-blown sands.[2] As a result of these climatic fluctuations the soils in this zone are arranged in a pattern which conforms to some degree with the relief. The watersheds are characterized by stretches of lateritic iron-stone, with rock inselbergs and in places prominent escarpments rising above them; old dunefields mantle long gentle slopes of the sedimentary basins, and heavier clays lie in the central hollows (Fig. IX).

These plains, lying between the deserts to the north and the forest to the south, are analogous to the loess belt of Europe. Both have long been zones of easy movement, both are unusually productive and owe their fertility at least in part to soils derived from wind- and water-laid deposits that accumulated under climates differing markedly from those of the present.

In the last 2,000 years the western Sudan has seen the rise

[1] D. Forde and R. Scott, *The Native Economies of Nigeria,* 1946. A very good general account of the native economies of the Hausa North is to be found in Chapter III.

[2] A. T. Grove, "The ancient erg of Hausaland and similar formations on the south side of the Sahara", *Geog. Jour.,* cxxiv, 1958, 528–33.

and fall of several loosely administered states and empires which were linked to the Mediterranean by caravan routes across the Sahara. Traders carried to Sudanese markets salt from Bilma and Taoudeni, cloth and metal-work from Europe, and they introduced to the African interior many elements of the Islamic life of the mediaeval Mediterranean coastlands. In spite of the intercourse between the lands north and south of the desert, agricultural techniques in the western Sudan do not seem to have been greatly improved. The plough, if it was ever intro-

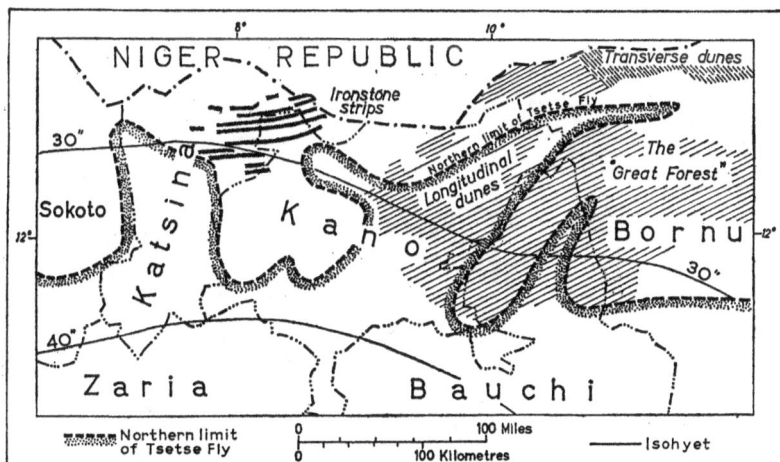

Fig. IX. The Kano region, Northern Nigeria: environmental setting.

duced, was never widely adopted, and cultivation is even now almost entirely by the hand-hoe.

In the Hausa States, which evolved nearly a thousand years ago, a period of great trading activity centred on Kano and Katsina started about the sixteenth century. The fortunes of these cities fluctuated but they have continued since that time to be nodal points in the economy of the surrounding country. Near the cities the land was heavily farmed, in part by slaves belonging to the city dwellers. Beyond lay a zone in the charge of governors who were responsible to the ruler of the city for the defence of their districts and for protecting trade-routes. Traders and tax-collectors carried to the city the surplus crops of the country. These fiefs of the Hausa, and later the Fulani, states of Katsina, Kano and of northern Zaria are contiguous and together they form a well-settled region in which the cultural pattern, though not uniform, is more consistent than that in most other parts of Africa of similar extent.

The region of heavy settlement, which for convenience will be referred to here as the Kano region, stretches eastwards from the water-parting of the Niger and Chad basins to western Bornu (Fig. X, below). Population densities exceed 400 to the square mile over about a thousand square miles in the vicinity of Kano city. They diminish away from this central

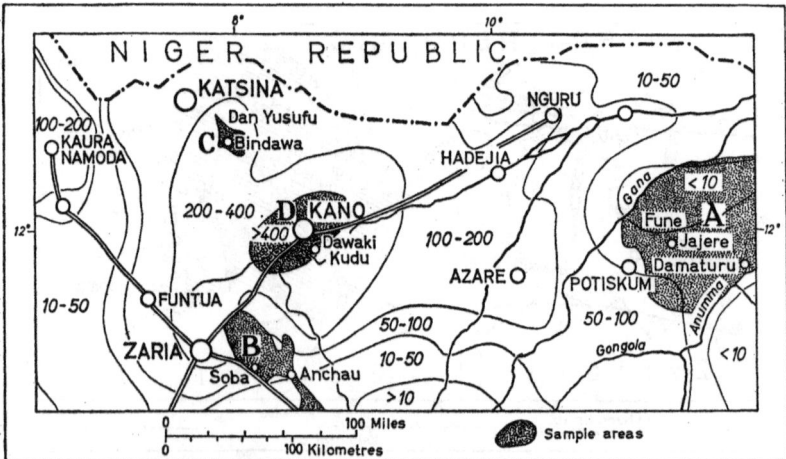

FIG. X. The Kano region, Northern Nigeria: population density (per square mile) and the location of sample areas. (A) Fune-Damaturu; (B) Anchau-Soba; (C) Dan Yusufu; (D) Kano.

area, but there are lesser concentrations of settlement, notably in areas north of Zaria and south-east of Katsina. The limits of this populous region can be set by population densities of less than 100 to the square mile. On the north they correspond approximately both to the frontier between Nigeria and the Republic of Niger, and to the former frontier of the Fulani Empire of Sokoto. The mean annual rainfall there is about 20 inches, and in some years crop failures caused by drought are severe. In the west, the sparsely settled country near the boundary between Sokoto and Katsina Provinces was for a long time a zone of conflict between the kingdoms of Katsina and Gobir.[1] It was regularly used as a routeway by raiders from Maradi, and following the Habe revolt in 1843 the area was largely depopulated due to the reprisals of Sidiku, the Fulani ruler of Katsina.[2] Although much of it has since been recolonized, a strip along the Sokoto border has been made into a Forest Reserve and remains unpopulated. In southern Zaria and the southern fringe of Kano Emirate dense woodland heavily infested with tsetse-fly and soils derived in part from lateritized Crystalline rocks provide a less congenial environment than further north. Furthermore, southern Zaria was for long regarded as the source of slaves by the northern states and its population suffered accordingly. East of Kano, sandy plains decline gently to the low country about Lake Chad, and the population density gradually diminishes towards the wide marchlands of Hausa and Kanuri states. The climate becomes drier in the same direction, wells are deeper and, paradoxically, the proportion of wet season swampland increases. But the low population density of "the great forest of Bornu" can be attributed mainly to the slave-raiding and warfare in this no-man's land between the states of Kano and Kanem and later between the Fulani and Bornu Empires.

South-west Bornu: Sparse Settlement and Immigration (Fig. XI, p. 120)

In western Bornu, population densities are about 25 to the square mile and only about one quarter of the land that could be cultivated is under crops and bush fallow. Into this region, with its great tracts of unsettled open woodland and grassland, Fulani herdsmen moved during the nineteenth century. They have adapted their seasonal movements to local water and grazing conditions, spending the rainy season with their herds on the well-drained crests of the ancient dunes, watering their cattle at the pools collecting in clay-floored inter-dunal hollows, and growing a few fields of millet to supplement their basic diet of milk. In the dry season they lead their herds to the banks of rivers such as the Gana to the north and the Gongola and

---

[1] H. Barth, *Travels and Discoveries in North and Central Africa*, London, 1858, IV, 113–20.

[2] S. J. Hogben, *Muhammadan Emirates of Nigeria*, London, 1930, 96–7.

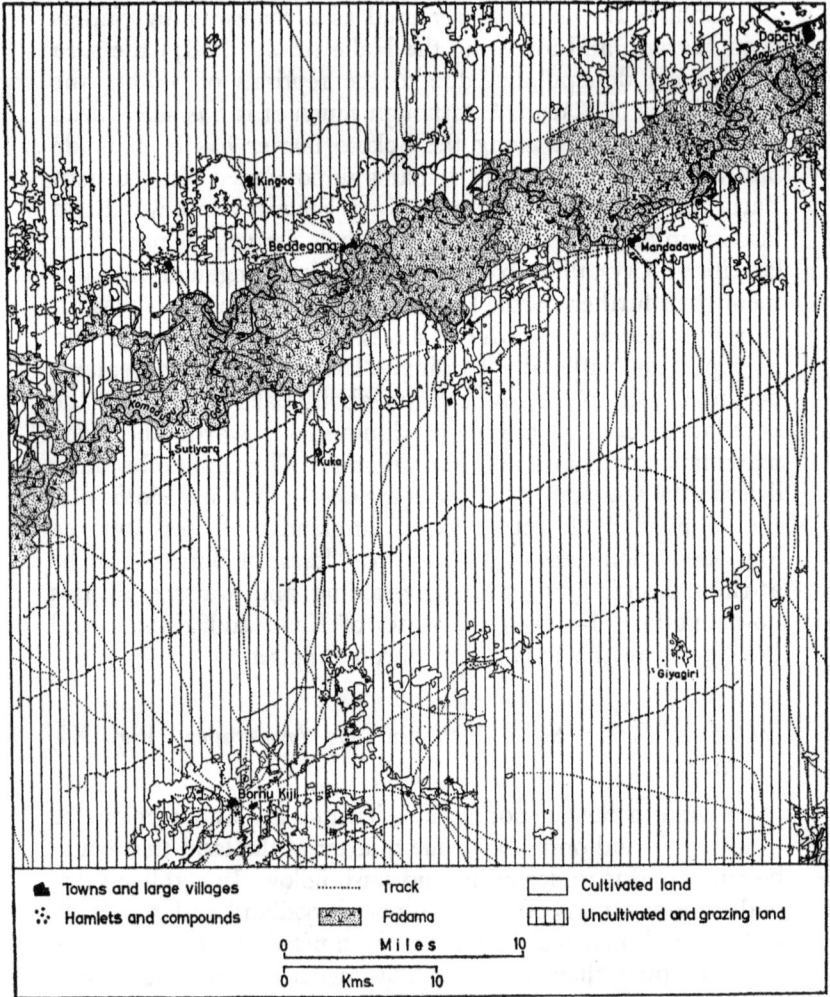

Fig. XI. Land use and settlement pattern in a part of the Fune-Damaturu area of Bornu Province. (Based on maps of the Directorate of Overseas Surveys.)

Anumma to the south, and only small groups remain behind on the lands occupied during the wet season.[1] After the rinderpest epidemic of 1897 which destroyed many herds, and again after

[1] D. J. Stenning, *Savannah Nomads*, London, 1959.

the very dry year of 1914, some families began to depend more on cereal growing, and for a time at least adopted a more settled way of life. In the Fune-Damaturu zone the leading herdsmen were persuaded by the administration about 40 years ago to settle in the wet season grazing lands as village chiefs. Many of them have gradually disposed of their cattle and now have much in common with non-Fulani agriculturists who have immigrated to the area in the meantime.

The population density of this Fune-Damaturu zone is about 25 persons to the square mile, of which the Fulani, numbering about 6,000, form between a fifth and a tenth. They own about 60,000 cattle, of which only one tenth remain in the zone throughout the year. The immigrant peoples, mainly Hausa and Kanuri, farm extensively, cropping a patch of land for a few years and then clearing another. Their farms are mainly distributed on the dune crests, but there is still so much land unfarmed that few disputes arise from cattle damaging crops.

The pastoralists depend for sustenance mainly on the milk from their cattle, and, as Stenning has shown, it is of the greatest importance to the Fulani family to maintain a balance between the size of its herd and the numbers of males and females constituting the family. The Fulani pastoral population is limited by the number of cattle that its combined dry and wet season grazing lands can support. This number is always difficult to assess, and it varies from year to year with the rainfall, but this zone would probably support more cattle than at present. There is, as yet, little co-operation between the pastoralist and sedentary cultivator in this sparsely settled area, and the arrangements for stubble-grazing which are an important feature elsewhere play little part in the agricultural economy. Nevertheless, the two groups are complementary to some degree in that the Fulani obtain a large proportion of the cereals they require from the cultivators in exchange for surplus milk and butter. Only occasionally are animals sold in order to purchase corn.

With the immigration and spread of cultivation in the last 40 years, woodland has been destroyed over wide tracts of country and the increase in population has been accompanied by an improvement of water supplies. Between Potiskum and Damaturu the level of ground-water has risen phenomenally in the last quarter of a century; water-levels in some wells have risen by more than a hundred feet and perennial springs have broken out to feed small lakes, thus providing opportunities for small-scale irrigation.[1] The form of the water-table indicates that the ground-water is largely replenished by seepage from the floors of valleys and it appears that the destruction of woodland, by reducing the losses by transpiration of water brought up from depth by the tree roots, has increased the volume left to percolate deeply into the pervious sedimentary rocks underlying the area. This example of environmental conditions being improved for agriculture as the population increases is perhaps unusual, but a similar rise in the water-table has also been noted in parts of Sokoto,[2] Zaria and Daura.

North-east Zaria: Moderate Population Density (Fig. XII)

Two hundred miles to the west, at the south-western corner of the Kano populous region, the village of Soba and the villages near Anchau in northern Zaria Province lie in a more heavily settled area, where the Sudan Savanna merges into the more humid and denser Guinea Savanna. The people are mainly Muslim Hausa with a minority of Maguzawa pagans. Nearly all of them grow guinea-corn and cotton, but the economies of the local communities vary, for while the Hausa are commonly more concerned with craft production than farming, the pagans concentrate on growing cereals. About 30 years ago the mean population density near Anchau was about 30 to the square mile. Since the British arrived in Zaria, the people had spread out from the walled villages where they had congregated for defence, and their farms and hamlets were scattered through the bush. The woodland is infested with tsetse-fly and in 1934 one-third of the population in the villages near Anchau were found to be infected with sleeping-sickness. Nash has described how a tsetse-free corridor 70 miles long and 10 miles wide was formed to link together the central fly-free

[1] J. D. Carter and W. Barber, "The Rise in the Water-Table in parts of Potiskum Division, Bornu Province", *Records Geol. Surv. Nigeria*, 1956, 5–10.

[2] R. M. Prothero, in an unpublished paper, has reported on several *fadama* in Sokoto Province that were formerly dry for part of the year, but which now hold water throughout the dry season.

areas of several villages.[1] The people were taken from the outlying hamlets and concentrated in this corridor to give a
population density there of 70 to the square mile, the minimum
required to cope with the re-slashing of cleared streams.

Before the resettlement of the villagers, a survey was made
of the hamlet of Gata near Anchau and it was found that more
than 2 acres per head were under cultivation, half under

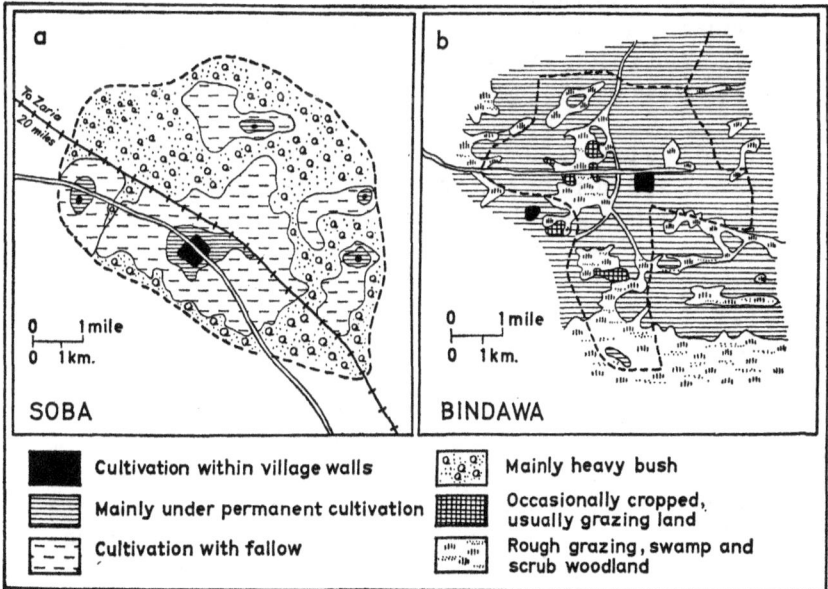

Fig. XII. Main categories of land use in the farmlands of Soba and
Bindawa villages.

guinea-corn and most of the remainder under cotton. This is
rather a large acreage for African hand farmers to cultivate.
Less than a quarter of the area under crops was under permanent cultivation. This land was manured by locally owned
cattle and by the herds of nomadic Fulani, and a large proportion of it was held by long-established members of the
community. Newcomers had only tiny plots of permanently
cultivated land but commonly farmed very large plots at some

[1] T. A. M. Nash, *The Anchau rural development and settlement scheme*, H.M.S.O.,
1948. Note map of Gata, Fig. 3.

distance from the centre of the hamlet. It was estimated that under the prevailing conditions each person needed a total of four acres of land, thus allowing a maximum population of 160 per square mile. Under these circumstances agricultural production is limited by the labour available rather than by any lack of cultivable land.

At Soba the population density is greater than that of the district near Anchau, with about 4,000 people occupying the 40 square miles within the boundaries of the village lands.[1] Most of the people live in a nucleated settlement, a *gari*, near the centre, and in four scattered hamlets. The cultivated land of the village is mainly concentrated within a mile or two of the *gari* and at a greater distance thick savanna woodland is broken only here and there by cultivated land. The pattern of land use is irregular but several concentric zones can be distinguished about the *gari* (see Fig. 2a). The village walls enclose about a hundred acres where small patches are well manured with household waste, and crops of vegetables, tobacco, maize and millet are grown. Outside the village walls, within about a half to three-quarters of a mile, nearly all the land is cultivated every year and its fertility is maintained by manure from locally owned donkeys, goats and sheep. Fulani herdsmen are invited and even paid to kraal their cattle on this land near the houses, as they move south at the end of the rainy season from southern Katsina and Kano Provinces towards the valley of the Kaduna River. The manure is distributed in a haphazard manner, and since it is not dug in until several months later, is less beneficial than it could be. Nevertheless, there is more co-operation in Soba between pastoralist and agriculturalist, to their mutual benefit, than there is in the more sparsely settled lands of western Bornu. Outside the manured land, in a third zone roughly a half to one mile from the *gari*, farms are cleared and cultivated for three or four years and the land reverts to fallow for at least five years. In the corresponding zone at Gata the fallow period was said to be three to six years but might last thirty or forty years, and in most places this fallow period varies greatly from one plot to another. In the outermost zone of Soba village, more than three or four miles from the *gari*, bush

[1] R. M. Prothero, "Land-use at Soba, Zaria Province, Northern Nigeria", *Econ. Geog.*, xxxiii, 72–86.

growth predominates, but the woodland bordering streams has been cleared in an attempt to eradicate tsetse-fly and reduce the incidence of sleeping-sickness. Concentric arrangements of land use, similar to those around the *gari*, are repeated on a smaller scale around the four hamlets of Soba, and they appear to be a common feature of settlements in areas with population densities of about 50–150 to the square mile.

In villages such as these, the chief exception to the concentric zoning is provided by the seasonally flooded *fadama* cropped with maize, tobacco and sugar-cane. In northern Zaria this swampland was originally worked by people coming from the congested areas near Kano, for the local villagers had not the skill to manage it. As the strangers often came only in the dry season, with no intention of settling permanently, a cash payment for the use of the land was introduced. Now the villagers have learned to grow *fadama* crops themselves, and they rent or buy patches of half or a quarter acre from those who own the *fadama*-land and formerly leased it to the Kano strangers.[1] *Fadama* in many villages is now fully utilized and is "scarce" in the economist's sense. The upland used for subsistence crops is still not bought and sold.

Northern Katsina: Dense Settlement, Land Impoverishment and Emigration (Fig. XII, p. 123)

Towards the central districts of the Kano region population densities increase, and all the inner agricultural zones surrounding villages have a greater radius. The proportion of village lands under yearly cultivation is larger, and at some critical figure of population density, the outermost zone of bush fallow farming is eliminated from the land-use pattern as a continuous feature. This critical figure varies with the soil conditions but it is probably of the order of 150 or 200 to the square mile. Where population densities are lower than this, land use is commonly unspecialized; land is not used for different purposes according to its inherent capabilities, but any particular patch may be under woodland at one time, rough grazing at another, cropped for a few years and then abandoned. In more heavily

[1] C. W. Cole, *Report on Land Tenure, Zaria Province*, Kaduna, 1949, 43 and 72–86.

settled areas, there is a closer relation of the land-use pattern to soil conditions.

Recent maps of north-eastern Katsina Province and the adjacent Emirate of Kazaure[1] distinguish between cultivated and uncultivated land. Over a total area of about 1,500 square miles the uncultivated land is arranged in strips each about a mile or two wide, broken but still clearly discernible, spaced about five miles apart and running across country for distances of 50 or 60 miles in a direction slightly south of west. This

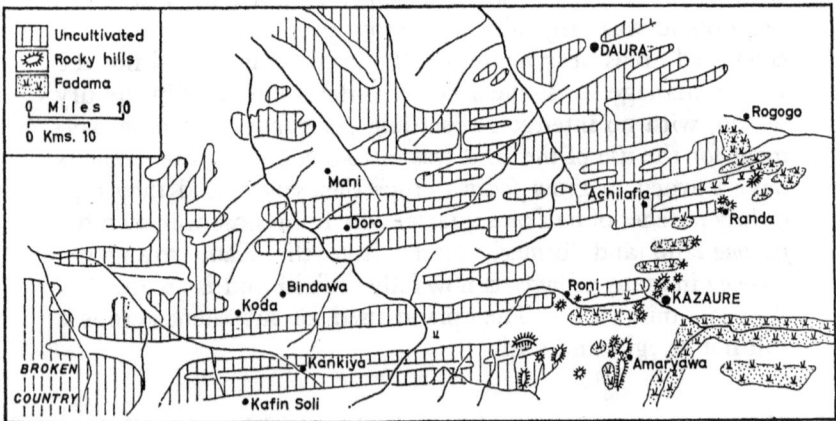

Fig. XIII. Detail of the pattern of ironstone strips and associated uncultivated land in parts of northern Kano and northern Katsina Provinces.

pattern is clearly controlled by soil differences. The uncultivated strips remain uncropped because their soils, which overlie lateritic ironstone at a shallow depth, are poor. Crops are planted on soils derived from aeolian sand which was carried west by the wind in a more arid period of the past. The sandy strips lie downwind of the gaps between a number of hills running north-east from Kazaure. The strips devoid of sand drift are in the lee of the hills (Fig. XIII).

In 1952, a land-use survey was made of Dan Yusufu, a district of 121 square miles which is believed to be fairly typical of this region, and which displays a fragment of this stripe pattern of

---

[1] Sheets 34, 35 and 36 prepared from air photographs by the Directorate of Overseas Surveys, Tolworth, Surrey; on a scale of 1:100,000.

land use.[1] More detailed studies were made of the pattern of cropping in Bindawa, one of the eight villages in Dan Yusufu, and of land-ownership in Illale, one of the ten hamlets in Bindawa. The proportion of land under cultivation is much greater than at Soba and there is little trace of the zoning of land use according to distance from the *gari*. Some garden crops are raised within the decaying walls of Bindawa, and the small plots immediately outside them are manured more heavily than those at a distance; but there is no encircling zone of bush fallow and woodland. Only about one third of the village people live in the *gari*; and the remainder live in compounds dispersed singly or in clusters through the hamlets.[2] All the cultivated land has people living near it, and all the land attractive to cultivators, with light sandy or loamy soils, is under crops. This explains why the regular soil pattern has been picked out so clearly on the maps mentioned.

About 58 per cent of the village land of Bindawa (that is the total area claimed by the village community) was under crops in 1952. About 6 per cent had been farmed within the preceding few years and was lying fallow, and nearly all the remainder consisted of rough grazing and scrub woodland. These figures are probably typical of Dan Yusufu as a whole and much of north-eastern Katsina Province and Kazaure Emirate. The average area of cultivated land per head is about 1·3 acres, and judging from the somewhat inadequate figures available for crop yields in the area, and the proportions of Bindawa devoted to different crops, this area of 1·3 acres produces in a normal year about 280 lb. of guinea-corn, 270 lb. of millet, 130 lb. of groundnuts plus some beans and other subsidiary crops such as cassava and maize. The market prices of corn vary widely from season to season, being much higher late in the dry season than immediately after the harvest, but the total value might be estimated as £6 or £7. The yield of 550 lb. of grain from the 1·3 acres of cultivated land per head compares with a basic

---

[1] A. T. Grove, *Land and Population in Katsina Province*, Kaduna, 1957.

[2] Since 1952 many of the people in Bindawa and other villages, who formerly lived in compounds dispersed through the farmland, have been brought close together to live in settlements built near to the roads. This brings them nearer to wells and schools and modern influences of all kinds. But the distant land may suffer from lack of manure, and trees near the settlements are felled for fuel.

grain consumption of about 700 lb. per head and does not take into account the corn required for seed.[1]

All the better soils in Bindawa are under cultivation and the remainder, nearly all of which have been cultivated at some time in the past, are used mainly for rough grazing and browsing. The village people, who number in all about 4,350, own more than 3,000 goats and 350 sheep. These feed on crop residues in the early dry season and browse on shrubs and trees in the uncultivated bush later in the year, while throughout the growing season they are tethered in the compounds. Donkeys carry their dung to the fields in the dry season, together with other household waste. With 60 horses and 400 donkeys, there are more large animals in Bindawa than in most villages of its size, because many are owned by members of the ruling class at the District Headquarters. Cattle, numbering 733, are owned by some 200 individuals but they are herded by only about 65 men, and many of the cattle spend a large part of the year attached to Fulani herds grazing outside the District. The total manure provided by these animals might amount to 2,000 or 3,000 tons and carefully conserved and distributed this would be enough to maintain fertility in half the village cropland. Quite small applications of farmyard manure appear to have beneficial results under Nigerian conditions.[2] The rough grazing land, on which the animals providing this manure partly depend, is now very poor and infested with weeds and probably contributes less to the village economy than it would if the numbers of stock using it were reduced. The soil is being severely eroded and the quality of the pasture is steadily deteriorating. There is little to attract pastoral Fulani to this heavily settled area of north-eastern Katsina and, for the most part, the northern limits of their seasonal movements lie further south.

The cultivated fields of this and other areas of long established, heavy settlement are characterized by the number of large trees providing food for stock or edible fruits. These were

[1] See W. E. McCulloch, "An inquiry into the dietaries of the Hausas and Town Fulani", *West Afr. Med. Jour.*, V.3, 8–22, 62–73, and B. M. Nicol, *Brit. Jour. Nutrit.*, III, 25 and VI, 34.

[2] K. T. Hartley and M. Greenwood, "The effect of small applications of farmyard manure on the yields of cereals in Nigeria", *Emp. Jour. of Experimental Agric.*, V, 113–21.

planted originally in the neighbourhood of compounds or to mark boundaries, or else were allowed to remain when other less useful trees were cleared and cultivation became permanent. They are owned by individuals and are sometimes bought and sold. Besides adding to the attractiveness of the landscape they provide a useful shade for certain crops, which also benefit from the manure of animals that congregate under the trees in the dry season. The unfarmed land is included mainly in fragments of the wide strips mentioned above, but there are numerous other smaller patches on poorly drained and eroded sites scattered through the village lands. Animals are moved frequently from one patch to another and from compounds to water-holes in the *fadama*, and arable fields are protected from them by hedges of cactus and various shrubs. The landscape of the heavily settled lands has been greatly modified by man.

The deceptively even picture presented by average figures conceals a range of variation amongst people and their possessions which cannot be disregarded. Every gradation of Islamic influence can be distinguished in villages as units; the Hausa-speaking people of a single village include Fulani and Habe, with admixtures of Touareg, Kanuri and other groups. Slavery has faded, but society remains well stratified and within any village the range in wealth and in size of holdings is well marked. The average holding of a family work-unit of six people in Bindawa consists of three plots of land totalling about eight acres; but in nearly every hamlet there are a few farmers with more than twenty-five acres. Most of them claim to be Fulani and own a large number of animals. Hamlet heads and District officials commonly fall into this class, and the latter employ labourers or depend on retainers for assistance in farming. A larger group of holdings, about 10 per cent of the total, are each made up of four or five plots covering between ten and twenty-five acres. More than half the holdings constituting about half the cultivated area are of five to ten acres and are made up of two or three plots. The smallest holdings, belonging mainly to artisans and craftsmen living in the *gari*, are less than five acres and occupy between 15 and 20 per cent of the cultivated area. Nearly every man is a farmer but nearly half also have another occupation as herdsman, trader, dyer, weaver, butcher, or drummer, and so on. These people spend at least a part of the dry season, when farm work in Bindawa is at a standstill, trading their wares in the local market-towns and in more distant parts. Some migrate southwards but the dry season exodus from Katsina Province is not on the same scale as that from Sokoto.[1] None the less it is probably important in helping to balance the grain deficit mentioned earlier.

The old system of usufructuary rights in land is being modified by new economic pressures in the villages where no uncultivated bush remains. In a sparsely settled area, a member of a community acquires the right to as much land as he needs and is capable of farming. If he departs from the village, his land reverts to the community and is available for reallocation by the village-head. In Bindawa and the surrounding districts where cultivable land is scarce, a farmer intending to leave his village for a year or two sells his land, pledges it, or places it in the care of a relative in case he should return. Buying and selling of land which took place 30 or 40 years ago only among the ruling class commonly takes place today. Prices vary from a few shillings to a few pounds an acre according to the quality of the land, its distance from the *gari* and the vendor's need for cash. On the fringes of the growing market-towns on the main roads in northern Katsina more than £15 per acre may be paid for farmland and prices of land generally seem to have been rising over the last decade.

In Dan Yusufu District with a population density of 307 persons to the square mile, pressure on the land may well have reached a limit. Population figures for Katsina Province as for the rest of Nigeria are unreliable, at least until 1952, but several districts there were given more than the usual attention in the census of 1931, and it is believed that the taxation records are probably more reliable there than in many less closely administered areas. The tax figures indicate that the population of Dan Yusufu District fell slightly between 1939 and 1951, while that of all the other districts in the province increased. The overall rate of increase was about 2 per cent per annum. While rates of increase were below average in the heavily settled districts adjacent to Dan Yusufu, according to both the

[1] R. M. Prothero, *Migrant Labour from Sokoto Province, Northern Nigeria*, Kaduna, 1959.

taxation records and a comparison of the intensive returns of 1931 with the returns of 1952, numbers in the less densely settled south-western parts of the province increased over the twelve-year period 1939–51 by more than 50 per cent. A drift of people from the heavily settled north-east to places with spare land has been in progress for at least 50 years, some moving only a short distance to neighbouring villages less congested than their own, others taking up land 50 or 60 miles away. The movements have been facilitated by the contacts made by people in their customary dry season journeyings; they have appreciated the opportunities in the less congested districts, have made friends there, and have turned to them for help when conditions in their own villages have become exceptionally difficult. Many people moved from north-eastern Katsina Province to towns and villages further south-west when the rainfall in that area was deficient in 1949 and again in the following year. Harvests were poor in Mani and neighbouring districts in 1959. From the heavily settled lands near Kano the seasonal exodus is said to vary from 10 per cent when there is a good harvest to 60 per cent of the people in a bad year.[1] Many of these migrants return to their former homes after a few months or years, but some settle down in the less congested villages or towns. Few villages in Katsina and western Kano Province now have much land to spare for strangers. Wide stretches of country north-west of Funtua, for example, that were largely uncultivated bush 20 years ago, are now planted with cotton. Although people from the congested districts may be able to acquire temporary rights to land here from individuals who hold more than they need, village chiefs acting for their communities now have little at their disposal, and migrants must go further afield, to Bauchi and north-west Bornu.

The Environs of Kano City: Intensive Farming in a Congested Area
(Fig. XIV, p. 133)

For 200 years Kano has been the commercial centre of Hausaland, and its importance has increased since the re-orientation of its trade and the construction of the railways from Lagos and Port Harcourt. Its population has grown from about

[1] C. W. Rowling, *Report on Land Tenure, Kano Province*, Kaduna, 1949, 16.

35,000 in the middle of the nineteenth century, to 50,000 in
1921 and 130,000 in 1952. In its vicinity lies the most heavily
settled region in the Sudan zone. Barth described its neighbourhood more than a century ago as one of the most fertile spots
on earth; the fields bordered by hedges and shaded by luxuriant
trees, fertile and well cared for, with clusters of neat huts
scattered about and having an air of comfort.[1] This description
applies at the present-day to much of the area within twenty-
five miles of the city, where population densities exceed 400
persons to the square mile. Practically no land lies fallow and
only small grazing commons remain uncultivated.

The main crops grown near Kano, as in Bindawa and west
of this central area, are guinea-corn, millet, groundnuts and
cowpeas. There is no systematic rotation of crops, but as in
Bindawa, intercropping is the almost invariable rule. When
water can be lifted from shallow wells, in small depressions and
alongside water-courses, small plots of about a quarter-acre are
irrigated to grow onions and garlic, wheat and rice, sugar-cane,
tomatoes, carrots and various other vegetables, for sale. The
returns from these intensively cultivated plots are several times
those from non-irrigated land, but the work is arduous and a
lot of manure is needed.[2] Manuring is everywhere more important than in less heavily populated areas. The droppings of
goats and sheep kept tethered in the compounds are used, as
in many other areas. More donkey manure is available than
in most places, because farmers living within twenty miles of
Kano keep these animals for carrying wood into the city and for
local trading. Other sources of manure are the composted
wastes from the Kano slaughter-house, old pit latrines, and
mud from the beds of streams which pass through the city and
act as sewers. The cattle owned locally do not contribute greatly
to local supplies of manure, because most of them are attached
to the herds of Fulani who pasture their herds outside the
congested districts.

In the congested districts near Kano, about 80 per cent of
the land is under cultivation. With the average size of holdings about four or five acres, there is less than one acre of
cultivated land per head. At the death of a land-holder, each of
his plots is commonly split up between the inheritors, and plots

[1] H. Barth, *op. cit.*, ii, 126–8.   [2] D. Forde and R. Scott, *op. cit.*, 146.

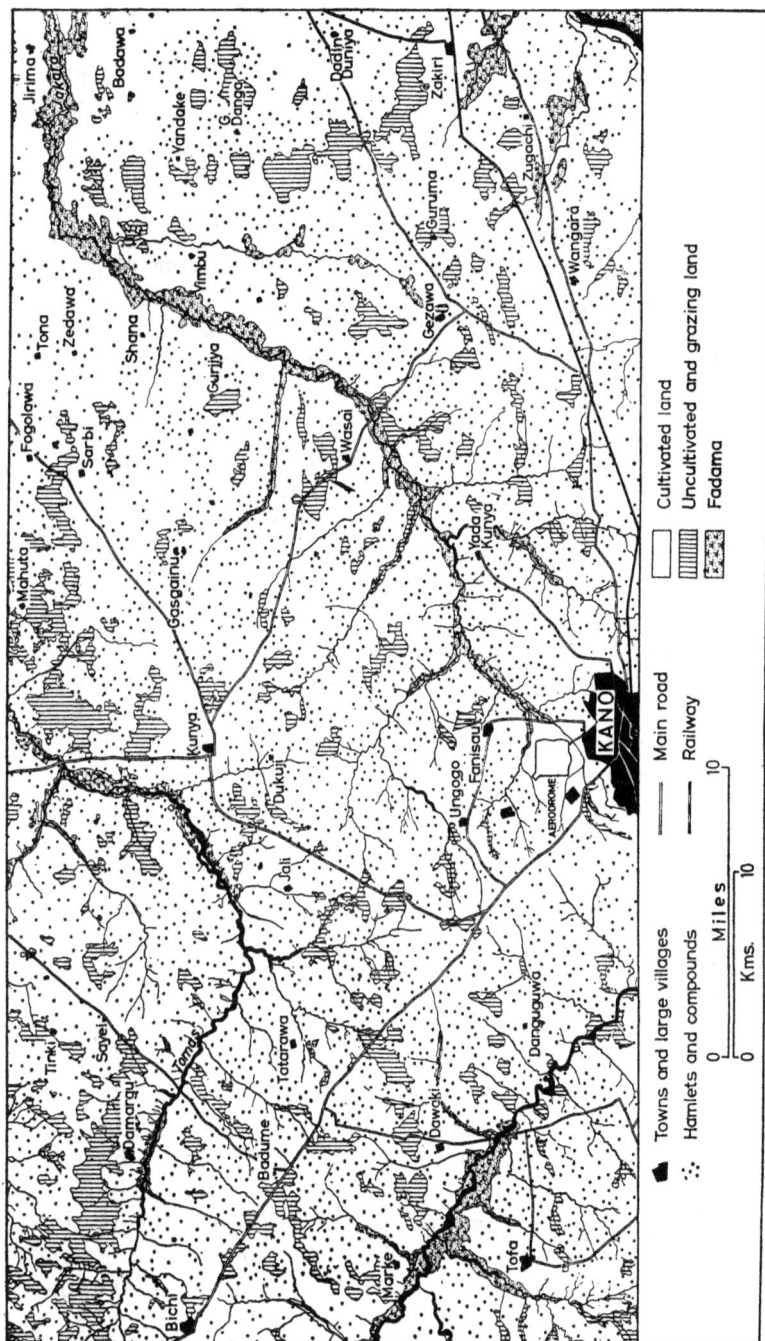

Fig. XIV. Land use and settlement in a part of the densely populated lands of Kano Province. (Based on maps of the Directorate of Overseas Surveys.)

are also subdivided as a result of part-sale. In Dawaki ta Kudu District, over a period of twenty years, out of a sample 320 plots, 25 per cent were subdivided, and over the same period, 25 per cent of 523 plots in Ungogo.[1] Some plots are now very small, but the average size of plots is about two acres and divisions are probably balanced by mergers. Under present conditions, with hoe cultivation the rule, subdivisions of plots does not seem to present a serious problem even in congested districts such as those near Kano and in Dan Yusufu District. In both areas a man's holdings are seldom found to be more than two miles apart, and waste of energy and time in moving from one plot to another, as a result of fragmentation, does not reach serious proportions. It is interesting to note that large farms of more than 100 acres exist in some of the more congested areas. Some are owned by chiefs, but many have been accumulated by traders. They probably provide the best opportunity for introducing improved methods of farming and they deserve detailed study.

In the very densely settled area within twenty miles of Kano farming is still the most important single activity, and it probably brings in more than half the income of the people living there. But crafts, wage-labour, transport and trading absorb more energy than at a greater distance, and food production is less important in the local economy than elsewhere. This applies to a lesser degree around all the towns of this region.

Summary and Conclusion

The growth of population in Northern Nigeria over the last fifty years has mainly affected rural areas. Towns have not increased in size at a great pace, and the increasing numbers have given greater densities in rural areas. Densities have increased at the greatest rate in areas that were sparsely settled as a result of unsettled conditions in earlier times, but are inherently attractive to cultivators and well served by modern communications. Immigration to west Bornu has been in progress for several years and will no doubt accelerate on the completion of the new railway line now under construction from Kuru to Maiduguri. As the area under cultivation

[1] C. W. Rowling, *op. cit.*, 12-13.

expands, the movements of Fulani cattle will be restricted as they have been further west and conditions for agriculture will probably come to resemble those in areas which are already heavily settled. In the south-west of the Kano area population has been increasing rapidly in the last few decades, and in the future as the menace of trypanosomiasis abates with the clearing of woodland, the extermination of game, and the inoculation of cattle, livestock will probably be incorporated more readily in the farming system than at present, allowing mixed farming to develop.

Mixed farming, whereby a farmer keeps cattle to provide manure for his fields and to draw a plough, has made considerable progress in the last thirty years, and in the seven years after the war, numbers of mixed farmers in Northern Nigeria increased from 2,000 to 10,000. Progress since 1952 is difficult to assess, but in 1960 more than 20,000 farmers were probably using ploughs drawn by cattle. Mixed farming has been most popular in areas with moderately heavy population densities of 150–200 persons to the square mile. In such areas woodland has largely been cleared and tsetse-fly do not breed easily; most of the land has been under cultivation for several years and tree-roots are no longer serious obstacles to the plough. With greater population densities difficulties are experienced by mixed farmers in acquiring holdings sufficiently large to justify the use of their relatively expensive equipment and the large size of work unit its employment entails.

The prospects of the very heavily settled lands vary according to their location with respect to large towns and cities. In the vicinity of Kano and Zaria, for example, fertility is maintained at least in part by manure from the city. Furthermore, the city-dwellers provide a ready market for cash-crops and meat, and there would appear to be excellent opportunities in the nearby congested rural areas for developing the use of artificial fertilizers and animal feedstuffs, such as groundnut cake. The outlook for the more remote rural districts with high population densities appears to be less promising. A high proportion of the land in such areas is under cultivation every year, but supplies of manure are not adequate to maintain fertility. The cattle population has fallen considerably over the decade 1950–60 and the condition of the soils is probably deteriorating. Communal grazing land has diminished with the extension of cropland and over large areas impoverishment and erosion are very serious. Pressure on the land is being relieved somewhat by people moving out seasonally and emigrating permanently to less congested areas and to the towns. The solution of the land-use problems of these heavily settled lands may well lie as much in the opportunities offered to the people in the growing towns of Hausaland and other parts of Nigeria, as in improvements in local agricultural practices and techniques.

10

Population, Land and Water in Central Sudan

K. M. BARBOUR

IN the earlier essay in this volume which discussed mapping the distribution of population in Sudan, frequent reference was made to the importance of permanent water supplies in determining the location of settlements. In areas with a long dry season, permanent villages can be built only where natural conditions provide a supply of water throughout the year, or alternatively where an artificial supply can be made available. Where such supplies cannot be obtained, men may occupy the land for a season, either to cultivate it or to graze their animals, but when the dry season comes they are forced to migrate to sites where water can be found. In consequence, as has long been recognized in Sudan, the shortage of water makes it impossible to exploit much of the country where the soil and rainfall are favourable for grazing or for the cultivation of unirrigated crops.[1] This has been the principal reason for the policy of developing rural water supplies in central Sudan that has been pursued by the Sudan Government since 1944. During the last fifteen years the Soil Conservation Branch of the Ministry of Agriculture has excavated more than 500 *hafirs* or surface-water reservoirs in areas of impermeable clay soils, the drilling teams of the Geological Survey have drilled deep bores and set pumps over them in areas where suitable water-bearing strata exist, and other engineers of the Public Works Department have built a number of dams on water-courses in hilly

[1] Sudan Government, *Soil Conservation Committee's Report*, Khartoum, 1944, 10–23.

areas where neither bores nor *hafirs* were practicable[1] (Fig. XV, below).

In voting substantial sums for these works (£E850,000 in the 1946/51 Development Programme, £E2,320,000 in the 1951/56 programme and £S860,000 in the 1957/58 programme),[2] the authorities in Sudan have not merely been attempting to develop or exploit natural resources that have hitherto gone to waste, important though such an objective may be held to be in

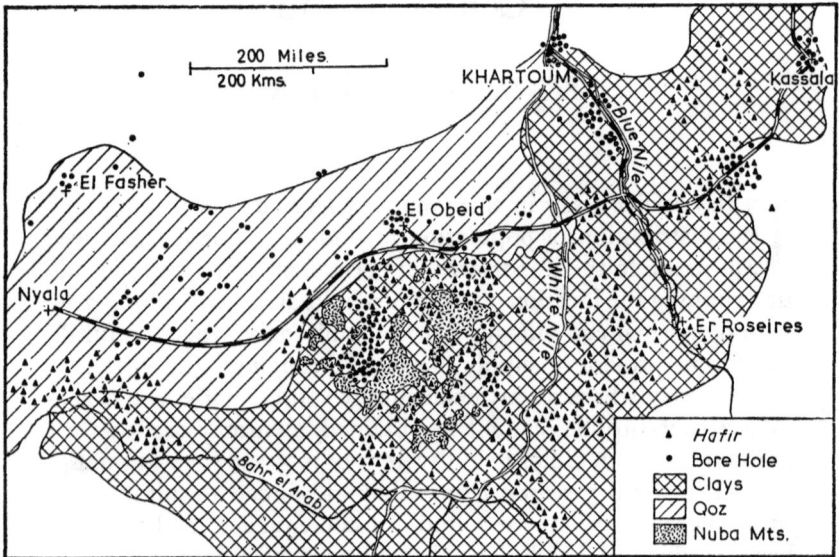

FIG. XV. The development of rural water supplies in central Sudan.

a large and generally poor country. Their two motives have been rather to prevent over-cultivation in areas where good natural water supplies are available (with its consequent risk of soil-deterioration and erosion), and to improve the country's grain supply, since in years of poor crops in the past the price of grain has fluctuated considerably.[3] To achieve these ends the Government has concentrated to a striking extent on the

[1] J. H. K. Jefferson, *Soil Conservation in the Sudan*, Khartoum, undated but c. 1955, 145.

[2] Republic of the Sudan, *Development Budget Estimates—1957/58 Development Budgets*, Khartoum, 1957, Tables I, IV and VI.

[3] J. H. K. Jefferson, "The Sudan's grain supply", *Sudan Notes and Records*, xxx, 1949, 77–100; *idem*, "*Harig* and *Mahal* cultivation", *ibid.*, xxx, 1949, 276–80.

creation of new water supplies, it being assumed that where both water and reasonably fertile soil are available, people will automatically take advantage of them; adequate communications to bring the people to the new lands and to transport their surplus crops will be provided, it is thought, by the road-clearing and the grading that precede the process of *hafir*-excavation, when tractors and excavators are brought to the selected sites along prepared traces.[1]

With such limited government help, the pioneering expected of the inhabitants of the villages beside the new bores or *hafirs* has clearly been of a very rugged type. It has involved setting up a home in an area devoid of most amenities, often far away from such limited services of health, education or justice as the state can provide in the longer-settled areas. New settlers have found themselves separated from friends and family and from the community in which they were reared, and even the maintenance of law and order has not always been wholly assured.

In consequence it is not surprising to learn that the development of rural water supplies has not produced many of the results that were originally expected. In the Nuba Mountains some new communities have grown up in the north, not far from Um Berembeita, where a number of wells and *hafirs* have been established, but elsewhere the Nuba have been reluctant to move permanently away from their homes around the hills. The new *hafirs* have not been wasted, for they have permitted crops to be grown and harvested where previously the land lay fallow, but they have not led to any significant change in the pattern of population distribution, and they have not much reduced the pressure on the land near the original settlements. In the southern part of Kassala Province and in parts of the Blue Nile Province away from the permanent rivers, many *hafirs* have been excavated and have led to the establishment of new settlements, but there is reason to doubt whether these are very stable or satisfactory elements of society, since the numbers of their inhabitants fluctuate irregularly. A similar situation has been noted in Tanganyika, where even when local inhabitants

---

[1] J. H. G. Lebon, "Current developments in the economy of the Central Sudan", *Natural Resources, food and population in Inter-Tropical Africa, International Geographical Union*, London, 1956, 57–66.

have been consulted in advance new water supplies lead to a very slow growth of population at new settlements. The Sudanese authorities are still far from accepting the view, now generally held in Tanganyika, that "all amenities in new settlement areas should be as accessible as in the area which the people are leaving. These amenities should include dispensaries, shops, schools, markets for cash-crops and livestock, court-houses, etc." [1]

The *hafirs* at Fangugu, to the south of Jebel Moya, have led to the growth of a permanent settlement,[2] but there has been no analysis made of the population in the village. Some of the villages near the *hafirs* in the Paloich area in Upper Nile Province are also occupied permanently.[3]

It would not be unfair, therefore, to say that the authorities in Sudan have achieved no more than a moderate success in the field of agricultural planning and social engineering. It is probably because the Gezira Scheme and other government irrigation schemes elsewhere have apparently been so successful that the difficulties inherent in bringing about lasting changes in the distribution of population through conscious planning have not been fully recognized.

The purpose of this essay is to analyse the relations between population, soil-types and water supplies, and so to suggest why the striking technical success of the *hafir*-digging policy has not achieved a comparable social result. The subject is one in which a wide range of accurate quantitative data will be required before any firm conclusions can be drawn; in the following pages the analyses of representative sites, collected single-handed by the writer, do little more than suggest possible lines of investigation.

The first point to consider is how settled cultivators in Sudan make use of the natural resources of the land. This requires investigation under three principal headings, namely the tribe,

[1] J. F. R. Hill and J. P. Moffett (ed.), *Tanganyika—A Review of its Resources and their Development*, Dar es Salaam, 1955, 259–60.

[2] J. H. G. Lebon, "Rural water supplies and the development of economy in the central Sudan", *Geografiska Annaler*, xxxviii, 1956, fig. IX, 92. The success of this settlement has perhaps been due to the scheme of controlled cultivation in the grassy plains to the south of it. This was in many ways the most interesting feature of the developments at Fangugu.

[3] Jefferson, *op. cit.*, 1955, 53.

ethnic group and traditions of the cultivators, with their numbers, the type or types of land that they are able to exploit, and the nature of the water supplies on which they have to rely, whether for drinking or for irrigation.

The Population

Certain demographic features are of particular significance in determining the character of an agricultural settlement, namely the tribal and cultural origin of its inhabitants, their numbers, and their age and sex structure. Tribal origin is important because the inhabitants of central Sudan, which is the part of the country where almost all the development of rural water supplies has taken place, are members of three rather distinct groups. These are the semi-autochthonous negroid peoples, such as the Fur or the many Nuba tribes, the Arabs, originally immigrants from the Arabian peninsula but now more or less mixed with the local peoples, and the Westerners, recent immigrants to Sudan from the west who are nominally making the pilgrimage to Mecca but may settle in Sudan for a number of years.[1]

Of these peoples the best cultivators are the native negroid tribes. Both the Fur and the Nuba have known invasion and persecution by Arabs, and in times of troubles they have been compelled to retreat to the hills to protect themselves. This has made them rather chary of outside contacts, and in the race to acquire education in Sudan today the Fur and Nuba have been left far behind the riverain tribes. Poverty of communications, moreover, has in general retarded their emergence from subsistence to participation in a money economy; nevertheless many of the Nuba now grow cotton, which is ginned locally and exported, while some of the Fur have for many years been growing coarse tobacco, which is sent to Omdurman and made into chewing snuff. The significance that these peoples attach to agriculture is well illustrated by the fact that during the rainy season the women do not confine themselves to looking after their homes and feeding their families, but also cultivate

[1] D. B. Mather, "Migration in the Sudan", in *Geographical Essays on British Tropical Lands*, edited by R. W. Steel and C. A. Fisher, London, 1956, 113–144.

pieces of ground near their homes, while their husbands are working in their main fields further away.[1]

The Arabs are to be found in all stages from the wholly nomadic pastoralist to the completely settled cultivator or even tenant in a scheme of irrigation, but generally they appear to be less interested in cultivation than the negroid tribes. A number of landless Ja'aliyin, brought from the Northern Province in 1950 to take up empty lands in the Gedaref District, very soon gave up and migrated either to the local towns or back to their homes. The Hamar of western Kordofan, on the other hand, are Arabs who settled on the land because they lost their animals in the Mahdiya; they find the Qoz sands relatively easy to cultivate, and it would be hard to say whether they sow, weed or harvest less effectively than the Fur, for instance, would do in a similar situation. The Hamar still practise rug-weaving and rope-making, crafts that are typical of animal-owners, but they know nothing of the peasants' crafts of metal working or pot baking.

The Westerners are a heterogeneous population, for they come from many tribes, usually moving as individuals or in small groups. They mostly come from settled tribes of cultivators, and so they are not afraid of hard work; both in the Gezira and in the Gash Delta they are much in demand as labourers in the areas most heavily infested with weeds, because of their willingness to undertake arduous tasks. They tend to travel without their families, and this makes them prone to drunkenness and hence to fighting; when in the Gezira they usually live in labour camps, and even when they settle in villages to cultivate on their own account the number of women in the community is usually very small. They are very ready to move from place to place, and to abandon any site where difficulties arise. Having no local tribal affiliations, the Westerners are ready to settle in any part of the country where they find land to cultivate; they are mainly to be found in the areas of clay soils, whether in the northern Nuba Mountains, along the Blue Nile towards Er Roseires or in southern Kassala Province.[2]

---

[1] S. F. Nadel, *The Nuba*, 1947. K. M. Barbour, "The Wadi Azum", *Geog. Journ.* cxx, 1954, 174–82.
[2] I. A. Hassoun, "Western migration and settlement in the Gezira", *Sudan Notes and Records*, xxxiii, 1952, 60–112.

Population, Land and Water in Central Sudan

The varied histories and cultures of the different groups suggest that their villages are likely to differ from one another in respect of their numbers of inhabitants, and also in age and sex structure. It is just in this kind of investigation, however, that the disadvantages of a sampling census, as recently conducted in Sudan, rather than a 100 per cent census, become apparent.[1] The returns of the First Population Census of Sudan, 1955–6, take as their smallest unit for the publication of figures by sexes the *omodia*, which is itself a group of up to twenty or

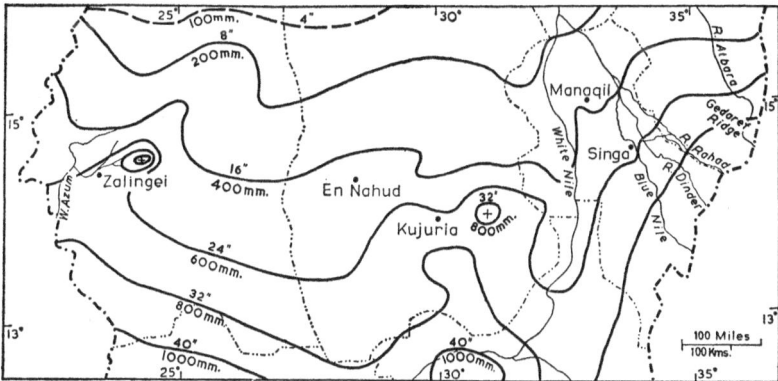

FIG. XVI. Location of sample villages in central Sudan, with selected isohyets. See also Fig. XIX.

even more villages when it occurs in a settled area, while for a breakdown of the figures into age-categories it is necessary to consult the figures for the census areas, whose average size approaches 10,000 square miles.[2] Pioneer villages are in many instances merely portions of long-settled *omodias*, and in consequence it is not possible to get from the census any figures at all for individual villages, and the distinctive demographic structures of the various *omodias* are also not generally available for study. Certain crude investigations were carried out by the writer a number of years ago, for individual villages or groups of villages in representative sites throughout central Sudan (Fig. XVI). The results of these are here presented, for what they are worth, in Table I on p. 144.

[1] *The 1953 Pilot Population Census for the First Population Census in Sudan*, Sudan Government Department of Social Affairs, Khartoum, 1955, 13–15.
[2] Barbour, chapter 8, above.

143

Table I: Estimates of Population in Sample Villages in Central Sudan, c. 1952

No.	Area	Number of Villages	Tribe	Adults				Children				Total
				M	%	F	%	M	%	F	%	
1	Western Darfur	3	Fur	127	17·5	237	32·7	157	21·7	204	28·1	725
2	Western Kordofan	1	Hamar Arab	77	20·1	115	29·9	67	17·4	125	32·6	384
3	Manaqil, Cent. Gezira	1	Mixed Arab	56	21·9	67	26·2	65	25·4	68	26·5	256
4	Blue Nile, nr. Singa	2	Mixed Arab	172	19·0	259	28·6	232	25·6	243	26·8	906
5	Khor el 'Atshan	10	Mixed Westerner	896	50·5	491	27·5	207	11·7	182	10·3	1,776
6	Gedaref Ridge	1	Mixed Westerner	173	35·6	125	25·7	98	20·1	90	18·6	486

In these figures the predominance of female adults in Nos. 1-4 is partly to be explained by the fact that girls are likely to be married almost immediately on attaining puberty, when aged 13 or even younger, and then to be classed with adults, whereas young men will continue to be regarded as boys until a later age, probably about 18. Another cause of the apparent excess of women is the custom that men go away for a few years to work in other parts of the country before settling down. There is also an overall predominance of women, probably to be explained by the fact that in primitive conditions girl children are easier to rear than boys.[1]

In the last two areas the number of children is much less than that of adults, and men are more numerous than women. These are communities where men migrating without wives are likely to settle; they can cultivate on their own account in the wet season, and then go and find work picking cotton in the Gezira after their own harvest has been reaped. The few women in these communities probably have plenty of opportunities to conceive offspring, but many of them are too old for child-bearing and the conditions of their existence do not favour the development of stable family life.

For the purposes of this paper, and by the kindness of the census authorities, figures have been specially extracted from the census returns for the *omodias* of which the villages studied above form part. (Table II.) While the authoritative census figures are for *omodias*, whereas the author's estimates were for villages or groups of villages, this does not make comparisons between the two sets of figures wholly inappropriate. This is because the first four *omodias* in Table II are wholly settled areas, like the first four villages or groups of villages in Table I; similarly the Khor el 'Atshan figures ought to resemble in character those for the rest of the area in which they lie, for the other villages of the *omodia*, situated beside the River Rahad, are also occupied by communities of mixed origins. Very much the same is true of the Gedaref area as has been said of Khor el 'Atshan. To make comparisons easier between the two tables, the figures for age groups

---

[1] K. J. Krotki, "Demographic Survey of Sudan", in *The Population of Sudan*, Report on the 6th Annual Conference of the Philosophical Society of Sudan, 1958, 24.

Under 1, 1–5, and *5–Puberty* have been added together in Table II.

Table II: 1955/56 Population Census—populations of the omodias which include the villages listed in Table I

No.	Census Area	Omodia No.	Adults				Children				Total
			M	%	F	%	M	%	F	%	
1	351	30	838	23·1	1,358	37·5	717	19·8	708	19·6	3,621
2	761	20	3,042	25·5	3,123	26·3	2,851	24·0	2,858	24·1	11,874
3	264	12	3,109	28·0	2,985	26·9	2,672	24·1	2,338	21·0	11,104
4	272	03	1,437	32·7	1,199	27·2	922	20·9	847	19·2	4,405
5	271	22	2,222	48·2	1,320	28·6	479	10·4	588	12·8	4,609
6	522	16	2,512	32·7	2,334	30·5	1,417	18·5	1,399	18·3	7,662

The first four sets of figures represent long-settled rather than pioneer communities. Their relevance to this essay is that they indicate the diversity of demographic conditions in different parts of central Sudan, and so draw attention to the need for research into the make-up of typical villages, so as to provide a base-line for the analysis of new communities. The latter two groups, on the other hand, are more representative of the new settlements, for at Khor el 'Atshan the whole basis of the interest taken by the Government in the villages and their fields was the fact that four *hafirs* had been excavated in 1947 and 1949 along the Khor el 'Atshan. This water-course usually dries out in the dry season, and since it has a clayey, not a sandy, bed there is at that time no way of getting water from wells in it. The *hafirs* were intended to make longer settlement possible in an area where some small villages had already existed, and so to form the basis of an agricultural experiment into controlled cropping. At Kabaros in Gedaref District the communities all appear to date from the present century. Along the ridge where the villages are situated water is obtained from shallow wells which penetrate into joints in the local basalts, but not far to the west in the clay-covered plains there are some recently excavated *hafirs* and some new villages beside them. These new villages, for which no statistical information is available, have been settled by peasants coming from the villages along the Gedaref Ridge; the latter may therefore be regarded as occupying an intermediate position between really long-settled villages, like those of Darfur, and true pioneering communities, like those at Khor el 'Atshan.

The Land

One of the most striking features of the land in central Sudan is the fact that there are very few areas of economic value where the soils have been formed *in situ* by the normal soil-forming processes. In this belt that lies between the Sahara desert and the tropical forest and woodland, almost every soil appears either to have been brought from the north, by the action of the wind, or else from the south, by the rivers. The latter have produced both the extensive lacustrine clays of the Gezira Clay Plain[1] and local terraces of silts and clays which are often easily irrigated and of high fertility.

These points may be illustrated from the areas where the populations listed in Table I have their farms. In western Darfur District, west of the volcanic Jebel Marra, schists, gneisses and other metamorphosed rocks break down to produce a thin sandy soil of low fertility, which is liable to sheet erosion. Such areas are of little use to man except for the rough grazing and firewood that they afford. Population is concentrated along the water-courses which drain Jebel Marra, because these are flanked by broad alluvial terraces in which particles of pumice and clay derived from the volcanic rocks combine to make a fertile soil which is easy to work. Where streams draining the local countryside flow into the great *wadis*, small alluvial fans are formed of silty-sandy soil, and these too are valuable for cultivation. Near Zalingei, a few miles to the east of the area illustrated, even the *wadi* bed is put to use for growing tobacco in the winter, since the roots of the tobacco plant can quite quickly reach down to the water-table. Apart from the heavy crops of grain that they produce in the summer, the alluvial terraces afford good sites for fruit gardens, in which citrus fruits, guavas and bananas flourish (Fig. XVII, p. 148).

In contrast to these conditions, the land in the second area considered, western Kordofan, is strikingly uniform. The fixed

[1] J. D. Tothill, "The origin of the Gezira clay plain", *Sudan Notes and Records*, xxvii, 1946, 153–83.

dunes or Qoz that cover the area have been gradually weathered, and are now only very gently undulating. The siting of villages within the area depends on the water supply rather

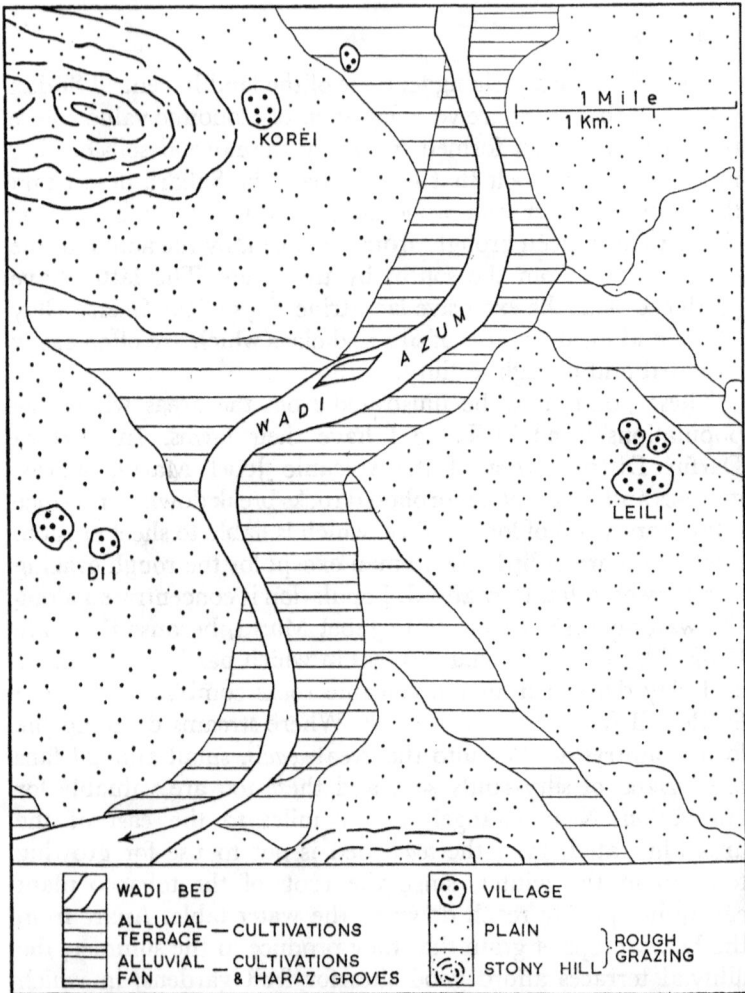

FIG. XVII. Land classification and use beside Wadi Azum.

than the soil, since the latter scarcely differs from one area to another. The soil is a well-drained reddish aeolian sand, low in plant nutrients but capable of supporting a surprisingly dense vegetation (in view of the low mean annual rainfall, *c.* 15 in. only) because the uncompacted sand permits plants to develop extensive root systems. The usual crops of the area are *Sorghum* and *Pennisetum*, but in the hollows of the dunes the percentage of clay particles at the surface is slightly higher and this enables the Hamar settled near En Nahud to grow a few cotton plants for sewing thread.

In the central Gezira, just to the west of the irrigated area, conditions were very different from those in the Qoz even before the coming of the Manaqil irrigation extension. The soil consisted of a very heavy dark cracking clay, forming an almost flat plain dipping very gently down to the west and north. With a rainfall unreliable in total and averaging 10–15 in. per annum, such an area is very near to the limit of cultivation. Indeed the local inhabitants would not be able to plant grain every year with a fair prospect of success if they had not learnt to construct ridges on the plain which impede the surface drainage and so compel the rain water to sink into the ground and wet it thoroughly. This resembles the Egyptian system of basin irrigation, carried out with rain water instead of the Nile flood. It is effective except where slightly sandy patches appear at the surface; these inhibit deep cracking of the clay, and so prevent the absorption of sufficient water to grow a crop. In an area of this kind agriculture is widespread, and only the occasional sandy soil conditions just described prevent its being practised throughout. There is a striking uniformity in the type and quality of the land, and hence of crops produced.

In the belt of country that lies on either side of the Blue Nile south of the irrigated Gezira Scheme, there is a greater diversity of agricultural soils than in the previous area, but the social conditions do not everywhere permit full use to be made of them. The soils of the plain are the same deep cracking clay as in the Manaqil area, with rather better possibilities for growing summer crops of grain towards the south where the rainfall is heavier. The bed of the Blue Nile is incised some 20 metres below the surface of the plain, and so between the level plain and the river there is a belt of much eroded land which is quite unsuited for agriculture (Fig. XVIII, p. 150). The Blue Nile flows in great loops, however, and is heavily charged with silt during its summer flood; in consequence the banks of the river and the loops of the meanders are covered with a rich silty soil. On the sloping banks crops of maize, beans and other vegetables may be grown after the subsidence of the annual flood without further irrigation, while on the level terraces

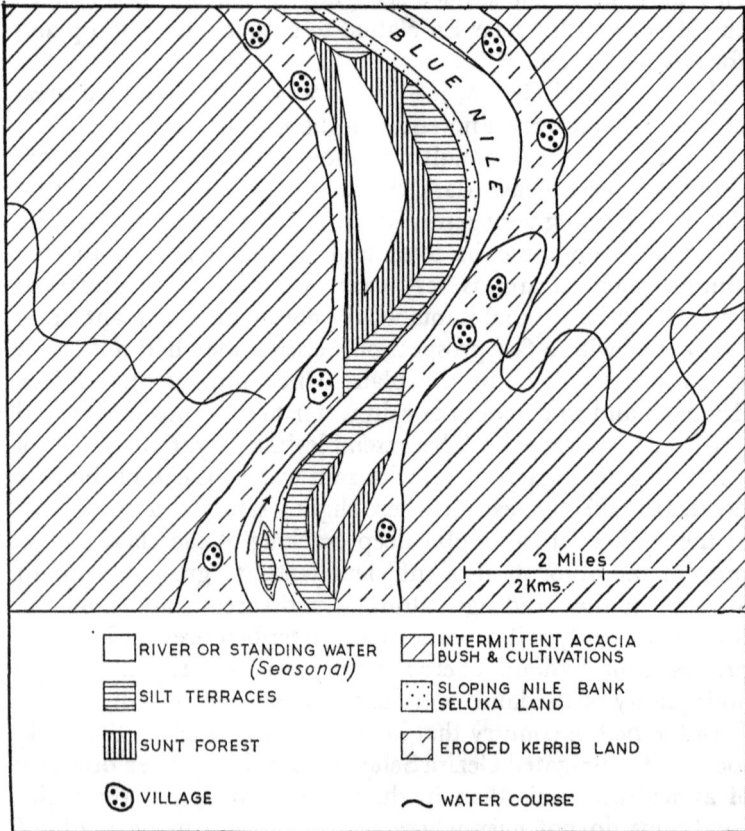

RIVER OR STANDING WATER
(Seasonal)

SILT TERRACES

SUNT FOREST

VILLAGE

INTERMITTENT ACACIA BUSH & CULTIVATIONS

SLOPING NILE BANK SELUKA LAND

ERODED KERRIB LAND

WATER COURSE

FIG. XVIII. Land classification and use beside Blue Nile.

pumps or water wheels may be set up to irrigate fruit trees, vegetables or other cash-crops.

Unfortunately these valuable soils do not make as great a contribution as they might to the diet of the local inhabitants. The natural vegetation of the river terraces consists of stands of *sunt* (*Acacia arabica* var. *nilotica*); these with the exception of narrow strips about 50–100 metres wide beside the river have been designated by the Government as forest reserves, to ensure the fuel supply of the towns, and hence the lands they occupy are not available for cultivation. The strips that have been cleared of forest make little contribution to the diet of the local inhabitants, for soon after the establishment of the Condominium at the end of the last century they were registered as

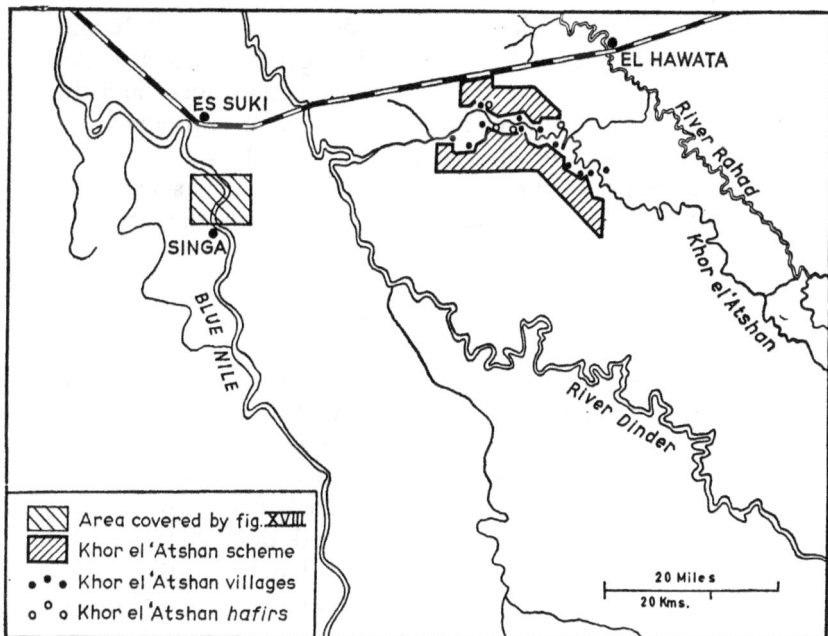

FIG. XIX. Location of Khor el 'Atshan scheme and of area shown in Fig. XVIII.

private land, in the names of a few families, and they are now chiefly used to grow cash-crops for the markets of the Gezira.

The Khor el 'Atshan settlements lie alongside an overflow channel which carries water in years of high flood from the River Rahad to the Dinder. By the time that the flood of the Rahad nears its peak the silt content of its water is much lower than in the early part of the flood, and in consequence there has been virtually no deposition of silt on the banks or bed of the Khor. In consequence there is virtually no variation in the soil available for cultivation, and poor drainage, which is always a potential drawback in otherwise fertile areas of heavy clay, periodically reduces yields. When it dries out at the end of the year, the bed of the Khor produces a growth of grass; this is of value as animal fodders, since the natural grasses of the plain become very unpalatable when they are dry (Fig. XIX, p. 151).

On the Gedaref Ridge the soil derived from the basalts consists of a heavy brown clay which is generally much better drained than the soils of the land between the Rahad and the Dinder. The local streams are much too small to produce any significant terraces or alluvial lands. The only variety of soil type that the area affords is that between the stony sides of the local hills and the deeper clay of the plains where the farmland is found.

Water Supplies

To the differences of soil in the several areas under discussion there are corresponding differences of water supply. These affect not only men's comfort but also the standard of life and health that they can enjoy. Where water is easily obtained at all times of the year, members of many tribes and communities will often gather in the dry season and then there will be opportunities of barter and commerce, but where the winter supply is inadequate it is sometimes necessary for a part or the whole of families to migrate elsewhere at considerable inconvenience. The chance to irrigate even a few patches of vegetables is much appreciated, since onions and okra or *bamia* (*Hibiscus esculentus*) and other pot herbs make a great difference to the flavour and nutritive value of a staple diet of grain with infrequent additions of meat.

In western Darfur there is usually water to be found in the beds of the great *wadis* only a few feet below the surface. This gives the local Fur a clean and reliable supply of water for domestic consumption, while cattle and camel-owning Arabs migrate to the *wadis* in the winter to water their beasts and to sell butter and milk in exchange for grain. The women use the water to irrigate small gardens of vegetables and tobacco, and many of the men have planted citrus and other fruit trees.

Population, Land and Water in Central Sudan

When there were many European officials in the province, especially in the headquarters at El Fasher, potatoes were grown as a cash-crop near Zalingei.

In western Kordofan, on the other hand, water supplies become very difficult towards the end of the dry season. Some villages have deep bores and water yards set up by the Government in recent years, but elsewhere use is made of the baobab trees as reservoirs where possible; when these run out a member of the family has to be sent to the nearest well centre every two or three days to water the animals and to bring back as many goat skins filled with water as the beasts can carry. There is no irrigation of either vegetables or fruit trees, though the sandy soils and the plentiful supplies of animal manure might make these easy to grow. Water melons also provide a useful source of liquid for animals and men.

In the central Gezira there were until the extension of irrigation two main sources of water—wells and surface tanks. The former tap the permeable sandstones of the Nubian Series which underlie the clay plain, and there find water that has entered these rocks from the Blue Nile further to the east. The latter are relatively scarce, being hand-excavated and representing, therefore, an expensive investment of human effort. The wells reach water some 100 ft. below the surface, and are therefore of no use for irrigation; the *hafirs* are found only in the larger settlements such as Manaqil, with its population of nearly 4,000 persons, and are used for drinking water but not for irrigation.

Beside the Blue Nile there is no shortage of water, providing that it can be raised to the level of the land. In general the silty soils near the river are irrigated by small pumps, with an intake diameter up to about 4 in., or else by animal-powered water wheels. The former will cost several hundred pounds to instal, but the latter are constructed from local materials, and can be paid for by giving the builder a share in the crop they produce. The level clay plain can readily be irrigated by the use of diesel pumps, which may supply schemes of several thousand acres. Such enterprises requiring capital are primarily geared to the production of cotton as a cash-crop, and their impact on the lives of the local population comes through the cash which they distribute to the tenants on the schemes.

Along the Khor el 'Atshan standing water is generally available in pools in the Khor itself until the end of the year. This is now supplemented by the four *hafirs* that were built in the area in 1947 and 1949. These provide ample water for human consumption and for domestic animals, which in fact are rather scarce apart from the small herd of cattle at Shamiya village. It would be physically possible to irrigate part of the Khor bed in the winter from the *hafirs*, but this is not done, principally because all along the Khor there is a tall stand of *sunt* trees, and these harbour monkeys and, in the winter, great flocks of nesting birds which would soon devour any vegetables growing nearby.

In the Gedaref Ridge water is obtained by shallow wells from joints in the Tertiary basalts. The supply is barely adequate for the domestic consumption of the existing population, and the few efforts that have been made to establish water wheels and irrigated gardens beside one or two of the streams have been abandoned. There are a few gardens near Gedaref itself, where the topography favours the concentration of the drainage into a limited area, but the recent rapid growth of the town's population makes it likely that all the water available will be required for domestic consumption.

Future Prospects

The facts presented above show that those peasants who are able to carry out even a little irrigation in the winter enjoy a better diet than those wholly dependent on summer crops. Where animals can be kept and give milk all the year, moreover, conditions are much more favourable for the rearing of young children. The relative volumes of water now employed for drinking, watering animals and growing vegetables and fruit trees are not known, but they could readily be determined according to the prevailing soil and climatic conditions.

Such is the importance of providing a balanced diet, if settlements are to grow and flourish, that future programmes for the extension of rural water supplies should clearly not confine themselves to providing drinking water according to a rather niggardly scale of 20 gallons per family per day, as Jefferson envisaged.[1] It should rather be assumed that pioneers will not

[1] Jefferson, *op. cit.*, 1955, 29.

be drawn to new areas as long as these are seen to be in many ways less attractive than the existing settled areas of the country. If the hitherto very thinly populated but reasonably well watered clay and sandy areas of central Sudan are to contribute to the wealth of the country, and not merely to constitute negative areas of little or no value, the provision of water should be on a much more generous scale than anything that has been attempted hitherto.

Now that a new Nile Waters Agreement has been signed dividing the available water supply between the Sudanese and the Egyptians, the time has come to consider bolder and more revolutionary ways of sharing the Nile waters amongst the Sudanese themselves. In the clays this may mean the construction ultimately of not one but several canals to carry water for drinking and for small irrigation projects. These could bring water from the Atbara across towards the Rahad, from the Rahad to the Dinder, from the Dinder to the Blue Nile, and from the Blue Nile to the White Nile. If belts of denser population could be created across these plains beside the new canals, perhaps as many as 500,000 Sudanese could be settled without increasing the present pressure on the land in any of the settled parts of the country.

Further west in the Qoz lands neither the relief nor the porous nature of the soil would permit the use of canals to distribute water. Yet for peasant agriculture, as opposed to mechanized cultivation, these easily cleared sandy areas have many advantages over the clays, not least the fact that good drainage makes the breeding of mosquitoes and other trying insects less serious. With a rainfall between 20 in. and 30 in. and the new railway just built from Rahad to Nyala, the southern Qoz presents good opportunities of cultivating ground-nuts and sesame and other cash-crops, but it can never support a stable and healthy population as long as even drinking water is hard to secure. Despite the great cost that would be involved, it is possible that one or more large pipe lines from the Nile along the new and projected railway lines would have a revolutionary effect on the population and prosperity of central and western Kordofan. Soils not very different from those of the Qoz support densities of population over 400 to the square mile round Kano in Nigeria. Without attaining figures of this order, it should be possible for western Kordofan to do rather better than its present density of not much more than 10.

Conclusion

Since the initial success of the Gezira Scheme many schemes of research and actual projects have been designed to extend settlement and increase agricultural production in Sudan. These have suffered from the lack of sociological research into the origins and traditions of the actual cultivating communities with their individual demographic characteristics. At the same time agricultural investigations into the main soil types of the country and the crops that they can support with differing amounts of rainfall need to be supplemented by large-scale local investigations into land use and water use, and into the gap between diets consumed and those required for a healthy existence. The justification for the expenditure needed is that pioneering in the conditions of the central Sudan is at present too uncomfortable, too insecure and too unrewarding to attract and retain a sufficient number of the Sudanese people.

11

Population Movements in East Africa[1]

A. W. SOUTHALL

Early Movements of Peoples

MOVEMENTS of population have been going on since the first appearance of man in East Africa. Physical types have been utterly transformed and are in most parts extremely mixed. Tribal communities have come and gone. One of the general results of recent research is to emphasize the fluidity of both physical and social boundaries. There have been large-scale, long-term corporate migrations of whole tribes and tribal groups, but there have also always been constant movements of individuals or families between one community and another. It is the movement of individuals which predominates today, though similar factors may operate in many thousands of individual cases. The rapidity and impermanence of contemporary movements is a new phenomenon. Migration has been channelled by the differing resources of the physical environment in relation to changing human needs, precipitated by war, famine and disease, influenced by the contrasting social structures and values of tribes and more recently by differentiation in education, wealth and opportunity. Our present purpose is to illustrate the operation of all these factors with concrete examples.

Tribal movements in the interior were eventually complemented by invasions of the coast. The movements of extant peoples cannot at present be very coherently linked with the discoveries of archaeology and it is better to wait until more of

[1] The areas occupied by the major tribes referred to in this essay are shown in Fig. XX, p. 162.

the detail is filled in.[1] The archaeological evidence necessarily relates primarily to racial groups, or physical stocks, while traditional evidence relates to language groups. It is essential to keep the two distinct. It appears that the earliest population of which there is any living trace was a sparse one of nomadic hunters and collectors, probably speaking "click" languages related to those of the present Bushmen. These are represented by the Hadza, round Lake Eyasi in northern Tanganyika, and by the Sandawe of Kondoa District in central Tanganyika, both of whom still speak "click" languages. Many East African peoples have legends of short-statured hunters having occupied their territory before them. Remnants of hunting groups still survive, but usually now speak languages related to those of their neighbours and often to a large extent absorbed into their social systems. There are, for example, the Twa in the forests of south-west Uganda, in Ruanda-Urundi and various parts of Tanganyika; there are the Boni, Sanye or Langulo in the semi-desert of north-west Kenya, and the Dorobo scattered among the Masai and other Nilo-Hamites. The early Bushmen-like population of click-speaking hunters and collectors was probably partly absorbed and incorporated by the later comers as they gradually encroached upon them and partly driven further south.

To judge from tribal tradition the coming of agriculture coincided very largely with the coming of the Bantu, although some Bantu groups remained hunters for a longer period and hunting continued as a major aspect of tribal economy nearly everywhere. The general movement of the Bantu was from north to south, although many particular subsidiary movements were not. After the Bantu came the Nilo-Hamitic pastoralists moving into north-western Kenya and north-eastern Uganda. The Hamitic Galla groups occupied north-east Kenya, pushing the Bantu south. In the mid-nineteenth century Somali pressure replaced Galla in the north-east. The Galla Boran were pushed westward in northern Kenya and the southward movement of the Somali was only halted by the strict measures of the colonial administration.

Small groups of Sudanic speakers moved into what is now

[1] See Sonia Cole, *The Prehistory of East Africa*, Harmondsworth, Middlesex, 1954, chapter 4.

north-west Uganda several centuries ago, while between them and the Nilo-Hamites the Nilotic Lwo peoples travelled south from the Sudan to occupy most of north central Uganda, passing on in large numbers also to settle all round Kavirondo Gulf. The supposed Hamitic element in the Hima-Tusi strata of the kingdoms in southern Uganda, Ruanda-Urundi and north-western Tanganyika remains an enigma in that no evidence for their migration from the north-east exists except that the unusual symbolic decorations of Hima huts are similar to those found on a megalith in central Abyssinia.[1] The unique cluster of the Iraqw, Gorowa, Alagwa and Burunge in north central Tanganyika speak similar dialects unrelated to any other African languages. Their general tradition is somewhat ambiguous but also indicates migration from the north.

Great parts of Tanganyika were almost empty, others were so transformed by slave-raiding, warfare, or tsetse-fly that their previous condition will never be known. The huge area of Nyamweziland, forming the present Districts of Tabora, Nzega and Kahama in western Tanganyika, was probably occupied only by wandering hunters until diverse groups mainly from the north and east but also from the south gradually settled it for cultivation.

The Nyika and other Bantu tribes of the coast, including the Teita, Giryama, Digo, Duruma, Jibana, Chonyi, Kamba, Kauma, Ribe, Rabai, Pokomo, Segeju[2] and even the Pare, Chagga and Bajun,[3] are all to some extent involved in the tradition of Shungwaya, the site of which is identified by some as near Port Durnford on the Somali coast just north of the Kenya border.[4] According to tradition, which is partly confirmed by historical records, all these people began to migrate south from Shungwaya in the sixteenth century. It is thought that Muslim pressure in Ethiopa led the Galla to attack

[1] C. M. Sekintu and K. P. Wachsmann, "Wall Patterns in Hima Huts", *Uganda Museum Occasional Paper* 1, Kampala, 1956, 1.

[2] E. C. Baker, "Notes on the History of the Wasegeju", *Tanganyika Notes and Records*, June 1949, 16–41.

[3] V. L. Grottanelli, *Pescatori del Oceano Indiano*, Rome, 1955.

[4] V. L. Grottanelli, "A Lost African Metropolis", *Deutsche Akademie der Wissenschaften zu Berlin Institut fur Orientforschung, Sonderdruck aus Afrikanistische Studien Diedrich Westermann zum 80 Geburtstag gewidmet*, Berlin 1955. A. H. J. Prins, *The Coastal Tribes of the North-Eastern Bantu, Ethnographic Survey of Africa*, London, 1952, 43.

A. W. Southall

Shungwaya and drive its peoples south. They are now in scattered occupation of the coast from the Bajun Islands north of Lamu to as far south as Pangani.

While the southward movement from Shungwaya was proceeding a spectacular contrary movement from south to north occurred. The Zimba, probably a Bantu people from near the present Zululand, moved north through what is now Portuguese East Africa devastating the countryside and (according to tradition) devouring its inhabitants. They sacked Kilwa in 1587 and two years later, together with the Portuguese, they destroyed Mombasa. Then they laid seige to Malindi, the Portuguese capital. Here they were attacked from the rear by the Segeju and finally dispersed.[1]

The remarkable Zimba incursion has left no identifiable trace,[2] but the much more recent Ngoni migration resulted in permanent settlement. Set upon their great trek north by the Zulu upheavals of the early nineteenth century, the Ngoni fought their way up into Tanganyika, depositing groups here and there along their route, reaching nearly to Lake Victoria, but with larger concentrations in Songea, Ulanga and Kilosa. The Makonde, Makua, Mwera and Mawia, all matrilineal groups from Mozambique, began to move into south-eastern Tanganyika during the second half of the nineteenth century.

The Masai penetrated furthest south of the Nilo-Hamitic peoples and came to occupy a unique position in the heart of East Africa after the main Bantu settlement had occurred. They were a comparatively small tribe, which numbers some 150,000 today including the Samburu and Kwavi, but had ranged over a vast territory with their huge herds. They occupied areas which do not appear to have attracted the Bantu agriculturalists and which seem for the most part to have been previously occupied only by small bands of hunting peoples. But here and there in Masailand there are traces of wells, irrigation works and large concentrated settlements which suggest a highly organized system of production and a complex social system the bearers of which are as yet unidentified.

[1] R. Coupland, *East Africa and its Invaders*, Oxford, 1938, 60–1.

[2] Zimba are, however, still to be found in north-west Mozambique. See Antonio Rita-Ferreira, *Agrupamento e Caracterização Etnica dos Indigenas de Moçambique*, Lisbon, 1958, 63–4 and 16 (map).

Population Movements in East Africa

During the nineteenth century the Masai sphere of operations extended from two degrees north to six degrees south, and from 34 to 40 degrees east. In this immense region over five hundred miles wide in either direction, there were on the mountains large tribal islands washed but not engulfed by the Masai sea: Arusha and Meru, Chagga, Pare and Sambaa, Kikuyu, Meru, Embu, Kamba and Teita. Colonial administration eventually confined the Masai to a small fraction of the area, permitting the other tribes to move gradually down on to the plains and the European farmers and their Kikuyu labourers to occupy the Rift Valley and its margins from Rumuruti to Longonot. This movement of peoples into areas formerly held or threatened by the Masai is one of the most important that has occurred in the interior of East Africa since colonial administration was established.

As examples of this we may cite the Chagga, Arusha, Pare and Iraqw. All these Tanganyika tribes have been increasing at a markedly faster rate than the population of the territory as a whole. There is the difficulty of unreliability in the early censuses of 1921, 1928 and 1931, but even on the firmer ground of comparison between 1948 and 1957 the same trend clearly appears, as is shown in the table below.[1]

Table 1: Percentage Increase of Population

	Tribes				Tanganyika
	Chagga	Arusha	Pare	Iraqw	
1921–31	21	13	27	94	22
1921–57	148	190	164	297	111
1948–57	34	31	27	32	17

It is not as though these tribes were likely to have been less

[1] *Report on the Native Census*, 1921, Government Printer, Dar es Salaam.
Native Census, 1928, Government Printer, Dar es Salaam.
Census of the Native Population, Government Printer, Dar es Salaam, 1932.
African Population of Tanganyika Territory, East African Statistical Department, 1950.
Tanganyika Population Census 1957, Part I, East African Statistical Department, 1958.

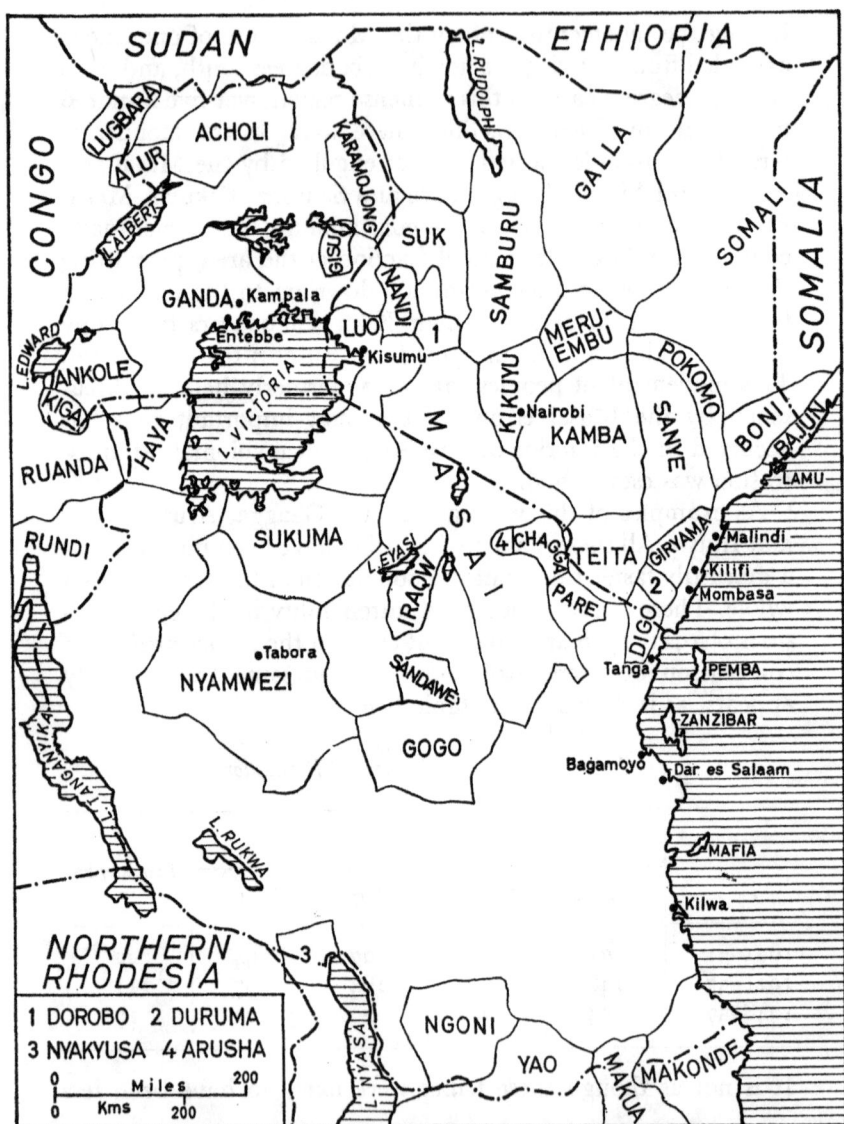

FIG. XX. Places and tribes to which references are made in Chapter II. (Boundaries of tribal areas after G. P. Murdock, *Africa: its Peoples and their Culture History*. New York, 1959, and J. E. Goldthorpe and F. B. Wilson, *Tribal Maps of East Africa and Zanzibar*. Kampala, 1960.)

well counted than other tribes in the early censuses, for the probability is rather the other way. The fact that imposition of peace upon the Masai permitted other peoples to spread into areas formerly terrorized by them, combined with the fact that these people were already in occupation of areas ecologically favoured from the point of view of modern peasant agriculture. They were little affected by the recurrent famines of other parts of Tanganyika and, thanks to their relative isolation, also by the devastating military campaigns of the first two decades of the century.

Movements along the Trade Routes

The great lakes acted as entrepôt regions as soon as trade routes reached them from the coast. Water transport was easier than foot safari although there was still serious risk of attack as well as of shipwreck. Drinking water and also food were more readily accessible. But the presence of Masai and Galla, combined with the rigours of the Taru Desert, discouraged the development of any regular caravan routes in East Africa north of Tanga and Kilimanjaro and so influenced the pattern of penetration from the coast. The southern route inland from Sofala was known from the sixteenth century. Farther north it was that from Bagamoyo and other nearby villages to Unyamwezi and Lake Tanganyika which had become by far the most important by the middle of the nineteenth century. Another ancient route ran from Kilwa up the Rovuma through Yao country to Lake Nyasa. The route from Tanga to Kilimanjaro and on in the direction of Lake Victoria involved running the gauntlet of the Masai before reaching Chagga country.

In 1848 Guillain[1] was told by a trader in Zanzibar that white men had never been heard of in Kikuyu, nor had Arabs or Swahili penetrated there before him, previous trade having been carried out by Nyika and Kamba. The Kamba claimed to have migrated from the south-east, near Kilimanjaro. It was they who maintained such communication as there was between the Kenya coast and the interior, for they were friendly with both the Nyika and the Kikuyu, as well as the Chagga

[1] Charles Guillain, *Documents sur l'Histoire, la Géographie et le Commerce de l'Afrique Orientale,* Paris, 1856, Pt. II, Tome 2, 279–97.

with whom they claimed kinship. But between their country and the coast lay the no man's land haunted by Masai and Galla raiders. It was also in 1848 that Rebmann first visited the Chagga. In 1849 Krapf first reached Kitui and on his second visit got as far as the Tana on the way to Embu and Kikuyu but nearly perished in the attempt. He heard vaguely of caravan routes from Chagga through Masailand, to Lake Manyara and to Ol Donyo Lengai, Burgenej (near Naivasha) and eight days further to "the sea".[1]

By 1871 New[2] was told of many different routes in the north used by caravans passing through Taveta, which was a junction for most of them. The route referred to by Krapf evidently reached Lake Victoria in Ukara. Further north routes passed through Mau and Nandi to Kisumu, Kakamega, Kitosh and Suk. Other caravans went inland from Kilifi and then joined the Mau route or went still further north past Donyo Sabuk to Kikuyu, or past Naivasha and Nakuru to Njemps on Lake Baringo. The Kitui Kamba were also reached from the Sabaki River route, or by starting up the Tana. All these routes seem to have been relatively little used and caused little movement of population or disturbance of tribal society until much later.

The direct route from Mombasa to the most populous and fertile parts of East Africa in the Kenya Highlands and round Lake Victoria did not become usual until after Thomson's exploration of 1883 and Bishop Hannington's fatal journey of 1885, especially when the Imperial British East Africa Company began to use it in 1889.

Thus it came about that Buganda, whose rich and well-organized state exerted a stronger attraction than any other single area of the interior, was only reached by the very roundabout route from Bagamoyo through Unyamwezi and Karagwe, a distance of well over a thousand miles. The largest and most important tribes of Kenya, the Kikuyu and Luo, remained almost untouched till the end of the century.

The main impact of external influence from the coast was restricted to a narrow strip of little more than twenty miles in the north hemmed in by inhospitable deserts and semi-deserts,

[1] J. L. Krapf, *Travels, Researches and Missionary Labours*, London, 1860.
[2] Charles New, *Life, Wanderings and Labours in Eastern Africa*, London, 1874, 462-6 and map.

only sustaining nomadic pastoralists largely immune from the temptations of trade, with little to offer and themselves more than a match for potential invaders. Further south, along what is now the coast of Tanganyika, the most intense influence was also in the innumerable small settlements on the coast itself. But along the Bagamoyo route, especially, the tentacles of trade spread wide and chain-reactions were set up in all directions as one group competed with another for ivory and slaves.[1]

The Nyamwezi were the tribe most influenced by the Bagamoyo route, as the Yao, Ngoni and Nyasa were by the southern route from Kilwa. The tradition that trade goods reached Buganda via Karagwe by about the end of the eighteenth century[2] would indicate that there was already considerable movement up and down the Unyamwezi route by then. It is suggested that the trade onward to Karagwe must have been undertaken by Swahili and Nyamwezi, rather than Arabs, at this early date. It seems that the earliest caravans, which were almost entirely of native Africans, provoked very little hostility. The coming of Arabs who regarded the local Africans as savages and were regarded by them as foreigners, and the growth in the size of caravans to hundreds if not thousands of men, inevitably led to intolerable pressure on local resources, constant fighting, which in itself encouraged the capture of slaves, and wholesale disturbance of the population.

In 1825 two Indians reached Unyamwezi and numerous Arabs began to use the route at about the same time. From the thirties the Sultan of Zanzibar was himself sending annual caravans to Unyamwezi as well as encouraging his subjects to do so. There were actually settlements of Arabs at Ujiji on Lake Tanganyika by 1845 and at Tabora by 1852. Tabora became the greatest centre of the caravan trade and of Arab settlement in the whole East African interior.[3] It can hardly

---

[1] See, for example, Heinrich Brode, *Tippoo Tib*, trans. H. Havelock, London, 1907.

[2] See Sir Apolo Kagwa, *Basekabaka be Buganda*, London, 1927.
Sir John Gray, "Trading Expeditions from the Coast to Lakes Tanganyika and Victoria before 1857", *Tanganyika Notes and Records*, XLVI, 1957, 80.
Sir John Gray, "Ahmed bin Ibrahim—the First Arab to reach Buganda", *Uganda Journal*, XI, No. 2, September 1947, 80.

[3] G. F. Sayers, *Handbook of Tanganyika Territory*, London, 1930, 42.

have been an accident that the Arabs established their inland headquarters near to the capital of Unyanyembe, the greatest of Nyamwezi chiefdoms, with whose ruling family the leading Arabs intermarried.[1]

The Tabora route and its network of subsidiary routes had a profound effect over most of Tanganyika, as well as the Eastern Congo, in accustoming persons from many tribes to prolonged travel and to working out the minimum requisites of safe passage along the routes they followed. From this evolved the special system of so-called joking relationships in Tanganyika, whereby the members of tribes travelling habitually on a particular route established understandings with all the tribes through whose territory they passed, on the basis of which each traveller could find fictional kin anywhere for assistance in destitution, sickness and death. This situation also created an urgent need for a *lingua franca*, which the Swahili-speaking traders supplied. Confirmed by the categorical support of the German administration, Swahili acquired a status as a national language in Tanganyika which no language in Kenya or Uganda has yet attained.[2] Travel and intercourse between tribes were thus greatly encouraged in Tanganyika and have continued under the pressure of new economic needs.

The Nyamwezi became the great travellers of Tanganyika and have remained so ever since. The caravan leader, Lief Ben Saeed,[3] a Nyamwezi born in Zanzibar early in the nineteenth century, is one of the earliest recorded indications of long-term settlement far from home. The Nyamwezi went through all the transformations of porters and leaders in ivory and slave caravans, to porters and explorers with German and later with British government officials and finally migrant labourers. As early as 1912 Nyamwezi labourers were reported as far north as Mombasa, Malindi and even Witu.[4] In all the censuses from 1924 to 1948 from six to eight thousand Nyam-

[1] e.g. H. Brode, *op. cit.*, 14.
R. F. Burton, *The Lake Regions of Central Africa*, London, 1860, II, 2–6.
[2] See W. H. Whiteley, "The Changing Position of Swahili in East Africa", *Africa*, XXVI, 1956, 343–53.
[3] J. Macqueen, "Visit of Lief Ben Saeed to the Great African Lake", *Journal of the Royal Geographical Society*, XV, 1845, 371–6.
[4] *Native Labour Commission*, 1912–13, Government Printer, Nairobi, 93.

wezi were recorded as a permanent element in the population of Zanzibar. But all the censuses have been taken out of the clove-picking season, so they do not reveal the much larger numbers of Nyamwezi who still stream to Zanzibar and Pemba every year for this purpose. The Manyema from the eastern Congo were also brought into Tanganyika by the Unyamwezi caravan route. They remain an important and stable element in many Tanganyika towns, numbering 27,000 in the Territory as a whole at the time of the 1957 census, but in Zanzibar their numbers dwindled from six to two thousand between 1924 and 1948. The Nyasa, Ngoni and Yao of the Kilwa route have also remained great travellers in Tanganyika but in Zanzibar their numbers have dwindled from 17,000 in 1924 to 9,000 in 1948.

The Nyamwezi remain very widely dispersed all over Tanganyika. They are found working in especially large numbers in the central, eastern and north-eastern districts, quite apart from their own home area. At the census of 1948 they were represented by over one thousand persons in sixteen out of the forty-seven administrative districts into which Tanganyika was at that time divided. At the 1957 census there were over a thousand of them in each of twenty-five of Tanganyika's fifty-eight districts. In Tanga there is a whole settlement of Nyamwezi who have lost all links with their tribal home. Over 4,000 were living in Dar es Salaam at the time of the 1957 census.

There is a marked contrast between the present high emigration of the Nyamwezi and the low emigration of their northern neighbours the Sukuma. This seems to be due to two general causes, historical and ecological. The influence of the Tabora caravan route was probably less felt by the Sukuma, whose country lay either north or east of the nearest routes radiating from Tabora. At the same time, both agricultural and pastoral opportunities have been much greater in Sukumaland, where there is a very high cattle population, large numbers of which are sold annually, and also the biggest cotton crop in Tanganyika. Most of Nyamweziland except the northern parts on the Sukuma border is infested with tsetse-fly and cattle cannot be kept, while for ecological reasons which still remain somewhat obscure cotton does not flourish either and the Nyamwezi have

A. W. Southall

never had a very successful cash-crop though in recent years the production of rice has increased.[1]

This is a clear case of the influence of ecological differences. It is in fact only recently that the Nyamwezi and Sukuma have been distinguished as different tribes. To Burton[2] in the middle of last century Usukuma was quite correctly the northern region of Nyamweziland as Utakama was the southern. No doubt the early Nyamwezi caravan porters included many Sukuma. But the modern post-colonial labour migration has been conditioned by the differing ecology of Sukumaland which gives it an economic advantage over Nyamweziland in the production of cattle and cotton.

The Classification of Modern Population Movements

We must now distinguish the character of different types of population movement more clearly. In pre-colonial times mass movement resulted from warfare, often but not always precipitated at some point by pressure on natural resources setting up a chain-reaction of one people on another. Individual movements resulted from personal reactions to misfortune or opportunity and affected only a small minority. Later came the greater movement resulting from trade along the routes from the coast and their interior networks.

Post-colonial movements may be seen in the context of the factors which cause people to leave home and the attractions which lead them to a particular destination. Broad distinctions can be made in East Africa today between areas of low emigration and primitive subsistence economy, areas of heavy emigration, which lack cash-crops or in which land is short, areas of low emigration and highly developed cash-cropping and, finally, areas of high economic and educational advancement with emigration at the professional level. These are type categories and often overlap empirically, especially in the case of the last. Some representative examples will be given.

[1] The Lake Province, whose cotton-growing areas are almost entirely Sukuma, produced 150,000 bales of cotton in 1957 out of a total crop of 167,000 bales for the whole of Tanganyika. The cotton crop of the Western Province, mainly a Nyamwezi area, was too negligible for mention. In the same year the Lake Province sold 91,000 cattle as against 30,000 from the Western Province and 232,000 from Tanganyika as a whole. [2] Loc. cit., 2–5.

Population Movements in East Africa

The following figures are extracted from census reports. The total number of persons of a particular tribe, in what may be regarded as its home districts, has been subtracted from the total for that tribe in the whole territory. The relation which the resulting figure bears to the territorial total has been called the emigration rate, expressed as a percentage of the tribal total.

Emigration Rates

Tanganyika

		Males	Females	Total
Nyamwezi	1948	15·0	9·4	12·1
	1957	17·5	12·7	15·0
Sukuma	1948	3·6	1·9	2·7
	1957	3·6	2·4	3·0
Chagga	1948	3·0	0·5	1·2
	1957	2·1	0·7	1·4
Haya	1948	5·7	1·9	3·2
	1957	3·8	2·6	3·2
Gogo	1948	4·7	2·0	3·3
	1957	7·9	3·7	5·7
Nyakyusa*	1948	9·2	3·3	6·1
	1957	8·5	3·8	5·9
Makonde	1948	3·4	1·7	2·5
	1957	8·7	5·9	7·3
Makua	1948	7·4	3·6	5·5
	1957	11·4	4·8	8·1

* See pp. 181 ff.

Kenya, 1948

	Males	Females	Total
Kikuyu (a)	33·0	24·3	28·7
Luo	14·1	4·8	9·3
Kamba	12·9	6·2	9·4
Nyika (a)	0·7	0·9	0·8
Masai	11·5	9·1	10·3
Kikuyu (b)	25·4	21·9	23·6
Nyika (b)	3·7	2·9	3·3

[Continued overleaf

A. W. Southall

	Males	Females	Total
Ganda	6·3	5·3	5·8
Acholi	4·5	2·1	3·3
Ankole	19·2	9·9	14·4
Lugbara	17·7	6·9	12·2
Karamojong	1·4	0·8	1·1
Gisu	10·5	8·8	9·6
Kiga	3·8	1·4	2·5

General Examples

The Karamojong of north-eastern Uganda are an extreme example of primitive subsistence economy, almost completely immune from modern population movements. This does not mean that economic or ecological pressures are absent, for few of these economies are in stable equilibrium. Nomadic pastoralists like the Karamojong live at very low population densities, yet their methods of exploiting the environment are usually such that deterioration of soil and vegetation is a serious problem. This also causes population movement. The southern part of Karamoja District was very little used by the Karamojong when administration began,[1] but since that time over 16,000 Suk have moved west into that part of the district from Kenya.

With the Karamojong may be classified all the nomadic or semi-nomadic pastoral Nilo-Hamites of north-eastern Uganda, Kenya and northern Tanganyika. Those mentioned in the census are the Karamojong and Sebei in Uganda; in Kenya the Suk, Samburu, Turkana and Kamasia; in Tanganyika the Masai, the Barabaig and other Tatog groups. Demographically similar are the Hamitic Galla and Rendille and the Semitic Somali, all of north-eastern Kenya. None of these tribes is really large by East African standards, but all of them occupy vast territories, amounting to three-quarters of Kenya alone and about a quarter of the total area of East Africa.

The Masai of Kenya themselves show a surprisingly high

[1] See J. Brasnett, "The Karasuk problem", *Uganda Journal*, XXII, 2, 1958, 113.

rate of emigration. The reason for this is their exclusion, as a tribe, from areas where they formerly roamed, such as the Uasin Gishu, Laikipia and Central Rift Valley. Much of the latter area was turned into vast European-owned stock farms into which the Masai have gone as herdsmen, and, it is said, because of the convenience of having agents on the spot for the planning of cattle theft. By 1912 Lord Delamere was already employing about 100 herdsmen, mostly Masai.[1]

In Tanganyika the Masai are found not only in the Masai District, but scattered in pockets of a few hundred to a couple of thousand in the ten adjacent districts of Arusha, Moshi, Pare, Korogwe, Handeni, Kilosa, Mpwapwa, Dodoma, Kondoa, and Mbulu. This accounts for all but 3·6 per cent of all Tanganyika Masai, so that as all these districts include areas traditionally roamed by Masai their emigration rate in Tanganyika is low.

The extreme case of migration is, not surprisingly, the Kikuyu. A major part of this movement has taken the form of Kikuyu families working by the month or squatting permanently on European farms all over the eastern part of the White Highlands. During the period of Mau Mau very large numbers of these were moved back into the Kikuyu tribal reserve, apart from those in various detention camps. It is quite impossible at present for Kikuyuland to support this population and it was only maintained by emergency measures until it was possible to permit a partial return into former areas of employment. For example, members of the Kikuyu, Embu and Meru tribes were forbidden to hold squatters' (resident labourer) contracts during the Mau Mau Emergency. In December 1956 this restriction was removed in the Rift Valley Province and by 1957 the numbers of these tribes in rural areas there had risen by 28 per cent.

In Nairobi City the percentage of Kikuyu, Embu and Meru in the total labour force fell from 47 to 22 between 1953 and 1956, as a result of the Mau Mau Emergency, while that of the Nyanza Province tribes (Luo, Luyia and Kisii) rose from 27 to 38 and that of the Kamba from 18 to 28. This double population movement, together with the coincident consolidation of all the Kikuyu of the reserves into large concentrated villages

[1] *Native Labour Commission*, 1912–13, Government Printer, Nairobi, p. 108.

of several hundred huts each, constitutes a revolutionary change in the whole social life of one of East Africa's most important tribes.

The Nairobi area is adjacent to the tribal lands of the Kikuyu. In the first set of figures (Kikuyu (*a*)) those in Nairobi District are all counted as part of the tribal movement. Even if they are excluded, the Kikuyu migration rate remains uniquely high (Kikuyu (*b*)). Nairobi District includes the areas surrounding the city itself. Males outnumber females by four to one among the Kikuyu of Nairobi District, as is characteristic of most African urban migration, so that the higher figures best represent the extent of tribal emigration.

The Chagga of Kilimanjaro exemplify low emigration with advanced cash-cropping, as also do the Sukuma with their production of cattle and cotton. The same factor is also operative in Buganda but combined with the export all over Uganda and beyond of highly educated professional men, often with their families. This practice grew up from the early years of this century by which time Buganda already possessed an élite of literate men unique in this part of Africa. Some of those who were proud to act as clerks to District Commissioners in those days are now among the most eminent figures in the country. It is not easy to separate the Ganda figures for income or occupation from those of other tribes, but, as some indication of their lead in skilled and professional activities, in 1954 the Ganda who form only one-sixth of the total population of Uganda provided 11 out of a total of 14 Africans in non-governmental legal services, 9 out of 12 in insurance, 260 out of 405 in printing and publishing, 122 out of 140 in government printing, 64 out of 163 in banks and 582 out of 1,307 in garages and motor sales. Their lead in these spheres is greatly assisted by the concentration of these activities in Buganda, but it also results in frequent employment of Ganda elsewhere, wherever such services are required. Clearly this population movement is small in numbers, but important for its quality.

Kenya

The Nyika group of tribes on the Kenya coast show an extremely low rate of external migration (Nyika (*a*)). However, as the Kikuyu have Nairobi on their doorstep, so the Nyika have the port of Mombasa right in the middle of their territory and, as the second town of Kenya, it is naturally the main employment attraction for them. The second set of figures (Nyika (*b*)) treats the Nyika on Mombasa Island as emigrants from their tribal area. The Nyika have not been greatly attracted to wage employment and large employers of labour at the coast have always had to rely considerably on tribes from the interior. But of the Nyika who are drawn into wage employment all are absorbed by Mombasa, the sugar and sisal estates, and the smaller towns of the coast. Shortage of land plays no part in inducing the Nyika to emigrate or seek employment. Population density is low in relation to soil fertility and rainfall and cash-crop production is also low by comparison with other agricultural areas of Kenya.

The other great migrant tribes of Kenya next to the Kikuyu are the Luo and the Kamba, though both are less than half the Kikuyu rate. The Luo country, despite its relative fertility, is far too small to support the rapidly increasing Luo tribe on the basis of peasant agriculture. Luo have been relied upon since the beginning of the century as one of Kenya's main sources of labour and they are found in every part of Kenya where any appreciable employment opportunities exist. They are found in smaller numbers in many of the towns of Tanganyika (582 in Dar es Salaam, 284 in Tanga, 225 in Moshi, 900 in Mwanza, etc.). They are probably the most wide-ranging of all Kenya tribes in their search for employment. About 10,000 Luo have migrated to Uganda for wage labour. They maintain close touch with their Kenya homes and visit them frequently. Nor, of course, is emigration permanent for most of them. As one goes another comes. The Luo have also spilled across the Tanganyika border into North Mara and Musoma Districts. This latter is a peasant migration with an equal balance of the sexes, not one in search of wage labour. It seems to have begun only shortly before the establishment of colonial administration,[1] but in these two districts their numbers had reached 53,332 in 1948 and 73,384 in 1957. Apart from relatively small

[1] The 1921 census mentions 30,000 Gaya in Mwanza District who may have been Luo, but neither Luo nor Gaya are mentioned in the censuses of 1928 and 1931.

favoured areas in the upland parts of Machakos District, much of Kamba country varies from dry scrub to semi-desert. The problem of erosion has been serious and many Kamba have taken to migrant labour since population growth led to serious pressure on the land. At the beginning of the century the Kamba were regarded as rich in cattle, with little incentive to go out to work. They have always displayed an unusual degree of manual dexterity and quickly came to prominence in the railway workshops, the army and in any other context where technical skill was required.[1] Some Kamba families have settled far from their main concentrations, on the edges of the Nyika territory at the coast, and they do a good deal of hunting in the arid region in between. They have always been noted hunters, and, if tribal traditions can be trusted on the point, Kamba hunting bands wandered very far in the past, for the Zaramo of Dar es Salaam claim descent from a force which drove back a party of Kamba who raided down the coast from Kenya and one of the chief ruling families of north-eastern Nyamwezi claims Kamba origin.

Tanganyika

The increasing migration of peoples from Mozambique into southern Tanganyika is illustrated by the figures for the Makua and Makonde. The total number of Makua in Tanganyika rose from 95,000 in 1948 to 123,000 in 1957, an increase of about 30 per cent. While no accurate figures are available for the period before 1948, the number of Makua taxpayers in Masasi District doubled between 1930 and 1948.[2] We must distinguish the peasant migration, which brought the Makua across the Portuguese border to settle mainly in Tanganyika's southern districts of Masasi, Lindi and Tunduru, from the labour migration whereby many of these, together with others from across the border, go further up the Tanganyika coast to work on the sisal estates as far north as Tanga District, where there were over two thousand Makua in 1957. The emigration

[1] The same facility appears in the remarkable industry which they have established in the production and sale of woodcarvings. See Walter Elkan, "The East African Trade in Woodcarvings", *Africa*, xxviii, 1958, 314–23.

[2] W. H. Whiteley, *Essays on the Makua*, MS. East African Institute of Social Research, 6.

rate indicated by the numbers of Makua living in Tanganyika outside their main districts of peasant settlement has risen considerably between 1948 and 1957 and the rate for males is one of the highest in Tanganyika. Much the same applies to the Makonde, whose total numbers in Tanganyika are three times those of the Makua, but whose emigration rate is not so high, although it seems to have risen rapidly between 1948 and 1957. The Makonde are mainly in Newala, Mtwara (Mikindani) and Lindi Districts, but they are found further north in numbers of over a thousand in each of the districts of Kisarawe, Dar es Salaam, Bagamoyo, Morogoro, Kilosa, Pangani and Tanga. It is noticeable that in all these latter districts Makonde males outnumber females heavily, whereas in Newala and Mtwara females outnumber males. This probably indicates the fact that in the districts further north most Makonde are in the migrant labour situation. The same contrast appears between the Makua in their main home districts of Masasi and Tunduru and those in the coastal districts further north where many men are employed without their wives and males outnumber females in some cases by over five to one.

It is not possible to give an emigration rate for the Ngoni on the basis of the census figures, because there are so many pockets of Ngoni settlement scattered about Tanganyika that they cannot be distinguished from Ngoni who have left home to work. But one of the best studies of migrant labour in East Africa concerns the Ngoni at Songea,[1] and many of its conclusions probably hold for other areas of Tanganyika. The Ngoni entered Tanganyika from the south in the mid-nineteenth century and now number 68,000 in the whole territory. When defeated by the Germans at the time of the Maji Maji Rebellion of 1905–6, the Ngoni were suddenly transformed from victorious raiders living off the country to settled peasant cultivators in a new state. Ngoni men were much engaged in head porterage, which for long remained essential in this remote south-western region of Tanganyika, four hundred miles from the sea, with very bad road communications and no railway. The Ngoni also took quickly to employment on the sisal estates and were already well known as far away as Tanga by

---

[1] P. H. Gulliver, *Labour Migration in a Rural Economy*, East African Studies No. 6, Kampala, 1955.

1914. Gulliver estimates that by 1924 about one quarter of the adult males of Songea District were away at work and in 1953 his samples showed about one third of Ngoni men away. Most spend from nine to eighteen months away on each trip and most make two trips in the course of their working lives. In 1953, 10 per cent of all men had been continuously away since 1945 and 8 per cent since 1939. Two thirds of those away were under 30. Before 1945 nearly half (46 per cent) of them were unmarried and nearly all the rest (47 per cent) left their wives at home, only 7 per cent taking them with them. The sample of trips after 1945 showed a drop in the percentage of bachelors (36 per cent), a slight fall in the percentage who left wives at home (43 per cent) and a big rise in the numbers taking wives with them (21 per cent).

The Songea Ngoni illustrate in microcosm most of the factors in labour migration which have already been mentioned. In nine out of ten sample areas there was a marked tendency for labour migration and income earned at home to vary inversely. It was the areas where average earnings were lowest that labour migration was highest. One area was exceptional in having the highest average earnings but also one of the highest rates of absenteeism. This proved to be an area of exceptional educational opportunity producing an export of skilled workers. It contained the diocesan headquarters of an important mission which had trained large numbers of artisans who had left home because of the higher wages paid for their qualifications in more advanced areas. Had it not been for their special education they would probably not have gone abroad because the cash-crop earnings of this area were relatively high.

Uganda

The major population movement in Uganda is the migration from Ruanda-Urundi, about which a good deal has been written.[1] It became established after the First World War and in 1927 a somewhat dubious estimate gave 46,000 immigrants entering Uganda by the south-west route. The numbers involved always fluctuate according to the relative prosperity of

---

[1] Audrey I. Richards (ed.), *Economic Development and Tribal Change*, Cambridge, 1954, gives a full account mainly from the Buganda point of view.

the areas of origin and destination in different years, but usually vary between forty and sixty thousand. There was little change during the depression years and a slow increase after the Second World War. In peak years such as 1946 nearly 140,000 men, women and children entered Uganda and less than half that number returned home.

The year 1957 was the first since 1948 in which the numbers returning were greater than those recorded entering. Even so the figures for the 1948–57 decade indicate a net increase of about 130,000 men, women and children staying in Uganda. These are not all Rwanda or Rundi; other tribes such as the Haya, Nyambo, Hangaza, Zinza and Ha of north-western Tanganyika are also involved. But the Rwanda-Rundi form the majority. The 1948 census of Uganda showed the following:

	Male	Female	Total
Rwanda	166,711	122,340	289,051
Rundi	42,887	13,617	56,504
TOTAL	209,598	135,957	345,555

All the Rundi must be considered of immigrant origin, but there were 60,000 Rwanda traditionally settled in the Bufumbira county of Kigezi, Uganda's south-western district, which is known as British Ruanda. The immigrant figures confirm a number of features found elsewhere. While in British Ruanda women far outnumber men, in Uganda's Rwanda-Rundi population as a whole men far outnumber women. Fewer women come from Urundi, which is farther away than Ruanda. Furthermore, the number of women has only become so great because the women who do come stay much longer than the men. On the two main migration routes from the south-west it was found that women stayed in Uganda from 48 to 50 months, but men only 8 to 14 months. From 86 to 98 per cent of the women expressed the intention of settling in Buganda, but only from 28 to 34 per cent of the men.[1]

The interesting aspect of this migration is that its objective is mainly rural, not urban, and the largest numbers work for

[1] A. I. Richards (ed.), *op. cit.*, 265 and 267.

African farmers or secure their own land, rather than working for the larger non-African firms. The Large numbers are, indeed, employed on the sugar estates, but the majority work on Ganda cotton or coffee farms, especially in Buganda's southern county of Buddu, which is not only nearest to Ruanda, but also is the richest coffee-growing area and which was comparatively sparsely populated so that there were exceptional opportunities for the new type of settlement stimulated by Buganda's unique system of *mailo*[1] land tenure. This enabled and encouraged migrants who stayed on to acquire their own land and to become prosperous peasants themselves.

A migration route from the north-west also developed after the First World War.[2] It involves mainly the Lugbara and Alur tribes. Both of them live partly in Uganda and partly in the Belgian Congo. In both cases Congolese migrants are included in the movement to Uganda. Consequently, the figures on p. 170 give a slightly exaggerated picture because some of the migrants originate from homes in the Congo and not in Uganda, and therefore should properly be related to the total Lugbara population of the Congo and not of Uganda. As in every other case where detailed research has been possible, it was found that this migration was very closely related to the varying opportunities in quite small areas.

Alur country consists of highland, midland and lowland regions. The highlands are the most densely populated, cattle are kept but there is no widely accepted cash-crop, although the potentialities of coffee growing have not been exploited. This is the region which supplies most of the migrant labour. In the midlands population density is lower, cotton growing has become very popular and the rate of emigration is very low. The lowlands have the lowest population density, heavy infestation with helminthic diseases, poor rainfall and rather low cotton production together with a good deal of fishing. This region has a much higher emigration rate than the midlands, but not so high as the highlands. The largest numbers of Alur migrants are found in the Buganda counties of Singo, Bulemezi and Busiro and in parts of Bunyoro. There are about 10,000 in

[1] See A. B. Mukwaya, *Land Tenure in Buganda*, East African Studies No. 1, Kampala, 1953.
[2] See A. W. Southall, "Alur Migrants", in A. I. Richards (ed.), *op. cit.*, 141–61.

Buganda. Some 5,000 Alur come to south Uganda every year from West Nile District and 2,000 more from the Congo.

Most of the Lugbara migration derives from the areas with the densest population, where land has begun to get short. Middleton[1] relates the incidence of migration to factors of altitude, climate and soil fertility, population density, cash-cropping and changes or variations in traditional social structure. As in Alur, cotton is unsuccessful in the highlands and there is more migration than in the midlands and lowlands where cotton is grown. Average income per head from sale of agricultural and animal products is twice as high in the latter as in the former. Population density in the county with the highest migration rate (26·5 per cent of adult males) is ten times as great as in the county of lowest migration (12·4 per cent of adult males). It is the reinforcing combination of high density and lack of a successful cash-crop which is particularly correlated with heavy migration. Longer-term migration, including a high proportion of women, is associated with areas whose traditional structure has been most disturbed. The long-term migration is mainly independent, whereas temporary migration is usually by contract to the sugar estates in south Uganda. Thus, among migrants from Aringa county, there were 25 women and 79 children to every 100 men and 80·5 per cent of the men were independent, while among migrants from Terego there were only 7 women and 36 children to every 100 men and 72·5 per cent of the latter were on contract. At the 1948 census there were 21,980 Lugbara altogether in areas of Uganda outside their home district: 10,000 in Bunyoro, 7,000 in Buganda and 3,000 in Busoga.

The other major labour supplying tribe in Uganda is Ankole. Traditional Ankole was a caste society in which the upper caste Hima, forming about one-tenth of the population, were mainly pastoral and the lower caste Iru mainly agricultural. The Hima have lost their former political dominance and the development of cash-crops has tended to make them a conservative and economically depressed caste by comparison with the more progressive Iru. The Hima have always been mobile and their distribution has been radically affected in

[1] J. F. M. Middleton, *Labour Migration and the Lugbara*, duplicated report to the Colonial Social Science Research Council, September 1952.

recent years by the ebb and flow of tsetse infestation in Ankole. Large numbers of them have migrated to other districts, wherever they could find good grass for their herds, or where there was a demand for their services as herdsmen. There are various schemes of remuneration as, for example, the herdsmen getting free milk and perhaps an occasional calf in return for his services. Traditionally the Kabakas and chiefs of Buganda always had Hima herdsmen, but the practice has now spread to every wealthy Ganda cattle owner. It has also spread to other tribes and areas, such as Busoga and Teso, so that almost anywhere in south Uganda where herds of cattle are found Hima are found in charge of them. This may be compared with the spread of Tusi, who are the southern counterparts of Hima in Ruanda, Urundi and Buha, all over Sukumaland and the parts of Nyamwezi country where cattle can be kept. These Tusi migrate with their herds rather than become herdsmen to others. They are extremely wealthy in real terms, but maintain a very simple traditional way of life. The Hima and Tusi population movement is of families, not of individuals. It takes place entirely within the African sector of society and does not show in the employment figures.

Much of Ankole is relatively dry and only a small part of the Iru population has been able to develop a prosperous cash-crop economy, the rest supplying their cash needs through migrant labour. In 1948 there were 56,000 Ankole of both sexes and all ages outside the district, 26,000 of these being in Mengo and 17,000 in Masaka Districts. Most of these must be employed on an informal basis by Ganda farmers, since only some 10,000[1] appear in the official figures of wage employment. Most of these latter are unskilled workers earning low wages.

Movement out of East Africa

The East African territories as a whole are almost certainly nett recipients of African population from neighbouring countries: Italian Somaliland, Ethiopia, Sudan, Belgian Congo, Ruanda-Urundi, Northern Rhodesia, Nyasaland and Portuguese East Africa. There is important immigration of Somali

[1] Rising to 14,000 in 1957.

Population Movements in East Africa

into Kenya, Alur and Lugbara from the Congo into Uganda, Rwanda and Rundi from Ruanda-Urundi into Uganda and Tanganyika, Ngoni, Yao and Nyasa from Nyasaland and Portuguese East Africa into Tanganyika and Makonde, Makua and Mawia from Portuguese East Africa into Tanganyika.

The largest movement out of East Africa is of labour migrants who cross the Lake Nyasa—Lake Tanganyika corridor in search of work mainly on the Northern Rhodesia Copperbelt and on the Rand. Gulliver[1] has collated the figures for this movement and analysed the differential factors responsible for it. In 1951 there were 19,110 Tanganyika Africans away in the south and in 1954 there were 20,630. Most of these came from Rungwe and Mbeya, Tanganyika's two south-western districts. The wages of labour are higher in the south than in Tanganyika and therefore attract those whose over-riding incentive is to earn money. Over 90 per cent of the Nyakyusa men of Rungwe who leave home go south. The Nyakyusa enjoy a higher standard of living than their neighbours in south-western Tanganyika and therefore need higher money earnings to maintain it. They are willing to make the necessary long journey on their own resources and to work both hard and underground in the mines. The alternative is lower wages in work such as that of the Tanganyika sisal estates, with the compensation that the work is less arduous, life on the rural estates is more placid than in the mining centres and towns of the south, they avoid underground work and can get free transport for themselves and their dependents through the recruiting organizations. It is this alternative which attracts nearly half the migrants from Mbeya District.

The southward migration of Nyakyusa only reached large proportions after the Second World War, with rising awareness of economic wants and with the diminished opportunity to work on the Lupa goldfields in Tanganyika which are just north of Nyakyusa country.

There is great variation in the incidence of labour migration within Nyakyusa country and, as in the case of the Alur, the reasons seem to be ecological. The Lake Plains of southern Nyakyusa offered the earliest and greatest cash-cropping

[1] P. H. Gulliver, "Nyakyusa Labour Migration", *Rhodes-Livingstone Journal*, XXI, 1957, 32.

attractions. Consequently, they became overcrowded and many were forced to go away to earn, especially young men who had not yet acquired land but desperately needed money and cattle for marriage. Here about one-third of all adult men were away at work, and about a half of the younger men, while 95 per cent of the younger men had been away at least once. The smallest exodus is from the Northern Uplands, where young men can still get land and good incomes can be made from coffee growing. Here only 10 per cent of all adult men and 16 per cent of the younger men were away. Half the younger had never been away and did not expect to do so.

Since the emigration rate of 8·5 per cent for the Nyakyusa in the table is based on movement within Tanganyika only, as in the case of the other tribes, it does not show the full extent of labour migration in Nyakyusa society. Gulliver's figure of 15,390 adult men away from Rungwe District in 1954 represents 15·4 per cent of the total number of Nyakyusa males of all ages in Tanganyika at the 1957 census.

Tribal Factors, Economic Policy, Migrant Labour and Urban Growth

At this point we must consider briefly whether tribe is the significant category as is implied by its constant use in the analysis so far. The concept of tribe itself is equivocal, but this problem cannot be dealt with fully here. Quite apart from the gradual weakening of tribal ties, the units of tribal awareness have been fundamentally altered by the influence of colonial administration. In spite of all this, tribe remains the most easily distinguishable and useful basis for dividing the vastly diverse population of East Africa into more meaningful units. Tribe is a convenient shorthand for differences of language, culture and traditional economy. For example, not all Masai-land is dry pasture, for there are also well-watered hills and rich forests. The Masai are pastoral nomads essentially because they are reared in a society which teaches them to be such and not because they are forced to be by their environment. Tribe is a rough criterion of distinction, but still the best available. Other increasingly important determinants, such as income and education, are of little use for lack of systematic data. They can sometimes be brought in to refine the tribal

Population Movements in East Africa

breakdown. In a study of population movement, tribe remains the fundamental clue to geographical origin.

It is in the coastal parts of Tanganyika that traditional tribal categories count for least. A number of factors contribute to this. It is there that the influence of Islam is strongest and that essentially non-tribal elements, such as Shirazi, Swahili and Arabs, are most influential, especially round the capital. At the same time, Tanganyika has no dominant tribes, such as the Ganda in Uganda, or even the Kikuyu or Luo in Kenya. Tribes which might exert strong influence, such as the Chagga, Sukuma, Haya, Nyamwezi, Hehe, Nyakyusa, Pare or Sambaa, are none of them near the main political and economic focus of the country at Dar es Salaam, many of them are actually in the most remote corners of the country and in any case they are mostly too small and as units altogether too numerous for any one to predominate over the rest. Furthermore, the transcendence of tribal divisions has become a positive plank in the Tanganyika African National Union platform, so that anyone who exalts tribalism is regarded by many as a traitor.

There is a marked divergence of territorial policies on the basis of differing human and natural resources. Omitting the prehistoric tribal movements, Tanganyika was the first to be affected by major modern movements, because the terrain and the state of the tribes favoured the development of caravan routes in Tanganyika, especially the Tabora route. To the large numbers moving as slaves and porters in trading caravans, and later as carriers for administrative officers, were gradually added those migrating to places of employment. Many Tanganyika tribes have retained ever since the habit of frequent long-distance migration.

The reaction to one another of African tribes on the one hand and on the other of the agents of change in the successive form of ivory and slave-traders, missionaries, explorers, chartered companies, colonial government officials and settlers depended a great deal on variations in tribal structure. The first distinction is between tribes possessing specialized political institutions in the person of chiefs with some degree of centralized power and acephalous societies without.

Both traders and administrators inevitably looked first for persons of power who could be paid or bribed to assist in the promotion of trade and the securing of order. Even missionaries were usually forced to concentrate on places where powerful chiefs could provide minimum security for their work or to wait for administrators to do so. These factors channelled the impact of change and the movements of population resulting from it.

Along the Bagamoyo route, traders aimed first at Unyamwezi, because there they could deal with large areas through their rulers instead of having to fight their way from village to village. From Unyamwezi they aimed at similarly attractive centres of power in the eastern Congo and at the most prominent East African rulers clustered in the Interlacustrine Kingdoms, especially Karagwe and Buganda. The personal idiosyncrasy of rulers, feuds between them and their differing relation to external events affected their reception of foreigners. Thus Bunyoro, through rivalry with Buganda, was hostile to the influx of foreigners from the East Coast, and Ruanda, with its powerful regime and its easily defended mountain country, held aloof from the trade routes which approached its borders.

The reaction of acephalous societies to foreign intervention was necessarily unco-ordinated, piecemeal and usually negative and hostile. The tribes of the immediate coastal hinterland were no match for Arab and Swahili bands. They were either decimated and broken by continual slave raids or had to retreat periodically into the forests, as was done by the Giryama and other Nyika peoples. Caravans from Tanga and Mombasa made their way as quickly as possible through the immediate hinterland, where there were no strongly organized tribes, first to Taveta, the junction of many different routes, and then in many cases to one of the Chagga chiefs capable of arranging for their reprovisioning before setting out into Masailand.

The nomadic pastoralists, like the Galla, Masai and other Nilo-Hamites, though politically acephalous, had age-organizations providing the basis for warrior bands which were more than a match for any but the largest caravans. Tribes like the Kamba and Kikuyu with a similar age-organization were less effective because more tied to settled agriculture. Their social structure did not permit the Kikuyu to win respect and recognition for any coherent tribal reaction to the beginnings of white settlement, as would have been the case where a strongly centralized political organization existed as in Buganda, or even Chagga. The warlike repute of the Masai enabled them to treat with Europeans on terms which no other Kenya tribe ever achieved. Although they lost much land in subsequent negotiation, vast areas still remained to them.

Social structure, economic way of life, density of population, intrinsic natural resources and climate not only conferred on each major tribal area a slightly different history in relation to modern change and population movement, but led to general differences in the overall development of the East African territories.

Early this century, all three territories passed through a period either of forced labour, or of heavy administrative pressure on the African population to go out to work for wages.[1] To this, of course, there was, again, a profoundly differing reaction from the various tribes. At this time all three territories also had great hopes for the future of plantation production, inevitably at that time managed by non-Africans and requiring African labour in large numbers.

What emerged after the First World War in addition to the continuing subsistence base was, in Uganda, an economy primarily dependent on peasant grown cash-crops; in Kenya, an economy mainly dependent on the production of non-African farms and plantations; and in Tanganyika, an intermediate situation with important peasant cash-cropping in some areas and important non-African estates and mines in others. This situation has persisted. If we consider the main export commodities in 1957, the almost entirely African produced cotton and coffee of Uganda formed 85 per cent of its total exports; the almost entirely non-African produced coffee, tea, sisal and sodium carbonate of Kenya accounted for 65 per cent of its exports; in Tanganyika the mainly African produced coffee, cotton, oilseeds, cashew, hides and skins formed 50 per cent and the non-African sisal, diamonds and metalliferous ores 35 per cent of total exports. These figures give a good picture of

[1] P. G. Powesland, *Economic Policy and Labour*, East African Studies No. 10, Kampala, 1957, pp. 18 ff.
Native Labour Commission, 1912–13, Nairobi.
J. F. R. Hill and J. P. Moffett (ed.), *Tanganyika—A review of its resources and their development*, Dar es Salaam, 1955, 267–8.

relative demands for wage labour with the following provisos. The demand for migrant labour is very heavy both in Kenya and Tanganyika. A distinctive feature of the Kenya labour force is the large number of "resident labourers", or squatters, who have become relatively permanent dwellers on European farms and in crown forests, though right outside their tribal areas and entirely without security for their holdings. It is the Kikuyu who are mainly involved in this system. The number of adult male squatters fell from 28,000 in 1948 to 22,000 in 1957. This change resulted largely from the Mau Mau Emergency and it is uncertain what the number of squatters will be in the future. They have been important because of their relative permanence, because they have their families with them to a greater extent than any other category of labourer and because of the large amount of labour supplied by their wives and children. In the years before the Mau Mau Emergency, though adult male squatters formed only about 7 per cent of Kenya's adult male labour force, their women provided from 20 to over 50 per cent of Kenya's female labour and from 20 to 25 per cent of its juvenile labour force.

Half a century of continuous demand for labour on Tanganyika's sisal estates, especially in Tanga Province, has produced a long-term core of almost permanent dwellers of very mixed tribal origin living around the plantation. In 1956, Gulliver estimated some 10,000 adult male alien settlers on tribal lands in Tanga, Pangani and Korogwe Districts, as against some 60,000 members of local tribes. These figures are exclusive of urban populations and of labour on sisal estates and in other rural wage employment. Among the alien settlers nearly every tribe in Tanganyika was represented, as well as many from beyond. Half the aliens had been continuously settled for 10 years or more. The reasons given for this situation are of general relevance: desire to continue in employment but at the same time to enjoy the amenities of African village life and to grow food, or to give up wage labour though with the possibility of taking it up again in time of need. All had started as sisal labourers. The opportunity for such settlement was provided by the sparse population of the coast, itself partly a reflection of the weakening and breaking of tribal ties which resulted from Arab and Swahili slave raiding and trade. The latter led to depopulation and economic stagnation or decline among neighbouring tribes and to lack of opposition to further settlement by other tribes such as is encountered in more strongly organized tribal communities.[1] Though Uganda's wage labour force appears relatively small, this is somewhat misleading. The vast peasant production of cotton and coffee has in fact also exerted a heavy influence which does not show in the figures. Those from Ruanda, Urundi and many other tribal areas, attracted to the cotton and coffee regions of Uganda, start off in effect as migrant labourers employed by African farmers on various informal systems of remuneration, but many of them also later acquire the use of land from their employers and become cash-crop producers themselves.

The total employed African labour force of Tanganyika in 1949 was 474,107, that of Kenya in 1948 was 385,567 and that of Uganda in 1949 was 158,631. The Uganda figure includes no females or juveniles, of whom there were extremely few (only 4,554 in 1950), but the Kenya figure includes 75,000 females and juveniles and the Tanganyika figure 62,000. It was suggested that there might have been 50,000 other labourers working informally for African farmers in Uganda in 1949. The total Kenya labour force had risen to 554,798 in 1957[2] and that of Uganda to 228,399 in 1958.[3] The Tanganyika figure of 474,107 for 1949 is the peak figure for the Tanganyika labour force, which fell to 413,000 by 1955 and stabilized at 430,547 in 1958.[4] These fluctuations are the outcome of three major factors: reduction in the sisal labour force since 1952, fluctuation in the demand for work, which rises in response to a bad crop season and falls in response to a good one, and a general long-term increase in the full prosperity of peasant agriculture which removes large numbers from the labour market. If we exclude domestics, who are not comparably estimated in the three territories, and the employees of African farmers, who are a distinctive phenomenon of Uganda, not accurately estimated there and hardly considered elsewhere, although small numbers are known to exist, we get perhaps the most adequately

---

[1] See Gulliver, *Alien Africans in the Tanga Region,* manuscript in library of East African Institute of Social Research.

[2] A rise of 43·9 per cent.   [3] A rise of 44 per cent.

[4] A fall of 9·2 per cent from 1949.

comparable figures for adult male employment of 416,611 for Kenya in 1957, 220,032 for Uganda in 1958 and 339,188 for Tanganyika in 1958. Relating these figures to those of the 1948 census, as the only comparable base for all the three territories, we get as percentages of the total adult male population: Kenya 33·2 per cent,[1] Tanganyika 18·3 per cent,[2] Uganda 15·9 per cent. Finally it must be remembered that immigrants from other territories form a much higher proportion of the total labour force in Uganda than they do elsewhere, the contrast being even more marked in the case of Kenya than Tanganyika. Thus Uganda not only has the lowest rate of adult male wage employment, coupled with the most prosperous level of agricultural production, but many of those employed are actually foreigners, so that the rate of employment, migrant labour and population movement among Uganda's own tribes is very low indeed. On the contrary, not only is the rate of employment highest in Kenya, but Kenya receives far fewer immigrant employees than either Uganda or Tanganyika, so that the full brunt of employment, labour migrancy and consequent population movement falls upon the tribes native to Kenya. Furthermore, the conservative pastoral tribes form a larger element in the population of Kenya than they do in either Uganda or Tanganyika, so that the incidence is extremely heavy on the main agricultural tribes of Kenya, especially the Kikuyu, Kamba, Luo and Luyia.

It is important to consider how far recent population movements have been related to the growth of towns. Rough indications of this will be the size of towns in relation to the total population and the proportion of the recorded employed population which is working in towns.

Urbanization, in the crude sense of the numbers of people

---

[1] The figure for Kenya's total adult male population does not include the tribes of the northern frontier, who are very isolated from the rest of Kenya and were only estimated without a genuine census. If we arbitrarily add 50,000 adult men to the territorial total, as 25 per cent of the estimated 200,000 population of the northern frontier tribes, the resulting percentage for adult males at work is 31·9 per cent instead of 33·2 per cent which makes little difference to the comparison.

[2] Tanganyika's peak male labour force of 396,516 in 1951 constituted 21·4 per cent of total adult males at the 1948 census. Tanganyika's 1958 figure of 339,188 constitutes only 15·1 per cent of total adult males at the 1957 census, but comparable figures for Kenya and Uganda cannot be given as recent censuses have not yet been completed.

living under urban conditions at any one time, has proceeded furthest in Kenya and least far in Uganda. At the 1948 census 2·7 per cent of the African population of Kenya was living in the nine towns recorded, each of which had African populations of over 1,500. In Tanganyika 1·5 per cent of the African population was in the eight towns recorded. But evidently several towns as large as those included were omitted. By 1957 thirteen towns were recorded in Tanganyika, all with African populations of over 4,000, so that the coverage was still less than in Kenya. The percentage of the total African population in them was 2·5. Dar es Salaam, Tanganyika's largest town, is over three times as large as Tanga, which in turn is more than twice as large as any other town. The African population of Dar es Salaam rose from 50,765 in 1948 to 93,363 in 1957. The African population of Kenya's two largest towns, Nairobi and Mombasa, rose respectively from 64,397 to 115,000 and from 42,853 to 89,854 in the same period. It is impossible to give any comparable figures for Uganda, because the main African population of its largest town, Kampala, lies outside the municipal boundaries and is therefore not included in the figures, but from available estimates the urban African population of Uganda would certainly be less than 2 per cent.

The low degree of urbanization in Uganda is related to the fact that such a preponderant part of Uganda's productive wealth lies in African peasant farming. Though Kenya has proportionately the largest urban African population, it seems that there is a larger core of long-term African residents in Tanganyika towns than there is in those of Kenya. This is probably due to the greater influence of the caravan routes in Tanganyika, which accustomed Africans to leaving home earlier than elsewhere, and to the integrating effect of Islamic and Swahili cultures, which provide a more favourable focus for multi-tribal urban life than exists elsewhere.

Figures for the proportion of the employed labour force working in towns can be given for Kenya and Uganda, but not for Tanganyika. In Kenya 31·5 per cent of the recorded adult male labour force was employed in nine main towns in 1948 and 36·1 per cent in 1957. In Uganda the proportion of the total employed in the five main towns rose from 26 per cent in 1951 to 28 per cent in 1958. It is interesting that, while a far higher proportion of Kenya's population gets drawn into paid employment than is the case in Uganda, the proportion of the paid labour force which is working in towns is less dissimilar.

Conclusion

We cannot here enter into the vast subject of the social effects of population movement in general and labour migration in particular. We can only refer briefly to a few salient characteristics. In prehistoric and proto-historic times tribes and sections of tribes usually moved slowly over long periods of time. Hunting peoples were gradually absorbed or forced into the most remote and inhospitable parts of the country. Some peoples were isolated, but most were in continuous interaction, constantly causing change, but only within the narrow limits of subsistence economy with a varying emphasis on pastoralism and agriculture. Climatic change and natural disaster often forced people to move, encouraging changes in their way of life in certain directions and limiting them in others. These natural forces exerted only a negative determination, in prohibiting types of behaviour for which the requisite resources were absent, while the positive stimuli were only taken up when also favoured by features of the social systems of the peoples concerned.

Trade followed by colonial rule has shaken people partly out of age-old patterns. The ease of movement for individuals is enormously increased, while the mass movement of whole peoples is often prevented by administrative control. A great part of the population is involved in the practice of migrant labour. Our figures show that those away from home at any one time are quite a small proportion of the total, though in many areas virtually every able-bodied male is involved at some time in his life. Far fewer women are involved, but those who do go tend to stay away longer than the average man.

The figures show that in the main labour migrating tribes the emigration rate for females is only a third or a half that of males. The exception to this is the Kikuyu, because of the special characteristics of the squatter system in Kenya. It is generally true that wherever migrant labour has become habitual, some of those involved in it have become more firmly attached to their place of work. These establish families, usually by getting women from their tribal homes, but sometimes by marrying local women in the area where they work. Such long-term workers are undoubtedly increasing, but still form only a small proportion of the total. So invariable is the predominance of men in labour migration to centres of wage employment that it is safe to assume that if the figures show a greater sex equality, the migration must be of a different nature, the objective probably being peasant settlement and cultivation. This is true of long-term peasant settlement in Buganda, by Rwanda, Rundi, Lugbara, Alur and other tribes, of the Luo movement into north-western Tanganyika and of many other smaller movements. Tribal systems, however radically transformed, still act as filters causing modern influences to affect each people differently in accordance with its traditional structure, values, natural resources and geographical position. So the uncentralized Masai formed no attraction for a capital city, though one grew up amongst them through the fortuitous siting of a railway camp, while the capital of the centralized Ganda state was such a magnet that a railway had to be built to it.

The extent to which people are drawn into labour migration depends on how far the appropriateness of their tribal economy to the resources of their country insulates them from new wants, and on whether new wants can be financed through increased production within the traditional framework or only by the earning of wages elsewhere. The strength of tribal community ties are the fundamental reason for the persistence of migrant labour in its African form.

If a man could find an adequate substitute community life outside the relatively closed circle of his tribe he would no longer have to oscillate so frequently between it and his place of work. As it is, considerations of economic, social and political security compel the great majority to retain their tribal stake however long they may absent themselves from home.[1] In addition, African family systems ensure for most a net economic advantage from the maintenance of two production units, one

---

[1] See J. van Velsen, "Labour Migration as a positive factor in the continuity of Tonga Tribal Society", paper presented to the International African Institute Seminar, East African Institute of Social Research, 1959.

based on his tribal home and operated by his wives and relatives for much of the time, the other based on his own cash-earning faculties away from home. The net advantage usually remains, however highly paid the absentee may be.[1]

Towns as such are of relatively small though growing importance in the actual numbers they attract. But they are pace makers of the new society, where change proceeds furthest and fastest and economic and class considerations most successfully supersede those of tribal origin.

BIBLIOGRAPHY

East African Statistical Department Quarterly Economic and Statistical Bulletins.

Annual Reports: Kenya Labour Department
Uganda Labour Department
Tanganyika Labour Department
Zanzibar Labour Department

Census: *Report on the Native Census*, 1921, Government Printer, Dar es Salaam.
Native Census, 1928, Government Printer, Dar es Salaam.
Census of the Native Population, 1931, Government Printer, Dar es Salaam.
African Population of Tanganyika Territory, East African Statistical Department, 1950.
Tanganyika Population Census, 1957, Part I, East African Statistical Department, 1958.
African Population of Kenya Colony and Protectorate, East African Statistical Department, 1950.
African Population of Uganda Protectorate, East African Statistical Department, 1950.
Annual Reports, Tanganyika Department of Agriculture.

---

[1] See E. H. Winter, *Bwamba Economy*, East African Studies No. 5, Kampala, 1955, 39.

12

Wage Labour and African Population Movements in Central Africa

J. CLYDE MITCHELL

IT is just a century ago that Dr. David Livingstone, missionary and explorer, was able personally to tell English audiences about the horrors of the slave-trade in central Africa. Slaving, in a grim sense, was one of the earlier forms of exploitation of Africa's natural resources, and through it, ironically, many of the tribal peoples of central Africa were able to enjoy a higher standard of living than would have been possible otherwise. The export of slaves, together with the ivory, beeswax and copper they transported to the coast, enabled the Bantu peoples of the interior to import goods which they themselves were unable to obtain from the resources they had at their command: items such as guns, powder, calico, beads and brass ornaments. It was Livingstone also who saw that legitimate trade therefore was likely to be the only real counter to the slave-trade though almost a half of a century was to pass before this could be shown to be true.

The Africa about which Livingstone reported to the Europe of the mid-nineteenth century was one in which a large number of tribal peoples lived almost entirely at subsistence level on the plateaux flanking the banks of the great Zambezi river. The earliest of their numbers had moved into this region many centuries earlier and had been subject themselves to a continual succession of invaders. The most recent of these, offshoots of the warlike Zulu people from Natal, were still terrorizing central Africa when Livingstone was there.

J. Clyde Mitchell

Most tribal groups were centred round chiefs who, in addition to being religious leaders, were also military commanders. The more powerful of these tribes, such as the Lozi, Bemba, the Lunda in the Luapula Valley and the various offshoots of the Zulu, such as the Ngoni and the Ndebele, were able to raid their weaker neighbours and to exact cattle and grain tribute from them. Between raids from more powerful neighbours, the weaker tribes pursued their livelihood by cultivating the soil with different techniques of ash-planting, hunting when cultivation did not demand their time, or tending their herds in those regions where cattle were able to flourish. The wants of the average tribesman were meagre. He was able himself to fashion out of iron weapons for defence and implements with which to wrest a living from the forest-covered plateaux, for the Bantu were aware of the techniques of smelting ore. He was able to clothe himself with bark-cloth from the forest or with the skins of animals killed in the chase. He built his houses from the natural products he had at his command in the bush; poles, mud and thatch. The grains he cultivated, the fish he caught, the animals he was able to kill in the chase, and the wild products of the forest he was able to gather, provided food enough at least to maintain the population if not to allow it to increase.

Each child was born into a society in which successful ways of meeting the challenge of hostile natural and human environments had been devised through centuries of adaptation and handed on from one generation to the next. He lived in a community in which he co-operated with kinsmen in religious observances, economic activities, ritual and recreation. He worshipped the spirits of his dead ancestors: his religion was thus an extension of his kinship system. He cultivated his gardens with his neighbours and relied on the ritual he practised with them to ensure that the spirits of the ancestors were ready to help in their worldly activities. A man danced at night with the villagers with whom he had hunted the day previously. He held cultivation rights in the land through a particular relationship with his chief, and he relied upon the chief to propitiate the tribal spirits in order that the rains should fall and the crops flourish. The social world of the tribesmen, in other words, was a single social unit in which a man co-operated with a limited number of kinsmen and neighbours and participated in activities which were all closely interconnected.

The first Europeans to follow Livingstone into South Central Africa who were not travellers and explorers, were themselves, like Livingstone, missionaries. They penetrated alone into the remote interior to make converts, winning the confidence of the people and learning their languages. These missionaries needed supplies of different sorts. They needed not only their own personal belongings but also cotton goods, beads and similar trade goods with which to reward the labour they employed to build their stations. They had to purchase most of their foodstuffs from the local villagers who wanted payment in kind not money. From the beginning, thus, the missionaries were more than teachers of the Gospel. They were also the first European employers of African labour, and the first to introduce these tribal people to the infinitely richer technological resources of the Western world.

Explorers, hunters and adventurers had also been stimulated by Livingstone's stories of the interior and soon more and more of these came hard upon the heels of the missionaries. Two of them, Hartley and Mauch in particular, returned in 1865 with tales of vast gold deposits in Southern Rhodesia. Interest in South Central Africa quickened and over the next twenty years many traders, prospectors and planters came seeking their fortunes. In 1878 the Tati Concessions Co. had obtained a mining concession from Lobengula the Ndebele king: this became a base from which further mineral wealth was sought in Southern Rhodesia. In the same year the African Lakes Corporation had been formed in Scotland to take over the trading activities of the Scotch mission in Nyasaland, and Buchanan, who had once been employed on one of the missions there, started growing coffee on his own account. The money economy was thus inevitably introduced.

Political developments followed on these first economic steps. In 1884 Germany had declared a protectorate over Demararaland and Namaqualand in South-West Africa and had also been showing interest in Tanganyika. This led to renewed interest on the part of the British Government in the territories in the interior. In 1889, Britain declared Nyasaland a protectorate. The previous year Rhodes's representative, Rudd, had obtained a concession from Lobengula, the Ndebele king, to mine in Mashonaland. Rhodes's Treaty with Lobengula enabled him to petition for a Royal Charter to set up the British South Africa Company which he did in 1889. In 1890 he was able to recruit about 200 pioneers to occupy Mashonaland and to begin farming and mining there. Various Company agents were then able to secure treaties with a number of the other chiefs occupying present-day Northern Rhodesia, so that by 1891 the Company was able to extend its activities beyond the Zambezi.

The political relationships between Black and White, however, had not been determined by these treaties, and in the decade which followed the European immigrants were able to consolidate their position of superiority over the indigenous Bantu people. In 1893 the Ndebele people in Southern Rhodesia raided an area occupied by some of the British South Africa Company pioneers and this led to a war in which the Ndebele people were routed and subjugated. Lobengula fled and died in exile. Three years later the remnants of the Ndebele people rose in rebellion and were subdued by force of arms. Immediately the Shona, who had for many years been the vassals of the Ndebele, also rose against the Whites and were likewise defeated. In Nyasaland in 1896 the Ngoni chief Gomani was taken into custody after his warriors had raided a mission station and was subsequently executed by an Imperial force. In 1898 an Imperial force took action against Mpeseni the Ngoni chief at Fort Jameson, and British South Africa Company authorities interfered with the succession of the Bemba paramount Chitimukulu to avoid bloodshed, so establishing their authority over the Bemba people. In the next year the powerful Lunda chief on the Luapula River yielded to an expedition despatched from Nyasaland.

By the turn of the century, the safety of intending settlers in British Central Africa had been secured and the region was on the brink of rapid settlement and economic expansion. At the time of the first census in 1911 there were 23,730 Europeans in Southern Rhodesia, 1,497 in Northern Rhodesia and 766 in Nyasaland. Ten years later the European population in Southern Rhodesia was 33,780, in Northern Rhodesia 3,634 and 1,431 in Nyasaland.[1] A large proportion of these in the earlier

[1] In Nyasaland it increased by only 500 to 1,975 in 1931 and then declined until

years were employed in administration and other services, but the economic development of the territories rested with the growing numbers of miners, farmers and traders.

Hopes of a second Witwatersrand in Southern Rhodesia ran high at the turn of the century, but it soon became obvious that the gold deposits there were less extensive than in South Africa. Other minerals were found, however, and these helped to centre the interest on mining. Coal had been discovered at Wankie in 1893 and began to be mined in 1903. Other minerals such as asbestos, chrome and a large number of others were discovered, but gold continued to be the most important mineral until about 1952. After this the value of other minerals, particularly asbestos, chrome and coal, increased considerably. In 1958 the value of asbestos mined was greater than gold (£8·6 million against £7·0 million), value of chrome mined about two-thirds of that of gold (£4·0 million), and coal about one-half of that of gold (£3·3 million). Gold in fact then represented only about one quarter of the value of all minerals mined (£25 million).

Interest switched from mining to ranching and farming before the First World War and the value of agricultural produce rose steadily against the value of mining products. Tobacco, which subsequently became of prime importance to Southern Rhodesia, was introduced in 1895 but only began to be important after the First World War. It has increased considerably following the Second World War and since it requires a large amount of hand labour has had a marked effect upon the distribution of labour.

Since 1938 manufacturing industries in Southern Rhodesia have expanded considerably and more and more labour has been attracted into the manufacturing towns of Salisbury and Bulawayo and the smaller towns like Umtali, Gwelo and Que Que. In 1938 the net output of mining in Southern Rhodesia was £7,696,000, agriculture £3,770,000 and manufacturing industries £2,332,000.[1] If we express subsequent expansion as

1945. Since then, however, the population has grown rapidly to an estimated 8,800 in June 1959. In Northern Rhodesia it increased to 13,846 in 1931 and since then has increased steadily to an estimated 73,000 in June 1959. In Southern Rhodesia it increased to 33,780 in 1921 and thereafter rose steadily to an estimated 215,000 in June 1959.

[1] C.A.S.O. 1959c: Table 1.

base 100 the growth of nett output of mining was 1938 = 100, 1942 = 122, 1947 = 98, 1952 = 263 and 1957 = 334. The growth of agricultural nett output was 1938 = 100, 1942 = 169, 1947 = 396, 1952 = 900 and 1957 = 1,315. On the other hand the nett output of manufacturing industries has grown thus: 1938 = 100, 1942 = 169, 1947 = 394; 1952 = 1,065 and 1957 = 1,860. By 1957 the nett output of manufacture was £43,176,000 which was almost equal to that of Agriculture (£45,086,000) and considerably more than that of mining (£25,764,000).

In Northern Rhodesia, on the other hand, mining has remained the main economic activity. Copper had been discovered in the hook of the Kafue between 1895 and 1899, but technical and transportation difficulties prevented its exploitation. It had also been discovered in 1899 at Kansanshi, while richer deposits were found in the Belgian Congo two years later.[1] Mining had started at Broken Hill for zinc and lead in 1902 and in the same year Collier had discovered the Bwana Mkubwa and the Roan Antelope copper deposits. By 1906—before the railway had reached the mineral area of Northern Rhodesia—zinc and copper was already providing 91 per cent of the value of exports from Northern Rhodesia. The mineral wealth of Northern Rhodesia could only begin to be exploited economically when the railway reached Broken Hill in 1906, and the Copperbelt in 1909: production increased rapidly after this date. The full copper deposits became attainable, however, only after 1923 when the world demand for copper revived and financiers were prepared to invest capital in extensive prospecting and the plant needed for the deep-level mining of the extensive sulphide ores. After an initial set-back during the economic recession of the 1930's the Coppermines have expanded their productivity ever since.[2] In 1956 Northern Rhodesia was the largest copper producer in the Commonwealth and the fourth largest in the world. The value of the mineral produced there in 1958 was £77 million, of which copper represented 91 per cent, cobalt 3·8 per cent, zinc 2·6 per cent and lead 1·2 per cent.

Nyasaland initially appeared to possess more agricultural potential than either Northern Rhodesia or Southern Rhodesia.

[1] Gann 1958: 120.   [2] Gann 1955 *passim*.

Labour and Population Movements in Central Africa

Coffee plantations were started as early as 1878 but declined owing to attacks by disease and pests combined with a fall of prices after 1900. Tea introduced in 1888 proved to be successful in the regions of high rainfall in the Shire Highlands and is responsible for 40 per cent of the value of agricultural production in Nyasaland today. Tobacco, introduced in 1889 and exported first in 1893, was initially produced mainly by Europeans. Increasingly, however, it is becoming a supplementary cash-crop for African subsistence cultivators. Tobacco contributes 35 per cent of the value of agricultural production in Nyasaland.

The flow of labour into and between the territories of the Federation has been profoundly affected by the degree of economic development in each. The per capita domestic product at factor cost (including subsistence output) for Southern Rhodesia in 1956 was £83 a year, for Northern Rhodesia it was £86 a year but in Nyasaland it was only £17. The average earnings of African employees in Southern Rhodesia in 1957 were £74, in Northern Rhodesia £100 but in Nyasaland £42.[1] These facts go a long way to explain the role of Nyasaland as an exporter of labour to the other territories of the Federation.

The Supply of Labour and Recruitment

The economic development in South Central Africa has only been possible through the availability of a large reservoir of cheap labour. But the supply of this labour has not been constant. In spite of the conspicuous poverty of the tribal Africans and the apparent abundance of men with no calls on their time, the entrepreneur has not always been able to count on a steady and sufficient flow of labour for his needs. Wage labour was foreign to the tribesmen of the late-nineteenth century and savoured to him somewhat of slavery. His needs were met entirely from the resources at his command: the trade goods he could acquire with money had no meaning for him so that he had no desire for it.

The earliest settlers in South Central Africa, therefore, like other pioneers who tried to establish modern enterprises

[1] Nyasaland Government 1959:51-3.

amongst tribal people living at a subsistence level,[1] found
themselves desperately short of labour in a land in which there
were many apparently idle men, and in which crude living
conditions demonstrated obviously that there was a pressing
need for the goods which the earnings of labour could buy.
Many of the early entrepreneurs were thus forced to bring
labour with them into areas in which there was already a sizeable local population. At the Kansanshi Mines in Northern
Rhodesia for example in 1913, 90 per cent of the labour was
non-local. The position at Broken Hill apparently was similar.[2]

The attitude of the early settlers to the reluctance of local
Africans to enter into wage-earning employment was that if he
did not respond to economic motives then, "the best way to
make him work was not to pamper him, but to tax him so that
he would learn the dignity of labour".[3] However much the
British South Africa Company may have sympathized with the
wishes of the settlers, the Imperial Government nevertheless
looked askance at any attempts at direct official pressure to
induce Africans into wage labour. Company officials in 1907
were instructed to "advise" natives to go to work but a Native
Affairs Committee in 1910 was opposed to "officials" showing
any interest in recruitment.[4] The imposition of tax which had
been tried in the Cape[5] however was one indirect way of achiev-
ing the same result. If tax had to be paid in cash[6] the only way
to obtain it in the absence of marketable crops or produce, was
to work for it. In Nyasaland a special provision enacted in 1901
allowed Africans employed by Europeans to pay only half the

[1] Sugar farmers close to densely settled Zululand had to import indentured
Indian labour. The gold mines on the Witwatersrand had to import Chinese
labour in 1904. Asian labour had to be used on the construction of the railway in
Uganda, and in the Congo Free State. In the French Congo labour had to be
forcibly recruited. Hailey, 1956:1357–1358. Macmillan 1949:171 writes: "The
history of European dealings with African labour is of a constant struggle to resolve
the paradox of actual shortage in presence of the deceptive appearance of plenty."
See also Moore 1951:14 ff.

[2] Gann 1958:123. See also Barber 1960:238.

[3] Gann 1958:91; 122. See also Orde Brown 1933:29. Moore 1951:67, refers
to taxation as "indirect coercion". Hailey 1956:677 writes: "There have
admittedly been instances . . . where the major considerations in the levy of direct
tax has proceeded not only from fiscal motives but from a desire to force Africans
into employment in European enterprise."

[4] Hailey 1956:1400.　　[5] Macmillan 1949:124; 172.

[6] Payment in kind had been abolished in Southern Rhodesia in 1895 and was
discouraged in the two northern territories.

ordinary tax. Those who were unable to pay the tax were liable to be made to work on public works until they had earned an equivalent, which was usually a month's wages. A hut tax had been imposed in Nyasaland in 1892, in north-eastern Rhodesia in 1900 and north-western Rhodesia in 1901, but it took several years before the tax could be collected effectively. By 1908 the number ferried across the Zambezi River from Northern to Southern Rhodesia at one point had almost reached the number being recruited.[1] It is unlikely that taxation was as efficacious as this in forcing men out to work: it was probably only accelerating a tendency which had shown up earlier. As Gann argues "taxation gave an enormous impetus to migration. It created a regular instead of a seasonal demand over the whole of the Territory, not just areas near to labour centres."[2]

A more direct method of securing labour was through recruitment. The gold mines in South Africa had similarly been short of African labour and had solved their problem by recruiting from both within South Africa and in the territories on her northern boundaries which would allow her to do so.

In 1903, following an agreement between the Imperial Government and the gold mines in South Africa, the Witwatersrand Native Labour Association started recruiting in Nyasaland. It ceased its operations, however, in 1913 when it was argued that the morbidity rates of "tropical" Africans on the mines was too high to make their employment profitable. It started recruiting again in 1935, initially through the London and Blantyre Supply Company, and since 1938 in its own name. In Northern and Southern Rhodesia recruitment for employment in South Africa started when the Low Grade Ore Commission in South Africa had recommended that labour should be sought further afield.[3] Southern Rhodesia, however, by this time was itself importing labour and soon ceased to be a source of labour for the South African gold mines.

Southern Rhodesia, in fact, had itself become a centre of employment at the beginning of the century so that in 1903 the British South Africa Company had set up a Native Labour Bureau to obtain labour for the farms and mines in Southern Rhodesia. Later when the mines in Northern Rhodesia

[1] Gann 1958:86.　　[2] Gann 1958:85.　　[3] Hailey 1956:1406.

developed in the mid-twenties it also supplied them with a considerable number of workers particularly from Nyasaland and the Eastern Province of Northern Rhodesia. Undoubtedly the Native Labour Bureau increased the supply of labour to Southern Rhodesia and to Northern Rhodesia but it seems that before the depression the majority of workers had begun to prefer to migrate voluntarily.[1] As labour requirements fell off during the economic recession of the early thirties, the Native Labour Bureau ceased operations.

When the demand for labour increased with the lifting of the recession, the copper mines of Northern Rhodesia found they were able to rely on the flow of free labour. Southern Rhodesia on the other hand found it necessary to stimulate further supplies by its Free Migrant Labour Transport Service[2] which it instigated in 1934. By this service migrants from certain points in Northern Rhodesia, Nyasaland and Portuguese East Africa could be transported free of charge to dispersal points a short distance within the Southern Rhodesian borders. The migrants, and their wives and children if they travel with them, are fed and accommodated along the routes until they reach the dispersal points, after which they are left to find their own employment.[3] There is no doubt that this service has done much not only to remove many of the considerable hardships formerly suffered by migrants on their trips to Southern Rhodesia, but also to direct much labour there which might otherwise have gone elsewhere. By 1953 no less than 71,549 men, women and children were transported into Southern Rhodesia and 43,434 out of it.[4] This appeared to be a peak year for the service: the number transported into and out of Southern Rhodesia since then has decreased.

In 1946 the need to secure more labour for Southern Rhodesia's rapidly expanding economy led to the formation of the Rhodesian Native Labour Supply Commission,[5] a state-

---

[1] Only 10 per cent of the Africans employed in the mining industry before the recession were supplied by the Rhodesian Native Labour Bureau. Hailey 1956: 1409.

[2] Known to Africans as "*Ulere*", which is the Nyanja word for "free".

[3] For a good description of *Ulere* services and their routes see Scott 1954a: 34–40.

[4] Southern Rhodesian Government 1959: Table XV.

[5] Known locally as "*Nthandizi*".

controlled organization which sought to recruit labour in Nyasaland and some districts of Mozambique for Southern Rhodesian employers. Most labour, however, prefers to seek work uncovenanted, and according to Scott less than one-tenth of all migrants into Southern Rhodesia since the War have been recruited.[1]

Labour migration between the territories of the Federation is now strictly controlled. In 1935 the Nyasaland Government had appointed a Commission of Enquiry into the effects of labour migration and its report drew attention to a number of the consequences of excessive migration.[2] Accordingly it sought to control migration and to regularize conditions for migrants through a number of agreements with Southern and Northern Rhodesia. Provisional covenants were signed in 1938 and 1942 and in 1947 a Tripartite Agreement between the three territories provided for the repatriation of workers after an agreed period[3] and for a system of Family Allowances and Deferred Pay.[4]

Labour recruitment is controlled in Southern Rhodesia by the Native Labour Regulations Act of 1939 and in general no recruiting is allowed in this territory. In Northern Rhodesia it is controlled by the Employment of Natives Ordinance of 1953 which embodies many of the provisions of the 1936 Recruiting of Indigenous Workers Convention of the International Labour Office. The Witwatersrand Native Labour Association is authorized to recruit 5,000 labourers in Barotseland, and another 500 in the Balovale District. Until recently this was the only recruiting which was allowed for labour outside Northern Rhodesia. There was some contraction of economic activities throughout the Federation after 1957 when the impact of the fall in copper prices began to be felt. Consequently in 1958, Southern Rhodesian farmers were allowed to tap labour registered on the labour exchanges in Northern Rhodesian towns where there was some unemployment. Internally

---

[1] Scott 1954a:32. [2] Nyasaland Government 1936.
[3] Two years for single men, though men whose wives are with them may be exempt from this provision.
[4] The provisions were included in the Migrant Workers Act of 1948 in Southern Rhodesia since repealed in May 1960; the African Migrant Workers Ordinance of 1948 (Cap. 233) in Northern Rhodesia; and the African Emigration and Immigrant Workers Ordinance of 1954 in Nyasaland.

the Northern Rhodesian Agricultural Development Society has a scheme whereby workers are flown from areas where there appears to be an excess of labour, such as the Northern Province, to Lusaka where most of the farming is centred. In Southern Rhodesia the fall-off in economic activities led to a decline in African employment with the result that some of the Free Migrant Labour Transport Services were withdrawn. The number of men, women and children brought into the territory thus fell dramatically from 56,044 in 1957 to 24,633 in 1958.[1] At the same time the Foreign Migratory Labour Act of 1958 made it illegal for labour from non-Federal territories to seek employment in the main urban areas of Southern Rhodesia (except Umtali). The object of this legislation was to control surplus labour in the urban areas and thus to provide greater employment opportunities for indigenous Africans. It was hoped that this might encourage indigenous labour to become permanent industrial workers which would be in line with the Government's policy in connection with the Native Land Husbandry Act of 1951.[2]

In Nyasaland recruiting is controlled by the African Emigration and Immigration Workers Ordinance of 1954. The Witwatersrand Native Labour Association is authorized to recruit for work on the gold fields in the Transvaal and the Orange Free State. It may not recruit in the Southern Province where its activities may compete with the local demand for labour, nor may it recruit during the agricultural season which is roughly between November and March. In 1957, it was limited to a quota of 16,000 but in 1958, following the failure of the Rhodesian Native Labour Supply Commission to recruit to its full quota the previous year, its quota was increased to 18,000.[3] Nyasaland Africans are declared prohibited immigrants in the Union of South Africa unless they have been recruited for work on the gold mines. Only those who have been able to become registered are entitled to work in proclaimed areas:[4] others can work in rural areas and mines only. Nyasaland Africans are therefore discouraged from going to South Africa under their own steam

---

[1] Southern Rhodesian Government 1958: Table XV.
[2] Southern Rhodesian Government 1959:11.
[3] Nyasaland Government 1959b:13.
[4] In general the main towns and their neighbourhoods.

and are more or less obliged to go under recruitment. The number being recruited for the South African gold mines therefore continues to increase while that recruited for work in Southern Rhodesia appears to be falling.

The Rhodesia Native Labour Supply Commission in 1957 was permitted to recruit up to 14,000 but it could only engage 6,945. In 1958 it could recruit 8,647 of the same quota. There is little doubt that where free movement is possible only a small proportion enters the labour market through recruitment. It is probable that most of those recruited are making their first trip to work. Frequently they do not have the resources to pay for their own travel on the first trip and need at least one recruited trip to enable them to build up capital for subsequent trips.[1]

Economic incentives have now come to be sufficient to ensure the flow of labour into most industries. Taxation and other administrative measures may have been a necessary stimulant to the flow before the range of wants of Africans had become diversified. Recruiting also is probably a necessary interim stage, but these inducements soon give way to normal economic incentives. We have seen that, in spite of a phenomenal expansion of the labour force since 1931, the copper mines have been able to meet their needs entirely from free labour. In the same way it is likely that as transportation facilities improve and the amount of circulation of money in the tribal areas goes up, African workers are more likely to exercise their free choice in seeking employment rather than accept the restrictions and obligations which recruitment puts upon them.

Population Growth and the Labour Supply

The supply of African labour however has not always responded directly to the demand. We have seen that initially the ordinary economic incentives were not effective and for a while the flow had to be stimulated by non-economic pressures such as taxation. The effective supply, therefore, for many years was far below the potential and employers had to import labour from territories in which wage-earning was an accepted part

[1] Watson 1958:52 describes this for the Mambwe.

J. Clyde Mitchell

of the life of the African people. In 1911 when the first census was taken there were 149 Africans from territories other than Northern Rhodesia, Nyasaland, Mozambique and Angola (i.e. probably from South Africa and Bechuanaland) employed to every 1,000 from Southern Rhodesia. By 1921 it had fallen to 29 per 1,000 and with some variation fell to 21 in 1941.[1] This

Table I: *The Distribution of Males of Working Age in Subsistence and Wage-earning Labour, Southern Rhodesia, 1911–56*

Date	De jure population (a)	S.R. Lab. force (b)	Males in employ (c)	Males avail. (d)	No. in subsist. (e)	Per cent (f)
1911	573,400	84,155	40,000	121,000	81,000	33·0
1921	770,000	147,316	58,600	162,000	103,400	36·2
1931	1,034,000	179,092	85,000	217,000	132,000	39·3
1941	1,388,000	299,510	146,000	292,000	146,000	50·0
1951	1,864,000	488,455	268,000	392,000	124,000	68·3
1956	2,160,000	564,962	297,000	454,000	157,000	65·4

(a) The *de jure*, i.e. the population which is normally domiciled in Southern Rhodesia, was obtained by computing the population growth from 1911 on the assumption it would have reached the *de jure* population in 1956 by an annual increase of 3 per cent per annum. The 1956 figure is based on the 1953–5 demographic survey and is probably the most reliable estimate we have. It seemed more desirable to proceed this way than to rely on doubtful population estimates made earlier.

(b) Males only, derived from the census returns taken in the years stated.

(c) The numbers recorded at the censuses as being employed in Southern Rhodesia corrected for the number employed in other territories of the Federation and in the Union of South Africa. According to C.A.S.O. 1959a:7, the number of males over puberty outside Southern Rhodesia was 27,000. I have assumed the figure to be 30,000 in 1956 and have applied it to the known number in Southern Rhodesia, i.e. 267,000. This yields a correction factor of 1·12 which I have applied to all other figures in this column.

(d) I assume that the working ages are between 15 and 50. Some of the males in employment are juveniles, i.e. under the age of 16, while some of those over 15 are in school. I assume these two tendencies cancel each other in my computation. There are probably some African males in employment over the age of 50 but the evidence we have is that by far the majority have left wage employment before this age.

(e) The difference between (c) and (d).

(f) (c) as a percentage of (d).

---

[1] The proportion rose again thereafter to a peak of 43 in 1951. Now, however, the circumstances were different and I see this increase as evidence, not of the unwillingness of Southern Rhodesian Africans to come on to the labour market, but of exactly the opposite—that the potential ceiling of supply had been reached.

then was a temporary phase, for Southern Rhodesian Africans were soon drawn into the money economy. The rate at which this took place is illustrated by estimates of the population growth in Southern Rhodesia set alongside the growth in the labour force as in Table I. As early as 1921, it seems that the labour requirements had reached the equivalent of 90 per cent of the total number of Southern Rhodesian males at that time: of the 162,000 males of working ages 58,600 were in wage-earning employment. Of these, 52,691 were employed in Southern Rhodesia so that at that stage Southern Rhodesia was drawing about 36 per cent of its labour requirements from its own territory and making up the rest from Nyasaland (30·4 per cent), Northern Rhodesia (21·2 per cent) and Mozambique (12·8 per cent). Thus something like 64 per cent of the adult males were then still in the tribal areas. The labour force grew relatively slowly until after the economic recession in the 1930's. After that date the rate of growth of the labour force has been at approximately 4·7 per cent per annum. The growth between 1931 and 1951 was higher (5·1 per cent per annum) than between 1951 and 1956 (2·95 per cent per annum). The consequence of this rapid growth of the labour force was that by the beginning of the Second World War the labour requirement in Southern Rhodesia was as great as the *total* number of Southern Rhodesian African males of working age, and could be met only if every adult male left the reserves and entered wage-earning employment. By 1956 the labour requirement exceeded the total number of Southern Rhodesian African males of working age by about 25 per cent.

Southern Rhodesian Africans have been drawn into wage-earning in increasing numbers. Until 1941 the numbers which were available to keep the economy of the tribal areas going was also increasing but slightly more slowly than the natural rate of increase (i.e. at 2 per cent against a natural increase of about 3 per cent per annum). Between 1941 and 1951 however the proportion of males in wage-earning employment appears to have reached no less than 68·3 per cent. This was probably due to the increased activity during the War and the expansion of industry immediately after the War. By 1956, however, it seems that the proportion in wage-earning employment had fallen slightly and a greater number was once again engaged in the

J. Clyde Mitchell

economy of the tribal areas. In 1951, the Native Land Husbandry Act was promulgated and this Act grants individual holdings to Africans. It is possible that the effect of the Act initially is to increase the number of Africans in the reserves since they are anxious to be assured of a holding in their tribal area.

In 1956 the *de jure* population in Northern Rhodesia was 2,130,000 and there were 267,000 African males of working ages in employment. These represented 59·8 per cent of the males of working ages.[1] In Nyasaland the number of males of working age appears to have been 577,000 in 1956 and of these 289,123 were employed in the Federation. I estimate that at least another 30,000 were employed in the Union of South Africa and elsewhere,[2] so that approximately 55 per cent of the available males were in wage employment, 30·8 per cent being employed outside Nyasaland.[3]

The Composition and Employment of the Labour Force

In May 1956 there were 1,037,343 Africans in wage-earning employment in the Federation.[4] This excludes the employees of African employers in rural areas, but includes those in urban areas. Of this total 971,719 or 94 per cent were males and 85,836 of these males, or 9 per cent, were juveniles.[5] Expressed differently, there were 74 females and 96 juveniles employed to every 1,000 adult males employed.

The sector of the economy which absorbed most African labour in the Federation was Agriculture and Forestry (34 per

[1] There were 254,267 employed in the Federation, according to C.A.S.O. 1957: Table IV. C.A.S.O. 1952:17, Table IV, shows 52,800 employed outside Northern Rhodesia. S.R.G. 1954: Table XLVIII shows that there were 46,240 employed in Southern Rhodesia. This suggests that the number in South Africa and elsewhere must have been about 6,500. Scott 1954b:433 gives a figure of 11,000 in South Africa, 7,000 in the Belgian Congo and 3,500 in Tanganyika. I have assumed approximately 12,500 in other territories for this calculation.

[2] Nyasaland Government 1959a:47 estimates that about 21,000 African males were in the Union of South Africa. This is almost certainly an underestimate.

[3] Comparable census material since 1911 is not available for Nyasaland, so that we cannot prepare a similar table for that territory. To do so for Northern Rhodesia would call for estimates of the number of Northern Rhodesian Africans employed in Belgian Congo and Tanganyika over the past forty-five years. This would entail more research than I can give to it at present.

[4] C.A.S.O. 1957.   [5] i.e. Males of the apparent age of 16 and less.

cent) followed by Services (22 per cent: Domestic Service represented 11 per cent and Other Services another 11 per cent); Manufacturing (11 per cent); Mining and Quarrying (10 per cent); Transport and Communication (3 per cent) and Electricity, Water and Sanitary Services (1 per cent). Juvenile males and females were not employed to the same degree in these different industrial sectors. Proportionately to adult males there were more juvenile males and women employed in Agriculture and Forestry, and in Private Domestic Service than in other sectors. Women and juveniles, frequently the wives and children of agricultural labourers, are employed in a variety of tasks in farming, as for example in weeding, sowing, tea-picking and tobacco sorting. Expressed per 1,000 male adults, the proportion of juvenile males and women employed in the different sectors were: Agriculture and Forestry 193 (160);[1] Mining and Quarrying 16 (7); Manufacturing 63 (35); Construction 26 (6); Electricity, Water and Sanitary Services 15 (4); Commerce and Finance 31 (10); Transport and Communication 8 (2); Private Domestic Service 204 (114); and Other Services 34 (77).

The number employed in each territory of the Federation depends of course on the wage-earning opportunities in it, hence directly on its degree of economic development. Of the 1,037,343 Africans employed in the Federation 59 per cent were employed in Southern Rhodesia, 25 per cent in Northern Rhodesia and 16 per cent in Nyasaland. In Southern Rhodesia and Nyasaland the majority are employed in Agriculture and Forestry (41 and 42 per cent respectively). In Northern Rhodesia only 16 per cent were so employed: instead rather more were employed in Mining and Quarrying (14 per cent as against 10 per cent in Southern Rhodesia and less than 0·5 per cent in Nyasaland) and in Construction (24 per cent as against 9 per cent in Southern Rhodesia and 15 per cent in Nyasaland). This difference in economic development is shown also in the proportion employed in urban areas.[2] In Southern Rhodesia and Nyasaland where Agriculture is more important than in Northern Rhodesia, 37 per cent and 19 per

---

[1] Rate for women in brackets.

[2] That is, all municipalities and townships and their neighbouring suburbs and mine townships with a non-African population of more than 1,200.

cent respectively of the African labour are employed in towns. In Northern Rhodesia on the other hand where mining is more important, 56 per cent are employed in towns. Of those employed in towns in Northern Rhodesia 70 per cent are on the Copperbelt (or 40 per cent of the total) and 78 per cent (or 43·5 per cent of the total) in mining towns.[1] The largest concentration of African labour in Southern Rhodesia is in the commercial and manufacturing towns of Salisbury and Bulawayo. Salisbury has 16·9 per cent of all African labour employed in Southern Rhodesia and 45·5 per cent of the labour employed in towns. Bulawayo has 11·1 per cent of the African labour force and 30 per cent of those employed in towns. Outside these two centres only Umtali and Gwelo employ an appreciable proportion of African labour employed in towns (6·1 and 4·8 per cent of the number employed in towns respectively).

The Origin of Labour

We have pointed out that the demand for labour varies in each territory according to the degree of economic development it has experienced. In Southern Rhodesia in 1956, for example, less than half of the African male labour force came from Southern Rhodesia itself. Northern Rhodesia was able to find 83 per cent of its requirement from within its own borders, while Nyasaland, where there has been least economic development, finds no less than 94 per cent of its labour force from among its own people. The trend of the proportion of Northern Rhodesian labour employed in Southern Rhodesia illustrates the relationships between local opportunities for earning wages and labour immigration. Between 1911, when the first census was taken, and 1931 the proportion of Northern Rhodesian Africans in the Southern Rhodesian male labour force remained constant at about one-fifth. In 1933, the copper mines in Northern Rhodesia, which had previously made an abortive start before the recession of 1930-2, recommenced production. Thereafter as copper production expanded in prospect of an impending war the economic development of Northern Rho-

---

[1] That is, the towns on the Copperbelt including Ndola, together with Broken Hill. The rest of the urban employed African population is distributed in Lusaka (15·4 per cent of the total) and Livingstone (6·5 per cent of the total).

Labour and Population Movements in Central Africa

desia received a fillip. Consequently the demand for African labour increased, not only on the mines, but throughout the territory. As wage-earning opportunities opened up nearer home the proportion of Northern Rhodesian Africans seeking employment in Southern Rhodesia fell off. In 1936, the proportion of Northern Rhodesian African males employed in Southern Rhodesia was 18·6 per cent—not far below the figure at which it had remained since 1911. Thereafter it fell steadily so that by 1956 it was only 7·2 per cent.[1]

Table II: Percentage of African Labour (Male and Female) by Origin, in the Three Territories of the Federation, May 1956

Country of Origin	S. Rhodesia	N. Rhodesia	Nyasaland	Federation
S. Rhodesia	49·3	0·8	0·0	29·2
N. Rhodesia	6·9	82·7	0·2	25·4
Nyasaland	21·8	7·9	94·5	29·7
Federal	*78·0*	*91·5*	*94·7*	*84·3*
Angola	0·4	2·2	0·0	0·8
Bechuanaland	0·3	0·0	0·0	0·1
Belgian Congo	0·0	1·6	0·0	0·4
Mozambique	20·1	1·4	4·7	12·9
Tanganyika	0·5	3·1	0·0	1·5
Others	0·2	0·0	0·0	0·1
Unspecified	0·6	0·2	0·4	0·2
Non-Federal	*22·1*	*8·5*	*5·1*	*16·0*

Source: Table II, *Report of the Census of Africans in Employment taken on 8th May 1956*, Item No. 9-6098.

Table II sets out the proportion of the total labour force which is derived from within the Federation and the territories

[1] Northern Rhodesian labour has not been drawn off greatly to other labour centres outside its own boundaries. The main labour centres outside Southern Rhodesia are the Union of South Africa and Tanganyika. We know that with increasing restrictive measures in South Africa since 1945, the flow of labour to the Union has been dropping off. The numbers employed in Tanganyika are too small to affect the argument.

neighbouring it. This table brings out the dependence of
Southern Rhodesia on outside labour, which we have noted
earlier, and the degree to which Northern Rhodesia and Nyasaland are independent of outside labour.

In Nyasaland 21·6 per cent of the labour force was made up
of juvenile males and women. The corresponding figures for
Southern and Northern Rhodesia are 16·0 per cent and 6·9 per
cent. In all three territories the tendency is for the greatest
proportion of female and male juvenile workers to be drawn
from the local population, or from the neighbouring foreign
territories, rather than from the other territories of the Federation. Thus, in Southern Rhodesia the highest proportion of
females and juvenile males is to be found amongst the working
population drawn from Southern Rhodesia. There is also a
fairly high proportion of females and juvenile males amongst
the working population drawn from Mozambique and Bechuanaland. The lowest proportion of females and juvenile
males are to be found in the working populations drawn from
Northern Rhodesia and Nyasaland. The same trend occurs in
the working population in Nyasaland, and to a considerably
smaller degree in Northern Rhodesia. This is because in each
territory there is a greater proportion of juveniles and females
to adult male workers in Agriculture and Private Domestic
Service than in other sectors of the economy. In Southern
Rhodesia and Nyasaland these two industries employ by far a
greater proportion of labour than others, and it is into these
sectors particularly that Southern Rhodesian and Mozambique
labour goes in Southern Rhodesia and Nyasaland labour in
Nyasaland. In Northern Rhodesia, however, Construction and
Mining employ most labour, and in these few women and
juveniles are employed. The majority of the labour force is
made up of adult males and they represent the potential on
which future developments will draw, and we examine the
distribution of labour from this point of view in the succeeding
pages.

Distribution of Labour in Industries according to Origin

The fact that certain industries in some of the territories employ more labour than others will affect the overall distribution

of labour by origin in the industries of the Federation as a whole. We know, for example, that in Southern Rhodesia and Nyasaland Agriculture and Forestry employs more labour than in Northern Rhodesia. We would expect that more Nyasalanders and Southern Rhodesian Africans would be employed in Agriculture than in other industries, merely because these are the biggest employers in their own territories.

To help us to examine the distribution of labour in industries according to its origin, we should compare the proportion of Africans from any particular territory employed in an industry, with the proportion in that industry as a whole. We know, for example, that of the 885,883 adult males employed in the Federation, 264,762 or 29·9 per cent were employed in Agriculture and Forestry.[1] Of the 241,558 African adult males from Northern Rhodesia employed in the Federation, only 39,650 or 16·4 per cent were employed in Agriculture and Forestry. Northern Rhodesian labour as a whole, thus is less concentrated in Agriculture and Forestry over the whole Federation than labour from other territories. The ratio of 29·9 to 16·4 gives us some measure of the degree to which Northern Rhodesian labour as a whole is less concentrated in Agriculture than labour from other territories.

In this way we are able to construct a series of index numbers which will show us the extent to which labour from different countries of origin is concentrated in the different industries in any particular territory. To do this we assume that the labour in any particular territory is distributed at random in all industries irrespective of its origin. We then compute the number of workers from each country of origin we would expect to find in any particular industry on this basis and compare our results with the actual numbers so employed. If we make the index 100 when the expected number coincides with the observed number, then a figure larger than 100 shows that labour from that country is concentrated in the industry we are examining, and conversely an index number of less than 100 shows that the labour is not concentrated there.[2]

---

[1] Virtually in Agriculture. Forestry absorbs only 5 per cent of African males in employment.

[2] Let N be the total number of African male adults employed in any territory, R be the number from any given country and I be the number employed in any

J. Clyde Mitchell

Since the distribution of labour as a whole in the Federation is likely to be affected by the industries which predominate in each of the territories and the degree to which these industries employ local labour, we need to examine the distribution of labour by country of origin in each territory separately. This is done in Table IIIA, IIIB and IIIc. The index number in this table therefore refers to the distribution of labour by country of origin within each territory, and not within the Federation as a whole.

In summary the main features of the table are:

In Southern Rhodesia

Local labour is employed predominantly in Other Services which include mainly the civil services, teaching and church work. It tends also to be concentrated in Commerce and Finance and to a slight extent in Manufacturing. It seems to be least concentrated in Electricity, Water and Sanitary Services, and in Mining and Quarrying.

Northern Rhodesian labour is concentrated particularly in Mining and Quarrying, Electricity, Water and Sanitary Services, and Transportation. It is least concentrated in Domestic Service and Commerce and Finance.

Nyasaland labour is concentrated in Electricity, Water and Sanitary Services, Agriculture and Forestry, and Mining and Quarrying. It is least concentrated in Other Services and Commerce and Finance.

Portuguese labour, 98·5 per cent of which in Southern Rhodesia comes from Mozambique, is concentrated in Electricity, Water and Sanitary Services, Agriculture and Forestry and Construction. It is least concentrated in Other Services and

given industry. Let O be the number of adult males from the country employed in the particular industry under consideration. The expected number of adult males from the country in question employed in the industry we are examining will be:

$$\frac{\text{N.I.R}}{\text{N}^2}$$

The Index number will be

$$\frac{100.\text{O.N}^2}{\text{N.I.R}} \text{ or } \frac{100.\text{O.N}}{\text{I.R}}$$

I used this type of measure to study the distribution of labour on the copper mines. Mitchell 1954b.

Table III: Distribution of the African Adult Male Labour Force in Industries by Country of Origin, May 1956
(Index 100 = Normal concentration)

A. SOUTHERN RHODESIA

	Territory of origin					
	S. Rhod.	N. Rhod.	Nyasa.	Port.	Other	Percentage
Agriculture and Forestry	86	79	120	121	41	36·3
Mining and Quarrying	64	213	113	92	453	11·4
Manufacturing	110	107	87	94	43	13·4
Construction	102	102	76	122	106	12·1
Electricity, Water, etc.	62	171	132	128	14	1·4
Commerce and Finance	147	60	64	57	35	5·6
Transportation	93	171	101	89	91	2·7
Domestic Service	106	63	110	96	39	10·2
Other Services	161	66	52	32	80	8·0
Percentage	45·9	7·7	24·0	20·6	1·7	*512,042*

B. NORTHERN RHODESIA

Agriculture and Forestry	74	100	103	163	61	14·0
Mining and Quarrying	26	90	137	88	232	15·2
Manufacturing	105	102	82	150	73	9·6
Construction	102	101	94	91	97	25·7
Electricity, Water, etc.	16	99	74	265	99	1·2
Commerce and Finance	160	104	107	58	47	5·7
Transportation	188	99	89	161	82	3·1
Domestic Service	240	102	116	61	71	10·5
Other Services	59	108	72	54	68	14·5
Percentage	0·8	83·3	8·1	3·6	5·2	*245,066*

C. NYASALAND

Agriculture and Forestry	19	19	96	149	94	34·2
Mining and Quarrying	0	0	108	27	0	0·4
Manufacturing	58	18	97	190	35	11·6
Construction	190	345	102	65	98	19·6
Electricity, Water, etc.	120	0	109	11	22	0·9
Commerce and Finance	59	80	105	33	27	8·2
Transportation	360	66	97	91	37	3·1
Domestic Service	204	105	102	59	34	7·1
Other Services	126	82	104	23	234	16·8
Percentage	0·1	0·3	94·8	4·8	0·4	*128,775*

Source: Computed from Table IV of *Report on the Census of Africans in Employment taken on 8th May 1956*, Item No. 9-6098. Figures in italics give the total labour force in each territory.

E.A.P.—P

Commerce and Finance. The small amount of labour from other territories, mainly Tanganyika[1] and Bechuanaland, is concentrated particularly in Mining and Quarrying and is little concentrated in other industries.

In Northern Rhodesia

Local labour is evenly distributed in most industries. There is a slight tendency for local labour to be concentrated in Other Services and to be least concentrated in Mining and Quarrying.

The small amount of labour from Southern Rhodesia is concentrated in Domestic Service, Transportation and Commerce and Finance. It is least concentrated in Electricity, Water and Sanitary Services, in Mining and Quarrying and in Other Services.

Nyasaland labour, the largest category of outside labour, is concentrated in Mining and Quarrying, and to some extent in Domestic Service. It is least concentrated in Other Services, Electricity, Water and Sanitary Services and in Transportation.

Portuguese labour, which in Northern Rhodesia comes mostly (65 per cent) from Angola, is concentrated mainly in Electricity, Water and Sanitary Services, in Agriculture and Forestry, in Transportation and least in Other Services, Commerce and Finance, and Domestic Services.

The labour from other territories, which includes 57·8 per cent from Tanganyika and 29·1 per cent from the Belgian Congo, is mostly concentrated in Mining and Quarrying and is least concentrated in Commerce and Finance and in Agriculture.

In Nyasaland

Local labour, which is in the overwhelming majority, is evenly distributed in most industries with a slight tendency to concentrate in Electricity, Water and Sanitary Services, and Mining and Quarrying, with the least concentration in Agriculture.

---

[1] These were 8,796 adult males from non-Federal countries excluding Mozambique and Angola. Of these, however, 3,426 or 38·5 per cent were returned as being from unspecified territories.

Labour and Population Movements in Central Africa

The small amount of Southern Rhodesian labour in Nyasaland is concentrated particularly in Transportation, Domestic Services and in Construction. It is least concentrated in Mining and Quarrying and Agriculture and Forestry.

The small amount of Northern Rhodesian labour in Nyasaland is concentrated mostly in Construction. Outside Domestic Services, in which there is a fair amount of concentration, Northern Rhodesian labour is not represented very strongly in other industries.

Portuguese labour, which comes entirely from Mozambique and which represents the largest source of labour in Nyasaland outside its own local supply, is concentrated in Manufacturing and Agriculture. Outside these industries it is not well represented.

The figures for labour from other territories in Nyasaland are not reliable since the greater number was returned as being from an unspecified territory.

The Distribution of Labour in Urban and Rural Areas according to Origin

With differences in distribution of the type we have described, we would expect that the labour from the different countries of origin to be distributed in town or country in accordance with the location of industries. Table IV sets out the indices of concentration for labour of different countries of origin in towns and country in the three territories of the Federation.

From this table we see that in Southern Rhodesia there is a tendency for local labour to be concentrated in the towns while Northern Rhodesian labour tends to be concentrated in rural areas. Nyasaland and Portuguese labour however is evenly distributed between towns and country though within the towns there is considerable variation. The small proportion of labour from non-Federal territories, excluding Mozambique and Angola, is concentrated mainly in the rural areas. It should be noted however that the African labour in the smaller mining towns is classified here as "rural" and that this explains the concentration of Northern Rhodesian and "Other Country"

Table IV: Distribution of Labour by Country of Origin in Main Towns and Rural Areas in the Territories of the Federation

(Index 100 = Normal concentration)

SOUTHERN RHODESIA

	S.R.	N.R.	Nya.	Port.	Other	Per-centage
Salisbury	85	28	128	134	35	19·6
Bulawayo	134	166	69	39	87	11·9
Umtali	118	9	21	193	17	2·1
Gwelo	174	56	43	25	35	1·9
Rural areas	95	112	102	101	122	65·8
Percentage	45·9	7·7	24·0	20·6	1·7	*512,042*

NORTHERN RHODESIA

	S.R.	N.R.	Nya.	Port.	Other	Per-centage
Copper mines	50	94	125	89	174	35·6
Ndola	182	94	127	106	136	8·6
Broken Hill	130	108	59	62	45	3·9
Lusaka	234	96	152	128	31	8·7
Livingstone	220	107	44	134	23	3·7
Rural areas	78	104	75	106	62	42·8
Percentage	0·8	83·3	8·1	3·6	5·2	*245,066*

NYASALAND

	S.R.	N.R.	Nya.	Port.	Other	Per-centage
Blantyre-Limbe	225	104	102	59	22	16·7
Zomba	295	58	104	15	53	4·7
Rural areas	66	100	99	114	118	78·3
Percentage	0·1	0·3	94·8	4·8	0·4	*128,775*

Source: *Report on the Census of Africans in Employment taken on 8th May 1956.* Salisbury, Central African Statistical Office.
Computed from Table V. African adult males only. The rural-urban proportions differ slightly from those quoted earlier (p. 207). In this table to save space I have excluded some of the smaller towns and have based this on adult males instead of all Africans in employment.

labour in rural areas. This is mainly in mining areas such as Wankie and Selukwe.

In Salisbury which has the largest labour force (91,911 adult males) there is a concentration of Portuguese and Nyasaland labour in relation to the composition of the labour force in Southern Rhodesia as a whole. Southern Rhodesian labour correspondingly is less concentrated in Salisbury while Northern Rhodesian labour is very thinly represented. In Bulawayo, on the other hand, Northern Rhodesian labour is moderately heavily concentrated while Nyasaland labour is less common. Portuguese labour is very thinly represented. In Umtali Portuguese labour is heavily concentrated and, while there is still a strong Southern Rhodesian element in the labour force, the Northern Rhodesian and Nyasaland elements are very poorly represented.

In Northern Rhodesia we see that there is a slight tendency for local labour and a more marked tendency for Portuguese labour to be concentrated in rural areas. The small proportion of Southern Rhodesian and the rather larger proportion of Nyasaland labour, on the other hand, appears to be concentrated in the towns. The Southern Rhodesian labour is concentrated mainly in the commercial towns of Livingstone, Lusaka and Ndola, and there is very little Southern Rhodesian labour on the copper mines. Local labour tends to be slightly concentrated in Broken Hill and Livingstone, but the difference between these towns and the copper mining towns and Lusaka in this respect is not great. Nyasaland labour is concentrated particularly in Lusaka and on the Copperbelt, while in Broken Hill and Livingstone there seems to be very little Nyasaland labour. Portuguese labour, on the other hand, is concentrated particularly in Livingstone and Lusaka while the copper mining towns have relatively little. Labour from other countries, particularly Tanganyika and the Congo, is heavily concentrated on the Copperbelt: very little is present in Broken Hill, Lusaka and Livingstone.

In Nyasaland local labour is evenly distributed between town and country. Portuguese labour which is the only other sizeable proportion of labour in Nyasaland, is concentrated particularly in the rural areas. The small proportion of Southern Rhodesian labour is distributed mainly in the two towns.

Labour from other countries, mainly Tanganyika, is concentrated in the rural areas particularly in the Northern Province.

Factors affecting the Distribution of Labour

There are, it is clear from the data presented here, distinct differences in the proportion of labour from different territories which is employed in specified industries or located in particular areas of the Federation. It is improbable that these differences are caused by chance factors. If a large number of unrelated factors were affecting the distribution of labour in the territories then the pattern of employment would approximate the random model we assumed in computing our index numbers. In this case the numbers would have varied in a narrow range around 100. In fact, about two-thirds of the index numbers fall outside the range of 80 to 120, which points to the operation of finite factors which determine the distribution of labour both in industry and region.

If the numbers involved were small some adventitious factor could easily determine the predominance of labour from a certain country of origin or industrial sector of some particular territory. For example, there were 104 adult males of Southern Rhodesian origin employed in Nyasaland. Of these only 12 (or 11·5 per cent) were employed in Transportation and Communication. In relation to the number of African males employed in Transportation and Communication as a whole in Nyasaland (3·2 per cent), this is very high and gives rise to the index figure of 360. Thus if a motor transport company should transfer a dozen of its Southern Rhodesian drivers to Nyasaland, an index figure of this magnitude could easily arise. The high proportion of Southern Rhodesian adult males in Domestic Service in Northern Rhodesia, (Index = 240) for example, is based on a total of 477. After the three territories were federated in 1953 a certain amount of interchange of European personnel between the three territories has taken place. If Europeans formerly employed in Southern Rhodesia took their domestic servants with them when they were transferred to Northern Rhodesia, then the number of Southern Rhodesian adult African males employed in Domestic Service in Northern Rhodesia becomes inflated by what is essentially an adventi-

…ribution of Labour in Industrial Groupings in the Federation according to Country of Origin, May 1956

(Index 100 = Normal concentration)

	Origin of Labour		
…strial Grouping	Local Territorial	Other Federal Territories	Outside the Federation
…nd Forestry; Mining …ying	87	132	132
…; Electricity, Water …ary Services; Trans- …ommunications; Do- …vice	106	86	92
…ng; Commerce and …ther Services	118	71	65

…ublished tabulations of the Census of Africans in Employment. …e courtesy of the Director of Census and Statistics. African male

…ustries in which skills need to be acquired and re- …l labour with a lower turn-over will tend to pre- …The more mobile labour needing fewer skills will …tween their tribal homes and industrial centres, …l to be restricted to those occupations and industries …kills they need are minimal.

Labour

…argued thus far that the concentration of labour …n countries in particular industries could be the …operation of specific and particular circumstances, …transfer of government officials from one territory …o that their domestic servants whom they take with …b a distribution involving small numbers. We have …that certain market factors such as the degree of …the relative stability of labour and the better …position of local over imported labour, may also …istribution of workers by country of origin in the …ustries in the Federation.

tious set of circumstances. The very high concentration of labour from non-Federal territories other than Mozambique and Angola in Southern Rhodesia (Index = 455) is probably due to Tanganyika labour on certain mines, such as the Wankie Collieries. The high index figure for the employment of "Other" labour in Northern Rhodesia (Index = 232) is certainly due to large numbers of Nyakyusa from southern Tanganyika who come deliberately to the copper mines, and it is likely that since 1954, when employment opportunities for Africans on the copper mines began to contract, that some of these have been coming to Wankie.

Where the numbers involved are small therefore,[1] chance factors may influence the apparent distribution of labour and the pattern may conceal the operation of a general principle.

We may seek a more general explanation of the distribution of labour by country of origin in the various industrial sectors of the economies of the territories in terms of the normal market factors in employment. If we compare the indices of concentration of local labour in the industrial sectors in Southern Rhodesia, Northern Rhodesia and Nyasaland with the indices for imported labour in these sectors, it emerges immediately that in the primary industries of Agriculture and Mining there is proportionately less local labour than imported. The effect is most clearly seen in Southern Rhodesia where the index number for local labour in Agriculture and Forestry is 86 and for Mining and Quarrying 64, against index numbers of 120 and 113 for Nyasaland labour and 121 and 92 for Portuguese labour. In Northern Rhodesia there is the same tendency. The number for local labour in Agriculture and Forestry is 100 and for Mining and Quarrying 90, while the corresponding indices for Nyasaland labour is 103 and 137, and for Portuguese labour 163 and 88. In Nyasaland the number employed in Mining and Quarrying is too small to be significant, but in Agriculture and Forestry the index figure for local labour is 96 and for Portuguese labour 149.

In Northern Rhodesia and Southern Rhodesia there is a

[1] Unless the index number is very large as in the case of "Other" labour in Mining in Southern Rhodesia it should be possible to compute a standard error of the index number and so determine when differences in the numbers are significant statistically. I have not been able to do this and invite attention of statisticians to the problem.

tendency for imported labour to be concentrated in the Electricity, Water and Sanitary Services, and a corresponding tendency for local labour to be disproportionately absent from them. In Southern Rhodesia, for example, the index for the employment of local labour in Electricity, Water and Sanitary Services is 62, while the corresponding indices for Northern Rhodesian, Nyasaland and Portuguese labour are 171, 132 and 128. In Northern Rhodesia the index for the employment of local labour in Electricity, Water and Sanitary Services is 99, while the figure for Portuguese labour is 265.[1]

As we move to secondary industry and the Services, however, we find that the general trend is for local labour to predominate over imported. In Manufacturing in Southern Rhodesia the index for local labour is 110, for Nyasaland labour 87, and Portuguese labour 94. In Northern Rhodesia the index figure is 102 for local labour and 82 for Nyasaland labour. The index for Portuguese labour in Manufacturing, however, is 150, which runs counter to the general trend but the numbers involved are small. In Nyasaland the index for local labour is 97 and for Portuguese labour 190. This does not contradict the tendency as strongly as it appears, however, since the Manufacturing Industries in Nyasaland are closely tied to plantation work, i.e. the packing and grading of tobacco and the processing of tea. These are centred in the Shire Highlands into which much Portuguese labour migrates.

No clear pattern of employment appears in Domestic Service except that Portuguese labour in general is much less concentrated in it than labour from the Federal territories.[2] Commerce and Finance has Portuguese and other foreign labour very much less highly concentrated in it than labour from the Federation. In Southern Rhodesia there is a tendency for local labour to be concentrated in Commerce and Finance as against Nyasaland and Northern Rhodesia, but in Northern Rhodesia the local labour does not seem to have the same advantage over Nyasaland and Southern Rhodesian labour.

In so far as Other Services are concerned there is a clear pattern in which local labour is dominant, and in which labour

[1] The Nyasaland index is 74, which runs counter to the general trend.
[2] This is probably because they cannot speak English—a disadvantage in English-speaking homes.

from other territories inside or o~ weakly represented. The pattern Rhodesia where the index for the in Other Services is 161, whereas i labour, 52 for Nyasaland labour In general, Portuguese labour i Other Services in all three terr other Federal territories.

Here we are dealing with gen more unskilled workers, with les wage-earning capacity, are empl ing and Quarrying than in Man Commerce and Finance and Oth where education and skills are employment of labour by coun Most are employed here as cle similar white-collar occupations.

The influence of skills and edu different territories is brought o average indices of concentration tory, from the other territories in t the Federation for groups of indu

In this table Agriculture and and Quarrying, are grouped tog general, there is the least require skills. At the other end of the sc and Finance and Other Service requiring most of all special skill The other industries are placed clear trend emerges in which centrated in the industries in v which require least skill and labour is concentrated in the i

It is likely that there is a low drawn from local sources.[1] W

[1] Unpublished data collected by Mrs. labour strength of a factory in Salisbury completing 60 months' service is 0·265 if 0·215 if he comes from within Southern from Salisbury; 0·097 if he comes fron Northern Rhodesia, and 0·094 when h

Table V:

In

Agricultur
and Qu
Constructi
and Sar
port and
mestic S
Manufactu
Finance

Source: U
Provided by
adults only.

in those ir
tained, lo
dominate.
circulate
but will te
where the

The Flow

We hav
from cert
result of tl
such as th
to another
them distu
also argue
education,
bargaining
affect the
various in

Labour and Population Movements in Central Africa

An examination of the material presented so far shows that a third factor, communication routes, also has a marked affect on the distribution of labour. In an earlier paper I was able to show that the composition of the African labour force on the copper mines of Northern Rhodesia was influenced considerably by the position of the mine in relation to the main road and rail services bringing labour to the area. A mine at the point of entry of a road from a particular region which supplies labour to the Copperbelt was likely to have a high proportion of labour from that region.[1] An examination of the distribution of labour in different regions in the Federation shows that a similar process is apparently at work here. The point is illustrated in Table IV. We examine the concentration of Portuguese labour in the three towns of Salisbury, Bulawayo and Umtali. The point of entry of most Mozambique labour into Southern Rhodesia is at Umtali. Salisbury lies 160 miles to the north-west of Umtali and Bulawayo another 250 miles south-west of Salisbury. The indices of concentration of Mozambique labour in these three towns, in order of distance from the border, is 193, 134 and 39. In the same way we can examine the concentration of Northern Rhodesian labour in the towns of Bulawayo, Salisbury and Umtali which lie in that order in distance from the main point of entry of Northern Rhodesian labour. The indices are 166, 28 and 9.[2] A similar process is shown in the concentration of Tanganyika and Congo labour in the towns of Northern Rhodesia where, as the distance increases from the Copperbelt which is the nearest point of inflow of labour from these areas, the indices are: copper mines, 174; Ndola, 136; Broken Hill, 45; Lusaka, 31; and Livingstone, 23.

I have attempted to check the generality of this relationship by examining the distribution of labour by country of origin in the districts of Southern Rhodesia. Southern Rhodesia has a large labour force spread over 37 districts. In order to simplify the table I have arranged the districts roughly in order of distance from the main points of inflow of labour from territories

[1] Mitchell 1954b. For a general discussion of the significance of transportation in labour migration see Niddrie 1954.

[2] Southern Rhodesian Government 1949 and Scott 1954a:40-42 drew attention to the same fact but did not examine it in any great detail.

neighbouring Southern Rhodesia. For Portuguese labour this is along the eastern boundary of Southern Rhodesia. The districts of Southern Rhodesia were arranged in four bands roughly of less than 100 miles, from 100 to 200 miles, from 200 to 300 miles, and lastly a zone including districts more than 300 miles from the border. In the same way the districts were arranged in four zones from the northern boundary of Southern Rhodesia for Nyasaland labour, and four zones from the north-western boundary for Northern Rhodesian labour. Indices of concentration were computed for each of these zones. The results are set out in Table VI. The classification of districts into these zones is admittedly crude, but the trend is clear enough. The proportion of labour from any one territory employed in districts in Southern Rhodesia falls off steadily as the distance from the main points of entry increases.

Table VI: Distribution of Labour in Southern Rhodesia by Country of Origin in Zones of Increasing Distance from the Main Point of Inflow of Labour

(Index 100 = Normal concentration)

Country of Origin	Distance from Point of Entry			
	Less than 100 miles	100 to 200 miles	200 to 300 miles	Over 300 miles
Portuguese Territories	180	124	54	21
Nyasaland	126	127	65	37
Northern Rhodesia	208	132	63	43

Source: Unpublished tabulations of the Census of Africans in Employment. Provided by the courtesy of the Director of Census and Statistics. African male adults only.

The correlation is by no means a perfect one. We see that the proportion of Nyasaland labour in the zone of districts approximately 100 to 200 miles from the main points of entry is the same as in the nearer districts. The districts in the second zone include Salisbury and Hartley where large numbers of African male adults are employed, and in these two districts the proportion of Nyasalanders is high. At the same time the districts of Wankie and Sebungwe have also been included in the second zone though in terms of the lines of communication they are very much more distant from Nyasaland than Salisbury and Hartley: the indices of concentration of Nyasaland labour in them is as low as 53 and 18 respectively. Selukwe, which is relatively distant from the main point of inflow of Nyasaland labour, has a relatively high index of concentration (114), while Mtoko which is very near one of the points of inflow has the surprisingly low index of 65. Similar anomalies occur in the tabulations for the Portuguese and Northern Rhodesian labour. For example, Buhera and Inyanga Districts are both relatively near the Mozambique border but the index of concentration of Portuguese labour in Buhera is only 4 and in Inyanga 69. Gutu (Index = 3), Chibi (Index = 8), and Ndanga (Index = 6) are all nearer as the crow flies to the Portuguese border than Bulawayo District (Index = 37), Nuanetsi (Index = 78) and Insiza (Index = 27), but the concentration of Portuguese labour in the latter is higher.[1] Northern Rhodesian labour is far less concentrated in Salisbury (Index = 29) than we would expect from its relative nearness to Northern Rhodesia, and much more in Gwanda (Index = 128) in view of its relative distance.

To some extent these anomalies are the product of the crudity of our method. The distance between a labour centre and the point of entry of labour to a territory depends on the lines of communication between the two points. The distance, as the crow flies, between Sebungwe (Index 37 for Northern Rhodesian labour) and the Northern Rhodesian border, for example, is not great but the main lines of transport by-pass Sebungwe entirely. It is not surprising therefore that Northern Rhodesian labour should be sparsely concentrated in Sebungwe. We are dealing in fact with a situation hypothesized by Stouffer where the proportion of labour reaching any point is related to the number of intervening opportunities it has experienced and not directly to the distance travelled.[2] This requires examination in

---

[1] The relationship of local supplies of labour to local demand is important here. This is discussed later on pp. 228–31.

[2] Stouffer 1940. A preliminary attempt to correlate the index of concentration of Portuguese and Northern Rhodesian labour in districts along the railway routes leading into Southern Rhodesia from their main points of entry, with the accumulated number of African male adults employed in those districts (as a measure of opportunities) suggests that the logarithm of the index number varies directly with the accumulated number of Africans employed. Using the figures for Northern

J. Clyde Mitchell

much greater detail which would be out of place here. Nevertheless even with the crude techniques we have used, the influence of the position of labour centres relative to the point of inflow of labour on the distribution of labour in the Federation has been demonstrated.

The Local Supply of Labour

Yet another factor determining the distribution of labour in Southern Rhodesia must be the amount of local labour available for employment. In those districts where economic activities have prospered, the local African population has been able to find employment, as it were, on its own doorstep. In other districts, on the other hand, where enterprises have not developed the local people must seek wage-earning employment elsewhere. Where enterprises have been very successful the demand for labour has outgrown the local supply and employers have had to seek their labour wider afield. We would expect to find that in areas where the local supply outstrips the demand that a high proportion of Southern Rhodesian labour would be employed, whereas where the demand exceeds the supply then the Southern Rhodesian labour must compete with labour from other territories. In Table VII I have set out the indices of concentration for labour in the districts of Southern Rhodesia, classified according to the degree to which the local supply of labour exceeds or falls short of demand. The relationship between the demand and the proportion of local labour is clearly brought out in the index of concentration of Southern Rhodesian labour. Where there is a large excess of the supply over demand then the proportion of Southern Rhodesian labour is considerably above the national average, while the proportion of labour from other territories is considerably below the national average. Where there is a large excess of demand over supply the proportion of Southern Rhodesian labour employed is lower than the national average and the proportion of labour

Rhodesian labour, very approximately the logarithm of the index is equal to
$$2.64 - 0.0167 \, P$$
where P is the accumulated number of African male adults employed at some point along the railway line, expressed as a percentage of the accumulated number at the most distant point, i.e. at Umtali.

Labour and Population Movements in Central Africa

Table VII: *Concentration of Local and other Labour in Districts in which the Demand for Labour falls short of or exceeds the Local Supply*

(Index 100 = Normal concentration)

Type of District	Origin of Labour				
	S. Rhod.	N. Rhod.	Nyasa.	Port.	Other
High demand	82	118	121	105	136
Moderate demand	112	67	83	111	56
Balanced	128	118	63	77	63
Moderate supply	126	105	59	93	63
Large supply	179	17	36	33	32

Note: The demand for each district was computed by relating the number of African adult males employed in each district to the number of males aged 15–50 normally resident in that district. It was assumed that 65 per cent of the males in working ages would be available for wage employment. This is based on the territorial average computed in Table I of this chapter. The districts in which there was a much greater demand for labour than was available in the local population were Salisbury, Bulawayo, Goromonzi, Hartley, Lomagundi, Mazoe and Wankie. Districts with a moderate excess of demand over supply were Bubi, Gwelo, Makoni, Marandellas, Wedza, Urungwe, Umtali and Fort Victoria. Districts where the demand was roughly equal to the supply were Belingwe, Gwanda, Insiza, Melsetter, Mrewa, Nyamandhlovu and Selukwe. Districts where the supply was moderately in excess of demand were Chipinga, Darwin, Lupane, Matobo, Sipolilo and Nuanetsi. Districts in which the supply was greatly in excess of the demand were Bikita, Buhera, Bulalima-Mangwe, Charter, Chibi, Chilimanzi, Gutu, Inyanga, Mtoko, Ndanga, Nkai and Sebungwe.

Source: The employment statistics were derived from unpublished records made available through the courtesy of the Director of Census and Statistics. The population for each district was obtained from C.A.S.O. 1959a: Table I adjusted to May 1956 (census date). I have assumed that 21 per cent of the total *de jure* population are males aged 15 to 50.

from other territories higher than the national averages.[1] In Bulawayo and Bubi Districts the proportion of Southern Rhodesian labour employed appears to be much higher than we might have expected from the numbers available from within those districts related to the labour opportunities in them. I think the explanation is that each district abuts another in which labour opportunities are small.[2] In the districts of Mount Darwin and

[1] The index of concentration appears to vary directly as the logarithm of the ratio of the number of African males employed in a district to the number available. On the basis of the curve so derived it appears that the proportion of Southern Rhodesian Africans begins to fall lower than the territorial average only when the local supply begins to fall lower than 40 per cent of the demand.

[2] Bulalima-Mangwe and Nkai.

229

Sipolilo, on the other hand, the proportion of Southern Rhodesian labour employed is rather less than we might have thought considering the amount of labour available in relation to the employment opportunities in the districts. In both these districts a relatively large number of Africans from other territories is employed. We can only conclude here that the local Africans prefer the more remunerative employment in the industrial centres and leave local employment to incoming migrants.

There is no direct relationship between the supply of local labour and the origin of labour which may compete with it. In high demand areas there is naturally a high proportion of labour from outside Southern Rhodesia, and conversely in high supply areas a low proportion of outside labour. But whether Northern Rhodesian, Portuguese or Nyasaland labour predominates in other areas depends, I think, predominantly on the geographical location of the districts. For example, in districts where there is a moderate demand for labour in relation to the local supply there is a tendency for the discrepancy to be made good with Portuguese labour (Table VII, Index = 111 as against 67 for Northern Rhodesian labour and 83 for Nyasaland labour). The explanation for this is, I think, that the demand falls mostly in the Marandellas, Makoni and Umtali Districts,[1] and this is near the point of main inflow of Portuguese labour. Similarly most of the areas in which the local supply approximately balances the local demand, Nyamandhlovu, Insiza, Belingwe and Gwanda, are near the main point of inflow of Northern Rhodesian labour. The apparent decrease in the proportion of Nyasaland labour employed as the supply of local labour increases is also, I think, spurious: the true explanation is more likely to be a geographical one. In general the areas in which there is the greatest demand for labour lie near the main points of inflow of Nyasaland labour and the areas with least demand are most remote from this point.

The composition of the labour force, therefore, at any point in the territory appears to be determined by a number of

---

[1] About half of the opportunities fall in this area. The rest are distributed in Urungwe, i.e. the Kariba Dam site, the Midlands, i.e. Gwelo, Bubi and Fort Victoria, all of which except Urungwe are relatively isolated from main streams of labour supplies. In Urungwe there are proportionately large numbers of Northern Rhodesian and Nyasaland labour working on Kariba, but the numbers are not sufficient to affect the indices.

tious set of circumstances. The very high concentration of labour from non-Federal territories other than Mozambique and Angola in Southern Rhodesia (Index = 455) is probably due to Tanganyika labour on certain mines, such as the Wankie Collieries. The high index figure for the employment of "Other" labour in Northern Rhodesia (Index = 232) is certainly due to large numbers of Nyakyusa from southern Tanganyika who come deliberately to the copper mines, and it is likely that since 1954, when employment opportunities for Africans on the copper mines began to contract, that some of these have been coming to Wankie.

Where the numbers involved are small therefore,[1] chance factors may influence the apparent distribution of labour and the pattern may conceal the operation of a general principle.

We may seek a more general explanation of the distribution of labour by country of origin in the various industrial sectors of the economies of the territories in terms of the normal market factors in employment. If we compare the indices of concentration of local labour in the industrial sectors in Southern Rhodesia, Northern Rhodesia and Nyasaland with the indices for imported labour in these sectors, it emerges immediately that in the primary industries of Agriculture and Mining there is proportionately less local labour than imported. The effect is most clearly seen in Southern Rhodesia where the index number for local labour in Agriculture and Forestry is 86 and for Mining and Quarrying 64, against index numbers of 120 and 113 for Nyasaland labour and 121 and 92 for Portuguese labour. In Northern Rhodesia there is the same tendency. The number for local labour in Agriculture and Forestry is 100 and for Mining and Quarrying 90, while the corresponding indices for Nyasaland labour is 103 and 137, and for Portuguese labour 163 and 88. In Nyasaland the number employed in Mining and Quarrying is too small to be significant, but in Agriculture and Forestry the index figure for local labour is 96 and for Portuguese labour 149.

In Northern Rhodesia and Southern Rhodesia there is a

---

[1] Unless the index number is very large as in the case of "Other" labour in Mining in Southern Rhodesia it should be possible to compute a standard error of the index number and so determine when differences in the numbers are significant statistically. I have not been able to do this and invite attention of statisticians to the problem.

tendency for imported labour to be concentrated in the Electricity, Water and Sanitary Services, and a corresponding tendency for local labour to be disproportionately absent from them. In Southern Rhodesia, for example, the index for the employment of local labour in Electricity, Water and Sanitary Services is 62, while the corresponding indices for Northern Rhodesian, Nyasaland and Portuguese labour are 171, 132 and 128. In Northern Rhodesia the index for the employment of local labour in Electricity, Water and Sanitary Services is 99, while the figure for Portuguese labour is 265.[1]

As we move to secondary industry and the Services, however, we find that the general trend is for local labour to predominate over imported. In Manufacturing in Southern Rhodesia the index for local labour is 110, for Nyasaland labour 87, and Portuguese labour 94. In Northern Rhodesia the index figure is 102 for local labour and 82 for Nyasaland labour. The index for Portuguese labour in Manufacturing, however, is 150, which runs counter to the general trend but the numbers involved are small. In Nyasaland the index for local labour is 97 and for Portuguese labour 190. This does not contradict the tendency as strongly as it appears, however, since the Manufacturing Industries in Nyasaland are closely tied to plantation work, i.e. the packing and grading of tobacco and the processing of tea. These are centred in the Shire Highlands into which much Portuguese labour migrates.

No clear pattern of employment appears in Domestic Service except that Portuguese labour in general is much less concentrated in it than labour from the Federal territories.[2] Commerce and Finance has Portuguese and other foreign labour very much less highly concentrated in it than labour from the Federation. In Southern Rhodesia there is a tendency for local labour to be concentrated in Commerce and Finance as against Nyasaland and Northern Rhodesia, but in Northern Rhodesia the local labour does not seem to have the same advantage over Nyasaland and Southern Rhodesian labour.

In so far as Other Services are concerned there is a clear pattern in which local labour is dominant, and in which labour

[1] The Nyasaland index is 74, which runs counter to the general trend.
[2] This is probably because they cannot speak English—a disadvantage in English-speaking homes.

Labour and Population Movements in Central Africa

from other territories inside or outside the Federation is only weakly represented. The pattern is most marked in Southern Rhodesia where the index for the employment of local labour in Other Services is 161, whereas it is 66 for Northern Rhodesian labour, 52 for Nyasaland labour and 32 for Portuguese labour. In general, Portuguese labour is less highly concentrated in Other Services in all three territories than labour from the other Federal territories.

Here we are dealing with general market factors. Broadly, more unskilled workers, with less education and hence lower wage-earning capacity, are employed in Agriculture and Mining and Quarrying than in Manufacture or more particularly Commerce and Finance and Other Services. In Other Services where education and skills are more essential the differential employment of labour by country of origin is most marked. Most are employed here as clerks, teachers, evangelists and similar white-collar occupations.

The influence of skills and education in selecting labour from different territories is brought out more clearly if we compute average indices of concentration of labour from within the territory, from the other territories in the Federation, and from outside the Federation for groups of industries. This is done in Table V.

In this table Agriculture and Forestry, together with Mining and Quarrying, are grouped together as industries in which, in general, there is the least requirement for special education and skills. At the other end of the scale, Manufacturing, Commerce and Finance and Other Services are grouped as the industries requiring most of all special skills and educational qualifications. The other industries are placed in a medial category. A very clear trend emerges in which extra-territorial labour is concentrated in the industries in which occupations predominate which require least skill and education, and local territorial labour is concentrated in the industries requiring most skills.

It is likely that there is a lower turn-over of labour when it is drawn from local sources.[1] We would expect, therefore, that

[1] Unpublished data collected by Mrs. T. S. Bell during a study of the African labour strength of a factory in Salisbury showed that the probability of a man's completing 60 months' service is 0·265 if he comes from within 60 miles of Salisbury; 0·215 if he comes from within Southern Rhodesia, but more than 60 miles away from Salisbury; 0·097 if he comes from Mozambique and the nearer parts of Northern Rhodesia, and 0·094 when he comes from farther afield.

J. Clyde Mitchell

Table V: *Distribution of Labour in Industrial Groupings in the Federation according to Country of Origin, May 1956*

(Index 100 = Normal concentration)

Industrial Grouping	Origin of Labour		
	Local Territorial	Other Federal Territories	Outside the Federation
Agriculture and Forestry; Mining and Quarrying	87	132	132
Construction; Electricity, Water and Sanitary Services; Transport and Communications; Domestic Service	106	86	92
Manufacturing; Commerce and Finance; Other Services	118	71	65

Source: Unpublished tabulations of the Census of Africans in Employment. Provided by the courtesy of the Director of Census and Statistics. African male adults only.

in those industries in which skills need to be acquired and retained, local labour with a lower turn-over will tend to predominate. The more mobile labour needing fewer skills will circulate between their tribal homes and industrial centres, but will tend to be restricted to those occupations and industries where the skills they need are minimal.

The Flow of Labour

We have argued thus far that the concentration of labour from certain countries in particular industries could be the result of the operation of specific and particular circumstances, such as the transfer of government officials from one territory to another so that their domestic servants whom they take with them disturb a distribution involving small numbers. We have also argued that certain market factors such as the degree of education, the relative stability of labour and the better bargaining position of local over imported labour, may also affect the distribution of workers by country of origin in the various industries in the Federation.

224

Labour and Population Movements in Central Africa

An examination of the material presented so far shows that a third factor, communication routes, also has a marked affect on the distribution of labour. In an earlier paper I was able to show that the composition of the African labour force on the copper mines of Northern Rhodesia was influenced considerably by the position of the mine in relation to the main road and rail services bringing labour to the area. A mine at the point of entry of a road from a particular region which supplies labour to the Copperbelt was likely to have a high proportion of labour from that region.[1] An examination of the distribution of labour in different regions in the Federation shows that a similar process is apparently at work here. The point is illustrated in Table IV. We examine the concentration of Portuguese labour in the three towns of Salisbury, Bulawayo and Umtali. The point of entry of most Mozambique labour into Southern Rhodesia is at Umtali. Salisbury lies 160 miles to the north-west of Umtali and Bulawayo another 250 miles south-west of Salisbury. The indices of concentration of Mozambique labour in these three towns, in order of distance from the border, is 193, 134 and 39. In the same way we can examine the concentration of Northern Rhodesian labour in the towns of Bulawayo, Salisbury and Umtali which lie in that order in distance from the main point of entry of Northern Rhodesian labour. The indices are 166, 28 and 9.[2] A similar process is shown in the concentration of Tanganyika and Congo labour in the towns of Northern Rhodesia where, as the distance increases from the Copperbelt which is the nearest point of inflow of labour from these areas, the indices are: copper mines, 174; Ndola, 136; Broken Hill, 45; Lusaka, 31; and Livingstone, 23.

I have attempted to check the generality of this relationship by examining the distribution of labour by country of origin in the districts of Southern Rhodesia. Southern Rhodesia has a large labour force spread over 37 districts. In order to simplify the table I have arranged the districts roughly in order of distance from the main points of inflow of labour from territories

---

[1] Mitchell 1954b. For a general discussion of the significance of transportation in labour migration see Niddrie 1954.

[2] Southern Rhodesian Government 1949 and Scott 1954a:40–42 drew attention to the same fact but did not examine it in any great detail.

neighbouring Southern Rhodesia. For Portuguese labour this is along the eastern boundary of Southern Rhodesia. The districts of Southern Rhodesia were arranged in four bands roughly of less than 100 miles, from 100 to 200 miles, from 200 to 300 miles, and lastly a zone including districts more than 300 miles from the border. In the same way the districts were arranged in four zones from the northern boundary of Southern Rhodesia for Nyasaland labour, and four zones from the north-western boundary for Northern Rhodesian labour. Indices of concentration were computed for each of these zones. The results are set out in Table VI. The classification of districts into these zones is admittedly crude, but the trend is clear enough. The proportion of labour from any one territory employed in districts in Southern Rhodesia falls off steadily as the distance from the main points of entry increases.

Table VI: Distribution of Labour in Southern Rhodesia by Country of Origin in Zones of Increasing Distance from the Main Point of Inflow of Labour

(Index 100 = Normal concentration)

Country of Origin	Distance from Point of Entry			
	Less than 100 miles	100 to 200 miles	200 to 300 miles	Over 300 miles
Portuguese Territories	180	124	54	21
Nyasaland	126	127	65	37
Northern Rhodesia	208	132	63	43

Source: Unpublished tabulations of the Census of Africans in Employment. Provided by the courtesy of the Director of Census and Statistics. African male adults only.

The correlation is by no means a perfect one. We see that the proportion of Nyasaland labour in the zone of districts approximately 100 to 200 miles from the main points of entry is the same as in the nearer districts. The districts in the second zone include Salisbury and Hartley where large numbers of African male adults are employed, and in these two districts the proportion of Nyasalanders is high. At the same time the districts of Wankie and Sebungwe have also been included in the second zone though in terms of the lines of communication they are

very much more distant from Nyasaland than Salisbury and Hartley: the indices of concentration of Nyasaland labour in them is as low as 53 and 18 respectively. Selukwe, which is relatively distant from the main point of inflow of Nyasaland labour, has a relatively high index of concentration (114), while Mtoko which is very near one of the points of inflow has the surprisingly low index of 65. Similar anomalies occur in the tabulations for the Portuguese and Northern Rhodesian labour. For example, Buhera and Inyanga Districts are both relatively near the Mozambique border but the index of concentration of Portuguese labour in Buhera is only 4 and in Inyanga 69. Gutu (Index = 3), Chibi (Index = 8), and Ndanga (Index = 6) are all nearer as the crow flies to the Portuguese border than Bulawayo District (Index = 37), Nuanetsi (Index = 78) and Insiza (Index = 27), but the concentration of Portuguese labour in the latter is higher.[1] Northern Rhodesian labour is far less concentrated in Salisbury (Index = 29) than we would expect from its relative nearness to Northern Rhodesia, and much more in Gwanda (Index = 128) in view of its relative distance.

To some extent these anomalies are the product of the crudity of our method. The distance between a labour centre and the point of entry of labour to a territory depends on the lines of communication between the two points. The distance, as the crow flies, between Sebungwe (Index 37 for Northern Rhodesian labour) and the Northern Rhodesian border, for example, is not great but the main lines of transport by-pass Sebungwe entirely. It is not surprising therefore that Northern Rhodesian labour should be sparsely concentrated in Sebungwe. We are dealing in fact with a situation hypothesized by Stouffer where the proportion of labour reaching any point is related to the number of intervening opportunities it has experienced and not directly to the distance travelled.[2] This requires examination in

---

[1] The relationship of local supplies of labour to local demand is important here. This is discussed later on pp. 228–31.

[2] Stouffer 1940. A preliminary attempt to correlate the index of concentration of Portuguese and Northern Rhodesian labour in districts along the railway routes leading into Southern Rhodesia from their main points of entry, with the accumulated number of African male adults employed in those districts (as a measure of opportunities) suggests that the logarithm of the index number varies directly with the accumulated number of Africans employed. Using the figures for Northern

much greater detail which would be out of place here. Nevertheless even with the crude techniques we have used, the influence of the position of labour centres relative to the point of inflow of labour on the distribution of labour in the Federation has been demonstrated.

The Local Supply of Labour

Yet another factor determining the distribution of labour in Southern Rhodesia must be the amount of local labour available for employment. In those districts where economic activities have prospered, the local African population has been able to find employment, as it were, on its own doorstep. In other districts, on the other hand, where enterprises have not developed the local people must seek wage-earning employment elsewhere. Where enterprises have been very successful the demand for labour has outgrown the local supply and employers have had to seek their labour wider afield. We would expect to find that in areas where the local supply outstrips the demand that a high proportion of Southern Rhodesian labour would be employed, whereas where the demand exceeds the supply then the Southern Rhodesian labour must compete with labour from other territories. In Table VII I have set out the indices of concentration for labour in the districts of Southern Rhodesia, classified according to the degree to which the local supply of labour exceeds or falls short of demand. The relationship between the demand and the proportion of local labour is clearly brought out in the index of concentration of Southern Rhodesian labour. Where there is a large excess of the supply over demand then the proportion of Southern Rhodesian labour is considerably above the national average, while the proportion of labour from other territories is considerably below the national average. Where there is a large excess of demand over supply the proportion of Southern Rhodesian labour employed is lower than the national average and the proportion of labour

Rhodesian labour, very approximately the logarithm of the index is equal to

$$2.64 - 0.0167 \, P$$

where P is the accumulated number of African male adults employed at some point along the railway line, expressed as a percentage of the accumulated number at the most distant point, i.e. at Umtali.

Table VII: *Concentration of Local and other Labour in Districts in which the Demand for Labour falls short of or exceeds the Local Supply*

(Index 100 = Normal concentration)

Type of District	Origin of Labour				
	S. Rhod.	N. Rhod.	Nyasa.	Port.	Other
High demand	82	118	121	105	136
Moderate demand	112	67	83	111	56
Balanced	128	118	63	77	63
Moderate supply	126	105	59	93	63
Large supply	179	17	36	33	32

Note: The demand for each district was computed by relating the number of African adult males employed in each district to the number of males aged 15–50 normally resident in that district. It was assumed that 65 per cent of the males in working ages would be available for wage employment. This is based on the territorial average computed in Table I of this chapter. The districts in which there was a much greater demand for labour than was available in the local population were Salisbury, Bulawayo, Goromonzi, Hartley, Lomagundi, Mazoe and Wankie. Districts with a moderate excess of demand over supply were Bubi, Gwelo, Makoni, Marandellas, Wedza, Urungwe, Umtali and Fort Victoria. Districts where the demand was roughly equal to the supply were Belingwe, Gwanda, Insiza, Melsetter, Mrewa, Nyamandhlovu and Selukwe. Districts where the supply was moderately in excess of demand were Chipinga, Darwin, Lupane, Matobo, Sipolilo and Nuanetsi. Districts in which the supply was greatly in excess of the demand were Bikita, Buhera, Bulalima-Mangwe, Charter, Chibi, Chilimanzi, Gutu, Inyanga, Mtoko, Ndanga, Nkai and Sebungwe.

Source: The employment statistics were derived from unpublished records made available through the courtesy of the Director of Census and Statistics. The population for each district was obtained from C.A.S.O. 1959a: Table I adjusted to May 1956 (census date). I have assumed that 21 per cent of the total *de jure* population are males aged 15 to 50.

from other territories higher than the national averages.[1] In Bulawayo and Bubi Districts the proportion of Southern Rhodesian labour employed appears to be much higher than we might have expected from the numbers available from within those districts related to the labour opportunities in them. I think the explanation is that each district abuts another in which labour opportunities are small.[2] In the districts of Mount Darwin and

[1] The index of concentration appears to vary directly as the logarithm of the ratio of the number of African males employed in a district to the number available. On the basis of the curve so derived it appears that the proportion of Southern Rhodesian Africans begins to fall lower than the territorial average only when the local supply begins to fall lower than 40 per cent of the demand.

[2] Bulalima-Mangwe and Nkai.

Sipolilo, on the other hand, the proportion of Southern Rhodesian labour employed is rather less than we might have thought considering the amount of labour available in relation to the employment opportunities in the districts. In both these districts a relatively large number of Africans from other territories is employed. We can only conclude here that the local Africans prefer the more remunerative employment in the industrial centres and leave local employment to incoming migrants.

There is no direct relationship between the supply of local labour and the origin of labour which may compete with it. In high demand areas there is naturally a high proportion of labour from outside Southern Rhodesia, and conversely in high supply areas a low proportion of outside labour. But whether Northern Rhodesian, Portuguese or Nyasaland labour predominates in other areas depends, I think, predominantly on the geographical location of the districts. For example, in districts where there is a moderate demand for labour in relation to the local supply there is a tendency for the discrepancy to be made good with Portuguese labour (Table VII, Index = 111 as against 67 for Northern Rhodesian labour and 83 for Nyasaland labour). The explanation for this is, I think, that the demand falls mostly in the Marandellas, Makoni and Umtali Districts,[1] and this is near the point of main inflow of Portuguese labour. Similarly most of the areas in which the local supply approximately balances the local demand, Nyamandhlovu, Insiza, Belingwe and Gwanda, are near the main point of inflow of Northern Rhodesian labour. The apparent decrease in the proportion of Nyasaland labour employed as the supply of local labour increases is also, I think, spurious: the true explanation is more likely to be a geographical one. In general the areas in which there is the greatest demand for labour lie near the main points of inflow of Nyasaland labour and the areas with least demand are most remote from this point.

The composition of the labour force, therefore, at any point in the territory appears to be determined by a number of

[1] About half of the opportunities fall in this area. The rest are distributed in Urungwe, i.e. the Kariba Dam site, the Midlands, i.e. Gwelo, Bubi and Fort Victoria, all of which except Urungwe are relatively isolated from main streams of labour supplies. In Urungwe there are proportionately large numbers of Northern Rhodesian and Nyasaland labour working on Kariba, but the numbers are not sufficient to affect the indices.

different factors. The degree to which the local demand for labour has outstripped the local supply determines the extent to which labour is likely to flow in from other territories.[1] The location of the point will determine the proportion of inflow of labour from each of the outside territories. General market factors will distort the geographically determined flow of labour by attracting less competitive labour into lower paid and less attractive occupations in industries wherever they are located. Finally the pattern may be influenced by a number of particular factors such as a tribal preference for a particular mine which has developed through historical associations, or the sort of patterns which may arise when domestic servants are taken from one territory to another when their employers are transferred. I have not been able to give a weighting to the various factors involved but I believe that it may be possible to erect a preliminary set of equations which could account approximately for the distribution of labour in Southern Rhodesia, and when the data becomes available, for Northern Rhodesia and Nyasaland as well.

Urbanization, Labour Migration and Social Change

Labour mobility and the changes in population distribution which accompany it are the natural concomitants of industrial development. Modern industrial organizations require a large number of workers and it is necessary for them to live near their place of work. The rise of industrialism in Western Europe thus has been characterized by a flow of population from the surrounding rural areas into the developing industrial towns. As industrialization proceeded the proportion living in urban agglomerations has increased. In South Central Africa superficially the situation appears to be similar, but there is a basic difference which has a marked effect on the growth of towns and consequently on rural development. In England during the early part of the nineteenth century, the growth of towns took place by what may be pictured as a series of concentric migratory contractions of rural populations into the larger industrial

---

[1] Presumably also from other areas in Southern Rhodesia where the local demand is not so high. Unfortunately there are no statistics which would enable us to study this internal movement of labour.

centres.[1] The larger industrial centres drew in towards themselves a number of workers and their families who were living
in the larger market towns on their perimeters. These towns in
turn made good their losses from surrounding villages, and the
villages from hamlets, the hamlets from the farms. Those being
drawn into the larger industrial centres were thus essentially
townsmen who had grown up in towns and who were accustomed to earning their living in towns. They themselves, and
their families, were quite dissociated from a rural way of life
and were in no way tied to a set of social relationships in rural
areas. Each step in the chain of movements in the larger town
represented a relatively small change for each person involved.
The farm hand took a job in the hamlet and was not much out
of touch with his kinsmen and friends amongst whom he had
lately lived. The hamlet dweller was already familiar with the
somewhat different pattern of life he would expect to find in the
village when he moved there.

In South Central Africa, however, industrialism and the type
of population concentration it demanded, was brought by
Europeans into a land where formerly the largest settlements
were villages, and where social relationships were fixed in terms
of a personally oriented kinship system. The tribal peoples were
inexorably drawn into the cash economy of which the industrial
system was a part, but they were drawn into it segmentally.
The tribesman needed money both for taxes and for the increasing range of goods it could buy. The industrialist needed the
labour of the tribesman: each served the interest of the other in
satisfying his needs. Initially the industrialist demanded few
skills from his labourers and they needed little training. The
labourer himself was still bound by social and religious ties to
his kinsmen in his rural area. From the beginning therefore the
contract between the employer and the African employee was
a temporary one: hence the *circulation* of labour rather than its
migration became its characteristic feature.

The distribution of labour at any one moment of time in
South Central Africa, thus, in contrast to England in the nineteenth century, is not the simple response of free labour to a
market situation in the sense that labour moves directly from

[1] Ashton 1955:15. For a general account of urbanization and its effects in South
and South Central Africa see Jones 1953.

a region or industry where there is an over-supply of labour to one where the demand is greater. Instead African workers are constantly migrating back and forth between industrial and tribal areas at intervals varying from a few months to several years. The pattern of distribution thus is maintained in spite of the movement, in the same way that the shape of an orographic cloud is maintained in spite of the passage of air through it. It is possible that migratory labour, because of its essential mobility, is more sensitive to changes in demand and supply so that the pattern of distribution is less affected by non-economic factors. The African tribesman seeking to satisfy definite monetary wants responds directly to market factors in taking employment at the nearest point, at the highest wage he can command, where there is least competition so that he can satisfy these wants quickly and with the least inconvenience and expenditure of effort to himself.

His participation in the cash economy in the towns (or on the farms), however, leaves his obligations and duties to his rural kinsmen and his general involvement in the tribal social system unchanged. He sees his ultimate security to lie amongst his tribesmen from whom he is able to claim support and succour in terms of his kinship relationship to many of them. He sees his position in the community ensured by his holding cultivation rights with them in a relationship which links him to his headman and his chief.[1] The cash he needs is to satisfy fringe wants not his basic subsistence needs. A tribesman can participate in both worlds by moving from one to the other: he can go off to town and earn the money he needs to buy cattle to enable his son to marry according to tribal custom, but he has no need to stay in town once his needs are met. There his labour is needed but the framework of social relationships in which it is set is part of a different world. In this way labour migration in South Central Africa is the product of a "plural" society: a consequence of the coexistence of two different modes of life in which a tribesman is able to play two disparate roles.

---

[1] Gluckman 1943; Orde Brown 1933:112; Watson 1958; International Labour Office 1958:138; van Velsen 1960:275; Gluckman 1960:66. This is characteristic of many tribal peoples who are becoming absorbed in a money economy. See Moore 1951:20ff. Quoting Raman, Moore writes (p. 25): "The Indian labourer is a peasant at heart and whenever he gets a chance he is likely to migrate back to the village."

J. Clyde Mitchell

The need for money is now universal among Africans however remote their tribal areas are from the industrial centres.
Everywhere Africans need money for a variety of purposes such
as for clothing, which takes up a large proportion of money
spent, for household goods such as the enamelware which is
replacing the traditional clay pottery, ploughs and hoes and
other agricultural implements, taxes, school and church fees,
and to an increasing extent for imported foodstuffs such as
sugar, wheaten flour, tea and coffee. Most of the traditional
exchanges of wealth such as at weddings and funerals are also
made in money nowadays.

At the same time the opportunities of earning money in the
tribal areas through exploiting their natural resources are
limited. The sale of crops yields an income in some areas, and
the sale of cattle and fish in others, but in general the majority
of Africans must look to wage-earning as the substantial source
of cash income.[1] The arrangement whereby Africans became
temporary workers at relatively low wage rates, but through
which they were able to meet their cash requirements, was no
doubt initially satisfactory to both tribesmen and entrepreneurs
alike. Entrepreneurs needed labour and were prepared to plan
on the assumption that this labour would of necessity be
unskilled. The tribesmen needed money and were prepared to
accept relatively rude living conditions and a rate of pay which
represented the marginal utility of their labour since the
economic support of their families and themselves in their old
age or infirmity was carried by the rural community.[2] But the
advantages to both parties began to fade when Africans came
to rely more and more upon their wages and less and less upon
subsistence production in the tribal areas. Entrepreneurs began
to demand greater skills, a lower turnover of labour and higher
productivity from their labour and African workers on their
part wanted higher wages and better living and working
conditions.

If we were dealing with a simple economic situation in which
labour mobility were a response to market factors alone, we

[1] Income and expenditure tables which show the main sources of money and
what it is used for, are given in studies such as Gluckman 1941; Allan and others
1948; Mitchell and Barnes 1950; E. L. B. and V. W. Turner 1955; Colson 1958;
White 1959.

[2] Hailey 1956:565; 1277-1278. Barber 1960:240; van Velsen 1960:277.

would have expected the distribution of the population between rural and urban areas gradually to have adjusted itself and reached some sort of balance. Instead the evidence we have shows that the circulation of labour between towns and tribal areas has been increasing from at least 1911. The fact that men seek wage employment when economic opportunities in their tribal areas are limited we can understand immediately. We need rather to explain why they continue to move between town and tribal area.

As in all social phenomena the causal nexus is complex, but we may approach it by looking at migration from both the tribal and urban points of view. Probably the most important single factor in the tribal area is the persistence of the tribal social system. The tribal social structure links together kinship relationships, cultivation rights, religious beliefs, allegiance to a chief and many other institutions in a single system so that each institution is inextricably involved in the other. The inter-dependence of these social institutions operates to provide a certain resilience to change since a change in one of them involves changes in the others. To some extent then it is difficult for a man to move out of the network of social relationships in which he is involved: from his point of view the town in which he works merely becomes a spatial extension of the tribal area. He is still involved in the affairs of his kinsmen in the rural area. He believes that the spirits of his ancestors centred in the rural areas still affect his doings in the town. He retains his cultivation rights in the tribal area for he knows that one day he will wish to return there. A man may have been forced out of a tribal area by his need for money, but he is constantly pulled back again by the network of social relationships and the social system out of which he has not escaped by mere absence.

The natural consequence of this is that if money opportunities arise locally tribesmen have the opportunity of remaining within the social system in which they have come to occupy positions and to play significant roles, and yet at the same time to earn the money they need. In these circumstances labour migration decreases. This is what happened amongst the Plateau Tonga where labour migration fell away as maize became an important cash-crop.[1] It happened also amongst the

[1] Colson 1958:64ff.

Luapula peoples where fishing became a lucrative activity
following the end of 1939–45 War,[1] and among the Mambwe
of Northern Rhodesia where the establishment of a locust
control unit provided opportunities for local wage employment.[2]

Most tribal communities however must face the alternative
and seek wage-earning employment in distant labour centres.
This involves the absence of many of the men in the most active
age groups for relatively long periods. The effects of this on
the rural community have often been exaggerated,[3] but it is
clear that it is impossible to generalize about them. Watson has
shown, for example, that amongst the Mambwe, by a sort of
division of labour amongst themselves, the kin-group has been
able to deploy some of its members in wage-earning in the
towns while others help the women to maintain the subsistence
economy.[4] They are thus able to achieve a higher standard of
living than would otherwise have been possible. van Velsen
has shown that among the Lakeside Tonga of Nyasaland a large
proportion of men is able to be absent because their subsistence
economy is based on cassava which needs less cultivation than
grain crops. The men absent in the towns are consulted in
village affairs and are looked upon as full members of the
community although they may have been away for many
years.[5] Amongst the Bemba of Northern Rhodesia on the other
hand, the young men play a vital part in pollarding the trees
to provide the material for the ash-planting system which the
Bemba practise. Among these people the absence of only a few
young men places an intolerable burden on those who remain,
and this leads to further migration and consequent severe impoverishment of the tribal areas.[6]

But even amongst the Bemba those in the towns look forward
to an eventual retirement in tribal areas.[7] The social structure
of village communities built up on the basis of kinship persists
in spite of the absence of a large proportion of the men. Garbett,

[1] Mitchell 1955:112.

[2] Watson 1958: 48–49. Barber 1960 documents this convincingly for Southern
and Northern Rhodesia.

[3] See for example Orde Brown 1933:100. Labour migration itself is a symptom
of a more general change in tribal life as it becomes involved in social, economic
and political relationships with the outside world.

[4] Watson 1958; 1959.   [5] van Velsen 1960:267.

[6] Richards 1939; 1940. Wilson 1941–2.

[7] Mitchell 1954a. McCulloch 1956: Table 39.

working in a Zezuru (Shona-speaking) community in Southern Rhodesia found that although the proportion of men away had increased considerably between 1948 and 1958, the basic kinship structure of the village has remained unchanged.[1]

The tribal system thus tends to accommodate itself to the new circumstances in which it finds itself. In many tribes a trip to the town has become a recognized symbol of a boy's becoming a man. He achieves adult status when he pays his first tax and goes off to earn his first wages: he shows by this that he is now an independent person in the tribe. In most tribes nearly every man has been out to work at some time in his lifetime. Thus labour migration has been accepted as part of the ordinary way of modern tribal life and is behaviour expected of young men when they reach adulthood.[2] The money returned by the migrants has become an important part of the economic life of the rural areas, providing for many of the consumer goods needed there and frequently providing the capital for whatever agricultural development has been possible in the tribal areas. The older men who return to their villages when their working days are over are able to take over the running of tribal affairs while the younger men in turn go out to earn money.

Part of the persistence of labour migration lies also in the conditions at the labour centres and the farms to which migrants go. Labour migration in South Central Africa is, as I have argued, an adjustment to a plural society. From the earliest days both European and African had assumed that the tribal areas was the normal place of residence for the African and that his stay in the towns was only temporary. The African's interest in town was primarily to earn money and he would return to his tribal area as soon as possible. This conception of the African as a temporary visitor to the industrial centres and to the farms

[1] Garbett 1960: Table 2.

[2] Mitchell 1959. Colson's description of the Tonga applies to many other tribes as well: "Labour migration is thought to be something for the young unmarried males who want adventure or seek to establish their independence of their kinsmen. It is not for married men who wish to be respected in their home communities." Colson 1958:65. Garbett found that 70·7 per cent of single men in the area he studied were absent in 1948 against 12·3 per cent of married men. In 1958 there were 83·4 per cent of the single men away and 49·6 per cent of the married. Garbett 1960: Table 8. Floyd 1959:28 reported that in Mrewa District 80·9 per cent of the single men were away but only 22·2 per cent of the married men were away.

was soon incorporated into the legal framework of the territory, and many of the laws dealing with Africans assume that his "normal" or "rightful" place of residence is in the tribal areas and that he is in the "European areas" only in the capacity of an employee.[1]

In the urban areas this point of view has led to inadequate family accommodation and a preponderance of housing for single men, a general lack of provision for old age care, inadequate provisions for land ownership and for invalidism.[2] These conditions have done nothing to encourage a settled family life in the towns. In Salisbury the proportion of men who have wives with them is 19 per cent[3] and in Bulawayo 31 per cent.[4] Many of the men in these towns of course are men who have never married, so that we cannot gauge directly from these figures the extent to which men have left their wives in rural areas. In a survey between 1951 and 1954 I found that in the mining towns of Northern Rhodesia where more married accommodation is available, of 4,436 married men 3,460 or 78 per cent had their wives with them, and 22 per cent had left their wives in the rural areas.[5] To some extent the proportion of men who have their wives with them in the towns is an index of the extent to which a pattern of social relationships is developing in towns which could counterbalance the social system in the tribal areas and serve to keep workers longer in towns. But several factors militate against this. The first is that since the employers in the past have been looking for unskilled manual labour, the tendency has been to attract young men particularly to industrial centres. There is usually a marked discrepancy of older men and of older children in the urban

[1] Mitchell 1956:698. Hailey 1956:565.

[2] For conditions in Southern Rhodesia see Ibbotson 1946. International Labour Office 1958:152 comments "Perhaps the migrant labour system largely survives not because of any impossibility of transforming Africans into stabilized workers, but mainly because Governments and employers have done nothing about it."

[3] C.A.S.O. 1959b. The numbers are not directly tabulated. I have estimated this proportion from the number of workers who are heads of households as against the number who are not.

[4] C.A.S.O. 1960:2.

[5] Unpublished preliminary results. These figures have not been adjusted for the differing sampling fractions in the various areas surveyed. Of the total 6,351 adult males in the survey 26·7 per cent had never married, 54·4 per cent were married and had their wives with them, 15·4 per cent were married but had left their wives in their tribal area, 3·1 per cent were widowers and 0·4 per cent were divorcees.

African communities. The age and sex structure of the towns therefore exhibits a characteristic "lop-sided hourglass" shape with a bulge on the side where there is an abnormally large proportion of younger men.[1] At the same time the circulation of the population between town and country leads to a considerable instability in residence, so that enduring patterns of social relationships on a neighbourhood basis cannot easily be built up. Lastly, the wide tribal hinterlands from which the growing industrial towns draw their labour means that their populations are heterogeneous and polyglot. This has a marked influence on the pattern of social relationships within which African town dwellers must live.

These features, combined with the legal restrictions on Africans living in towns, hamper the development of a well-entrenched social system for Africans in towns which would serve as a counter-balancing effect to the pull of the rural social system. In this way the nature of the urban communities acts rather in unison with the pull from the rural areas to bring labour migrants constantly back to the tribal homes.

There are thus several factors, economic, political and social, which maintain the circulation of labour in South Central Africa. These are, in different ways, the manifestation of a "plural" society—a society in which peoples pursue their activities in partially isolated social systems, but who derive mutual benefits from a segmental co-operation in the economic field. Moore in a general review writes:

> In view of the universal discontinuity between the non-industrial economies and full-scale urban industrialism, it is understandable that a great variety of transitional or compromise forms of economic activity have grown up in different areas. The compromises allow, at whatever level of efficiency and stability, the coexistence of traditional social relationships that formed the security-giving context of individual behaviour and some degree of economic modernization. The most common of these compromise devices, the one that appears time and again not only in colonial areas but in Latin America, China and India, is the migratory labour system.[2]

How long the circulation will persist of course depends on

[1] Diagrams are presented in Mitchell 1954a; McCulloch 1956; Bettison 1959 and relevant statistics in C.A.S.O. 1959b; 1960.
[2] Moore 1951:29.

J. Clyde Mitchell

changes in the larger social system of which it is a part. Under certain circumstances, no doubt, it could continue for ever. There are certain basic trends, however, which tend to slow down the circulation of the population between town and country. These are that the population is increasing rapidly while at the same time the standard of living is rising. The birth rate of the African population of Southern Rhodesia in 1953–5 was 44·8 while the death rate was 14·4 per thousand.[1] In Northern Rhodesia the birth rate in 1950 was 56·8 per thousand while the death rate was 32·2 per thousand.[2] This suggests a rate of natural increase of the order of 2·5 to 3·0 per cent per annum, which implies the doubling of the population every generation. The probabilities are that the birth rate is not likely to change for some years to come[3] while the death rate, due to improved medical facilities and a decline in the prejudice against using them, will decrease. Thus we can expect a sustained, if not an accelerated rate of population increase over, say, the next 25 years.

At the same time the level of consumption in both rural areas and urban areas is rising, and it is clear that the tribal areas which even at present levels of consumption are over-crowded, will no longer be able to support greater populations. It seems inevitable thus that production in the rural areas must be increased to balance industrial development in the towns. Industry and rural development at present compete for the same working population—that of the able-bodied and physically active young men. One of the keys to increased production in both rural and urban areas is the division of labour between those who have skills in the industrial sector, and those who have skills in farming: this implies an investment of time and training and subsequently the maximum use of labour where it is most productive.

The extent to which there has been a slowing down of the

[1] C.A.S.O. 1959b: Table IV.
[2] C.A.S.O. 1952:8. See also Chapter 4 in this book.
[3] It is commonly assumed that the birth rate, as in Britain, will decline when standards of living improve and urbanization increases. The evidence we have, however, is that this happens when there is a considerable shift in the values surrounding the position of family relationships in the social system and the significance of material goods as symbols of prestige in a community. The initial response to improved social conditions therefore tends to be an increased rather than a lowered birth rate.

circulation of labour in response to the population pressure in the reserves and the more efficient use of labour in towns is difficult to determine. Some direct attempts to do this have been made by trying to gauge the degree to which Africans in towns are becoming permanently "urbanized".[1] Human beings react to diverse social and personal pressures and move in and out of town and tribal areas in response to them. Consequently there seems to be no foolproof way of foretelling how many are going to remain in town over a given period, and how many will return to their tribal homes. We know that a substantial proportion of African men and women in the towns of Northern Rhodesia, for example, have spent more than 10 years away from their tribal areas.[2] We also know that a substantial proportion of the same people have spent more than two-thirds of their adult lives in town rather than in their tribal areas[3] and have therefore presumably chosen urban life, in preference to rural life. This is indirect evidence of how people have behaved in the past. Substantially fewer, however, see themselves living in the towns for ever.[4]

The danger of allowing a permanent population to develop in the towns in an economy based almost entirely on mineral extraction has been in the mind of the Northern Rhodesian Government since economic recession in the early thirties.[5] At that time the African urban population had fallen from 32,000 in November 1930 to 9,300 in June 1933.[6] Thus some 23,000 were able to slip back unobtrusively to their tribal homes and stay there until things improved. But a permanently urbanized population could be an embarrassment

---

[1] Wilson 1941–2; Mitchell 1954a; 1956; McCulloch 1956.

[2] At Ndola the percentage as 45·8; on the Roan Antelope Copper Mine 40·5; at Luanshya 42·2; at Broken Hill in 1954, 46·0. (Mitchell 1956:703.) In Livingstone it was 47·1. (McCulloch 1956:29.)

[3] At Ndola the percentage was 40·3; on the Roan Antelope Mine 26·7; at Luanshya 44·6; at Broken Hill in 1954, 32·9. (Mitchell 1956:703.) In Livingstone it was 32·8. (McCulloch 1956.)

[4] The percentage of men who looked upon themselves as likely to live in town for the rest of their days were: at Ndola 12·7; on the Roan Antelope Copper Mine 6·5; at Luanshya 7·9; at Broken Hill in 1954, 6·6. (Mitchell 1956:708.) In Livingstone it was 10·1. (McCulloch 1956:59.)

[5] Hailey 1956:1390. These fears were echoed again recently. See Northern Rhodesian Government 1959b:2.

[6] Gann 1955:7. Macmillan 1949:184 gives the figures from 31,942 in 1929 to 7,523 in July 1932.

in the future if it could not melt away quite so unobtrusively.[1] I know of no explicit statement of policy in this matter, nevertheless it is clear that the Northern Rhodesian Government envisages an African population permanently resident in towns.[2] In 1957, Article 43 of the Northern Rhodesian Order in Council was amended to allow Africans to lease plots in urban areas, so that they may now build and own houses in town.[3] At the same time it has introduced a Housing Loan Scheme whereby Africans are able to borrow money to build their own homes.

Yet the extent to which Northern Rhodesia still relies on tribal areas as a reservoir into which surplus workers and their families may be poured when they are no longer needed in town, is strikingly illustrated by the fact that when the newly founded mine at Bancroft went out of production following the fall in copper prices in 1957, only 380, or 17·5 per cent, of the 2,164 African employees found work on other mines. The remaining 1,784 with their families, making in all 4,500 persons, were repatriated to their tribal homes.[4] A total of 4,500 persons no doubt scattered over many tribal areas had little impact on them, but the wider implications are clear.

Development plans should, of course, take their consequential ramifications into account, but planning authorities do not always appear to do so. One of the more ambitious schemes of rural development, the Southern Rhodesian Government intention to grant individual land-holdings to Africans in the reserves, clearly recognizes that the carrying capacity of the reserves is limited and that there must be a flow of excess population from the land to the towns.[5] At present it is not certain that industrial development will be able to sustain its

---

[1] Hailey 1956:1390. See also Orde Brown 1933:112ff.

[2] The policy of the mining industry, however, is to foster the "stabilization of labour by reducing labour turn-over and encouraging long-service, while at the same time avoiding 'detribalization' and urbanization". It hopes to achieve this paradoxical aim by paying pensions to long-service employees and encouraging them to return to their tribal areas when they retire. See Prain 1956:307.

[3] Northern Rhodesian Government 1958:iv.

[4] Northern Rhodesian Government 1959b:1.

[5] Southern Rhodesian Government 1955:14. Floyd 1959:37. The Southern Rhodesian Government has introduced home ownership schemes in the larger towns and has taken action to reduce the flow of non-Federal Africans into the towns.

rate of expansion to keep pace with the numbers who are likely to seek employment when the tribal areas have reached capacity. Many industries have been able to hold their own on a world market only because of low labour costs. If these increase, as they are bound to as standards of living rise, the possibility is that industry will use its labour more efficiently and reduce the number employed. This happened in the mining industry of Northern Rhodesia where the African labour force was dropped from 52,299 in 1955 to 37,923 in 1958,[1] the majority of which decline was on the Copperbelt. Production during the same period has been maintained: the earnings of the mineworkers increased from an average of £124 to an average of £200 per African worker per annum.[2] This has meant not only a concentration of the purchasing power in the hands of a smaller proportion of Africans, but also that some 14,000 African workers have been obliged to seek work in other industries or to go back to a semi-subsistence existence in their tribal homes. This clearly runs counter to the process by which the circulation of labour may finally be reduced.

The circulation of labour thus seems to be a phenomenon of a different order from its distribution. We are able to explain the salient features of the pattern of distribution of labour by means of a few general economic principles. We need assume little more than that in seeking employment, Africans tend to maximize their benefits they are able to derive from a given market situation. The distribution of labour in industries and in regions either in terms of distance from the point of inflow, or in terms of local opportunities, is nothing more than an expression of this. Departures from the general rules appear to be explained by particular circumstances rather than by principles of another order.

The circulation of labour, however, is essentially, I have argued, a feature of a "plural" society in which African workers participate in the economic sector of the larger Central African society, and are thus involved segmentally as employees only in social relationships with Europeans. At the same time they are involved in a tribal social system centred in the reserves from which they come. They are able to satisfy their cash needs and

[1] Northern Rhodesian Government 1959a: Appendix 1:57.
[2] Northern Rhodesian Chamber of Mines, 1959.

fulfil their social obligations by circulating between the two areas.

Labour circulation does not depend entirely on economic conditions: it is rather part of a larger totality in which Africans try to solve the problem of meeting two sets of opposed obligations by participating segmentally in each—in the one as a migrant worker and in the other as a part-time tribesman. From this we may argue that although improvements in the economic status of Africans in both rural and urban areas are undoubtedly a *necessary* condition for the slowing down of the tempo of the circulation of labour, it is by no means a *sufficient* condition. Social and political factors are involved also. Moore writes, "Industry comes wrapped in a bundle. Although it may initially enter a new culture in the form of a few isolated strands, its substantial development depends upon a roughly parallel or collateral development of the whole complex." [1] Functional holism may be taken too far, but it seems certain that the vision of an African Birmingham in the midst of a tribal Arcadia is bound surely to fade.

BIBLIOGRAPHY

ALLAN, W. *et al.*
  1948 *Land Holding and Land Usage among the Plateau Tonga of the Mazabuka District*, Rhodes-Livingstone Paper No. 14.
ASHTON, T. S.
  1955 *An Economic History of England: The Eighteenth Century*, London, Methuen & Co.
BARBER, W. J.
  1960 "Economic Rationality and Behaviour Patterns in an Underdeveloped Area: A Case Study of African Economic Behaviour in the Rhodesias", *Economic Development and Cultural Change*, VIII, 237–251.
BETTISON, D.
  1959 *Numerical Data on African Dwellers in Lusaka, Northern Rhodesia*, Rhodes-Livingstone Communication No. 16, Lusaka.
CENTRAL AFRICAN STATISTICAL OFFICE
  1952 *The 1950 Demographic Survey of the African Population of Northern Rhodesia*, Salisbury.
  1957 *Report of the Census of Africans in Employment taken on 8th May 1956*, Item No. 9-6098, Salisbury.
  1959a *The 1953–1955 Demographic Sample Survey of Indigenous African Population of Southern Rhodesia*, Salisbury.

---

[1] Moore 1951:188.

Labour and Population Movements in Central Africa

1959b *First Report of the Salisbury African Demographic Survey August–September 1958*, Salisbury.
1959c *Report on the Census of Industrial Production 1957–8*, Salisbury.
1960 *Report on Bulawayo African Demographic Survey held in May 1959*, Salisbury.

COLSON, E.
1958 *Marriage and the Family among the Plateau Tonga of Northern Rhodesia*, Manchester. Manchester University Press for Rhodes-Livingstone Institute.

FLOYD, B. N.
1959 "Changing Pattern of African Land Use in Southern Rhodesia", *Rhodes-Livingstone Journal*, xxv, 20–39.

GANN, L. H.
1954 "The End of the Slave Trade in British Central Africa: 1889–1912", *Rhodes-Livingstone Journal*, xvi, 27–51.
1955 "The Northern Rhodesian Copper Industry and the World of Copper: 1923–1952", *Rhodes-Livingstone Journal*, xviii, 1–18.
1958 *The Birth of a Plural Society*, Manchester. Manchester University Press for Rhodes-Livingstone Institute.

GARBETT, G. KINGSLEY
1960 *Growth and Change in a Shona Ward*. Occasional Paper from the University College of Rhodesia and Nyasaland. African Studies No. 1.

GLUCKMAN, M.
1941 *Economy of the Central Barotse Plain*, Rhodes-Livingstone Paper No. 7.
1943 *Essays on Lozi Land and Royal Property*, Rhodes-Livingstone Paper No. 10.
1960 "Tribalism in Modern British Central Africa", *Cahiers d'Etudes Africaines*, VI Section: Sciences Economiques et Sociales: Ecole Pratique des Hautes Etudes: Sorbonne, 55–70.

GULLIVER, P.
1957 "Nyakyusa Labour Migration", *Rhodes-Livingstone Journal*, xxi, 32–63.

HAILEY, LORD
1950 *Native Administration in the British African Territories. Part II. Central Africa: Zanzibar, Nyasaland, Northern Rhodesia*, London, H.M.S.O.
1956 *An African Survey: Revised Edition*, London, Oxford University Press.

IBBOTSON, P.
1946 "Urbanization in Southern Rhodesia", *Africa*, xvi, 73–82.

INTERNATIONAL LABOUR OFFICE
1958 *African Labour Survey*, Studies and Reports. New Series, No. 48, Geneva: International Labour Office.

JONES, J. D. RHEINALLT
1953 "The Effects of Urbanization in South and Central Africa", *African Affairs*, lvii, 37–44.

MACMILLAN, W. M.
1949 *Africa Emergent*, Harmondsworth, Middlesex.

J. Clyde Mitchell

McCulloch, M.
1956 *A Social Survey of the African Population of Livingstone*, Rhodes-Livingstone Paper No. 26.

Mason, P.
1959 *The Birth of a Dilemma*, London, Oxford University Press, for Institute of Race Relations.

Mitchell, J. C.
1954a *African Urbanization in Ndola and Luanshya*, Rhodes-Livingstone Communication No. 6.

1954b "The Distribution of African Labour by Area of Origin on the Coppermines of Northern Rhodesia", *Rhodes-Livingstone Journal*, xiv, 30–6.

1955 "The Tribes in the Towns" in Brelsford, W. V., *The Tribes of Northern Rhodesia*, Lusaka, Government Printer.

1956 "Urbanization, Detribalization and Stabilization in Southern Africa: A Problem of Definition and Measurement", in Forde, D. (ed.), *Social Implications of Industrialization and Urbanization in Africa South of the Sahara*, U.N.E.S.C.O. Tensions and Technology Series, 693–711.

1959 "Labour Migration in Africa South of the Sahara: The Causes of Labour Migration", *Bulletin of the Inter-African Labour Institute*, vi, 1: 12–46.

Mitchell, J. C., and Barnes, J. A.
1950 *The Lamba Village: A Report on a Social Survey*, Communication No. 24 (n.s.), School of African Studies, University of Cape Town.

Moore, W. E.
1951 *Industrialization and Labour*, New York, Cornell University Press.

Niddrie, D.
1954 "The Road to Work: A Survey of the Influence of Transport on Migrant Labour in Central Africa", *Rhodes-Livingstone Journal*, xv, 31–42.

Northern Rhodesian Chamber of Mines
1959 *Yearbook of the Northern Rhodesian Chamber of Mines*, Kitwe.

Northern Rhodesian Government
1951 *Census 1951: The European, Coloured and Asiatic Population and Africans in Employment as disclosed by the Census taken on 8th May 1951*, Lusaka, Government Printer.

1958 *African Affairs. Annual Report for the Year 1957*, Lusaka, Government Printer.

1959a *Annual Report of the Department of Labour for the Year 1958*, Lusaka, Government Printer.

1959b *African Affairs. Annual Report for the Year 1958*, Lusaka, Government Printer.

Nyasaland Government
1936 *Report of the Committee appointed by His Excellency the Governor to Enquire into Emigrant Labour, 1935*, Zomba, Government Printer.

1959a *Report of an Economic Survey of Nyasaland 1958–1959*, Zomba, Government Printer.

Labour and Population Movements in Central Africa

1959b *Report of the Labour Department for the Year 1958*, Zomba, Government Printer.

ORDE BROWN, G. ST. J.
1933 *The African Labourer*, London, Oxford University Press, for International African Institute.

PRAIN, R. L.
1956 "The Stabilization of Labour in the Rhodesian Copperbelt", *African Affairs*, LV, 305–12.

READ, M.
1942 "Migrant Labour in Africa and its Effects on Tribal Life", *International Labour Review*, XIV, 605–31.

RHODESIAN INSTITUTE OF AFRICAN AFFAIRS
1958 *The Progress of Africans in Southern Rhodesia*, Bulawayo.

RICHARDS, A. I.
1939 *Land, Labour and Diet in Northern Rhodesia*, London, Oxford University Press, for International African Institute.
1940 *Bemba Marriage and Present Economic Conditions*, Rhodes-Livingstone Paper No. 4.

SCOTT, P.
1954a "Migrant Labour in Southern Rhodesia", *Geographical Review*, XLIV, 29–48.
1954b "The Role of Northern Rhodesia in African Labour Migration", *Geographical Review*, XLIV, 432–4.

SOUTHERN RHODESIAN GOVERNMENT
1949 *Report on the Census of Population of Southern Rhodesia held on 7th May 1946*, Salisbury, Government Printer.
1954 *Census of Population 1951*, Salisbury, Government Printer.
1955 *What the Native Land Husbandry Act means to the Rural African and to Southern Rhodesia: A Five-Year Plan that will Revolutionize African Agriculture*, Salisbury, Government Printer.
1958 *Report of the Labour Department for the year ended 31 December 1957*, Salisbury, Government Printer.
1959 *Report of the Secretary for Labour, Social Welfare and Housing for the year ended 31 December 1958*, Salisbury, Government Printer.

STOUFFER, S. A.
1940 "Intervening Opportunities: A Theory relating Mobility and Distance", *American Sociological Review*, V, 845–67.

TURNER, E. L. B. and V. W.
1955 "Money Economy among the Mwinilunga Ndembu. A Study of some Individual Cash Budgets", *Rhodes-Livingstone Journal*, XVIII, 19–37.

VAN VELSEN, J.
1960 "Labour Migration as a Positive Factor in the Continuity of Tonga Tribal Society", *Economic Development and Cultural Change*, VIII, 265–278.

WATSON, W.
1958 *Tribal Cohesion in a Money Economy*, Manchester. Manchester University Press for Rhodes-Livingstone Institute.

J. Clyde Mitchell

WATON, W.
  1959 "Labour Migration in Africa South of the Sahara: Migrant Labour
         and Detribalization", *Bulletin of the Inter-Africa Labour Institute*, VI,
         2: 8–32.
WHITE, C. M. N.
  1959 *A Preliminary Survey of Luvale Rural Economy*, Rhodes-Livingstone
         Paper No. 29.
WILSON, G.
  1941–2 *An Essay on the Economics of Detribalization in Northern Rhodesia*,
         Rhodes-Livingstone Papers Nos. 5 and 6.

13

The Towns of Tropical Africa

R. W. STEEL

Introduction

"Towns will certainly be the crux of the native problem in the tropics," wrote Julian Huxley in *Africa View*, his record of a journey in East Africa in 1929 and 1930.[1] His foresight was remarkable, especially as he could not anticipate the effects of the Second World War and its aftermath. During the last quarter of a century, and particularly since the end of the war, there has been a very rapid growth in the size and population of towns in many parts of tropical Africa, and Africans are increasingly remaining in towns for long periods and even becoming permanent residents in them. Towns have in fact become, in the words of the East Africa Royal Commission Report of 1955, "the centres of social and intellectual life, of economic enterprise and of political activity".[2]

The emergence of the town as a form of settlement pattern is something new over much of tropical Africa, and towns have of recent years received considerable attention not only from political leaders and government departments but also from sociologists, economists, geographers, statisticians and others. I.N.C.I.D.I., the International Institute of Differing Civilizations, devoted its annual meeting in 1952 to a discussion of "the 'pull' exerted by urban and industrial centres in countries in course of industrialization".[3] The Colonial Office Summer

[1] *Africa View*, London, 1931, 217.
[2] *East Africa Royal Commission, 1953–1955, Report*, Cmd. 9475, H.M.S.O., 250.
[3] *Record of the XXVIIth meeting held in Florence on the 4th, 5th, 6th, 7th & 8th June, 1952*, I.N.C.I.D.I. (International Institute of Differing Civilizations), Brussels, 1952.

Conference of 1954 was concerned with industrial development and town growth; it was said to have been the first time that such subjects had ever been studied intensively by British colonial administrators.[1] The East Africa Royal Commission of 1953–5 devoted much time and space to a study of the "conditions for urban development".[2] In 1956 U.N.E.S.C.O., with the collaboration of bodies such as the International African Institute, published a comprehensive report on the social implications of industrialization and urbanization in Africa south of the Sahara.[3] Detailed papers and special reports on individual territories and towns have also appeared, so providing a growing volume of information on the typical problems of the towns of tropical Africa.

At this stage, therefore, it seems appropriate to attempt a general appraisal of the situation, approached from the standpoint of the geographer, with a stress on the facts of distribution and their implications and on the significance of the town in the study and understanding of the African landscape today. The emphasis will be on British areas, especially on those of which the writer has personal knowledge, though there will also be references to the broadly similar trends and influences that can be observed elsewhere in Africa, especially in those French and Belgian areas of comparable economic and political development.

The African Town

The distinction between town and village, in the Western sense, depends largely upon difference in economic organization and administrative functions, and some of these considerations apply, though often with significant modifications, to town and country in tropical Africa. E. A. Boateng, for example, has shown that in Ghana the function that tradition-

[1] Colonial Office Summer Conference on African Administration, Sixth session, 23rd August–4th September 1954. Industrial development and town growth (African No. 1183). The report, though printed, is marked "not for publication" but can be consulted in certain libraries with good collections of African literature.

[2] *Op. cit.*, 200–50. See also "Report of the Conference on urban problems in East and Central Africa held at Ndola, Northern Rhodesia, in February, 1958', *Journal of African Administration*, x, 1958, 182–251.

[3] *Social Implications of Industrialization and Urbanization in Africa south of the Sahara*, U.N.E.S.C.O., 1956.

ally distinguishes a town from a village is the social one:[1] a town is a settlement which is the seat of a chief, so that it is the political, administrative and social centre of tribal life. A village is usually an offshoot of a town, and though it may have its own administrative head, it continues to look to the parent town as the source of its social, political and spiritual life. But many of the distinctions and criteria of urban geography in Western Europe and North America cannot be fairly or directly applied to a study of towns in tropical Africa with their vastly different historical, social and economic conditions.[2] Moreover it must be recognized that for most of tropical Africa there is a lack of the documentary information and statistical data that can be taken for granted in many other parts of the world. In the present state of knowledge, reliance may need to be placed upon very indifferent and quite inadequate criteria if any general picture of the pattern of urban development is to be obtained. The fact that detail is now available for a few towns, such as Accra and Jinja or, in non-British territories, Elisabethville, Libreville or Thiès, only underlines the extreme paucity of the information for African urban areas as a whole.[3] In a different way, the contrast between a general survey and a more detailed regional analysis is emphasized by the juxtaposition of the present essay with the paper by N. C. Mitchel on the Yoruba towns of western Nigeria.

[1] E. A. Boateng, "Recent changes in settlement in south-east Gold Coast" *Transactions and Papers, 1955*, Institute of British Geographers, XXI, 1955, 157–69. There is also some discussion of urban functions in West Africa in W. B. Morgan, "The 'grassland towns' of the Eastern Region of Nigeria", *Transactions and Papers, 1957*, Institute of British Geographers, XXIII, 1957, 213–24.

[2] See, for example, A. E. Smailes, *The Geography of Towns*, London, 1953, and "Some reflections on the geographical description and analysis of townscapes", *Transactions and Papers, 1955*, Institute of British Geographers, XXI, 1955, 99–115; and G. Taylor, *Urban Geography; a Study of Site, Evolution, Pattern and Classification in Villages, Towns and Cities*, London, 1949. Among works that deal specifically with African towns, reference may be made to J. Dresch, "Villes congolaises: étude de géographie urbaine et sociale", *Le Revue de Géographie Humaine et d'Ethnologie*, I, 1948, 3; K. M. Buchanan and J. C. Pugh, *Land and People in Nigeria*, 1955, 63 et seq.; and M. Heymans, *L'urbanisme au Congo Belge*, Brussels, 1951.

[3] Ioné Acquah, *Accra Survey: a Social Survey of the Capital of Ghana*, London, 1958; C. & R. Sofer, *Jinja Transformed: a Social Survey of a Multi-racial Society*, Kampala, 1955; Ann E. Larimore, *The Alien Town: Patterns of Settlement in Busoga, Uganda. An Essay in Cultural Geography*, Chicago, 1958; Alice Chapelier, *Elisabethville: essai de géographie humaine*, Brussels, 1957; Guy Lasserre, *Libreville: la ville et sa région. Etude de géographie humaine*, Paris, 1958; G. Savonnet, *La ville de Thiès: étude de géographie urbaine*, St. Louis, 1953.

R. W. Steel

For initial working purposes, it is not easy to do better than to take crude population totals as an indication of the number of towns and the degree of urbanization in a particular area. But, as in Europe, there is as yet no agreed figure for systematic application throughout tropical Africa. Thus in the Belgian Congo and Ruanda-Urundi a town is a non-agricultural centre with 1,000 or more inhabitants.[1] In the Nigerian census of 1931, as R. M. Prothero has pointed out,[2] the division between urban and rural was fixed at 2,000: but for the 1952-3 census of Nigeria, towns were defined as "those which are considered by the Residents of the various provinces to be urban centres, each containing a population of 5,000 or more in a compact area". But quite apart from the arbitrary nature of any particular figure, numerical differentiation is far from satisfactory, for there are many occasions when the special functions of a settlement give it legitimate urban status, despite the small size of its population. Thus, as in the Ghanaian example already given, a chief's headquarters ought, in terms of its functions, to be enumerated as a town, even though it may have few permanent inhabitants or imposing buildings. Similarly some district headquarters, established by a European administration, may never attain high population rank, yet they clearly provide the areas and peoples surrounding them with those administrative and social services that are rightly associated with towns. Usually, of course, such administrative centres acquire other functions—commercial, educational, cultural, and the like—and frequently they become the largest concentrations of population in the districts that they serve. Herein, indeed, is one of the major difficulties of making a functional classification of urban settlements in tropical African towns. So many of them are multifunctional and so few have really specialized functions. In this, as in several other respects, they contrast markedly with towns elsewhere in the world; and these differences must constantly be kept in mind if the student of African towns is to appreciate fully their peculiarities and their special features.

[1] G. T. Trewartha and W. Zelinsky, "The population geography of Belgian Africa", *Annals of the Association of American Geographers*, XLIV, 1954, 176.

[2] R. M. Prothero, "The population census of Northern Nigeria, 1952: problems and results", *Population Studies*, X, 1956, 179.

The Towns of Tropical Africa

African Towns in the Past

Nowhere are the essential contrasts between urban development in tropical Africa and that of Western Europe better shown than by a consideration of the African towns of the past. The great majority of the towns of Africa today owe their origin in large measure—at least outside West Africa—to non-African initiative. This general statement is not invalidated by the existence of ancient cities and towns on and near the shores of the Indian Ocean, such as Zanzibar, since these were mostly Arab creations that were concerned with trade across the Indian Ocean.

In West Africa the situation is rather different and there are several cases of long-established towns founded by the indigenous peoples. The outstanding examples are those of the Yoruba of western Nigeria, discussed by N. C. Mitchel elsewhere in this volume.[1] Towns like Abeokuta, Ife, Iwo, Ogbomosho, Oshogbo, Oyo and, above all, Ibadan, have for many years played a leading role in the development of the Yoruba states, and in the 1952 census 47 per cent of the population of the Western Region was recorded as living in settlements of 5,000 or more inhabitants.[2] By contrast the Ibo, the dominant tribe east of the Niger, have never been town-dwellers and only 14 per cent of the population of the Eastern Region were classed as urban in the 1953 census.

Northern Nigeria, though with an urban population of only 9 per cent in 1952, has, like Yorubaland, its old-established towns, the centres of the Moslem emirates, such as Kano (130,000 inhabitants in the city in 1952, with perhaps 2,000,000 or more regarding it as their capital), Katsina (53,000), Sokoto (48,000), Zaria (54,000) and Yerwa-Maiduguri (55,000). Kano's history is known to go back for many centuries,[3] during which the city itself appears to have changed little,

[1] See also C. D. Forde, *The Yoruba-speaking Peoples of South-Western Nigeria* (Ethnographic Survey of Africa, London, 1951). Reference is made to some of the special features of the towns of West Africa in R. W. Steel, "Some problems of population in British West Africa", in R. W. Steel and C. A. Fisher (editors), *Geographical Essays on British Tropical Lands*, London, 1956, 19–50, especially 39–48.

[2] These figures and others quoted in this paragraph and elsewhere are taken from the Reports of the Nigerian Census, Lagos, 1953–6.

[3] See M. F. Perham, *Native Administration in Nigeria*, Oxford, 1933, especially pp. 83–6.

except for the wider roads driven through in places and for the large new buildings that are to some extent harmonized with their setting. In 1824 Hugh Clapperton, expecting "a city of surprising grandeur" [1] from the "flourishing description" given by the Arabs, was disappointed to find "the houses nearly a quarter of a mile from the walls, and in many parts scattered into detached groups, between large stagnant pools of water". But he noted the busy market in this "great emporium of the kingdom of Haussa" and estimated the population to be "from 30,000 to 40,000 resident inhabitants, of whom more than one-half are slaves": to these there had to be added the "strangers who come here in crowds during the dry months from all parts of Africa, from the Mediterranean and the Mountains of the Moon, and from Sennar and Ashantee". Thirty years later Kano was visited by another traveller, Heinrich Barth, who estimated the population as nearly 60,000 and was greatly impressed by this "central point of commerce" and "great storehouse of information". [2]

Outside Nigeria there were very few other towns in West Africa up to the beginning of the twentieth century. Along the edge of the Sahara, where the nomads and traders of the desert met the more settled peoples of the Sudan, there were commercial centres like Ségou, Gao and Timbuktu. Ségou was a Bambara town of considerable age, the capital of the Bambara kingdom from 1660 to 1861. Gao, the capital of the Songhai Empire, was founded in the ninth or tenth century, but never recovered from its occupation by the Moors in 1591. Timbuktu, established by the Tuareg during the twelfth century, was regularly visited by traders and scholars from all over North Africa, including Egypt, from about 1300. It had a population of 45,000 in the sixteenth century, when it was visited by Leo Africanus, but like Gao suffered from Moorish and later Fulani conquest. The French explorer Rene Caillié was bitterly disappointed by the squalor and ugliness of the town in 1828, and Barth, who spent six months in Timbuktu in 1853–4 and

[1] The quotations are taken from D. Denham, H. Clapperton and W. Oudney, *Narrative of Travels and Discoveries in Northern and Central Africa in the Years 1822, 1823 and 1824*, London, 1826.

[2] Heinrich Barth, *Travels and Discoveries in North and Central Africa, 1849–55*, vol. II, 1857–8, 96; quoted in R. M. Prothero, "Heinrich Barth and the Western Sudan", *Geographical Journal*, cxxiv, 1958, 326–39.

completed a plan of the town, described "this mysterious city" as a "desert place" and noted that, unlike Kano, it had no manufacturing but depended almost wholly upon trade in gold, salt and kola nuts. When the town was occupied by the French in 1894 it was ruined and half-empty, and its population today is only about 6,000.

Kumasi, the headquarters of the paramount chief of the Ashanti, one of the more powerful and warlike of the tribes of the interior, was known as a considerable town from the time of the first European contacts with the Gold Coast. T. E. Bowdich, who visited it in 1817, wrote that "the average resident population of Coomassie is not more than from 12 to 15,000",[1] but during the nineteenth century it suffered many vicissitudes and immediately after the seventh and last of the Anglo-Ashanti wars, that of 1900, the first census of Ashanti (1901) returned a population of only 3,000.[2] Kumasi's great twentieth-century growth—from nearly 19,000 in 1911 to 35,829 in 1931, 70,705 in 1948, and possibly 90,000 today—is due to many different factors, including the general economic development of Ghana, the spread of a communications network, and the extension of government services: in other words, to the activities of the British administration and of European commercial concerns as well as to the work of the Ashanti people themselves. The same admixture of European and African achievement can be seen today in most other sizeable West African towns with important administrative or commercial functions. Accra, for example, grew up on the site of a small fishing settlement, not far from the stronghold of Christiansborg Castle, purchased by the British from the Danes in 1867. With the transference of government headquarters in 1876 from Cape Coast Castle to Accra, and with the establishment of cocoa farming in the interior to the north of the town, its growth has been considerable and, at times, very rapid, so

---

[1] T. E. Bowdich, *Mission from Cape Coast Castle to Ashantee*, 1817. Joseph Dupuis in his *Journal of a Residence in Ashantee*, 1824, it should be noted, estimated Kumasi's population at more than 200,000—an obvious exaggeration. See R. W. Steel, "The towns of Ashanti: a geographical study", *Compte Rendu de XVIᵉ Congrès International de Géographie, Lisbonne, 1949*, Lisbon, 1952, 81–93. See also K. A. J. Nyarko, "The development of Kumasi", *Bulletin of the Ghana Geographical Association*, IV, 1959, 3–8.

[2] R. W. Steel, *ibid.*, 85.

that today it has more than 150,000 inhabitants and is the scene of much new building, especially since Ghana became independent in 1957.[1] The same concentration of urban growth in modern times and during a period of European administration can be seen in Nigeria at Lagos, where population has spilled over from the overcrowded island in the lagoon to the mainland at Apapa, Iddo and elsewhere. Similar tendencies are visible in Sierra Leone at Freetown which was first established in 1787 as a settlement for liberated slaves on a previously uninhabited site.

Elsewhere in tropical Africa the general picture is very different from that of parts of West Africa. Away from the coasts there are few large settlements. This is especially true of those areas where lawlessness prevailed and where formal government, and law and order, were established only during the latter years of the nineteenth century. J. Dresch has noted that in the Congo basin the Bantu nowhere built settlements of greater size or complexity than the agricultural village before the coming of the European;[2] and G. T. Trewartha and W. Zelinsky emphasize that every one of "the 167 towns of the Belgian Congo and the 14 of Ruanda-Urundi was located, planned and built by Belgians with Africans playing a passive role".[3] Indeed over most of tropical Africa there seem to have been relatively few villages in the past; the usual pattern of settlement was the isolated group of huts, or, more commonly, the scattering of homesteads throughout the countryside, especially in districts that were not immediately adjacent to the routes followed by slavers or other traders. Even today nucleated settlement remains a comparative rarity over many parts of tropical Africa, particularly in the Congo basin, East Africa, Ethiopia and Sudan.[4]

European penetration of the interior—with all its consequences in terms of administration, economic development,

[1] E. A. Boateng, "The growth and functions of Accra", *Bulletin of the Ghana Geographical Association*, IV, 1959, 4–15; Ioné Acquah, *op. cit.*

[2] Dresch, *loc. cit.*

[3] Trewartha and Zelinsky, *loc. cit.* (footnote 12).

[4] This explains the break with Kikuyu tradition that the policy of "villagization" introduced during the Mau Mau Emergency represented. See G. B. Masefield, "A comparison between settlement in villages and isolated homesteads in Africa", *Journal of African Administration*, VII, 1955, 64–8.

settlement and communications—is, moreover, a very recent occurrence. On the West Coast, parts of which were long referred to as "the White Man's Grave", there was little incentive to move inland, and in other parts of Africa, individual travellers, traders, government officials and missionaries explored and pioneered during the nineteenth century. Some achieved fame like the Scottish missionary David Livingstone, others acquired notoriety like the German agent Karl Peters, but the majority remained unknown with their work unrecorded, unless they happened, like T. J. Alldridge in Sierra Leone, to publish accounts of their travels and discoveries.[1] It has been only during the last 60 or 70 years that the effective establishment of law and order has taken place in most parts of tropical Africa. Thus the Protectorate over the hinterland of Sierra Leone was declared only in 1898, and the British penetrated beyond the Gold Coast Colony, first into Ashanti and then into the Northern Territories, only early in the present century.

The situation in East Africa was broadly similar: only the stimulus of the humanitarians in their campaigns against the Arab-controlled slave-trade, strengthened perhaps by fear of the Germans as political rivals in their base of German East Africa, induced British penetration on any scale into the Lake Victoria basin and the costly construction of the Uganda Railway from Mombasa on the Indian Ocean to Kisumu on the Kavirondo Gulf of Lake Victoria. Nairobi, incidentally, owed its origin and growth directly to the building of this railway. It was selected as a suitable place for a railway headquarters and workshops with ample space and an adequate water supply.[2] Since then there has been remarkable development so that Nairobi, with a population of more than 230,000 inhabitants and many fine modern buildings, became at its fiftieth anniversary in 1950 the first tropical African city to be given a Royal Charter.

Farther south, in what is now the Federation of Rhodesia and Nyasaland, Europeans entered from the south, again at a

[1] T. J. Alldridge, *The Sherbro and its Hinterland*, London, 1901, and *A Transformed Colony: Sierra Leone, as it was, and as it is. Its Progress, Peoples, Native Customs and Undeveloped Wealth*, London, 1910.

[2] R. W. Walmsley, *Nairobi: the Geography of a New City*, Nairobi, 1957, and L. W. Thornton White, L. Silberman and P. R. Anderson, *Nairobi: Master Plan for a Colonial Capital*, H.M.S.O., London, 1948.

relatively late date. The first permanent European settlement in Southern Rhodesia—the London Missionary Society's station at Inyati, 40 miles north of Bulawayo—celebrated the centenary of its establishment in 1959: and not until 1890 did the "Pioneers" push northward to found Salisbury, while Bulawayo was established even more recently in 1893. The township of Livingstone, the capital of Northern Rhodesia until 1935, grew up close by the Victoria Falls railway bridge over the Zambezi, completed in 1903. The line continued north-eastward and northward past the mining centre of Broken Hill and through the then uninhabited district now known as the Copperbelt into the mineral-bearing province of Katanga in the Belgian Congo: but the large mining developments on the Copperbelt, and the consequential urban growth, have been wholly concentrated into the past three decades.[1]

The Distribution of Towns today

Fig. XXI (p. 259) shows the distribution in tropical Africa (excluding Sudan, Ethiopia and Somalia) of settlements with 5,000 or more inhabitants according to a post-war census or a recent estimate of population. Unreliable though many of the figures may be, they suffice to give the broad pattern of towns over a large part of the continent. The clustering in parts of West Africa, especially in the Yoruba country, is noteworthy, as is the size of cities such as Ibadan (459,000), Lagos (267,000) and Accra (136,000) in British areas, and Dakar (228,000) and Abidjan (120,000) in French West Africa. But the other tropical areas are not as completely different from some parts of West Africa as they would have been only 30 or 40 years ago. There is an appreciable scatter of towns throughout British East Africa, some of fair size, such as Nairobi, Mombasa and Dar es Salaam. In the Federation of Rhodesia and Nyasaland, Bulawayo has become a large industrial and communications centre, and Salisbury, the Federal capital, claims to be the most rapidly developing town in Africa south of the Sahara. Other growing towns like Brazzaville, Léopoldville, Stanleyville, Elisabethville and Bukavu (formerly Costermansville) are

[1] R. W. Steel, "The Copperbelt of Northern Rhodesia", *Geography*, XLII, 1957, 83–92.

important centres of administration, commerce and communications, with considerable European, as well as African, populations. But elsewhere in the territories formerly known as the
Belgian Congo and French Equatorial Africa, and in the Portuguese territories of Mozambique and Angola, there is a striking
lack of urban settlements, apart from coastal ports such as
Beira and Lourenço Marques: and even in these countries it is

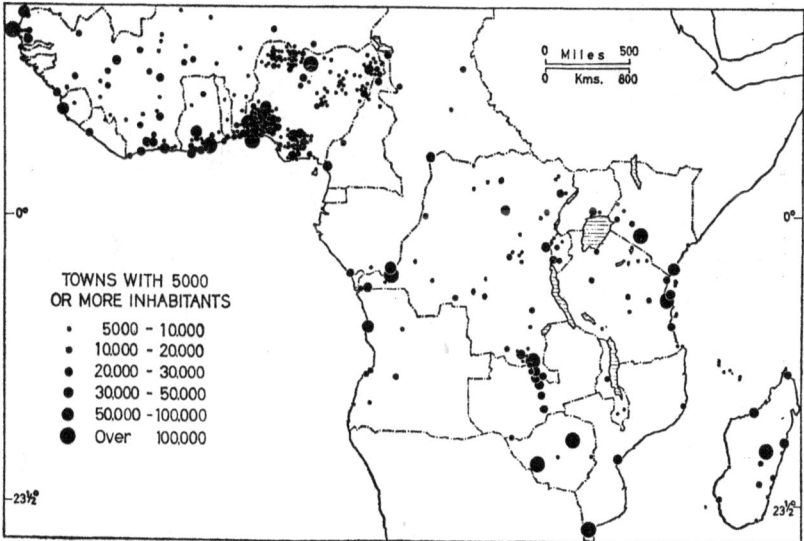

FIG. XXI. Tropical Africa: the distribution of towns with 5,000 or
more inhabitants (all races). (The information is based largely on
data taken from G. T. Trewartha and W. Zelinsky, "Population
patterns in tropical Africa", *Annals of the Association of American
Geographers*, XLIV, 1954, 135–62.)

possible to discern the tendency towards urbanization that is so
apparent in adjoining territories.

Fig. XXI has been designed to indicate the broad facts of distribution and to show the size of individual towns in tropical
Africa. But it is equally important to obtain a sense of perspective and to realize what proportion of the total population
can properly be classified as "urban". G. T. Trewartha and
W. Zelinsky estimated that about 10 years ago only 7·1 per
cent (or about 8½ million people) of the total population of

tropical Africa (121 millions) lived in towns with 5,000 or more inhabitants:[1] and thus they considered that in their general survey of population patterns in tropical Africa "the relative numerical insignificance of city dwellers does not entitle them to detailed discussion".

In a specific study of African towns, however, "numerical

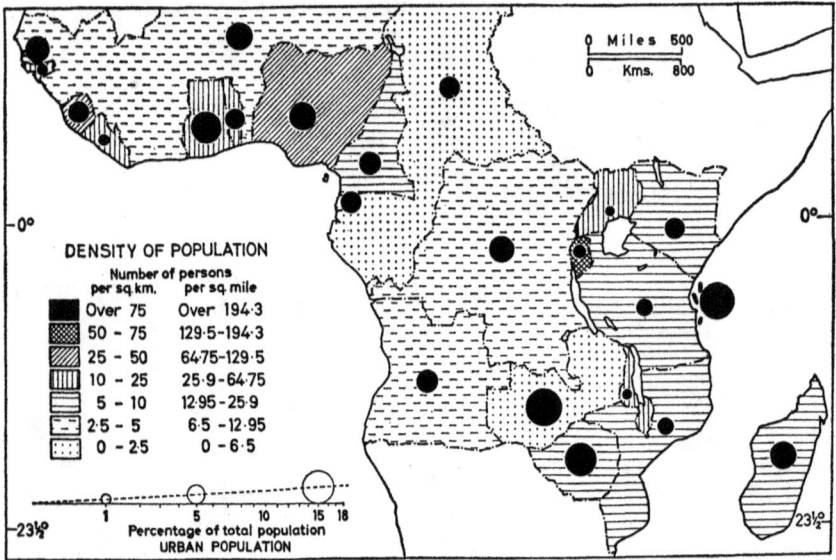

FIG. XXII. Tropical Africa: urban population in relation to density of population. More detailed information is available for the density of population in tropical Africa, but to have shown it on this map would have been confusing. (The figures on which this map is based are given in Table I and are taken largely from G. T. Trewartha and W. Zelinsky, "Population patterns in tropical Africa", *Annals of the Association of American Geographers*, XLIV, 1954, 135–62.)

insignificance" must not be emphasized unduly, and even though they are not much concerned with urban population, Trewartha and Zelinsky refer to the importance of the definite regional contrasts brought out by the size and spacing of towns.[2] Fig. XXII (above) attempts to bring together in a single map the proportion of the urban population in individual territories

[1] G. T. Trewartha and W. Zelinsky, "Population patterns in tropical Africa", *Annals of the Association of American Geographers*, XLIV, 1954, 144.

[2] *Ibid.*, 146.

and the average density of population for the same areas. The figures on which the map is based, taken generally from those given by Trewartha and Zelinsky, are given in summary form in Table I. Those of the urban figures are 10 years old and so

Table I: *Urban Population: Percentage of Total Population*

Country	Density of population (per sq. km.)	Urban population (thousands)	Percentage of total population
Northern Rhodesia	3	332	18·4
Zanzibar	100	45	17·0
Southern Rhodesia	7	276	12·8
Ghana	20	499	12·0
French West Africa	4	1,537	9·6
Nigeria	37	2,936	9·4
Belgian Congo	6	925	8·0
Gambia	29	20	7·7
Angola	3	249	6·1
French Cameroons	7	173	5·8
Spanish Guinea and Fernando Po	8	11	5·5
French Equatorial Africa	2	234	5·3
French Togoland	19	49	4·8
Kenya	11	253	4·8
Sierra Leone	29	96	4·8
Mozambique	8	160	2·8
Tanganyika	10	208	2·7
Ruanda-Urundi	85	62	1·6
Portuguese Guinea	16	7	1·4
Liberia	11	20	1·2
Nyasaland	23	22	1·1
Uganda	24	38	0·7

Note: The figures of density of population are based on the latest census data or official estimates as given in the United Nations, *Demographic Yearbook, 1958*, New York, 1958. The other figures are those given by G. T. Trewartha and W. Zelinsky, *op. cit.* The political territories are those in existence in mid-1958. No attempt has been made to give information for the political units of 1961, since in many cases reliable statistics are not available.

are, in nearly every instance, rather too small: and, like the density figures, they refer to whole territories, many of which are very large in area and variable in the degree of urbanization, so that they completely obscure many regional differences. More detailed and accurate figures, applicable for smaller areas, would, if generally available, help to clarify the picture and put it into much sharper focus. In default of such additional information, the map suggests such correlations as seem reasonable in the light of general geographical and statistical knowledge, while at the same time revealing certain surprises and anomalies.

Four main classes of territories may be recognized:

(i) those with fairly high densities of population and with urban populations above the general tropical African figure of 7·1 per cent;

(ii) those with relatively high density figures and little or no development of towns;

(iii) those with low density figures but a relatively high proportion of urban population; and

(iv) those with a low overall density figure and an urban population considerably below the average figure of 7·1 per cent.

In the first category are included countries like Nigeria and Ghana, where marked economic development has been matched by reasonable urban growth. Many districts have large total and rural populations along with considerable urban concentrations. But Nigeria illustrates the way in which overall figures obscure significant regional contrasts: the general figure (85 per square mile) hides the marked differences, noted earlier in this essay, between the Yoruba towns of the Western Region, the essentially rural landscape of the Ibo areas of the Eastern Region, and the relatively sparsely peopled areas of parts of the Northern Region.

The second class is represented by territories such as Ruanda-Urundi, Nyasaland and Uganda, each with quite high average densities of population but with hardly any development of towns. The scattered rural dwelling is the characteristic pattern of settlement, and there has as yet been no economic development of a special character, such as mining, that gives rise to large concentrations of people in towns.

It is this type of development that largely explains the contrast between general density of population and proportion of urban population in the countries forming the third group.

The Towns of Tropical Africa

Both Rhodesias and the areas formerly known as the Belgian Congo and French West Africa are good examples. Northern Rhodesia, with only 6 persons to the square mile, is one of the most sparsely peopled parts of tropical Africa, yet its urban population exceeds that of any other territory. This situation is largely explained by the great concentration of both Africans and Europeans in the Copperbelt during the last 30 years. The position in Southern Rhodesia is broadly comparable as a result of the growth of industrial towns in the High Veld area of the "Midlands" between Salisbury and Bulawayo, the two most rapidly developing of all. The Belgian Congo figures emphasize the contrast between the vast rural, sparsely populated, town-less parts of the Congo Basin on the one hand and the urban growth of Léopoldville, Stanleyville, and the Katanga towns such as Elisabethville and Jadotville on the other.

French West Africa is different again, though it must be admitted that general figures for so vast an area completely ignore some very important and marked regional contrasts. The area as a whole has only 3 per cent of its employed workers engaged in mining and only another 4 per cent in other forms of industry, yet some of its towns have grown tremendously during recent years and have served as great attractions for those seeking work from districts adjacent to them and from areas far away. Dakar, for example, has nearly a quarter of a million people (including 50,000 Europeans—a remarkable concentration for a tropical town), compared with less than 90,000 before the Second World War. Abidjan and Bamako each have more than 100,000 inhabitants, and Conakry and Porto Novo over 60,000. The amazing contrasts between rapidly growing and overcrowded towns and sparsely peopled and poorly developed rural districts may well account for some of the political developments in this part of Africa during recent months.

The final category—countries with low density of population and limited town growth—includes undeveloped areas like Angola and much of former French Equatorial Africa: if more statistical breakdown were available, parts of French West Africa (such as Mauritania, Niger and the French Sudan) could be added. In none of these areas is there likely to be much urban development in the forseeable future. The group also includes Kenya and Tanganyika, both of which have large, almost uninhabited tracts and, as yet, only restricted development of towns outside their capitals and principal ports.

Another aspect of African towns today that needs emphasis is their very mixed racial composition which is often directly reflected in their social life, their economic organization and their political structure. Some reference to the resultant problems is made later in this essay. It will be sufficient here to refer to the great contrasts between different towns in tropical Africa —between, say, the essentially European and characteristically French creation of Dakar, the almost wholly African town of Ibadan, the European domination of modern Salisbury, especially in the central area, and the markedly multi-racial aspect of Nairobi where Asian influences are almost as important as European in creating the town of today, even in central Nairobi. By themselves maps and statistics may fail to bring out significant differences of this nature, just as they can do little to underline the peculiar nature of many of tropical Africa's urban problems or to suggest the many reasons that account for the sudden economic, social and political upsurge of urban communities in Africa at the present day.

The Reasons for the Growth of Towns

African towns often grow for the same reasons as their counterparts in extra-tropical areas, but sometimes the significant reasons are different and these may even be peculiar to African conditions. The advantages of living in towns are broadly the same in tropical Africa and in Western Europe. A concentration of people can be provided with services and facilities which cannot be supplied, easily or economically, to people who are scattered throughout a rural area. Water supply, drainage, sewerage and sanitation, as well as schools, hospitals, clinics and shops can clearly be made available more readily and cheaply to an urban population than to every member of a widely dispersed community. To an African the prospect of such services may seem even more desirable than it is to a European, who perhaps is apt to take them for granted. African women, who, with their children, are usually the drawers of water in the community and who often need to walk great distances during the dry season to remote water-holes (round journeys of 10 or more miles are by no means uncommon), are not slow to recognize that the time and energy saved by the provision of piped or static water supplies can be diverted to the care of their farms or of their children or to other domestic duties. Common sense, as well as medical propaganda, suggests the value to health and general well-being of clean compounds, tidy streets and hygienic markets. Though there undoubtedly was a time when the virtues of education and medical services needed to be preached, and when victims had to be persuaded to submit themselves to the ministrations offered by governments or Christian missions, the situation is now entirely different. Today the demand for schools and hospitals far exceeds the supply almost everywhere. There is a widespread realization that those who can profit most from the services available are generally those living in the towns where the facilities have been placed. The zeal for increased educational opportunities may indeed be one of the most potent factors making for the ever-growing movement of African families from rural districts to urban areas at the present time.

Another magnet that draws Africans to the towns is the prospect of paid employment offered by many urban areas. In the countryside employment for wages is still quite unusual outside those districts where there is a traditional use of migrant labour on the farms, such as Buganda in East Africa or Ashanti in Ghana. In the towns, there is often a wide range of occupations. Government departments and European business concerns need clerks, storekeepers, porters, labourers and domestic servants. If a town is a communications centre there is a demand for railway workers, lorry drivers and mechanics, and for dock labour in the case of ports. Where secondary industry develops, new outlets are created which may prevent unemployment or underemployment with their accompanying social and political problems. Industrial development, in the broadest sense, has been especially responsible for the townward movement of people during post-war years in the case of some of the larger places like Bulawayo, Salisbury, Nairobi, Mombasa, Dar es Salaam, Lagos and Accra.

A less tangible, yet no less potent, factor in creating larger urban populations in tropical Africa arises from the real enthusiasm and zeal for urban life that are shown by many African communities today. There is a growing belief that no young man has really "seen life" until he has gone to the towns for a period of employment, and that such an experience is an essential prelude to the attainment of the status of manhood in tribal society. I. Schapera has described this attitude in his study of the movement of labour from Bechuanaland,[1] and his account could be paralleled in many other territories. One of the most striking features of this mid-twentieth century revolution that is transforming so many peoples and places in tropical Africa is the remarkable way in which predominantly agricultural and rural peoples are adapting their activities and ways of life to a considerable degree of industrialization and urbanization. Moreover there is, as yet, no indication that either the extent or the speed of this change is becoming any less: indeed some of the signs suggest that the present tendencies are becoming even more marked in certain territories.

There are, therefore, many different ways of explaining the great movement of Africans into towns during the past half century and, in particular, during the last 20 years. So great has this movement been that many towns now have more inhabitants than they can properly support or regularly employ. In Tanganyika, for example, it is reported[2] "there is a perceptible drift of Africans from the country districts to the towns, in many cases the numbers involved bearing no relation to the industrial or commercial opportunities offered by the town". It is these jobless people who often directly cause much of the unrest and create many of the problems of the urban areas, including political agitation, petty thieving, prostitution and juvenile delinquency. Exclusion of elements of the population that are "surplus to requirements" is politically dangerous to propose, and is administratively very difficult to organize. In some cases the development of secondary industry and of other activities can absorb some of the unemployed population, at least temporarily, but there remains the problem of the con-

---

[1] I. Schapera, *Migrant Labour and Tribal Life*, London, 1947. See also H. Ashton, *The Basuto*, London, 1952.

[2] *Report of Her Majesty's Government to the General Assembly of the United Nations on the Administration of Tanganyika, 1951*, Col. No. 287, H.M.S.O., 1952, para. 678.

siderable "unemployable" element in most towns—the sick, the aged, the destitute and those incapable of doing regular work. The scale of this problem is likely to increase in the future if the free and easy movement of people between town and country is reduced. It seems bound to happen in a country like Southern Rhodesia where real efforts are being made to establish a stabilized urban population on the one hand and an equally fixed, virtually free-holding, rural population on the other.[1] Desirable though some of these developments may be, it is questionable whether the Southern Rhodesian Government has adequately foreseen some of the likely consequences of its policy, particularly in relation to the urban population.

Some Major Problems of Urban Areas

The concentration of considerable numbers of people in relatively restricted areas gives rise to problems that deserve careful study in any part of the world. In a continent like Africa where there is little tradition of urban living, and in the tropics where the nature of the physical environment creates its own special difficulties, the problems of urban communities demand particularly close attention from governments and local authorities on the one hand, and from social and political scientists, economists and geographers on the other. Recognition of the urgency of these problems accounts for the considerable space devoted to the survey of the conditions for urban development in the East Africa Royal Commission's Report.[2] There is also an important section in the revised edition of Lord Hailey's *An African Survey*, though the discussion is in general directed to "the special problems created by the growth of the urban populations which have come into being as the result of the activities of Europeans, or (as in East Africa) of the activities of the European and Asian communities".[3]

Information is lacking, as has been stated before, for many important aspects of town growth and urban life in tropical

[1] The Southern Rhodesian Native Land Husbandry Act, No. 52 of 1951. See also *What the Native Land Husbandry Act means to the Rural African and to Southern Rhodesia: a Five-year Plan that will Revolutionize African Agriculture*, Salisbury, 1955.
[2] *East Africa Royal Commission, 1953–1955, Report*, 200–50.
[3] Lord Hailey, *An African Survey: Revised 1956: a Study of Problems arising in Africa South of the Sahara*, London, 1957, 564–86. The quotation is on pp. 564–5.

Africa. The time may come when sufficient data will be available to permit a full-scale appraisal of the problems relating to the distribution, size and growth of towns and to their diverse and varying functions. Already these matters can be studied for individual towns or groups of towns, as has been done by many different kinds of workers (including N. C. Mitchel in his essay on the Yoruba towns in this volume).[1] But for tropical African towns as a whole, it is possible as yet only to assess the importance of some of the problems that are of a practical administrative, rather than of an intellectual, character. The remainder of this essay is, therefore, devoted to some consideration of a selection of the physical, economic, social and political problems of African towns at the present time.

Physical Problems

Many problems are directly caused by the physical siting of towns, and some are peculiar to the conditions of a tropical environment. Town sites have possibly been as fortuitously selected in the African tropics as in any other part of the world. The European officer of the past, for example, probably had only a rudimentary knowledge of local conditions as he chose the position of his station or *boma*. Perhaps sometimes his choice was determined more by a desire for a lofty and airy eminence for his own residence and office than by consideration of the interests and convenience of the people for whom he was responsible. Occasionally directions were, deliberately or inadvertently, misunderstood: this is said to be the case with Salisbury whose apparently well-chosen site at the foot of a *kopje* lies 12 miles south-eastward of the site where the Pioneers under Colonel Pennefather were meant to establish their camp. Nairobi was originally selected in a suitable place for the erection of railway workshops. When it replaced Mombasa as the capital of Kenya in 1905, Major J. W. Pringle reported that "as a station site, the level ground commends itself to the engineer. As a site for the future capital of East Africa and for

[1] See, for example, those given in footnote 3 on page 251, but many others could be cited. For fuller bibliographical details see the bibliography compiled by J. Comhaire, *Urban conditions in Africa. Select Reading List on Urban Problems in Africa*, London, 1952.

permanent buildings for Europeans, the sanitary engineer and the medical expert condemn it."[1] Although subsequent events have proved Nairobi's drawbacks to be less marked than were feared at first, the creation of a healthy city has taken time and money, and very real problems of water supply and drainage have had to be faced.

Grave physical problems occur even where sites have been carefully selected with probable future growth in mind. In 1935 Lusaka became the capital of Northern Rhodesia in a relatively central position in the territory as a whole, replacing Livingstone by the Zambezi river and on the southern border of the country. Considerable care was taken over the choice of the site and the early planning of the settlement. But this has not prevented very great expenditure during recent years for the installation of an adequate water supply and an effective drainage system as the town has increased its population and extended its buildings over an ever-widening area.

Water supply, drainage, sewerage and supplies of building material or of foodstuffs are, in fact, generally much more serious problems in tropical towns than in other parts of the world. Drainage, for example, is a particular difficulty in tropical countries where rainfall is highly seasonal in its distribution. Wide and deep storm-drains are often necessary alongside the main streets to deal with the occasional torrential downpours of tropical storms; and costly water-storage schemes may be essential where there is a lengthy dry season, even in a place like Freetown, Sierra Leone, with an annual rainfall exceeding 150 inches.

The seriousness of physical conditions in tropical towns is, however, underlined by the extent of disease and the speed with which it may spread, especially in countries where health services are often still rudimentary. Slum clearance, the reduction of overcrowding, the maintenance of health in the poorer quarters of the town, and the adequate provision of medical facilities are thus even more important in Lagos or Dar es Salaam than they are in London, New York or, for that matter, Johannesburg.

---

[1] Quoted in R. W. Walmsley, *op. cit.*, 19.

R. W. Steel

Economic incentives have been largely responsible for the influx of people into towns during recent years. There are considerable economic problems in communities where the tradition of working for regular wages is usually quite new and where there is little experience of dealing with the economic consequences of the congregation of fair numbers of people within a restricted area. Food, for example, is often high priced and sometimes very hard to buy; housing may be difficult and gross overcrowding may result; rent-profiteering is common, even in slum property; the journey to work may be long and tedious, especially where local transport services are poor or in those towns with many European residents where the African housing areas may be very distant from the main districts of employment.[1]

Two inter-related sets of problems may be mentioned because of their particular significance, those relating to the stabilization of economy and the stabilization of labour. The need for a broadening of the economy of most tropical territories has been widely recognized in recent years. There are all too many examples of countries whose prosperity depends upon the production of a particular crop or the output of a single mine. The problem of the single-commodity economy remains even where Marketing Boards and Producers' Associations have been established or where there has been some development of secondary industry. Ghana's welfare depends largely upon the world demand for cocoa, Northern Rhodesia's economy is dominated by copper, parts of Tanganyika are prosperous or depressed in terms of the price of either sisal or coffee. Nowhere are the consequences of a slump felt more than in the towns, even where an agricultural commodity is primarily responsible, for the demand for the services that a town renders to the community at large results in considerable measure from the prosperity or otherwise of the farmers in surrounding areas. Where a mineral is the basis of the economy, the effects in the towns of

---

[1] In Salisbury, for example, while the Harari African Township is very close to the principal industrial area of the city, the municipality's African housing area at Mabouku (formerly Donnybrook) is some miles distant and is served by an irregular and expensive bus service.

a fall in demand are even greater and more immediate. The world depression of the thirties, for example, hit the Copperbelt of Northern Rhodesia in the very early days of its development. Fortunately at that period the Africans employed as labourers in the constructional stages could readily be absorbed back into the tribal life of the reserves whence they came. The Europeans who had come especially into the area in anticipation of the steady development of mining were the principal sufferers. Subsequently economic conditions improved, and those Europeans who had remained were able to benefit from the renewal of mining and of its associated occupations. There was also a return of African workers with an increased demand for labour.[1]

Latterly the Copperbelt mining companies have pursued a deliberate policy of establishing a stabilized labour force and a permanent urbanized community that now numbers about a quarter of a million. Thus an ever-increasing population is wholly dependent upon the mines, and more and more Africans are permanently living away from their former homes in the reserves. Any decline in employment has, therefore, very grave consequences, especially in those towns where most of the inhabitants rely upon one particular occupation. Some of the older Copperbelt towns like Nkana-Kitwe, Nchanga-Chingola, Mufulira and Luanshya-Roan Antelope have developed other occupations, such as secondary industry, transport, and municipal services, but even they are largely dependent upon copper which remains the key to the whole economy of Northern Rhodesia and accounts for over four-fifths of the total value of the country's exports.

Stabilization of labour, accepted now not only in the Copperbelt but also in other parts of the Federation of Rhodesia and

[1] For early developments on the Copperbelt, see J. Merle Davis (editor) *Modern Industry and the African*, London, 1933. This book is the report of "an enquiry into the effect of the copper mines of Central Africa upon native society and the work of Christian missions made under the auspices of the Department of Social and Industrial Research of the International Missionary Council". A later discussion, largely though not exclusively concerned with the mining centre of Broken Hill (not on the Copperbelt) in 1939-40, is Godfrey Wilson's *An essay on the economics of detribalization in Northern Rhodesia*, Rhodes-Livingstone Papers, Livingstone, No. 5, 1941 and No. 6, 1942. See also A. Lynn Saffrey, *Report on some Aspects of African Living Conditions in the Copperbelt of Northern Rhodesia*, Lusaka, 1943.

Nyasaland, and for long practised in the Katanga province of the Belgian Congo, clearly results in certain social and economic benefits. It helps to produce over the years a skilled body of workers, a contented labour force, and a stable social and political community.[1] But it also creates economic difficulties, especially, as has already been suggested, in times of commercial recession, and it carries with it a host of important corollaries, to many of which little attention has so far been given. If, for example, there is to be the complete break between urban and rural communities which legislation like the Native Land Husbandry Act of Southern Rhodesia seems to envisage, the Government and other employers of labour must accept the fact that higher wages will have to be paid, if the urban worker is to maintain an adequate standard of living. Provision must also be made for illness, unemployment and—ultimately—retirement in a society that will no longer be able to do what it used to do, and return its sick and aged members to the reserves. There must in fact be the creation of those economic circumstances that will make possible the proper social provision for a permanent urban population, along the lines suggested by the East Africa Royal Commission's study of the "conditions for urban development". Africans must be helped to lead satisfactory lives as permanent town dwellers, and government policy must be aimed at the building up of "integrated urban communities—communities in which all persons of whatever race can participate in the social, economic and political life of the town in accordance with their individual abilities".[2] While it may be long before the Welfare State can be created in any part of tropical Africa, there is already an urgent need for many of its provisions, particularly for the people who live in towns—European and Asian as well as African—and who are usually particularly exposed to the vicissitudes of economic development.

---

[1] Cf. G. St. J. Orde Browne, *The African Labourer*, London, 1933; see also Lord Hailey, *op. cit.*, 1387–92, and J. D. Rheinallt Jones, "The effect of urbanization in South and Central Africa", *African Affairs*, LII, 1953, 37–44.

[2] *Journal of African Administration*, x, 1958, 189.

The Towns of Tropical Africa

Social Problems

Social problems in the new urban communities of tropical Africa arise not only from the nature of their economic structure and organization, but also from the mixing together in the towns of many different tribes as well as of different races. The mingling of tribes in urban areas is the result of the widespread movements of labour described elsewhere in this volume by A. W. Southall and J. C. Mitchell.[1] In Freetown, Sierra Leone, fifteen or more tribes from the interior are represented in fair numbers in the community, and an elaborate organization has been created for their administration.[2] Every Ghanaian town of any size has its *zongo* where African strangers live: sometimes the *zongo* contains more people than the rest of the township.[3] In Nigeria the immigrants' quarter is known as *sabon gari* ("new town"). East and Central African towns often have a fair variety of tribes, sometimes living in groups, at other times scattered indiscriminately through the town. Usually local government functions satisfactorily with little inter-tribal feeling,[4] but at times there is considerable tribal tension, and many post-war disturbances in the towns and elsewhere have had tribal rivalries as their immediate, though not necessarily their deeper, causes. But while there has been some revival of tribalism in countries such as Nigeria, there are also very clear signs of detribalization, with its effects as visible in the areas whence the townsmen have come as in the towns themselves.[5] Detribalization is probably an inevitable result of the change from a community life based on agriculture in the rural areas

[1] See also A. I. Richards (editor), *Economic Development and Tribal Change*, Cambridge, 1954.

[2] See M. Banton, *West African City: a Study of Tribal Life in Freetown*, London, 1957. R. L. Buell in *The Native Problem in Africa*, 2 volumes, New York, 1928, wrote on page 879: "Freetown has made perhaps more successful attempts to group together natives living in industrialized conditions under tribal authority than any other city of Africa."

[3] R. W. Steel, "The population of Ashanti: a geographical analysis", *Geographical Journal*, CXII, 1948, 64–77, and "The towns of Ashanti: a geographical study", *op. cit.*, 1952, especially 91–2.

[4] See, for example, A. W. Southall and P. C. W. Gutkind, *Townsmen in the Making: Kampala and its Suburbs*, East African Studies, 9, 1957. Another study of Kampala, earlier and very different, is E. S. Munger's *Relational Patterns of Kampala*, Uganda, Chicago, 1951.

[5] There is an excellent study of detribalization in Tanganyika by M. J. B. Molohan, *Detribalization*, Dar es Salaam, 1957.

R. W. Steel

to the very different social and economic conditions of urban life. "The urban resident has moved from a world where ties are largely personal to one in which his obligations are to an increasing extent impersonal." [1] From this arise many of the problems of urban administration, social organization and cultural development to which sociologists and government officials have rightly given much attention in recent years. [2]

Racial diversity is much more characteristic of the towns of East Africa, the Federation of Rhodesia and Nyasaland and the Belgian Congo, than of those of West Africa where, apart from some French cities like Dakar, the number of European residents is usually small. On the eastern side of Africa a fairly high proportion of the immigrant communities live in the towns. In Tanganyika, for example, the census of 1948 revealed that, whereas only 2 per cent of the African population lived in urban areas, 50 per cent of the Europeans and 70 per cent of the Asians lived in 18 of the largest towns, and of the rest the majority were to be found in the remaining townships. [3]

Where different races live at relatively close quarters in towns, many problems arise through social contact and economic competition that are never likely to develop where the communities are more widely scattered, as in rural areas. Ideas about the zoning and segregation of different races have changed greatly during the present century. Professor W. J. Simpson, who reported on planning problems in Nairobi, Kampala and elsewhere in East Africa in 1913, [4] advocated complete segregation of racial groups in the towns. This policy was quite specifically abandoned in the Devonshire White Paper of 1923. [5]

It is now the view of the competent medical authorities that, as a sanitation measure, segregation of Europeans and Asiatics is not

[1] Hailey, *op. cit.*, 564.
[2] Of the numerous references that could be given, see especially J. Clyde Mitchell, "A note on the urbanization of Africans on the Copperbelt", *Rhodes-Livingstone Journal*, xii (1951), and *African urbanization in Ndola and Luanshya*, Rhodes-Livingstone Communication No. 6 (1954). See also E. Hellman, "Urban areas" in *Handbook on Race Relations in South Africa*, Cape Town, 1949, 229–74.
[3] *East Africa Royal Commission, 1953–55, Report, op. cit.*
[4] Quoted in *Nairobi: Master Plan for a Colonial Capital, op. cit.*
[5] *Indians in Kenya*, Cmd. 1922, 1923. The memorandum, in the name of the Duke of Devonshire, included a considered statement on inter-racial relations in Africa.

absolutely essential for the preservation of the health of the community; the rigid enforcement of sanitary, police and building regulations will suffice. It may well prove that in practice the different races will, by a natural affinity, keep together in separate quarters, but to effect such separation by legislative enactment except on the strongest sanitary grounds, would not, in the opinion of His Majesty's Government, be justifiable.

As the White Paper suggested, differences in living standards largely account for the comparative isolation of different racial groups in tropical towns. Most Europeans in tropical Africa are able to maintain a high standard of living, and their housing conditions are generally very good. Few Africans, and not many Asians, can afford to live in predominantly European areas, whether or not there is any restrictive legislation. Thus in practice the racial diversity of many towns is often still clearly reflected in the nature of the layout and building types and in the general separation of the races. There have, however, been significant modifications in certain countries during recent years as a result of changing social ideas and of political pressure. Former exclusively European quarters have become "official areas" with African, West Indian and Asian as well as European residents. In some countries suburban areas are described in terms of their housing as first, second or third class, whereas in the past they were called European, Asian and African. In the Federation of Rhodesia and Nyasaland, where the question of racial contact is a particularly live issue, some slight concessions have been made since the establishment of Federation, though for most practical purposes segregation is still very much a reality in the towns.

Despite the importance of the non-African elements in the urban populations of tropical Africa today, and notwithstanding the small proportion of the total African population to be found in the towns, it is the African inhabitants who dominate nearly all African towns in terms of numbers, as the figures given in Table I indicate. Even in towns like Jinja and Kampala, where Asians form considerable and very powerful minorities, Africans easily outnumber peoples of all other races.

R. W. Steel

Political Problems

African towns have many problems of a political nature. Some are fascinating problems in political geography, about which but little is known as yet. While the new Federations and closer associations of tropical Africa have not given rise to quite such controversial issues relating to the selection of federal capitals as has been the case in the West Indian Federation, there was nevertheless some spirited, and possibly justifiable, opposition to the choice of Salisbury as both a Federal and a territorial capital. Lagos has not been made the Federal capital of Nigeria without much keen and bitter inter-regional and inter-tribal debate, while Nairobi's dual position as capital of Kenya and, since 1948, as headquarters of the East Africa High Commission has been repeatedly criticized in Tanganyika and Uganda. Even in Ghana, Accra's position and status have been questioned by some parties and groups in the country, and it is significant that it is the Ashanti town of Kumasi that is the centre of opposition to the government established by the Convention People's Party.

Of more immediate and practical importance are the day-to-day problems of administration in towns where officials are dealing with the highly mixed urban populations who have so recently been thrown together, with no common tradition or shared experiences to help in the creation of really live communities. For many years the need for special methods in urban areas was barely admitted by government officials who appeared to regard the towns as unfortunate, and indeed unnecessary, nuisances and as untidy blots in their otherwise neat pattern of rural Native Administration. Even where embryonic town councils—Public Health Committees and Sanitary Boards as they were often called—were established, their powers were severely limited, and in some instances the claims of large African communities for consideration by the local authorities were ignored, even where they were of long standing and of proved stability.[1] It is encouraging to see how

[1] Of many examples that could be given, that of the Kumasi *zongo* in Ashanti may be quoted. See M. Fortes, R. W. Steel and P. Ady, "Ashanti Survey, 1945–46: an experiment in social research", *Geographical Journal*, cx, 1947, 149–79, especially 161–2.

The Towns of Tropical Africa

during recent years the problems of urban administration have been studied and tackled by governments with a new awareness of their importance. Several governments have put forward specific proposals for new towns. In Northern Rhodesia, for example, not only is the stabilization of population in the Copperbelt being actively pushed forward, but urbanization has been accepted as part of its 10-year development plans and new African townships are being created in the reserves to provide additional employment in new areas and to help in the evolution of an African middle class. In Southern Rhodesia the building up of a permanent and much enlarged urban population is both an inevitable and a highly desirable corollary of the Native Land Husbandry Act.[1] Outside the tropics, in the Union of South Africa the Tomlinson Report[2] has made it clear that the establishment of a hundred new Bantu towns is essential if *apartheid* is to become a practicable policy of the Nationalist Government. It remains to be seen how effective these plans will be, but they may well be signs of the shape of things to come. The recognition of these and other plans for urban development, and the consideration of the problems that must inevitably accompany them, call for earnest effort and study by the governments concerned and by all who are interested in the progress of tropical Africa. The problems are vast enough and sufficiently pressing to demand a real inter-disciplinary approach to them on the part of geographers, sociologists, demographers, planners and all who are concerned with this new and significant phenomenon of the tropical African landscape, the African town.

The African town of the mid-twentieth century has clearly come to stay, and many towns will grow with striking rapidity in years to come. There is unlikely ever to be a predominance of the urban population in most parts of tropical Africa—and it is, therefore, important to keep a sense of perspective: yet increasingly the towns will contain a growing and a stabilized African population, along with a high proportion of the

[1] The Southern Rhodesian Native Land Husbandry Act, No. 52 of 1951. See the reference in footnote 1 on p. 267.

[2] *Summary of the Report of the Commission for the Socio-Economic Development of the Bantu Areas within the Union of South Africa* ("The Tomlinson Report"), U.G. 61/1955, Pretoria, 1955.

continent's non-African inhabitants. Predominantly agricultural and rural though tropical Africa is, and is likely to remain, the African townsman and townswoman will undoubtedly be making an ever-increasing, and probably quite disproportionate, contribution to the political life, the economic organization and the social progress of the territories in which they live.

14

Yoruba Towns

N. C. MITCHEL

Introduction

THE Yoruba peoples form one of the largest tribal groups in Nigeria and in the census taken in 1952 they numbered about 5,000,000. Most of them live in the Western Region where the provinces of Abeokuta, Ibadan, Ijebu, Ondo and Oyo are predominantly Yoruba, and in the Federal Territory of Lagos. In all these areas they account for more than 70 per cent of the total population. They are the dominant element in the population of Kabba and Ilorin provinces in the Northern Region, while outside Nigeria there are important groups in Dahomey. One of the most distinctive features of the Yoruba is their high degree of urbanization. Almost half of Nigeria's total urban population (5·66 million) is concentrated in Yorubaland (2·77 million). Both the size and number of their towns are unique in tropical Africa. Of the Western Region's 128 towns, 107 are in the Yoruba provinces; five of these have populations of over 100,000, and Ibadan, with a population of 459,196, is the largest town in tropical Africa (Fig. XXIII, p. 280). In addition, the Federal Territory has 7 towns including Lagos with a population of 286,407. Outside Yorubaland, Kano is the only town in Nigeria with a population exceeding 100,000, while the largest town in the Eastern Region is Onitsha with 76,921. Yoruba towns are even more remarkable in view of the fact that urbanization is indigenous. With the possible exception of Lagos, there are no new towns which follow the more usual colonial pattern of growth through administration, trade and mining, as in other parts of Nigeria.

Instead, these functions have been added to the existing towns which were established before the colonial era.

There are varying degrees of urbanization within Yorubaland itself. Ibadan and Oyo provinces and Lagos are more highly urbanized than Ijebu and Abeokuta. Within each province there are also important variations. Small towns

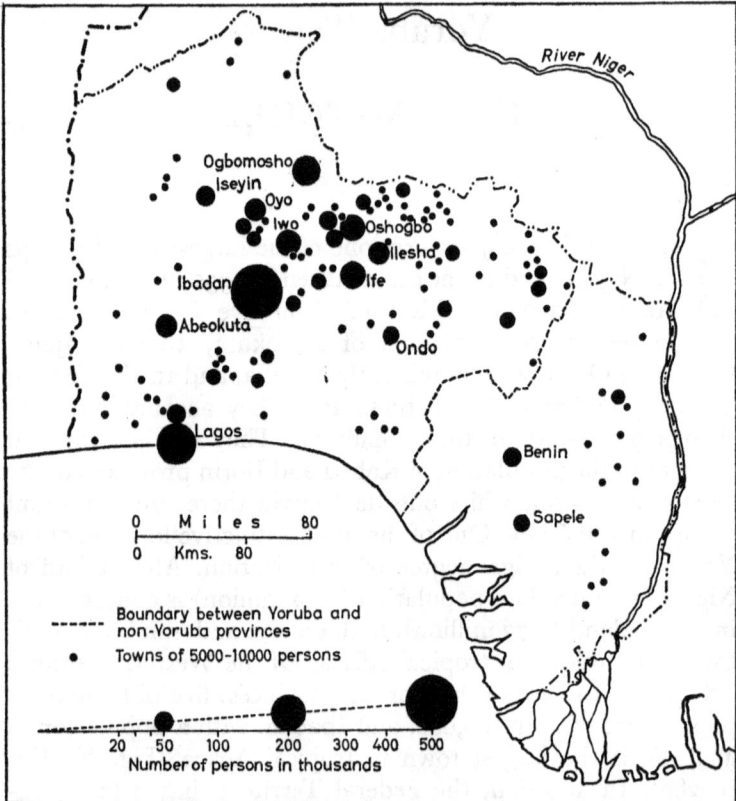

FIG. XXIII. The distribution of towns in the Western Region of Nigeria (1952 census).

(population under 10,000) are far the most numerous, especially in Abeokuta, Ondo and Ijebu provinces. However, only 25 per cent of the Yoruba urban population lives in them while just over 50 per cent is in 9 large towns, each with over 100,000 people. Ibadan and Lagos together account for 26 per cent of

Yoruba Towns

the total urban population. No single factor explains the overall high degree of urbanization or the variations within Yorubaland. The indigenous towns owe their distribution and growth to a combination of physical, historical, political and social factors.[1] The economic factor gained in importance when wider trade relations, better communications and cash-crop farming were developed under the colonial administration. Today the principal areas of town development coincide with the core area of high population density among the Yoruba in the "Cocoa Belt", which is the most prosperous part of the Western Region.

Samples of urban occupations taken in 1952 suggest that the agricultural element is the most distinctive feature of the majority of Yoruba towns. For example, 92 per cent of working males in the small town of Eruwa (8,154) are engaged in agriculture and in the large towns of Ogbomosho (139,535), Oshogbo (122,728) and Iwo (100,006) agriculture employs between 60 per cent and 70 per cent of working males. Even in Ibadan, with its many functions which will be discussed later, the figure is 35 per cent. Some towns, however, contrast with this and have a surprisingly varied occupational structure. Abeokuta has 27 per cent in trading and clerical occupations and only 15 per cent in agriculture. Ijebu-ode has 28 per cent in trading and 20 per cent each in crafts and agriculture. In view of the general importance of this non-urban characteristic it may well be asked if the term "town" is applicable to Yoruba settlements. Moreover, many so-called towns lack the services normally associated with urban status in other parts of the world. But size cannot be ignored and a compact settlement of over 100,000 people can scarcely be called a village although 70 per cent of its male population is engaged in agriculture. When more studies of functions become available, an "agricultural town" may become an accepted term in its Yoruba context.

Some note must be taken of the administrative definition of a town in the census which ignores traditional Yoruba

[1] Miller has emphasized the fortunate climatic position of south-western Nigeria with both early and late rains which permit two harvests in the year. Gourou has stressed the importance of the cultural and historical factors.
R. Miller, "The climate of Nigeria", *Geography*, xxxvii, No. 178, 1952, 203.
P. Gourou, *The Tropical World*, London, 1953, 86 (trans. E. D. Laborde).

terminology. In Yorubaland an *ilu* is regarded as the equivalent of a town. It possesses certain features and performs functions which distinguish it from the *ileto*, *abule* and *aba* which are the villages and hamlets. An inhabitant of an *ilu* will be offended if his settlement is referred to as an *abule*. The Yoruba say that a settlement is an *ilu* if it has a ruling hierarchy and performs administrative functions. An *ilu* may have a smaller population than the 5,000 set by the census for town status and yet be more important in local estimation than a settlement like Agege (12,844) listed as a town in the census, but whose inhabitants regard it as a large village which is undergoing rapid growth as a roadside market. It can be argued, of course, that the economic changes brought about by new roads, markets and crops have reduced the value of the traditional terminology. The census definition took into account current trends and, despite its shortcomings, gives a useful guide to the urban centres.

Origins and Early Growth

The accounts of travellers show that in the nineteenth century Yoruba towns were both large and numerous. Even before this, the Portuguese explorers, d'Aveiro and Pereira, had received reports of towns that were almost certainly Yoruba.[1] Despite the lack of records, there can be little doubt that the present well-developed sense of community among the Yoruba, expressed in their desire to live in large compact settlements, is of long standing. Their traditions point to Ife as the parent settlement from which various groups founded new towns in both the forest and savanna. Ife, which became the spiritual capital of Yorubaland under the Oni, was a forest town whereas Old Oyo was in the savanna where it developed as the political capital under the Alafin. Under the Oyos, Yorubaland was well organized and probably reached the zenith of its power and influence before the eighteenth century. By the early nineteenth century the impact of Fulani invaders from the north and internal dissensions resulted in the decline of Yoruba power. Refugees moved southward from abandoned towns, in-

---

[1] W. Bascom, "Urbanization among the Yoruba", *American Journal of Sociology*, LX, 5, 1955, 447.

cluding the capital, Old Oyo, to the towns and villages in the transition zone between savanna and forest. Those who went to Ife were permitted to settle as a colony within the town walls and this area, Modakeke, remains a distinct section of the modern town. The Egbas suffered most from the impact of these refugees. They were forced to abandon much of their northern lands and concentrate for survival in Abeokuta, which was settled about 1830, not as a single town but as a collection of small towns and villages, over 140 of them in close juxtaposition.[1] The Egbas in their turn expanded at the expense of other groups, the Aworis and Egbados. On the savanna of western Yorubaland, many small towns sought the protective sites of rock domes and plateaux in the face of Fulani expansion and Dahomeyan raids.

In the early nineteenth century the Portuguese chose Lagos as a centre for their slave-trade. It soon became the largest slave port on the West Coast, and remained so until some British control was established by the appointment of a Consul in 1851. It became a Crown Colony in 1862. Since it developed as part of an African response to a European demand for slaves, it may be termed a semi-indigenous town. It is not typical, either in growth or plan, of the indigenous town of the interior, although its influence has penetrated Yorubaland in many diverse ways, for example, in architecture and in building materials. Its unique site has given it distinctive character and at least to some extent has controlled its development.

Study of the influence of historical factors on the present urban pattern suggests that the development of the indigenous Yoruba town took place in four stages. The origin of many towns was a hunters' encampment to which newcomers were attracted by reason of good farmland, population pressure in the parent town, or a good trading position (e.g. Shaki, Iseyin, Ilora and Fiditi). The second stage was one of consolidation and growth. Bascom suggests that during this period some towns became metropolitan in that they served as centres for an entire kingdom (e.g. Oyo, Ife and Ilesha).[2] Regular communications and administrators (Ajeles) linked them to outlying towns. Inter-tribal warfare, invasion and the collapse of

---

[1] A Hinderer, *Seventeen Years in the Yoruba Country*, London, 1872, 215.
[2] Bascom, *loc. cit.*, 452.

central authority in the nineteenth century all contributed to the next stage when survival depended on adequate defence, political affiliations and size of population. New towns were formed during this period, both from war camps and from concentrations of population for protection. Ikirun is an example of the former, beginning as the Ibadan base for operations against Ilorin and Ekiti; today it is a town of 26,000 inhabitants. One of the best examples of a defensive nucleation is Old Idanre in Ondo province, situated at the foot of Orosun, a rock dome 3,089 feet high. The nineteenth century also saw the weakening of links between smaller settlements and parent towns. A growing centre like Ibadan was able to subdue by conquest or by treaty towns which owed allegiance to the metropolitan centres of Ife and Ilesha and to bring them within its own sphere of influence.[1] The fourth and present stage began with the British administration, when protection was no longer of prime importance. Instead, new administrative and economic factors began to influence town development. On the whole, the colonial administration did not directly initiate changes in the settlement pattern except to encourage some small towns on protective sites in the savanna to move to more accessible sites; Okeiho was laid out on a new site in 1917, and Igbetti moved from its site on a rock dome as early as 1905.

Morphology

The limits of an indigenous town were clearly marked by protective earthworks in the form of walls and ditches. These existed prior to the inter-tribal wars of the nineteenth century which gave them added importance. Some towns, like Ife and Ilesha, show traces of more than one wall, but Yoruba earthworks were never so imposing as the walls and gateways of towns like Kano and Zaria. Sir Richard Burton, when he visited Abeokuta in 1860, made some caustic comments on its "celebrated defences".[2] His description gives a clear picture of the nature and extent of the outer limits of a large town

---

[1] Ibadan had about 90 tributary towns and villages in 1893. Under British Administration, this extensive area became a division of Oyo province. Relations with Oyo were always strained and, in 1951, it was made a separate province.

[2] Sir Richard Burton, *Abeokuta and the Cameroons Mountains*, London, 1863, 68.

which occupied a precarious position between the Dahomeyans in the west and the Ibadans in the north.

To the northwards, in the direction of the hostile Ibadan, the walls are three in number and the external circumference may be 20 miles. . . . It is a marvel that man should be stopped by such an obstacle. The wall is hardened mud, good material but only five to six feet high . . . it is approached by an equally inefficient moat or ditch, perhaps five feet broad, wet and half-choked with bushes. The large entrances, exclusive of those leading to farms, are five in number.

Small towns, especially on the savanna, often had an outer ring of woodland (*igbo ile*) in addition to their wall to give greater protection or, as at Shaki, there might be a narrow strip of woodland within its walls, which could be cultivated in times of siege. Towns had at least four gates, the most important being elaborate constructions with recognized toll collectors. The gates were named after important adjoining towns or important personages. Ibadan had its Iwo, Abeokuta, Oyo and Iddo (Lagos) gates, and Abeokuta its Alake's gate. Town walls, besides indicating defensive functions, also show the various stages of a town's growth. As a town expanded outwards towards its original wall, so the need arose to build a new one to enclose additional land for future expansion and to ensure adequate land for the growing of food crops in times of danger. According to tradition, Ibadan had outgrown its original wall by the middle of the nineteenth century. Its later one, which was a marked feature when the British assumed control, was built in the 1850's and was known as Odi Ibikunle (Ibikunle's wall) after the Bale (chief) who began it. Today, the area within the outer walls of most indigenous towns is still not entirely built on, but some towns have extended beyond their old walls at one or more places. In Ibadan in 1908, 23 per cent of the land within the walls was built up and another 14 per cent had very scattered dwellings.[1] Now 45 per cent of this land is occupied by dwellings and the town has extended westwards beyond the line of the walls.

Within their walls, towns were laid out with marked uniformity, but with the physical features of the site giving each

[1] These figures are based on one of the first published maps of Ibadan.

N. C. Mitchel

some distinction.[1] The focus of most towns was the "Afin" or Bale's compound, which was the largest in the town and invariably built opposite the market place. Markets were often impressive in size, and trade relations were widespread, even during the tribal wars. The bulk of the retail trade was, and still is, in the hands of women and under them the market lay-out was highly organized. The larger and more important a town, the more subsidiary markets it had, and a town was especially important if it had a well-developed night market.[2]

The central market was the focus of the principal roads which led from the gates, with a network of smaller ones and innumerable winding paths which intersected between groups of compounds. The rectangular thatched compound enclosing an extensive inner courtyard was the traditional form of building. Compounds were of two kinds, either the large "savanna" type, still seen in Okeiho and Shaki, or a smaller, more compact, "forest" type. With the exception of roofing material, their plan and appearance has not altered much since they were first described by missionaries over a hundred years ago. They, and not the roads, were the most important element in the Yoruba town plan. Each compound was the visible expression of a lineage or extended family, and might have between 20 and 2,000 inhabitants but with an average of between 100 and 200.[3] The town was composed of groups of these compounds formed into quarters, each with a quarter chief under the Bale. The size of each often depended on the prestige of its chief, and, as a result, could vary considerably within each town and from town to town. It was possible for a town like Shaki, with a population of just over 13,000 in 1929, to have more quarters (27) than a larger town like Iseyin (17) with twice the popula-

[1] Both Frobenius and Johnson emphasize the uniformity of Yoruba town plans.
L. Frobenius, *The Voice of Africa*, I, 1912, 220.
S. Johnson, *The History of the Yorubas*, London, 1921, 12.
[2] This is still true today. In Ilora, for example, there is one main market and two subsidiary markets daily, but only a small night market due to competition from the large one in nearby Oyo.
R. M. C. Welldon, "The human geography of a Yoruba township in South-west Nigeria", B.Litt. thesis, Oxford, 1957, 63.
[3] According to Lloyd there are 500 compounds in Iwo (population 100,006): Welldon obtained a figure of 138 for Ilora (population 26,122).
P. C. Lloyd, "The traditional political system of the Yoruba", *Southwestern Journal of Anthropology*, x, 4, 1954, 375.
Welldon, *op. cit.*, II, Fig. 17.

tion. As in most towns, new quarters have been added and existing ones extended as population increased so that Shaki now has 41 quarters and Iseyin 26. Iseyin received a group of Ijebu immigrants soon after its foundation, and still has an Ijebu quarter; later, small neighbouring villages joined the growing town, and their names remain in the present town quarter. Ibadan's growth was never so clear-cut, and Hayley, in his report on administrative reforms, sums up the haphazard way in which the town grew, when he states that there are "65 traditional quarters in Ibadan, undefined and undefinable".[1]

In addition to their trade connections, Yoruba towns had a craft basis but, unlike towns in Northern Nigeria, there were no quarters exclusive to particular crafts. Scattered through a town, traditional crafts, especially among the Oyo Yoruba, showed great diversity and have maintained themselves to a surprising degree in competition with imported goods. However, important changes are taking place and some towns are becoming more specialized in certain crafts, as in Iseyin where 16 per cent of working males are engaged in the weaving of cotton cloth while women dye and spin. The cloth is exported in quantity to the Ibadan market. In the face of this kind of competition, weaving is declining in nearby smaller towns. Woodcarving is a dying art in most towns and the modern carpenter is replacing the older craftsman. Blacksmiths still flourish for there is always a demand for farm implements.

The main basis of the majority of Yoruba towns is still agricultural. It is no longer imperative to keep land within the walls in reserve for food crops, but in small plots, especially along stream banks, women still grow vegetables, melons and sugar cane. One hundred years ago the main farmland lay outside the walls usually within a radius of 5 or 6 miles, which was considered to be a reasonable distance for farmers to walk to and from their fields each day. If the rural area around a town was considered to be safe, farming operations were extended beyond this limit and farmers remained on their farms for varying lengths of time. In the 1850's this was especially true

---

[1] J. Hayley, *Final Report on Ibadan Divisional Reforms*, Ibadan, 1952, 3.
An Ibadan quarter chief could give a newcomer land anywhere within the wall; consequently, his followers were not closely grouped in a compact quarter.

of Ibadan and many chiefs in the town owned what were, in effect, extensive plantations worked by slaves. Today farming activities have been greatly extended and "town farmers" may only return to their parent town for a few annual festivals. Many of Ibadan's farmers now live and work up to 30 miles away. The map of the farmland of Ilora gives some indication

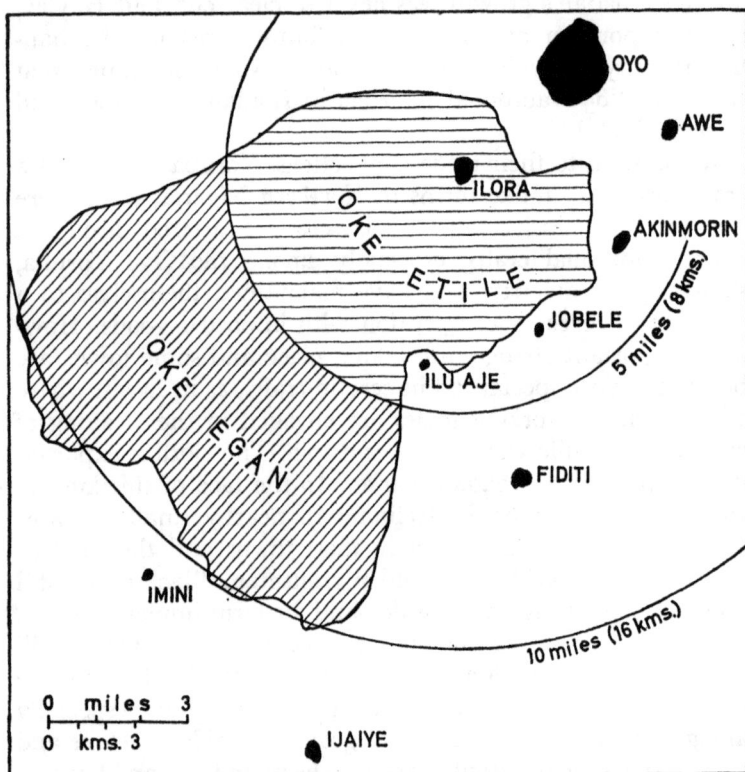

FIG. XXIV. Ilora town and its farmland (after Welldon).

of the extent of its farming activities (Fig. XXIV). The *oke etile* or "home-farm" corresponds with the original inner ring of land within a radius of 5 miles from Ilora and the *oke egan* or "forest farm" corresponds with the more recently farmed areas. The expansion of farmland has been to the south-west, away from the neighbouring and larger town of Oyo.

The traditional Yoruba town plan can still be seen, but is

being modified by changing conditions. Walls and ditches are mostly gone. Many roads and paths have been widened and straightened, the main roads even have a tarred surface and roads are beginning to influence town lay-outs. The old compounds backed on to the roads but modern roads and new forms of transport mean that dwellings and shops compete for the favoured roadside sites. In particular, along the main roads on the outskirts, ribbon development is taking place, partly hastened by the advance of gully erosion in the older sections of the towns.[1] These outskirts usually have some of the most recent and most imposing buildings. In the interior of Yorubaland buildings in "Lagos style" are now common, a blending of African and European architecture inspired originally by freed slaves who had returned from Latin America or Freetown. Bungalows have been built in many towns since the 1930's by people with Lagos contacts but storeyed houses are more recent in the interior. Both types of building may have walls of sun-dried mud blocks covered with a thin coating of cement often painted or, in the case of the most elaborate ones, of cement blocks. Roofing material consists of corrugated iron sheets, locally known as "pan", which are long lasting and easy to replace. These new types of building are rapidly replacing the traditional compound, except in the poorer and less accessible parts of the savanna. Both house style and roofing materials are general indications of the wealth of the individual and the community, but even a rather poor savanna town like Shaki has 30 per cent of its buildings, both compounds and individual dwellings, roofed in "pan". More and more the trend is towards the individual dwelling.[2] The old town plan is further modified by the addition of schools, churches, mosques, wells, dispensaries, trading stores, courts and the ubiquitous petrol-filling stations.

The direct and indirect effects of European contacts on the

[1] In 1949 the Annual Report for Oyo Division stressed the urgency of combatting erosion in the town centre of Ilora. It was pointed out that extensive gully erosion was about to wash the mosque and the market place into the stream and that roads in the centre were half their former width. Welldon, writing in 1954, records that gullies and ruins were still there and were hastening the outward spread of the town.

[2] The insistence by Christian missionaries on the single family unit is also a factor which should be taken into consideration when explaining this trend.

morphology of Yoruba towns may best be seen from the detailed examination of one town. Ibadan is an obvious example for, of the many indigenous towns, it has undergone the greatest expansion and change and yet is much more representative of the indigenous town than is Lagos. It originated as a small forest settlement only in the late eighteenth or early nineteenth century but it has developed in the urban tradition associated with the Yoruba farming, trading and craft economy with modern problems and trends which are relevant to other expanding Yoruba towns.

Ibadan (Fig. XXV)

Ibadan's defence works, almost 11 miles in circumference, are no longer prominent; the remains of the walls are nowhere more than three feet in height and are mostly overgrown with vegetation. In the early years of the British Administration, however, they were a visible divide between the indigenous town and the new European sections being built to the west and north-east. This division is reflected in the present-day morphology. The indigenous town has developed under the Ibadan Native Administration, which was formed in 1897, while land outside the walls which was needed for residential and other purposes was acquired from the Native Administration and later declared Crown Land under direct control of the Colonial Government. It has encroached on the indigenous town in a few places, but to no significant extent.

Urban density figures illustrate the contrast between these two parts of modern Ibadan. At least 400,000 people live within the 8·7 square miles of the indigenous town. Crown Land in the immediate vicinity of the indigenous town takes up 8·3 square miles but here densities of less than 5 persons per acre contrast with a mean density of 80 persons per acre for the indigenous town. A more relevant indication of density in the indigenous town is obtained if this is calculated on the amount of built-up land within the walls. This gives a mean density of 150 persons per acre.[1] It is high, but overcrowding is not com-

[1] Welldon obtained a figure of 109 persons per acre of built-up land for Ilora and 101 for Fiditi (*op. cit.*, p. 57). Ogbomosho has 120, Oyo 80 and Abeokuta only 35. The older and more compact towns like Ilora and Ogbomosho have higher

parable with that in parts of Lagos where, in an area of
69 acres on Lagos island, the average density is 306 persons per
acre with resultant slum conditions. In Ibadan in 1908 closely

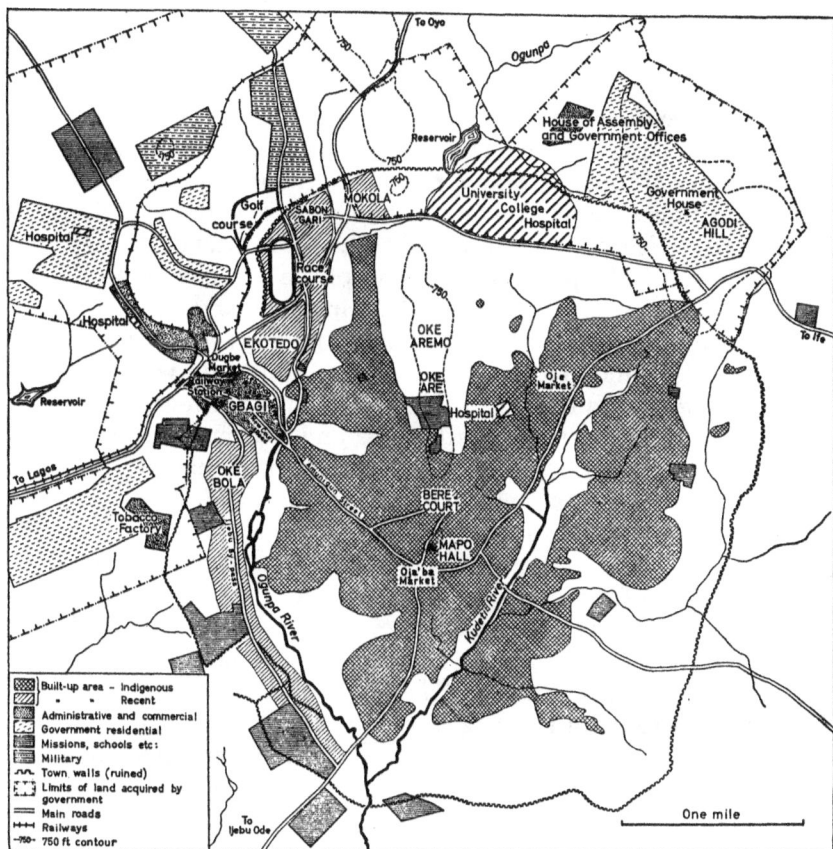

FIG. XXV. The morphology of Ibadan.

grouped compounds occupied almost 2 square miles and scattered compounds an additional 1·2 square miles. The town
population was about 175,000 in that year, giving a density of
135 per acre for the densely populated sections and 86 per acre

densities than the nineteenth-century towns like Oyo and Abeokuta. The more
compact old towns like . . . . Abeokuta. In this respect, however, Ibadan is a
special case.

for the entire settled area.[1] This is only a rough estimate for it is impossible to give precise meaning to phrases like "sparsely populated with scattered compounds" appearing on the 1908 map and estimates of population are suspect. Population increase has been mostly absorbed by expansion into the area shown as sparsely populated in 1908 and though the town has doubled its built-up area its population has trebled and consequently densities are greater.

Ibadan's original town wall is supposed to have enclosed half a square mile on Oke Mapo, the southernmost hill on the Oke Aremo ridge. According to tradition, it passed through Bere Square, which occupies the col between Oke Mapo and Oke Are (Fig. XXVI, p. 293). The focus of the old town was, and still is, the large Oja'ba market, the principal market in Ibadan and one of the largest in Yorubaland. By 1893 the town had spread along the southern slopes of Oke Mapo and westwards to the Ogunpa valley and Inalende. The area north-east of the ridge had only scattered settlements and Oje market, one of Ibadan's old ones, was still known as the "bush market". The Aremo ridge, rising steeply some 200 feet above the surrounding countryside, tended to make contact between the areas to the east and west difficult and even today serves to isolate the more inaccessible of the old town's quarters from the new western sections. In the past settlement avoided it owing to poor water supplies, the rapid erosion of steep slopes, and lack of space for the grouping of compounds. The first settlements on the ridge itself were those of the Lagos traders, Shepherd and Gomez. Today there is a mission school, a small number of private residences, and a wireless relay station, but most of the ridge is covered with a forestry plantation. Streams have influenced the settlement pattern, their marshy and malarial valleys being unsuitable for settlement. With the canalizing of stream courses and the draining of marshes by the Public Works Department in the 1930's, settlement is now developing in the valleys and the streams no longer form marked divides between different sections of the town.

[1] Governor Moloney estimated Ibadan's population to be 150,000 in 1890. Millson put the figure at 120,000.

Sir A. Moloney, "Notes on Yorubaland and the Colony and Protectorate of Lagos, West Africa", *Proceedings of the Royal Geographical Society, New Series*, XII, 1890, 596.

A. Millson, "The Yoruba Country, West Africa", *ibid.*, XIII, 1891, 582.

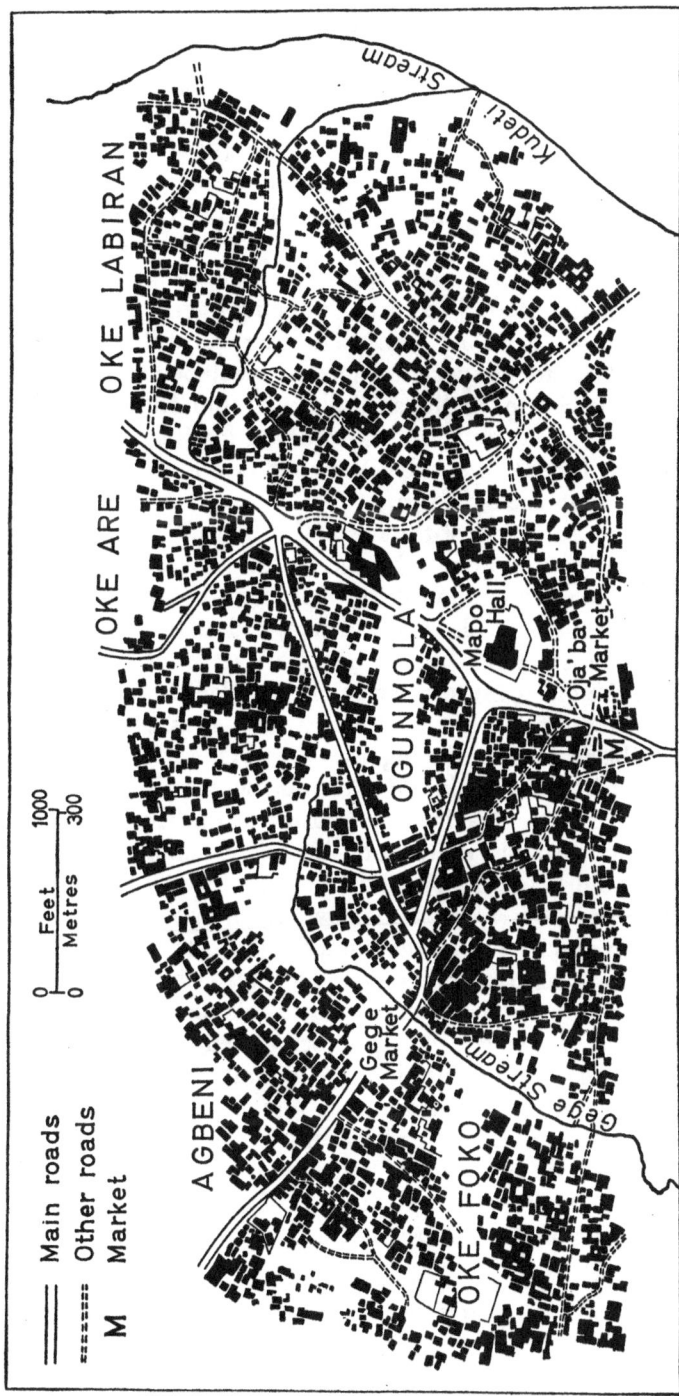

FIG. XXVI. Ibadan: an example of the indigenous urban pattern.

Main roads
Other roads
M Market

AGBENI

OKE FOKO

Gege Market

Gege Stream

OKE ARE

OKE LABIRAN

Kudeti Stream

OGUNMOLA

Mapo Hall

Oja 'ba Market

Feet   1000
0
Metres   300
0

The old town has retained some of its character and the majority of Ibadan's 2,000 compounds are found here.[1] Old crafts scattered throughout the town are still well represented despite the appearance of a variety of new occupations, among them bicycle-repairing and tailoring. Only bicycle- and motor-repairing show any marked tendency to localization, not unnaturally, along the main roads. Most of the 35 per cent of working males referred to earlier as being engaged in agriculture come from the old town. The markets still retain their importance although specialization has developed among them. Oje now specializes in the sale of cloth from Iseyin, Oja'ba's large night market provides cooked food for the town's many temporary inhabitants and Gege has developed as a meat market serving the old town.

With the exception of the hospital in Adeoyo, the old town was not influenced greatly by the British Administration until the 1930's when considerable development took place. As well as stream control, roads were widened, and dual-carriage ways, Ogunmola Street and King George V Avenue, were built through the old town to the east of the ridge. Mapo Hall, the headquarters of the town administration, was built opposite the Oja'ba market on the highest part of Oke Mapo. By 1937, 29 wells had been sunk. The general increase in wealth was beginning to have its effects on housing at this time. The post-war era has brought even more significant changes in roofing material and house design. Thatch has virtually disappeared and storeyed houses and bungalows are now more numerous than compounds. It was the compound which had given the town its homogeneous character and a heterogeneous townscape is now developing. To keep pace with this modern expansion, the Native Administration has formulated many new rules relating to building, sanitation, the lay-out of markets and the canalizing of streams. For example, no roof thatch is permitted without the consent of the Administration. Plans for new building require ratification; houses must not exceed half and commercial buildings three-quarters of the area of their site, and building materials are specified. Even the size of living

---

[1] Native Administration Tax Returns, 1954. On this basis there are about 19,000 dwellings of all kinds in the indigenous town, with an average of about 20 persons per unit.

rooms is regulated. There are also market rules laying out specifications for the size and arrangement of stalls. Ibadan is not alone among Yoruba towns in maintaining control of its modern development. There are other progressive Native Administrations influencing town character and growth elsewhere in Yorubaland.

Four important factors hastened Ibadan's growth in the twentieth century. The railway from Lagos reached the town in 1901 and prepared the way for an influx of new people—both African and non-African—new ideas and commerce. The first trading firms were, in fact, African, but the larger European firms quickly recognized the importance of the town's central position in the interior. Cash-crop farming was introduced, beginning with rubber and followed by cocoa and palm kernels. Ibadan became the principal buying and distributing centre for the "Cocoa Belt". Thirdly came the development of road transport, especially since 1945. Today Ibadan acts as an entrepôt for Yorubaland with lorry service to all parts of Nigeria, to Ghana and to French territory. Lastly, Ibadan became the headquarters of the Western Provinces and is now the capital of the Western Region. The assumption of these administrative functions, allied to an excellent nodal position, ensures its future importance and growth.

The arrival of newcomers in Ibadan, especially after the coming of the railway, created many problems for the British Administration and has had a permanent effect on the town's morphology. The apportionment of land was a difficult problem. Natives of Ibadan frequently leased land to European firms and Lebanese traders without authority and there were many alleged attempts on the part of native newcomers to take improper possession of valuable land within the walls. In the early years of the twentieth century there does not appear to have been any opposition to newcomers settling in the town, except for Lagos Yorubas who sheltered behind their British nationality to exclude them from any liability to local taxation or judicial control by the Ibadan Native Administration. With increasing numbers of "strangers"—as all non-Ibadans were called—haphazard development and settlement could no longer be permitted. The Native Administration was encouraged to grant land to certain "stranger" groups to avoid the erection of further temporary, insanitary camps of grass huts. The construction of the first planned settlement, in which uniform building lots were allocated, was begun in 1917. This was the *Sabon Gari* ("new town"); it was completed in 1920 and is a predominantly Hausa settlement.[1] With the construction of other planned settlements, notably Mokola, Ekotedo and part of Inalende, the contrast in morphology between them and the

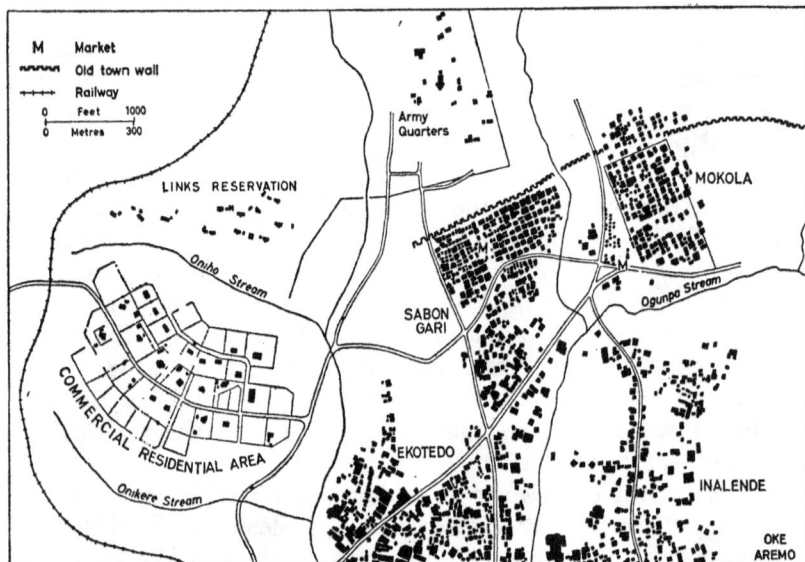

FIG. XXVII. Ibadan: an example of the recent urban pattern.

older town developed and tribal segregation was accepted (Fig. XXVII).

The presence of a *Sabon Gari* reflects the importance of the trade connections of a Yoruba town with Northern Nigeria. The permanent population of Ibadan's *Sabon Gari* is mainly concerned with the large and profitable trade in kola nuts and cattle carried on between Northern and Southern Nigeria. Before 1930, other Northern Nigerians also congregated there and it became so badly overcrowded that new land had to be

[1] In the towns of Northern Nigeria the *Sabon Gari* is a planned settlement for Southern Nigerians.

found for its non-Hausa inhabitants. This presented a problem, for there was little land left in existing "stranger" settlements within the walls, and expansion outside them was restricted by Crown Land development. Nupe and Igbirra peoples were finally settled at Mokola adjoining the *Sabon Gari* on what was, in fact, Crown Land although within the walls. By 1946 Mokola in turn had become congested and had to be extended to provide land for people from Ilorin. This was on the steep slopes of the Oke Aremo ridge, and the consequent clearing of vegetation resulted in an increasingly serious problem of erosion control. The planning of a settlement like Mokola refers only to the allocation of building plots on an approved site and dwellings are not provided. Because Mokola is on Crown Land, its inhabitants have permission to build only temporary dwellings for the land could be requisitioned at any time. The fact that substantial storey houses are being erected, in addition to the many inferior thatched buildings, indicates the resolve of its inhabitants to make the settlement a permanent one. Now even Ijebu and Ibadan people hold plots for speculative building. Sample densities of population range between 100 and 135 persons per acre. There is overcrowding since Nupe labourers and traders and Igbirra farmers have sought to augment their small incomes by letting rooms to Ibos, Edos and other newcomers, thus making the number of people per dwelling unit higher than the average for the town. One house visited, a small thatched one, had in it 35 people, Nupe, Ibo, Edo and Ilorins, an indication of the amount of tribal intermixing that is now taking place in what was intended as a settlement for various northern tribes. Similarly, people from Eastern Nigeria have entered Ekotedo and Inalende which were established as planned settlements for Yoruba from outside Ibadan. In this way economic factors are helping to break down tribal separation at least in the newer parts of Ibadan.

Apart from planned settlements for "strangers", a commercial sector has also developed within the walls. Architecturally Gbagi is the most impressive addition to the indigenous town. On the site of what was farmland, it was leased by the Native Administration to various trading firms—European, Asiatic and to a lesser extent African. It was extended in the 1930's to the Ogunpa stream in the north and to the Oyo road. At the suggestion of the British Administration all Lebanese in Ibadan were concentrated in Gbagi Street which is now known as Lebanon Street and today 70 per cent of all trading stores in Gbagi are owned by Lebanese, who deal mainly in textiles. As good customers of the large European firms, they have been allowed to overflow into New Court Road, the second of Gbagi's main streets. This was originally reserved for European firms—British, French, Swiss and German, but they are also found in Lebanon Street today. In both the main streets of Gbagi there are also a few Indian and Syrian firms. About thirty small African stores overflow into Gbagi from Amunigun and Agbeni Streets, the principal area for small-scale African enterprises. Gbagi is also a residential area, for the majority of Levantines and Indians and a few Europeans live above or at the rear of their stores. Its character changes uphill away from the Ogunpa valley and the old town until the Crown Land in the west is reached. In this zone there are banks, offices, motor show-rooms and garages and a post office. A new ten-storey office block is indicative of the increasing demands for business accommodation in a small commercial core. In the face of these demands it is likely that Gbagi will experience further vertical extension.

Another area within the walls which has developed its own character is along the road which runs from Ibadan to Ijebu-ode. Until the draining of the Ogunpa marshes and the building of a new road to link the roads to Lagos and Ijebu-ode, this area was thinly populated. Over a hundred years ago land grants had been made to various Christian missions to develop in the area, but development has been most rapid since 1945. There has been much speculative building on the part of the Ijebus who constructed large storeyed houses in the style which originated in Lagos and spread inland via Ijebu-ode. Local building rules have affected their plan, for a regulation narrow frontage of 50 feet has meant that they can be little more than a double line of rooms opening off a central hallway. A house may have as many as twenty-four rooms which are let individually at high rents. This area is not only residential, it contains in addition schools, businesses and cinemas. Modern industry, which is generally absent in Yoruba towns apart from Lagos, is represented here by a factory owned by an Ijebu for the retreading of tyres. Nearby is one of the largest tobacco factories in Africa, owned by the Nigerian Tobacco Company. Factories for fruit-canning and plastics have recently been established on the outskirts of Ibadan near Moor Plantation. Further development may be expected now that the new Lagos–Ibadan road, via Shagamu and Ijebu-ode, has been opened.

Outside the walls development has been controlled by a series of land acquisitions in relation to particular needs. The first of these was in 1893, when Agodi became the administrative and residential sector. The railway came next, and the station was built near the Iddo gate and so affected development in Dugbe and Ekotedo, as well as in Gbagi. The British Cotton Growing Association in 1904 asked for 15,000 acres, and were granted 5,000 by the Native Administration on which to grow cotton and thus employ the town's liberated slaves. This plan came to nothing as the slaves never materialized, having been completely absorbed into the social structure of the town. In 1913, only 150 acres were in use, and the Governor recommended that the remainder be returned to the Native Administration. 3,000 acres were retained and formed the nucleus of what is today Moor Plantation, a Department of Agriculture Research Station. In 1917, a "Township" was established which included the railway station and adjacent residential areas. The Township Ordinance encouraged but did not compel Europeans to live in an area where special rules for public health could be enforced. Such "Townships" are not typical of Yoruba towns, and were created only in towns like Lagos, Ibadan and Ijebu-ode which were commercially important for Europeans.[1] Ibadan's "Township" was abolished in 1936 when there was no further need for it as European residential areas had become too widely scattered.

Various other developments have taken place during this century. Land was acquired for the Eleiyele waterworks in 1911 and the Ogunpa reservoir in 1934. In 1906 a racecourse was laid out and a golf course in 1929. The Recreational Club, which was the centre of the European community's social activities, moved to its present site in 1930. European residential

[1] In 1931 there were 221 Europeans in Ibadan, by 1952 the number had risen to 721 and today it is well over 1,000.

areas continued to grow. Europeans engaged in commerce settled in the Old Reservation and government officials in Agodi and in the New Reservation which was laid out in 1938. In common with European residential areas in other Nigerian towns, Ibadan's were characterized by uniformity of house type and road pattern. A building-free zone of 440 yards' width surrounded each of them and was cleared of vegetation, in accordance with the then accepted theory that mosquitoes were unable to reach buildings across a clearing of this distance. Today, Africans in senior posts occupy houses in all the principal residential areas, and the Recreational Club is open to all members of the community. New demands have been made on the Crown Lands, especially since 1945. As capital of the Western Region, Ibadan now has a House of Assembly and a House of Chiefs which have been built near the Secretariat in Agodi and are linked with western parts of the town by the new and imposing Queen Elizabeth highway. A new hospital, the most modern in Nigeria, has been built on Crown Land within the walls. New educational demands for land have been met at some distance from the town. The University College, for example, has 5 square miles for its present and future requirements.

Ibadan is no longer an indigenous Yoruba town contained within defensive walls. The new Ibadan that has emerged in the last 60 years is a much larger unit of complex character. The old town's irregular nucleated layout is in marked contrast with the more recent additions within the walls and on Crown Land outside. Oke Mapo and its large market have been replaced by Gbagi as the main commercial focus of the town. The concentration of newcomers in areas west of the Oke Aremo ridge has encouraged the growth of sectional interests in the town and this ridge now divides an essentially wage-earning and salaried part of the community from the older farming and craft section. Petty trading, however, transcends all boundaries. The majority of immigrants have come from other parts of Yorubaland. They and their descendants may account for as much as 30 per cent of the town's present population whereas those from outside Yorubaland, although they make an important contribution to the town's character, account for only 5 per cent of the total population. The immigrant factor has been responsible for the town's very rapid growth. Whereas the population of large indigenous towns like Ogbomosho and Oshogbo have, at the most, doubled since 1893, that of Ibadan has trebled.[1] One of the most significant pointers to the future size of the population is that over 50 per cent of the present population is under 14 years of age. Apart from a very high rate of natural increase, the drift from the rural areas may be expected to increase in the future. It is evident that the urban trend in Western Nigeria is accelerating and that well-established centres like Ibadan and Lagos are attracting population at a faster rate than smaller towns.

In Nigeria, the brief era of colonial administration is at an end. In as far as it affected Ibadan, it may be criticized for not initiating greater changes in the indigenous town, but development through the Native Administration ensured that changes would not be too rapid and unsettling. Capital for development has always been limited and whereas the new impressive buildings on Crown Lands have received priority, any such development within the indigenous town has largely been in the hands of commercial enterprise. During the period of British Administration some degree of planning was initiated but problems relating to housing, sanitation, water supply and erosion control are far from being solved. More than ever this still rapidly growing town will require intelligent planning if these problems are not to multiply in the future.

[1] The population of Lagos has increased six times since 1891.

15

A Geographical Analysis of Boundaries in Inter-Tropical Africa[1]

K. M. BARBOUR

THE rapid emergence in the last few years of a number of independent states in Africa makes this an appropriate time to take a look at the political map of the continent, since the many unions, federations and other associations of states that are currently under discussion suggest that the present pattern of countries and boundaries may not be destined to endure for long. It is not here intended to recommend what changes should be made in Africa's boundaries, still less to forecast what shifts are likely to occur in the future. There are various physical and social problems connected with these boundaries, however, concerned both with their initial establishment and their current effects. By drawing attention to these it is hoped to stimulate enquiry and research into the geographical as well as the historical aspects of boundary-making.

The boundaries of Africa owe their existence, almost without exception, to the wave of empire-building in the continent that took place in the latter part of the nineteenth century. Penetration of the African interior had begun with the Portuguese journeys up the Zambezi in the early part of the sixteenth century, had continued with the Egyptian invasion of the Nile Valley in 1821, and was carried a stage further by the gradual extension of British and French interest in West Africa during

[1] The author wishes to thank the Central Research Fund of London University for a field-work grant which led to the writing of this essay.

the middle of the nineteenth century. Nevertheless it was the appearance of the Belgians and Germans on the scene in the 1880's that provoked the rapid extension of European influence in Africa, culminating in the "Scramble for Africa" and the Treaty of Berlin of 1885. After this very little of the continent remained independent, unless the American negro colony of Liberia, founded in 1821, be granted this title. Of the many possible lines of investigation in connection with the frontiers of Africa, three are here suggested as being of particular geographical interest. These are the types of line used in boundaries between states, the relationships between boundaries and tribal territories, and the relationships between boundaries and the distribution of population.

Types of Boundary

There is an interesting series of maps showing stages in the assignment of Africa to the several colonial powers printed in Stamp's regional geography of the continent.[1] The types or characters of these frontiers clearly differ greatly. Fawcett,[2] following Lord Curzon's Romanes Lecture of 1907,[3] has classified frontier types as follows:

(1) Natural barriers, which may consist of
    (a) the sea
    (b) a desert
    (c) mountains
    (d) forest
    (e) swamp
(2) River boundaries
(3) Artificial boundaries, which may consist of
    (a) pure astronomical lines
    (b) geometrical lines
    (c) lines of reference

Such a classification is not wholly applicable to tropical Africa, where the balance of types of line employed is rather different from other continents. Watersheds, in particular, which are much employed in the continent, are classified by

---

[1] L. D. Stamp, *Africa*, 1953, Figs. 6–13.
[2] C. B. Fawcett, *Frontiers*, 1918.
[3] Lord Curzon, *Frontiers*, Romanes Lecture, Oxford, 1907.

Fawcett merely as instances of lines of reference, whereas it may be argued that they constitute lines related to relief features, comparable therefore with rivers, etc. From a study of the individual treaties defining boundaries in Africa, most of which are to be found in Hertslet's *Map of Africa by Treaty*,[1] the following alternative classification has been drawn up, and Fig. XXVIII has been constructed from it.

A = Astronomical line, i.e. parallel or meridian
M = Mathematical line, i.e. straight line, arc of circle, line
   equidistant from a named line, etc.
   Mr = Mathematical line defined by reference to relief
   Mh = Mathematical line defined by reference to fea-
      ture of human occupation
R = Relief feature
   Rf = foot of mountain chain
   Rl = edge of lake or lagoon
   Rs = stream or river, usually the centre line
   Rw = watershed
I = One of the above which is also an inter-tribal boundary

The map shows, as would be expected, that astronomical and other mathematical lines are usually, though not always, to be found in thinly inhabited areas such as the Sahara Desert. Those lines, on the other hand, which are defined in relation to features of the human occupation of the land, are generally to be found in areas which were both settled and known when the boundaries were drawn up. The relative proportions of the different types of boundary, calculated very approximately, is as follows: Astronomical lines, 44 per cent; Mathematical lines, 30 per cent; Relief features, 26 per cent.

In another continent, these proportions would clearly be different. In Australia there are no international boundaries, and the state boundaries, if indeed they may be regarded as comparable, have an exceptionally high proportion of astronomical lines. In Europe the period of occupation, of disputes about frontiers, and of shifts one way or another has been so long that the astronomical line is scarcely employed at all between sovereign states; rivers and mountain barriers, on the other hand, are widely used.

[1] Sir E. Hertslet, *The Map of Africa by Treaty*, 3rd edn., 1909.

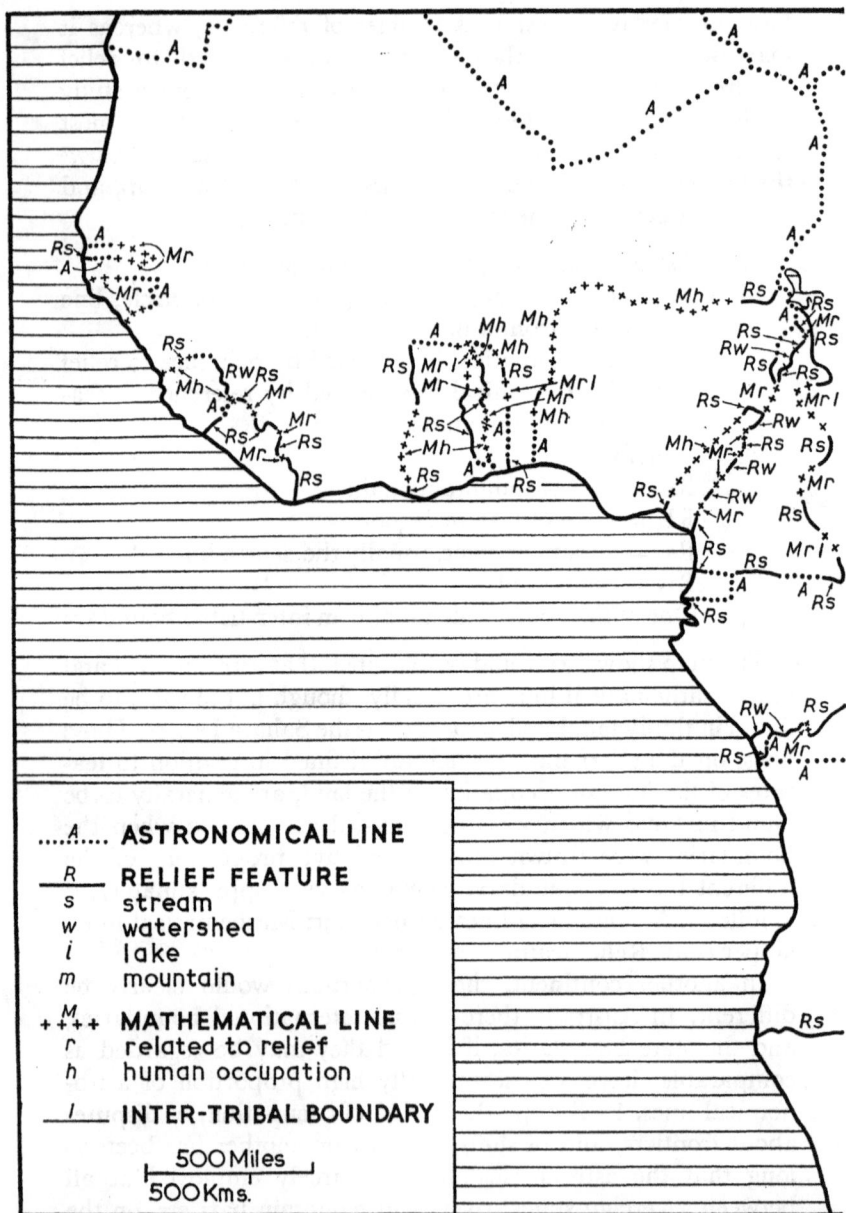

FIG. XXVIII. Tropical Africa:

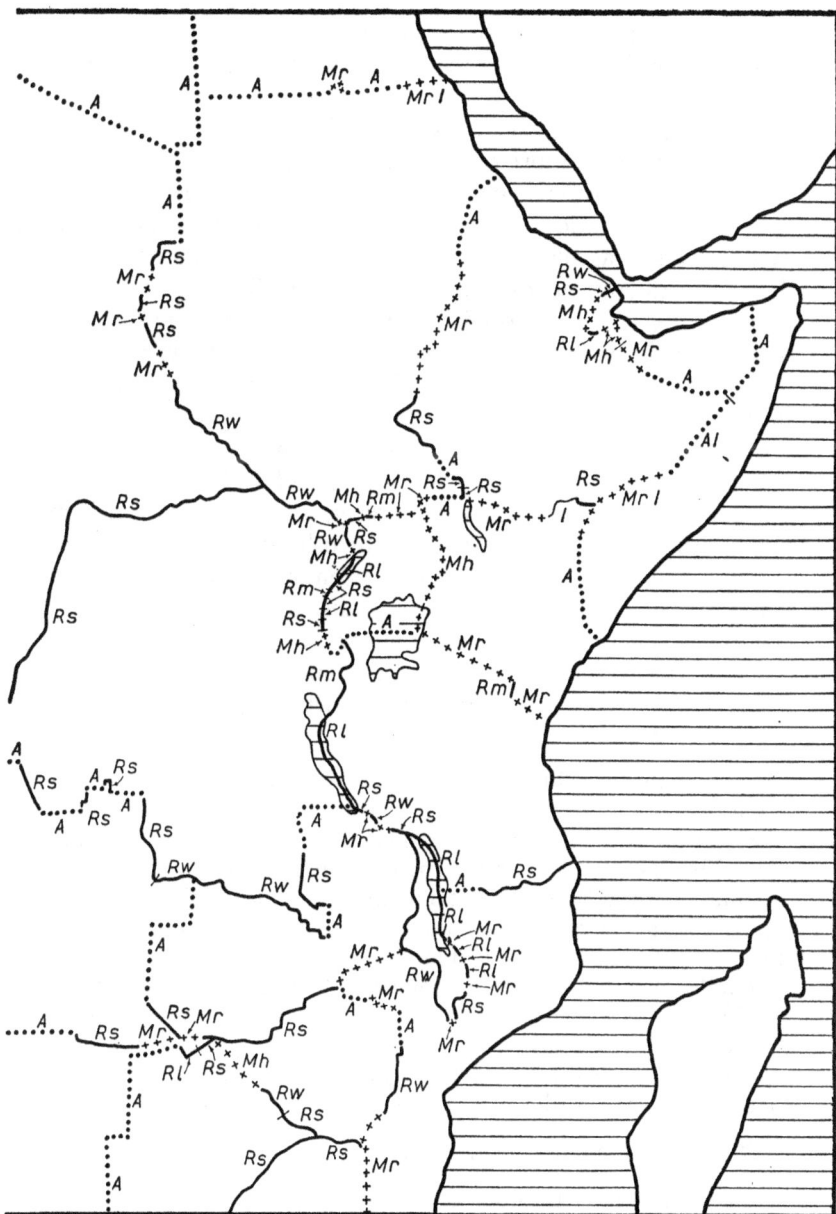

types of international boundary.

K. M. Barbour

The reason why watersheds are so much more important in Africa appears to be that the early exploration of the continent consisted primarily of a series of attempts to elucidate the drainage pattern of the continent.[1] Given the river systems with their mouths more or less easily mappable at the coast, it was clear that watersheds between their basins must lie somewhere in the interior. It was quite common, therefore, for colonial powers to agree to use a watershed as a boundary before it had been discovered or mapped. Thus in 1894 Great Britain acknowledged King Leopold's authority in the Congo Basin to extend to the watershed (or mountain ridges) of the adjacent basins, particularly that of the Nile on the north.[2] How little this paid heed to the convenience of the native peoples may be judged from a message sent in 1900 to Zemu or Zemiu, a Zande chief from the south-west of what is now Sudan. He was thought to rule on both sides of the boundary, and was sent a British flag with a message to fly it in British territory. "You are aware of the boundaries that have been arranged between the English, the French and the Belgians, and that the Anglo-Egyptian sphere of influence begins from where the rivers and streams rise which flow to the north and the Nile." [3] On the other hand, watersheds had their drawbacks too, as was well recognized:

If it should be held that the occupation of the sea-coast entitles a nation to the possession of the inland territory . . . questions must arise, in the state of our geographical knowledge, as to what that inland territory is. A decision which might give us (if we decide to maintain our Oil River district Treaties) the valley of the Niger . . . might give to the Sultan of Zanzibar that Kilimanjaro country, in the possession of which the Cabinet decided recently we must not be forestalled by other nations. It would seem, on the other hand, to be fatal to our resistance to the Portuguese claims on Lake Nyassa. It would leave the Congo Basin, a very wide geographical expression, undefined. . . . Still a watershed is capable of geographical definition, and if the position of the law above alluded to is correct, it

[1] J. N. L. Baker, *A History of Geographical Discovery and Exploration*, 1931, Chapter XIV, 302–63.

[2] Agreement between Great Britain and His Majesty King Leopold, Sovereign of the Independent State of the Congo, 12/5/1894, Article I(a), and Article II, printed in Hertslet, *op. cit.*, vol. II, 584.

[3] R. Wingate to Lord Cromer, 12/10/1902, F.O. 10/776.

Analysis of Boundaries in Inter-Tropical Africa

might form the basis for the demarcation inland of coastal possessions.[1]

Of the other types of boundary employed, the astronomical lines could similarly be agreed on at a conference table many miles away from where they were to be applied, albeit with some ludicrous results if the surveyors proved unable to make their calculations agree. This happened when the Anglo-German boundary was being demarcated between Nigeria and the Cameroons in 1903, since the two parties were using different methods of determining longitude by observation of the moon.[2] By the use of wireless time signals this type of error has now been virtually eliminated. Where boundaries based on astronomical lines run across settled ground, or across routes followed by nomadic tribes in their annual migrations, they can be most inappropriate. This was recognized in the boundary between Egypt and the Anglo-Egyptian Sudan, for having first been defined as the 22nd parallel of latitude,[3] it was subsequently altered to a less direct line which brought the whole of the grazing grounds of certain Beja tribes into the Sudan, and similarly gave the Egyptians authority over all the territory of an Arab tribe, the Ababda.

The use of rivers as boundaries involved few technical difficulties, except in areas where streams are liable to change their courses, or where a river was known in part, but not all, of its length when agreement was initially reached. Thus the German, Dr. Karl Peters, was once suspected of claiming falsely that a river had changed its course, presumably for the sake of gaining some territory, or at least of obtaining a bargaining counter for use elsewhere.[4] And in discussions relating to the Sudan-Abyssinian frontier it was proposed to use the Pibor River, but "if the Pibor River does not go as far as the 6th degree (of latitude north), its course to Meridian 34° E of

[1] Memorandum by C. L. Hill dated 20/10/1884, in F.O. Confidential Print 5023.

[2] Hertslet, *op. cit.*, III, 933.

[3] Agreement between the British Government and the Government of the Khedive of Egypt, relative to the future administration of Sudan, Article I, section (1), printed in Sir Harold MacMichael, *The Anglo-Egyptian Sudan*, 1934, 67.

[4] C. S. Smith, Consul at Zanzibar, to Earl of Rosebery, 30/12/1892, and later documents, including Anglo-German Protocol of 25/7/1893, signed in Berlin. F.O. 2/76.

Greenwich shall be the frontier".[1] When through uncertainty of the local topography a suspicion arose that the drainage system did not follow a normal pattern, further difficulties were experienced. Thus the Anglo-French treaty of 1882 declared that France was to control the Mellacoree River and Great Britain the Scarcies River, but

if the water communication at Mahela shall be found to open into the Mellacoree as well as the Scarcies River, the line shall start on the coast from the centre of the stream which joins the sea at Mahela, and shall be continued so as to assign to Great Britain the communication with the Scarcies River and to France that with the Mellacoree River.[2]

Despite these difficulties there was no doubt that boundary lines which actually followed rivers or other physical features had many advantages over lines of reference or mathematical lines which were defined as running at some stated distance from a river or a road. When the Belgians were trying to establish the boundary of the leased Lado enclave, in what is now southern Sudan, as a line running 40 miles west of the Nile, the Marquess of Lansdowne drafted a prudent memorandum on the wisdom of adhering to lines defined by physical geography:

To mark out a line of this nature (40 miles west of the Nile) in an unexplored tropical country is a notoriously difficult, expensive and laborious task, and the exact trace to be followed is likely to be a subject of much discussion and argument between the members of the Commission of Delimitation. His Majesty's Government are unable to believe that the tract of country to be gained or lost by either party is of sufficient value to justify the rejection of a plan which provides a distinct frontier easy both to ascertain and observe.[3]

Boundaries and Tribal Distributions

Frontiers of whatever kind are defined by treaty so as to make it possible to determine precisely on the ground just where the boundary between two territories lies. To a certain extent, therefore, boundaries merely reflect in precise topographical terms what has already been decided on admin-

---

[1] Mr. Warrington to Viscount Cromer, 26/5/1899, F.O. 1/44.
[2] Hertslet, *op. cit.*, II, p. 735.
[3] Marquess of Lansdowne to Mr. Phipps, 3/6/1902, F.O. 10/776.

istrative grounds to be the most sensible line to adopt. It would be unreasonable to assume in every case that lines so defined pay no heed to the convenience of local tribes or peoples. Nevertheless for a large part of the continent it has come about in practice that the present political boundaries divide tribes or language groups, and place them under two or even more administrations (Fig. XXIX).

This is not to say that the boundaries in Africa were drawn up with complete disregard for the feelings or interests of the local inhabitants, for in as much as territorial claims were generally based on treaties made with native chiefs, the lines between colonies usually reflected the prior existence, at least near the coast, of some sort of division between separate native political units. The care that was, at best, taken by the European authorities is well illustrated in a memorandum on the "formalities of occupation", which was drawn up in connection with the Berlin Conference of 1884. The writer stressed the need to establish the degree of authority of the representatives on the European side, the care that must be taken to sign agreements with none but the rightful owners of land, the necessity of consulting *all* kings, head chiefs or sub-chiefs who might claim authority, and the value of using good interpreters who could ensure that native peoples knew what was going on when they entered into agreements.[1]

Where a boundary which had been decided on appeared to disrupt the way of life of the local inhabitants, attempts were often made to mitigate the evils and inconveniences arising from the division of a tribe or of its lands. In the Anglo-French Agreement on the division of Somaliland there is a clause which states: "The subjects of both parties are at liberty to cross frontiers and graze their cattle, but wherever they go they must obey the Governor of the country where they are, and the wells remain open for both countries."[2] Similarly in the Anglo-French Agreement of 11/5/1905 concerning the boundary between the Gold Coast and the adjoining territory, it was provided "The villagers near the frontier shall retain the right to use the arable and pasture lands, springs and watering

---

[1] Memorandum by A. W. L. Hemming, inclosure No. 220, dated 11/12/1884, F.O. Confidential Print 5051.

[2] Hertslet, *op. cit.*, II, 429.

1 Regibat	39 Karachi	77 Adamawa	115 Azande	153 Aushi
2 Delim	40 Tribu	78 Mundang	116 Mundu	154 Tabwa
3 Serer	41 Kebu	79 Vere	117 Madi	155 Lungu
4 Malinke	42 Egba	80 Dari	118 Alur	156 Iwa
5 Banyun	43 Buem	81 Kotopo	119 Nyoro	157 Lambya
6 Balante	44 Fon	82 Laka	120 Toro	158 Nyakyusa
7 Biafada	45 Ewe	83 Mbere	121 Nkole	159 Tumbuka
8 Fouta Djalon	46 Popo	84 Chamba	122 Chiga	160 Mombera
9 Susu	47 Gun	85 Ndoro	123 Berta	161 Chewa
10 Valunka	48 Tienga	86 Kentu	124 Koma	162 Yao
11 Koranko	49 Sokoto	87 Fungon	125 Anuak	163 Makonde
12 Temne	50 Adarawa	88 Mambila	126 Murle	164 Makua
13 Toma	51 Tazarawa	89 Wum	127 Suri	165 Mbunda
14 Gola	52 Ifora	90 Ekoi	128 Resniat	166 Nsenga
15 Kpelle	53 Asben	91 Ododop	129 Turkana	167 Kunda
16 Ngere	54 Azjer	92 Mum	130 Karamojong	168 Nyanja
17 Grebo	55 Teda	93 Bamilere	131 Sabei	169 Mbukushu
18 Bakwe	56 Bideyat	94 Kosi	132 Wanga	170 Tawara
19 Assini	57 Kharga	95 Kpe	133 Luo	171 Zimba
20 Anyi	58 Barabra	96 Baya	134 Afar	172 Ambo
21 Brong	59 Ababra	97 Koko	135 Esa	173 Nukwe
22 Nafana	60 Amer	98 Ngumba	136 Ogaben	174 Subia
23 Ligbi Degha	61 Zaghawa	99 Seke	137 Somali	175 Manyika
24 Dagari	62 Tama	100 Fang	138 Snebelle	176 Ndau
25 Grunshi	63 Masalit	101 Dzem	139 W. Somali	177 Kung
26 Busansi	64 Manga	102 Sanga	140 Boran	178 Koba
27 Gurma	65 Moba	103 Bonjo	141 Boni	179 Hiechware
28 Gurensi	66 Kanembu	104 Bwaka	142 Segeju	180 Nbelle
29 Manprusi	67 Shuwa	105 Banziri	143 Chagwa	181 Venda
30 Moba	68 Kotoko	106 Yakoma	144 Masai	182 Hlengwe
31 Chakossi	69 Musgu	107 Bangi	145 Digo	183 Ngwato
32 Bomba	70 Mandara	108 Teke	146 Chokwe	184 Tlokwa
33 Bargu	71 Wakura	109 Vili	147 Mbagani	185 Thonga
34 Dagomba	72 Matakam	110 Yombe	148 Lunda	186 Nusan
35 Konkomba	73 Kapsiki	111 Sundi	149 Luval	187 Kgatla
36 Basari	74 Gude	112 Kongo	150 Ndembu	
37 Basila	75 Tuburi	113 Yaka	151 Kaonde	
38 Atyuti	76 Masa	114 Ndogo	152 Lamba	

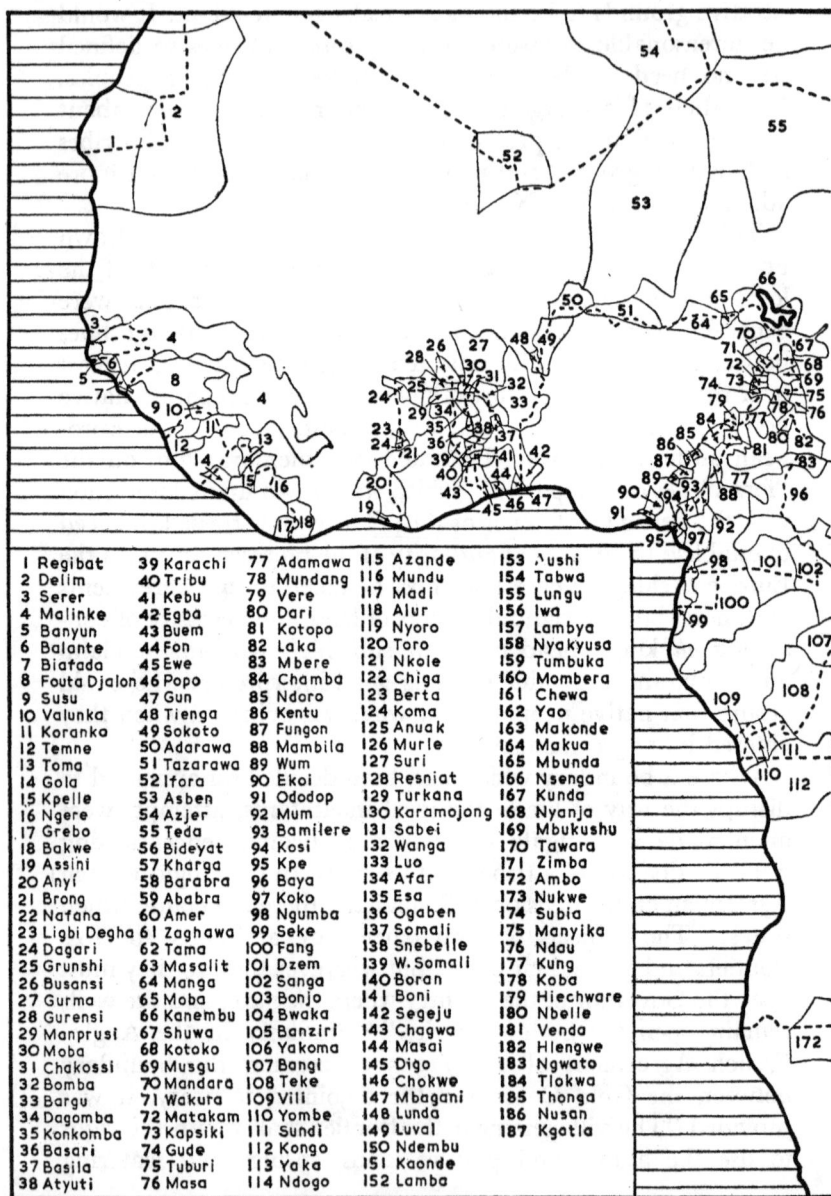

FIG. XXIX. Tropical Africa: tribal territories divided by

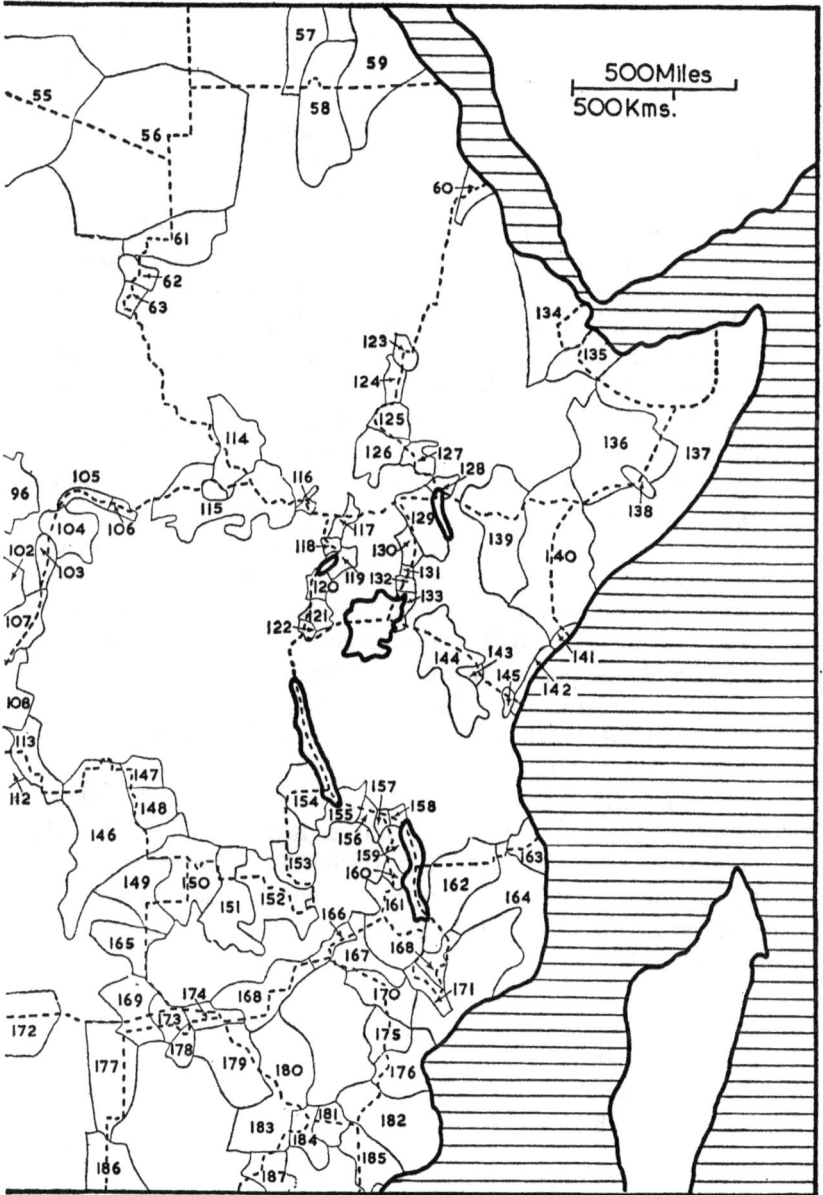

international boundaries. Mainly after Murdock (see Fig. XX).

places which they have heretofore used . . ."." even if these lay in the other's territory.[1] And in the Agreement of 1/2/1903, a further clause states: "The undersigned have agreed that the natives who would not be satisfied by the attribution of their town either to England or to France shall be allowed to move to the side of the boundary which they may select within one year from the signing of the final agreement."[2]

Yet the European powers were not always able to take into account the convenience of local peoples, even when information was available about them, as may be seen from a study of the negotiations with Germany which preceded a general settlement of claims in East Africa. In a letter exceptional for its period, revealing incidentally the close ties of knowledge and sympathy between the early missionaries in Nyasaland and the local Africans, J. W. Moir had submitted that the proposed Anglo-German frontier along the "Stevenson Road" from Lake Nyasa to Lake Tanganyika would be an unworkable boundary: "The road runs right through the very heart of several tribes, and it would be absurd to allow one half of such a tribe, because situated south of the road, to be British, while compelling the other half to submit to the Germans, of whom the natives know positively nothing." Such a boundary "would exclude the Northern Wa Nkonde, who have been uninterruptedly our friends for the last 11 years", and who had helped the British against the Arabs.[3]

No notice appears to have been taken of this appeal, for when the Anglo-German Agreement was signed the line adopted consisted of a number of short stretches, variously defined, which though running slightly to the north of the Stevenson Road yet divided the lands of the Wa Nkonde and of several other tribes.[4]

It would be misleading, however, to suggest that a simple list can be drawn up to distinguish between frontiers where the tribal distribution was taken into account, and those where it was disregarded. The term tribe is capable of several meanings: it may be used for a group of persons who speak the

[1] Hertslet, *op. cit.*, II, 841.   [2] *Ibid.*, 806.
[3] African Lakes Company to Marquess of Salisbury, F.O. Confidential Print, 6146, No. 69, 20/6/1890.
[4] Anglo-German Agreement, 1/7/1890, printed in Hertslet, *op. cit.*, III, 899.

same language and observe a generally similar pattern of dress and customs, or it may mean all the persons who acknowledge a common political head, whether they are culturally identical or not. Nadel, for example, wrote of the Nupe:

> What is the social reality to which the term Nupe people or Nupe tribe refers? The three meanings of *Nupe*, people, language and country, do not coincide. . . . Politically the Nupe people are scattered over several countries, seven Emirates or chieftainships today and four or five in pre-European times. . . . If the Nupe tribe is thus not a local group in the strict sense of the word, it is not a linguistic term either.[1]

This difficulty of definition continues to trouble investigators, for Goody, in an account of researches carried out in 1950 and 1952, writes: "I went to West Africa looking for a tribe called the 'Lobi'. . . . In fact I never found a group of people who replied to my questions 'We are Lobi'." [2]

Since the establishment of European power in the African continent it has been found convenient, particularly in the British dependencies, with their tradition of "indirect rule", to group together persons of the same speech and customs, and to make use, if possible, of a titular head to transmit orders, collect taxes and perform other administrative duties. This has meant that groups speaking the same language, who formerly had little sense of unity and were perhaps often at war with one another, have in many instances been welded together and given a sense of political homogeneity that they never possessed before.[3] Such a reduction in the number of small separate political units has clearly been to the benefit of the people of Africa, as a first step towards the creation of larger viable states. Where a political boundary has divided persons speaking the same tongue, however, a coalescence of this sort has generally not been possible, particularly since the inhabitants of French and British colonies, for instance, learn different European languages and have been introduced to significantly different political ideas.

[1] S. F. Nadel, *A Black Byzantium*, 1942, 12 and 13.
[2] J. R. Goody, *The Social Organization of the Lowiili*, 1956, 16.
[3] Lord Hailey's *African Survey*, revised 1956, 498 shows how the modern political unification of Bechuanaland has been the outcome of the establishment of a British Protectorate with a central administration.

K. M. Barbour

On the West Coast of Africa, where many of the political boundaries divide members of the same tribe, the changing nature of European interest in the continent has in part been the explanation of this division. The early European settlements were devoted to trade, not military conquest, and in favourable areas such as the drier and healthier Gold Coast they settled in great numbers, each station entering into an agreement with the local native chief. The forested country along the coast did not lend itself to the establishment or maintenance of large native kingdoms, and a visitor to West Africa in the 1860's remarked: "The state of the river (the Niger delta) is that of perfect anarchy. Some Europeans sigh for the order and responsibility of a single ruler—others . . . prefer not to pay the comeys or customs which royalty would demand and enforce." [1] Such traders had no occasion to concern themselves with the tribe or language of the people with whom they had dealings, and debased forms of English or French were in use as means of communication. Already in 1820 a traveller could report: "At Old Calabar different European languages are understood, and the English language is spoken, taught, read and written; they [the natives] keep regular mercantile accounts in our language." [2]

Yet despite the multiplicity of small African states, it was essentially people and kingdoms of Africa that the Europeans first undertook to protect and rule, rather than arbitrary slices of the African soil. When around 1882 German political interest in the continent began to be felt, it became obvious that it would no longer be possible to allow the various African states to evolve gradually without coming under foreign political control. Great Britain, which had hitherto refused to accept the submission of native chiefs to the British Crown, now set about entering into agreements with native chiefs whereby they assigned their lands, without defining them at all precisely, to the protection of Her Majesty Queen Victoria.

Thus in Sierra Leone the slightly comical course of events was as follows: In 1825 Sir Samuel Turner had signed an agreement with the King of Sherboro (or Sherbro) which put his kingdom under British protection. The home government had

[1] "An F.R.G.S." (Sir Richard Burton), *Wanderings in West Africa*, 1863, 246.
[2] Quoted in W. Hutton, *A Voyage to Africa*, 1820, 398.

disavowed this treaty, but had never announced their decision, either in Sierra Leone or to the king concerned. When in 1879 rival claims were being put forward by the Liberians to the territory in question, the problem arose whether the British could rely on their earlier agreements to support their claim to the kingdom concerned.[1] An example of a typical treaty with a tribe of the interior is given by Miss Perham in her study of the life of Lord Lugard.[2] The treaty between the King of Nikki (which was the capital of Borgu) and the Royal Niger Company referred specifically to the fact that Hausa was the language employed at the court of Nikki, and to the fact that the kingdom was a part but not the whole of the Hausa state of Borgu. Today most of Borgu is in Ilorin Province of Nigeria, but Nikki was assigned to France by the Anglo-French Convention of 14/6/1898.[3]

When such treaties precede boundary-making, the native political organization may be said to have determined where boundaries shall run, at least on the local scale. Unfortunately by the time the continent was divided several centuries of slave trade had so disrupted the older kingdoms that very few retained an effective existence. The Sultan of Sokoto, the King of Buganda, the Sultan of Darfur and the Chiefs of Barotseland and Matabeleland, to take a few outstanding examples, all ruled over large areas at the time when they accepted foreign protection, and with the exception of Lobengula they all achieved a *modus vivendi* with their new masters which preserved the identity, if not the whole territory, of their lands. Yet even these rulers cannot be said to have ruled over homogeneous territories all of whose inhabitants spoke the same tongue,[4] and so it is not surprising that the modern much larger states into which the continent is divided are much more diverse. The extensive but nebulous domain of the Sultan of Zanzibar on

---

[1] S. Rowe to F.O., 12/2/1879, F.O. 84/1558.

[2] M. Perham, *Lugard—The Years of Adventure*, 1956, 516.

[3] Hertslet, *op. cit.*, II, 785.

[4] "As in the case of all the great native kingdoms of South Africa, the extent of the kingdom (of Barotseland) is far greater than that of the original tribal territory, and includes vast areas over which the King exercises an indirect authority analogous to that which the paramount sovereign exercised over vassals in the feudal system."

From a memorandum on questions pending in the African Department, 15/11/1900, F.O. Confidential Print 7439.

the east coast of Africa cannot properly be compared with the kingdoms just discussed, since it was by trade rather than by military expeditions that the Sultan extended his nominal sway.

The Boundaries of Africa and the Distribution of Population

Fig. XXIX, while indicating very clearly that many of the boundaries of Africa divide persons of the same tribe or tongue, gives no indication of the number of persons involved by these divisions, nor does it reveal how far the boundaries of Africa pass through more or less densely inhabited parts of the continent. Fig. XXX has therefore been constructed to show, in a very general way, the relationship between the present density of population in tropical Africa and the political boundaries.

Such a map poses a number of problems. First, there is the question whether the current distribution of population resembles that of 75 years ago, when the boundaries were being demarcated. For the urban population this is clearly not the case, but for rural areas it is more difficult to judge, in view of the absence of maps of the distribution of the native populations at the time when the Europeans divided the continent. Sir Harry Johnston's map of the density of native population in Uganda in 1902 is quite unique in this respect, and its accuracy is clearly open to question.[1] Secondly there is the question of the reliability of Fig. XXX itself. As Prothero reminds us in Chapter 6 above, the mapping of the population in intertropical Africa is most uneven, and not every part of the map is therefore equally trustworthy. Thirdly the map is at so small a scale that while it can hint at various practical problems posed by boundaries, it cannot provide the evidence to decide an argument one way or another. In an ideal account of the boundaries of a state or region, it would be necessary to present, at least for critical areas, portions of the topographic map at scales of 1 : 1,000,000 or even larger, and portions of population maps to match, if such existed. From these the reader might be able to appreciate how the boundaries affect, or at least are relevant to the study of, the daily lives of the frontier peoples. Since in such a study local knowledge and investiga-

[1] Sir H. Johnston, *The Uganda Protectorate*, 1902, plate IV.

tion are almost certain to be necessary, the following instances are chosen from areas known personally to the writer.

In the extreme south-west of Sudan, the densely wooded land along the Nile-Congo watershed is occupied by the Zande tribe, a term given to a loose amalgam of Africans now speaking a language of the Sudanic group.[1] As we have already seen, these people live on either side of the line which was chosen in 1885 to be the boundary of the Congo State, and they are at present divided so that about 29 per cent of their number live in Sudan, 68 per cent in the Congo and the remainder in Oubangui-Chari in the French Union. This was a purely fortuitous division, since the European powers knew very little about the area when the boundary was drawn. From the Zande point of view, however, the inadequacy of European geographical knowledge of that time is clearly revealed. The topography of the area is that there are many streams rather steeply and narrowly incised into the lateritic ironstone plateau,[2] and the soils most favourable for cultivation are situated on the flanks of the streams.[3] Before the coming of the Europeans the Azande were therefore widely dispersed throughout their region, being in fact quite recent arrivals, by warlike penetration, from further west. A frontier sited by the Europeans along the Nile-Congo watershed inevitably had the effect of dividing the tribe.

Again, in the west of Sudan between Darfur and Wadai, where the dry season lasts for 7 to 8 months of the year, many of the people, whether animal owners or cultivators, move in the winter to the vicinity of the large sandy *wadis*, to drink from the shallow wells in their beds.[4] Along these *wadis*, moreover, they find the most favourable alluvial soils for summer cultivation, and so the population map for any season of the year will pick out the drainage lines, with large areas much less densely inhabited in between. Nevertheless the boundary between Sudan and French Equatorial Africa, which was originally defined by agreement between Great Britain as the traditional division

[1] P. T. W. Baxter and A. Butt, *The Azande*, Ethnographic Survey of Africa, 1953.

[2] C. G. T. Morison, A. C. Hoyle, and J. F. Hope Simpson, "Tropical Soil-Vegetation Catenas and Mosaics", *Jnl. of Ecology*, xxxvi, 1948, Fig. 1, 10.

[3] P. de Schlippe, *Shifting Cultivation in Africa*, 1956, Chapter IV.

[4] K. M. Barbour, "The Wadi Azum", *Geographical Journal*, cxx, 1954, 174–182.

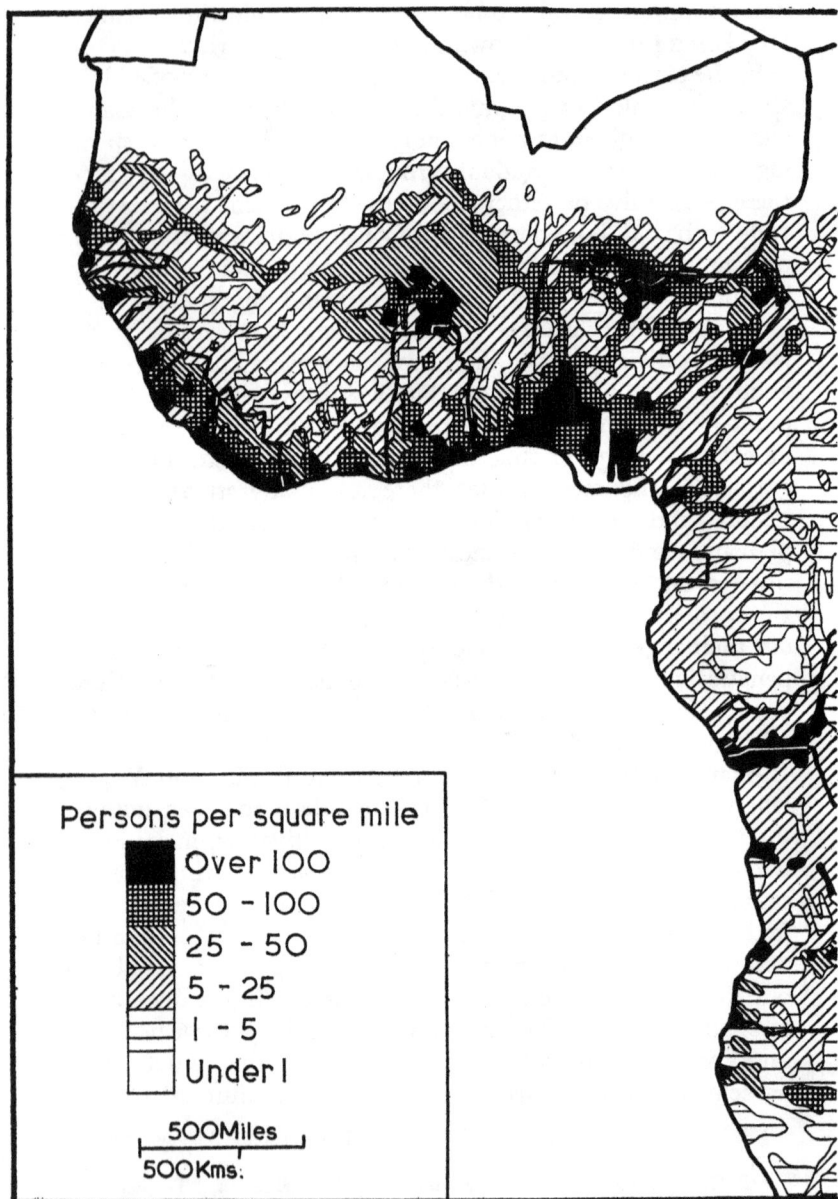

Persons per square mile

Over 100
50 - 100
25 - 50
5 - 25
1 - 5
Under 1

500 Miles
500 Kms:

Fig. XXX. Tropical Africa: international boundaries in

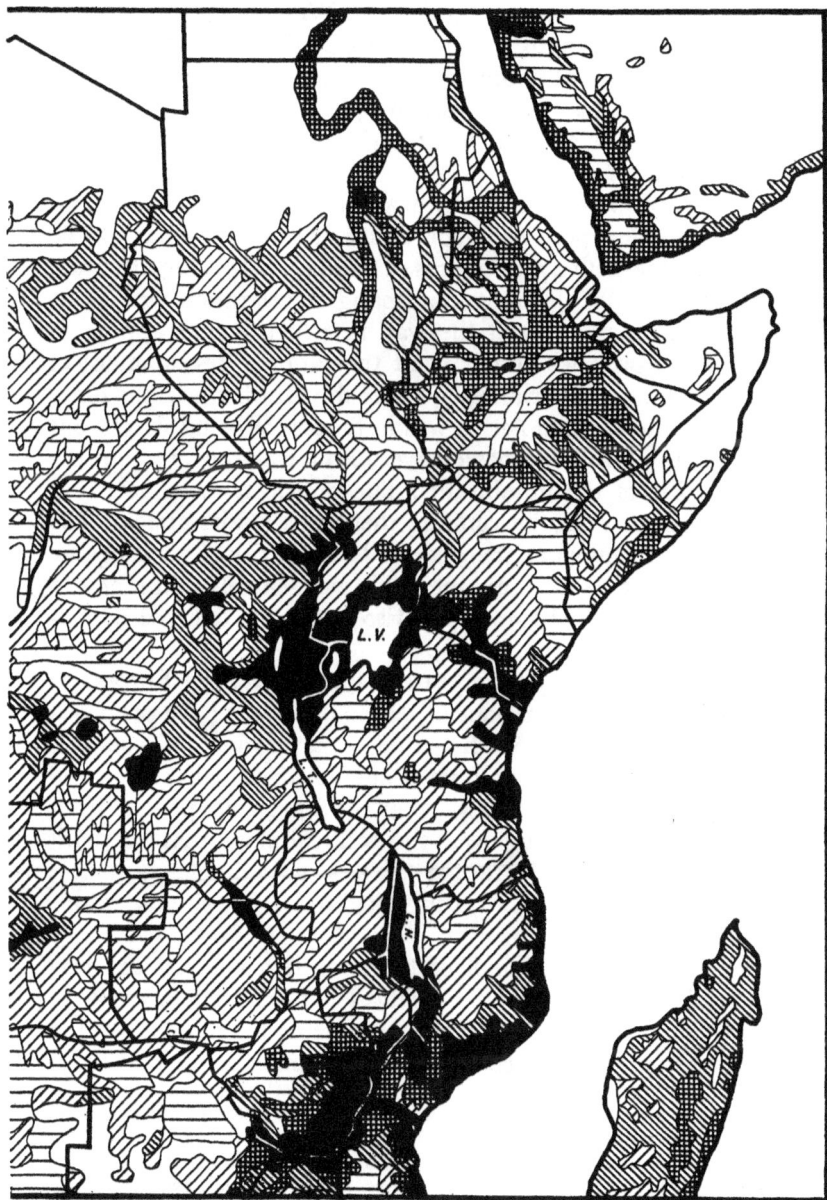

relation to the density of population.

Mainly after *The Times Atlas of the World*, vol. 1, 1958, plate V.

between the kingdoms of Darfur and Wadai,[1] has been sited for much of its length along the Wadis Kaja and Tini.[2] This convenient physical boundary proves therefore to be more of a magnet than a barrier between peoples, and in addition there are numerous tribes which cross the frontier in their annual migrations.

These are two only of many examples that could be adduced of frontiers that pose problems which will one day have to be solved by the native inhabitants of Africa. In drawing attention to them it is difficult to avoid a feeling of frustration, or at least of cynical resignation, at the way in which events appear to conspire to obstruct and prevent the rational development of the human and material resources of the continent. In the nineteenth century, when Africa was in process of being shared out between the European powers, very little was known about the ways of life of the inhabitants. The prospect, moreover, that they might one day be running their own affairs appeared so remote that even when there seemed to be a risk of dividing one section of a tribe from another, this was scarcely considered a matter to reckon with in comparison with the delicate adjustments of European politics.

During the first 35 or 40 years of this century the Europeans gradually became conscious of the complexity of the problems they had taken on. At this time considerations of prestige, combined with inertia and pre-occupation with what appeared to be more important tasks, kept the European powers from undertaking the tidying up of the political map of Africa, with the exception of the transfer of a large triangle of useless desert from Sudan to Libya in 1934, and a few similar minor rectifications.[3]

Now in the second half of the twentieth century the raw material for serious frontier analysis is beginning to come to hand. Aerial photography is revolutionizing the mapping of the continent, population censuses are becoming more numerous

[1] Declaration relative to the British and French spheres of influence in Central Africa, dated 21/3/1899. C. 9134 (1899).

[2] Notes exchanged between the United Kingdom and France ... defining the boundary between French Equatorial Africa and the Anglo-Egyptian Sudan, dated 21/1/1924. Cmd. 2221 (1924).

[3] Exchange of notes between United Kingdom, Egypt and Italy respecting the boundary between the Sudan and Libya, dated 20/7/1934. Cmd. 4694 (1934).

and more reliable, the anthropologists have enormously increased our understanding of the ways of life of many of the African tribes, agriculturalists, botanists and soil scientists are giving us a much deeper understanding of the physical background of the continent, and geographers are beginning to produce regional studies which draw together the many threads to give an overall view of Africa and its problems. By now, however, the seed of national consciousness has taken firm root in the African soil, particularly among the educated classes, whose members are rejecting narrow tribalism. Any attempt to re-draw boundaries today would have to deal with all the former difficulties, together with the certainty that any unrequited loss of territory would almost certainly provoke political troubles far more serious than those it was hoped to remedy.

From an academic point of view, political geography in Africa and the study of the composition and boundaries of states are just beginning to appear as fruitful and significant lines of investigation.[1] Politically, however, the problems associated with the boundaries of Africa remain as untouchable as ever before. All we can hope to gain from this kind of work is that as new masters become responsible for the destinies of Africa, they will appreciate the fact that decisions taken without an adequate basis of factual knowledge may build up problems for their successors just as difficult and persistent as those presented by the boundaries of Africa today.

[1] e.g., J. F. V. Prescott, "Nigeria's Regional Boundary Problems", *Geographical Review*, XLIX, 1959, 485–505.

Index

Index

Barth, H., 119n., 132, 132n., 254, 254n.
Bascom, W., 282n., 283, 283n.
Baxter, P. T. W., 319n.
Bechuanaland, 206, 211–12, 216, 266
Beja people, Sudan, 309
Belgian Congo, 54, 70, 75, 166, 178–81, 184, 198, 211, 216–19, 225, 252, 256, 258–9, 261–3, 272, 274, 319
Belgians, 2, 256, 304, 308, 310
Belgium, 31, 77, 104
Belingwe, Southern Rhodesia, 229–230
Bell, T. S., 223n.
Bemba people, Northern Rhodesia, 115, 194, 196, 236
Berlin, Treaty of, 304, 311
Bettison, D., 239n.
Bimoba people, Ghana, 87
Bindawa, Nigeria, 123, 127–30, 132
Blantyre-Limbe, Nyasaland, 218
Blue Nile, 110–11, 142, 149–50, 153, 155
Blue Nile Province, Sudan, 105–6, 110, 139
Boateng, E. A., 250, 251n., 256n.
Boni people, Kenya, 158
Boran people, Kenya, 158
Bornu Province, Nigeria, 118–20, 124, 131, 134
boundaries, 5, 157, 303 ff.
    distribution of population and, 318–19
    movements of population and, 319
    origin of, 308 ff.
    re-alignment of, 322–3
    tribal distributions and, 310–18
    types of, 304–10
Bowdich, T. E., 255, 255n.
Brasnett, J., 170n.
Brazzaville, 25, 258
British, 1, 2, 68, 100, 166, 195, 250, 283, 285, 294–5, 298, 301, 303, 308, 314–15

British East Africa, 17–30, 49–61, 77, 258
British West Africa, 8
Brode, H., 165n., 166n.
Broken Hill, Northern Rhodesia, 198, 200, 210n., 218, 219, 225, 258
Buchanan, K. M., 251n.
budget surveys, 12
Buell, R. L., 273n.
Buganda, 21, 164, 172, 177–80, 184–5, 191, 265, 317
Buhera, Southern Rhodesia, 227, 229
Bukavu (Costermansville), 77, 258
Bulawayo, 39, 197, 210, 218, 219, 225, 227, 229, 238, 258, 263, 265
Bunyoro, Uganda, 178–9, 184
Burgdörfer, F., 69, 69n., 78n.
Burton, Sir R. F., 166n., 168, 284, 284n., 316n.
Burunge people, Tanganyika, 159
Busoga, Uganda, 179–80
Butt, A., 319n.

Caillié, R., 254
Carter, J. D., 122n.
censuses,
    accuracy and errors of, 13
    administrative units and, 19, 73
    analysis of, 12, 23
    categories of data in, 8, 11, 12, 14, 19, 21–2, 27
    inter-censal estimates, 13
    pilot, 15n., 21
    post-war, 3, 7–8, 9, 13–15, 31–2, 73
    pre-war, 7, 8, 19–20, 32–4
    problems of, 8, 10, 21
    sample, 4, 10–12, 23–7, 39–40, 101
    training of staff, 10–11, 15n., 22, 24, 28
Central Africa, 31, 193–248, 273
Central African Statistical Office, 33, 36, 43, 197n., 206, 208n., 218n., 238, 239n., 240n.

Index

Index

328

Index

Index

Index

Index

Index

Index

Index

Waganda people, Uganda, 51
Walmsley, R. W., 257n., 269n.
Wankie, Southern Rhodesia, 197,
219, 221, 226, 229
Waschmann, K. P., 159n.
water supplies, 109, 121–2, 137 ff.
Watson, W., 205n., 233n., 236,
236n.
Welldon, R. M. C., 286n., 290n.
Wemba people, Tanganyika, 55
West Africa, 4, 7–15, 77, 84, 110,
115, 253, 255–6, 258, 274, 303,
316
Western Province, Tanganyika, 54–
55, 57, 59
Western Region, Nigeria, 9, 11,
251, 253, 262, 279–301
Westerners in Sudan, 141–2, 144
White, C. M. N., 234n.
White Nile, 111, 155
Whitely, W. H., 166n., 174n.
Wilkinson, H. R., 112n.
Wilson, F. B., 162
Wilson, G., 236n., 241n., 271n.
Winter, E. H., 192n.
Witwatersrand Native Labour Asso-
ciation, 201, 203–4
World Health Organization, 25, 81

Yao people, Tanganyika, 163, 165,
167, 181
Yoruba people, Nigeria, 5, 251, 253,
258, 262, 268, 279–301

Zaghawa language, 106
Zalingei, Sudan, 147, 153
Zambezi river, 31, 40, 193, 196, 201,
258, 269, 303
Zande district, Sudan, 103, 111,
308, 319
Zanzibar, 17–30, 49–61, 163, 165–
167, 253, 261
Zaramo people, Tanganyika, 174
Zaria, Nigeria, 117–19, 122–5, 135,
253, 284
Zein M. Omar, 114n.
Zelinsky, W., 70, 70n., 252n., 256,
256n., 259, 260, 260n., 261
Zezeru (Shona) people, Southern
Rhodesia, 237
Zigua people, Tanganyika, 55
Zimba people, East Africa, 160
Zinza people, Tanganyika, 177
Zomba, Nyasaland, 47, 218
Zongo, Ghana, 273
Zuarungu, 84, 93
Zulu people, 160, 193–4

For Product Safety Concerns and Information please contact our EU
representative GPSR@taylorandfrancis.com
Taylor & Francis Verlag GmbH, Kaufingerstraße 24, 80331 München, Germany

www.ingramcontent.com/pod-product-compliance
Lightning Source LLC
Chambersburg PA
CBHW070902080426
R18103500001B/R181035PG41932CBX00012B/3

* 9 7 8 1 0 3 2 5 4 8 2 0 3 *